Becoming Brazuca

Brazilian Immigration to the United States

Clémence Jouët-Pastré and Leticia J. Braga, editors

Published by Harvard University David Rockefeller Center for Latin American Studies

Distributed by Harvard University Press
Cambridge, Massachusetts
London, England
2008

Printed in the United States of America

Library of Congress Cataloging-In-Publication Data

Becoming Brazuca : Brazilian immigration to the United States / Clémence Jouët-Pastré and Leticia J. Braga, editors.

p. ; cm.

Includes bibliographical references and index.
ISBN-13: 978-0-674-02802-9
ISBN-10: 0-674-02802-3

1. Brazil—Emigration and immigration. 2. United States—Emigration and immigration. 3. Immigrants—United States. 4. Brazilians—United States. 5. Brazilian Americans—Cultural assimilation. I. Jouët-Pastré, Clémence. II. Braga, Leticia J. III. David Rockefeller Center for Latin American Studies.

E184.B68 B42 2008
305.86/98

Contents

A New Generation of People and Research

Prologue: The Diasporic Experience

Carola Suárez-Orozco

Processes of globalization are rapidly transforming not only economies but cultures and societies as well. International flows of trade and capital along with large-scale political, religious, and ethnic upheavals have lead to unprecedented levels of worldwide migration. Consequently, at the beginning of the new millennium, there are over 200 million immigrants and refugees worldwide. In the United States, the new immigration began in 1965, accelerating to the rate of approximately one million individuals entering the country each year. Currently there are an estimated 35.7 million people who were born abroad (U.S. Census Bureau 2006) and well over 56 million who are of so-called foreign stock—as the first-generation immigrants and second-generation U.S.-born children of immigrants are referred to (U.S. Census 2000). While 12.4 percent of the population is foreign-born in the United States, this is considerably less than in several post-industrial nations—37.3% in Luxemburg; 23.1% in Australia; 18.2% in Canada, for example (OECD 2003), as well as proportionally less than during the last great migratory wave of the 1880s to the 1920s.

The new immigrants to North America are extremely diverse and their experiences resist facile generalizations. Nearly three quarters of these new immigrants come from Latin America, Asia, and the Caribbean (U.S. Census, 2000). They bring with them a wide array of languages, religions, cultural beliefs and practices. Some have highly educated professional backgrounds, while others are illiterate and low-skilled, struggling in the lowest-paid sectors of the service economy. Some are escaping political, religious, or ethnic persecution; others are lured by the promise of better jobs and the hope for better educational opportunities. Some people have officially sanctioned Homeland Security[1] documentation; some do not; and still others are families with mixed documentation whereby some siblings are documented while others are not. Some come to settle permanently and others move from one migrant work camp to another. Some engage in transnational strategies of living both "here and there"—that is, shuttling between their country of birth and their country of choice (Levitt 2001). The immigrant journey today follows complex paths bifurcating into divergent experiences and varied outcomes—some thrive with immigration while others struggle, all too quickly joining the "rainbow underclasses" (Portes and Zhou 1993).

Large-scale migration from Brazil to the United States is a relatively new phenomenon. Indeed, Brazil has historically been a host society for immigrants from many nations rather than a sending nation. Given the recent significant increases in the Brazilian population in the United States, there is to date far too little systematic work done on the Brazilian immigrant experience. Several reasons may account for this neglect. First, Brazilians are fairly new arrivals in the United States: as such, despite their ambivalence and resistance, they are often subsumed within a larger Latino or Hispanic designation. Many Brazilians cast off this label, citing language differences and a general sense of not belonging to an underclass as primary reasons. Others argue that Brazil is in Latin America and given that this identity seems to be imposed upon Brazilians within the receiving culture, it may be politically strategic to make an alliance with the Spanish-speaking immigrants. How this drama will be resolved remains to be seen.

Research on immigrant origin groups tends to be focused on so-called problem populations or on model minorities (Lee 1996). Research abounds on the poor performance of Latinos in the educational system or on particular groups in the penal system or in gangs. Conversely, researchers also look towards the other end of the continuum—the so-called model minority that routinely overachieves. Yet groups that tend neither to overachieve nor to dramatically underachieve are often under-researched—no doubt contributing to the woeful understudy of Brazilians.

It should be noted that this perspective has recently begun to change in areas in which Brazilians are highly concentrated; in the Greater Boston region for example, local communities and the media voice concerns about the newcomers' lack of Homeland Security documentation and worry that they may be draining resources. The Brazilian diasporic experience is an area of research ripe for cultivation. Hence this volume is an important addition to our understanding of the phenomenon.

The goal of research should be to capture the migratory experience in all of its subtleties—understanding that there are many common denominators of experience between the groups of origin while recognizing the specificity of experience of particular groups as well as individuals. To paraphrase the famed anthropologist Clyde Kluckhohn, every immigrant is like all other immigrants, like some other immigrants, and like no other immigrants (Kluckhohn, 1949). The accomplished researcher should strive to capture that reality. Brazilians certainly exhibit characteristics that make them quite different from Mexicans or Argentines, but do they share any migratory parallels? How are particular groups similar to others? How may they be different? And how can we account for these differences? Only by considering diverse groups can we begin to answer these types of questions.

Combining "outsider" (*etic*) and "insider" (*emic*) approaches to diverse populations is important in the phases of recruitment, instrument development, data collection and analysis (Cooper et al. 1998). Taking into consideration a perspective gained from research in Brazil provides a frame of comparison that is essential. What are the cultural patterns that are "imported"? Which may arise from the contact of cultures? What is derivative of the migratory process? What is transient and what tends to be sustained? The chapters in this volume provide several examples of the ways crucial knowledge is culled by the practice of combining *etic* and *emic* viewpoints.

Researchers should consider the historical, political, economic, social, and cultural forces at work not simply within the host country but also in the sending countries. Within the sending context, for example, various factors can greatly affect the post-migratory adjustment: the circumstances surrounding the migration (e.g., political crises or wars); the socioeconomic background of the immigrants; whether or not there has been a rural to urban shift; as well as how cohesive the family is and whether or not families were separated as a result of the migration. Within the receiving context, the available networks of social relations; whether or not the newcomers are documented; neighborhood and school segregation; the availability of work for adults; the quality of schools for children; as well as the ethos of reception towards the particular immigrant group and the disparagement and social mirroring they may encounter, all will contribute to variable pathways of adjustment. In the United States, post-9/11 hostility to migrants is on the rise. Subsequent draconian immigration policies force undocumented parents to choose between having their children grow up far away from them in Brazil or have them develop at their side in an undocumented limbo. Further, given the color spectrum represented by Brazilian society, keeping this reality in mind is essential while conducting research into the adaptation of Brazilian immigrants in a racially conscious society.

Research should also consider sources of resilience that arise from the migratory experience. For example, are such inoculating traits as hope, perseverance, and capacity to delay gratification more often found among immigrants than among their native-born peers? This shift to a consideration of both challenges and strengths has the potential to deepen our understanding considerably. Here research that considers Brazilian community resources is crucial. What cultural practices contribute to strengthening community resilience in the diaspora? What is the role of political activity both in the local immigrant community as well as back in Brazil in sustaining a transcultural experience? What role do religious and spiritual practices play in the community? How do the Brazilian media strengthen transnational contact, information exchange, and community solidarity? What is the role of community restaurants, dance and music performances, and sports events in maintaining cultural pride and connectedness?

In order to successfully capture the complexity of the Brazilian migratory experience, insights contributed from a variety disciplines are essential. The social sciences—sociology, anthropology, psychology, political science, economics, linguistics, history, and education—all have explanatory value. However, the insights gained from the arts, including literature, poetry, plays, film, and music, also shed important light on the experiences both in the point of origin as well as in the diaspora.

Clearly, the perspectives of a variety of disciplines both in Brazil as well as in North American host societies are essential to begin to fill in the mosaic of the Brazilian immigrant experience. In this volume, the reader is treated to an extraordinarily rich interdisciplinary view of what has until just recently been the nearly invisible Brazilian immigrant community. These chapters represent emerging scholarship of the most eminent Brazilian and American researchers of the Brazilian diasporic experience. The book provides a much needed view into the richness and complexity of the Brazilian-North American community.

Notes

1. Homeland Security is the U.S. Government agency responsible for granting immigration privileges and documentation (officially replacing the Immigration and Naturalization Service after the September 11, 2001 World Trade Center attack).
2. "Hispanic" and "Latino" are terms that are often used interchangeably. Hispanic is a term the Census Bureau began using in the 1970s. This term, however, connotes a link to the Iberian Peninsula (and most specifically, Spain). The term Latino has increasingly been designated as the more 'politically correct' term that privileges a link to Latin America from which the bulk of this rapidly growing minority group actually originates.

References

Cooper, C. R., Jackson, J. F., Azmitia, M., and Lopez, E. M. 1998. "Multiple Selves, Multiple Worlds: Three Useful Strategies for Research with Ethnic Minority Youth on Identity, Relationship and Opportunity Structures." In *Studying Minority Adolescents: Conceptual, Methodological, and Theoretical Issues*, pp. 111–125. Eds. V. McLoyd and L. Steinberg. Mahwah, NJ: Lawrence Erlbaum.

Kluckhohn, C. 1949. *Mirror for Man: The Relation of Anthropology to Modern Life*. New York: Whitssley House.

Lee, S. 1996. *Unraveling the "Model Minority" Stereotype: Listening to Asian American Youth*. New York: Teachers College Press.

Levitt, P. 2001. *The Transnational Villagers*. Berkeley: University of California Press.

OECD. 2003. *Trends in International Migration*. Paris: Organization for Economic Co-operation and Development.

Portes, A., and Zhou, M. 1993. "The New Second Generation: Segmented Assimilation and Its Variants." *The Annals of the American Academy of Political & Social Science* 530:74–96.

U.S. Census Bureau. 2006. *The 2005 American Community Survey*. Washington, D.C. Internet Release Date August 2006.

———. 2000. *Profile of the Foreign-born Population in the United States*. Washington, D.C.: U.S. Census Department of Commerce.

Biographical Information

Editors

Clémence Jouët-Pastré obtained her Ph.D. in Translation Studies from Universidade de São Paulo, Brazil, and has taught at Stanford University and Princeton University. She directs the Portuguese Language Program at Harvard and is currently the Undergraduate Advisor in Portuguese. She has published widely on intercultural communication, second language pedagogy, and multicultural education. She is co-editor of *Giving Voice to a Nascent Community: Exploring Brazilian Immigration to the U.S. through Research and Practice* (DRCLAS, 2004), and co-author of a language textbook, *Ponto de Encontro: Portuguese as a World Language* (Prentice-Hall, 2007).

Leticia J. Braga has a B.A. in Psychology and a minor in Education from the College of William and Mary. She received an Ed.M. in International Education from, and is currently a doctoral candidate in, Human Development and Psychology at the Harvard Graduate School of Education; she is the Teaching Fellow for "Portuguese and the Community," a service/learning course. Her articles have appeared in *ReVista*, published by the David Rockefeller Center at Harvard University, and she is co-author of *Community-Based Learning: A Window into the Portuguese-Speaking Communities of New England* (Hispania, 2005).

Contributors

Darién J. Davis is Associate Professor of Latin American history at Middlebury College. His current work is on trans-nationality and Brazilian performers. He is the author of two books on race and nationality in twentieth century Brazil. His forthcoming book with Michigan State University Press is entitled *White Face, Black Mask: Africaneity and the Early Social History of Popular Music in Brazil.* He is also editor of *Beyond Slavery: The Multifaceted Legacy of Africans in Latin America and the Caribbean* (2006); *Slavery and Beyond: The African Impact on Latin America and the Caribbean* (1995) and co-editor of *Companion to Latino Literatures* (2007). He has published a number of articles on Brazilians in the United States.

Bernadete Beserra (Associate professor at the Federal University of Ceará, Brazil) received her Ph.D. from the Department of Anthropology at the University of California, Riverside, in 2000. She is the author of *Brazilian Immigrants in the United States: Cultural Imperialism and Social Class* (LFB Scholarly Publishing, New York, 2003), and researches and publishes in the areas of international migration and racism, Brazilians and Latinos in the United States, and racism and class in the Northeast of Brazil. Professor Beserra is also a member of the editorial board of *Latin American Perspectives.*

Paul Freston is Byker Chair in Sociology at Calvin College, Michigan, and professor of sociology in the post-graduate program in social sciences at the Universidade Federal de São Carlos, Brazil. He is the author, amongst others, of *Evangelicals and Politics in Asia, Africa and Latin America* (Cambridge University Press, 2001).

Márcia Guimarães holds a B.S. in Psychology and an M.A. in Intercultural Relations from Lesley University, MA. She is a certified independent trainer for Parent's Place and for Federation for Children with Special Needs. She is currently a Teaching Assistant in Portuguese at Harvard University and also works as a cross-cultural independent consultant for Brazilian immigrants in the area of mental health in a community center in Allston-Brighton area. She has strong research interests especially on the psychological impact of immigration for women.

Tiago Jansen is an occupational physician who is now a doctoral student at the Work Environment Department of UMASS Lowell, with a major in Work Environment Policy. He is a research assistant in the project Collaboration for a Better Work Environment for Brazilians (COBWEB). He now studies Brazilian immigration to the United States.

Joshua Kirshner is a Ph.D. candidate in City and Regional Planning at Cornell. He is currently writing a dissertation on internal migration, urban growth, and the challenges of integration and social exclusion in the city of Santa Cruz, Bolivia. Kirshner received his A.B. in Social Anthropology from Harvard College and an M.A. in Urban Planning from UCLA. He has done research on a variety of issues related to migration, labor, and employment.

Solange de Azambuja Lira is Associate Professor of Education in the Division of Language and Literacy at Lesley University. She has a Doctorate in Linguistics from the University of Pennsylvania and teaches courses in second-language acquisition in the teacher preparation programs. Her areas of expertise include sociolinguistics, Creole linguistics, second-language acquisition, literacy, and Portuguese syntax. She is the author of numerous articles and a book published by Peter Lang, *The Subject in Brazilian Portuguese* (1996), as well as a chapter in *The Other Before Me: A Bicultural Dialogue in Reflections of Multiculturalism* (1997), published by Intercultural Press. Professor Lira is a native speaker of Portuguese and has been an educator for twenty-five years.

Márcia Loureiro is a career diplomat. She completed the Preparatory Course to the Diplomatic Career, Rio Branco Institute (Brasilia, 1986), and a Master's of Science in Foreign Service Program, Edmund A. Walsh School of Foreign Service, Georgetown University (Washington, D.C., 1993). In the Brazilian Foreign Service, Marcia Loureiro has worked in several areas since 1987, such as trade promotion, scientific and technological cooperation, diplomatic planning, consular and juridical affairs, and assistance to Brazilian nationals abroad.

Cileine de Lourenço is Associate Professor of Latin American Studies and Spanish, Department of English and Cultural Studies at Bryant University. Her research has focused on representations of gender and race in Latin American cultural production in relation to construction of national identities. Her interest in race, gender, class, and national identity has presently led her to a collaborative work on Brazilian immigrant women and construction of identity.

Maxine L. Margolis is Professor Emerita of Anthropology and Latin American Studies at the University of Florida in Gainesville and Senior Research Associate at the Institute of Latin American Studies at Columbia University. She is the author or co-editor of seven books, most recently, *Little Brazil: An Ethnography of Brazilian Immigrants in New York City* (Princeton University Press, 1994), *An Invisible Minority: Brazilians in New York City* (Allyn & Bacon, 1998), and *True to Her Nature: Changing Advice to American Women* (Waveland 2000).

Ana Cristina Braga Martes is a Professor of Sociology at the Getúlio Vargas Social and Legal Foundation at the School of Business Administration in São Paulo. In 2002 she held a position as visiting researcher at Boston University, and from 1994 to 1996 as visiting scholar at the Massachusetts Institute of Technology. With a B.A. in Social Science from UNESP, she also holds master's and doctorate degrees from São Paulo University. In 2000 she published *Brazilians in the United States: A Study of Immigrants in Massachusetts.* She has several published articles on Brazilian emigration, both in Brazil and abroad.

Judith McDonnell is Associate Professor of Sociology, Department of History and Social Sciences at Bryant University. Her research has focused on racial and ethnic inequality in the United States, emphasizing housing, racialization, residential segregation, and institutional discrimination. Her recent research has focused on identity negotiation among Brazilian immigrant women.

Kátia Maria Santos Mota, Ph.D. in Portuguese-Brazilian Studies at Brown University, is a Professor at the State University of Bahia (Universidade do Estado da Bahia) in the School of Education and Researcher in the field of Sociolinguistics and Language Education. She has published articles on Bilingual Education and Language Diversity, and has recently edited two books on Intercultural Communication in Foreign Language Classrooms and Language Minorities.

Ana Y. Ramos-Zayas earned a B.A. in Economics and Latin American Studies from Yale College and an M.A./Ph.D. in Anthropology from Columbia University. Ramos-Zayas is Associate Professor of Anthropology and Latino & Hispanic Caribbean Studies at Rutgers University in New Brunswick. She is the author of *National Performances: The Politics of Class, Race, and Space in Puerto Rican Chicago* (The University of Chicago Press, 2003) and co-author of *Latino Crossings: Mexicans, Puerto Ricans, and the Politics of Race and Citizenship* (Routledge, 2003), and has written various articles on critical race theory, urban space, and diasporic identities among Latinos in the United States. Her current ethnographic research examines the intersection of urban neoliberalism, race, and the anthropology of emotions among Puerto Ricans and Brazilians in New Jersey.

Branca Telles Ribeiro is a multilingual Associate Professor in the School of Education at Lesley University. Dr. Ribeiro is an experienced educator and the Research Coordinator for the Doctoral Program at Lesley University. She has a doctorate in Linguistics from Georgetown University and is a specialist in applied linguistics, cross-cultural communication, and discourse analysis. She has published extensively in the USA and internationally. Several of her recent articles have been co-authored with her research team and published in the United States, Germany, and France. Her book, published by the Oxford University Press in 1994, received very positive reviews from researchers in anthropology, psychology, and linguistics. She has been a researcher at TERC (Cambridge, MA) where she studied teachers' conversations on their teaching practice.

Teresa Sales is a Professor of Sociology at UNICAMP University. She has authored *Brasileiros longe de casa* (São Paulo, Cortez, 1999); *Agreste, agrestes* (Rio de Janeiro, Paz e Terra, 1982); and *Cassacos e Corumbas* (São Paulo, Ática, 1977). She was a Visiting Scholar at the Center for International Studies at MIT in 1990–91 and 1995–96. She edited the *Revista brasileira de estudos de população* from 1993–96, was a member of the editing board for *Revista brasileira de Estudos Sociais,* and is currently a board member of *Travessia–revista do migrante.*

Carlos Eduardo Siqueira, MD, ScD, is research assistant professor at the Department of Work Environment at the University of Massachusetts Lowell, where he has researched the political economy of the migration of hazards between developed and developing countries, and healthcare and immigrant workers' work environment policy issues.

Sueli Siqueira is Professor of Sociology at the Vale do Rio Doce University in Governador Valadares, Brazil. She is the author of *Trabalho e Violência–Desvendando a Realidade Social* (2000) *A Produção do Trabalho e a Pesquisa Científica na Construção do Conhecimento* (2004), and *No Caminho das Ciências Sociais para Compreender o Mundo Contemporâneo* (2008). She coordinates the Center for Studies on UNIVALE's Regional Development and is a member of the sister city committee responsible for establishing an agreement between Governador Valadares and Framingham, Massachusetts.

Carola Suárez-Orozco is Professor of Applied Psychology at New York University's Steinhardt School of Culture, Education, and Human Development and Co-Director of Immigration Studies at NYU. She is the author of *Learning a New Land: Immigrant Students in American Society* (with Marcelo Suárez-Orozco and Irina Todorova, Harvard University Press, 2008); *Children of Immigration* (with Marcelo Suárez-Orozco, Harvard University Press, 2001) and *Transformations: Migration, Family Life, and Achievement Motivation Among Latino Adolescents* (with Marcelo Suárez-Orozco, Stanford University Press, 1995).

Else R. P. Vieira is a Reader in Brazilian and Comparative Latin American Studies at Queen Mary, University of London; former Visiting Professor at the Centre for Brazilian Studies, University of Oxford (1999); and a Senior Research Fellow at the University of Nottingham (2001–02), with a previous career in Comparative Literature at the Federal University of Minas Gerais, Brazil. Among her major projects, she is the Director of Research and Editor of the website The Sights and Images of Dispossession: The Fight for the Land and the Emerging Culture of the MST (landless-voices.org). Her present AHRB-funded project involves a comparative study of documentaries in Brazil and Argentina.

Acknowledgments

This volume stems from presentations made at the "First National Conference on Brazilian Immigration to the United States," held at Harvard University during the Spring 2005 semester. Such projects typically involve many people from start to finish, and we would like to thank all who have helped us along the way, with special acknowledgment to those without whom the project would not have come to fruition.

We would like to thank Merilee S. Grindle, director of the David Rockefeller Center for Latin American Studies, for her continued support. The wonderful staff at the Center has been an integral part of this project. June Erlick has offered her knowledge, professionalism, and friendship from beginning to end. Also, Anita Safran's experience and eye for detail were critical during the editing and final stages of publication. Research for this book was also made possible by the Brazil Studies Program and the generous support of the Jorge Paulo Lemann Fund.

Professor Carola Suárez-Orozco inspired us to organize numerous events that worked to build fruitful bridges between academia and the Brazilian community. Professor Doris Sommer was a constant source of inspiration, creativity, and guidance. João Kulcsár first opened the doors to the community for us and motivated youths to create beautiful artwork that inspired the cover for this volume.

We could not conclude without thanking all of the authors for their time, patience and for working judiciously throughout this long trajectory to bring this volume to life. Finally, our heartfelt thanks to the Brazilian community, many of whom graciously contributed their time, stories, and lives to this project.

Introduction: Interdisciplinary Perspectives on Becoming Brazuca

Leticia J. Braga and Clémence Jouët-Pastré

"When you realize that someone's disappeared it's because they're already there [in the U.S.] . . . everyone here has or knows someone there."
—resident of Governador Valadares, Brazil

Brazilian immigrants are an interesting case study because their similarities to and differences from other immigrant groups illustrate both normative trends and new areas of interest in the study of the wave of immigration to the United States that has taken place since the 1960s. Unlike most immigrant groups from Latin America, Brazilians speak Portuguese, come from higher socioeconomic classes, and have an ethnic and racial self-identification that does not easily fall into the American "Hispanic" or "Black" categories in which they are often placed; see, for example, Martes and Fleischer (2003) and Marrow (2003). One perceived cultural difference is that, while social class is a major explicit component of a person's identity in Brazil, race is a much more salient explicit component of identity in the United States. Learning to navigate the American racial hierarchy and defining the status of one's ethnic group within this system are issues common to other immigrant groups as well, such as West Indians (Waters 1999), and data from an array of new immigrant groups are necessary to see how traditional forms of racial identity are being upheld or contested in the United States. Many current topics of study in Brazilian immigration, including transnational religious and political ties, remittances, and educational opportunities for first- and subsequent-generation immigrants, serve to illustrate broader patterns and offer methodological and theoretical perspectives that are applicable to the greater study of immigration as a global phenomenon.

Throughout the 19th century, Brazil was a receiving country of immigration flows. Between 1880 and 1915, about 31 million immigrants settled in the Americas; their favorite destination was the United States (21.4 million), with Argentina coming in second (4.2 million) and Brazil in third, with 2.9 million immigrants (Oliveira 2001). Starting four years prior to the country's independence from Portugal in 1822, Portuguese King Dom

João VI allocated land to Germans in the Northeast and to Swiss in the Southeast, with the goal of developing a model of small family farms rather than the traditional plantations based on slave labor (Seyferth 1996). After the transatlantic slave traffic was forbidden in 1850, the Brazilian Empire passed a law that donated unfarmed land to foreigners (Seyferth 1996; 2000). At the same time, the world's demand for coffee was growing and the elite class of the state of São Paulo, a center of coffee production, was desperate for cheap labor. In 1886, two years before abolition, a group of eminent coffee producers created a society—SPI (Sociedade Promotora da Imigração)—to promote immigration. The government of São Paulo subsidized immigration by providing free tickets to Brazil, free transportation from the Port of Santos to the farms and, in some cases, free meals for the first six months (Alvim 2000). Nationally, Brazilian officials launched an aggressive campaign to recruit immigrants in European countries as a result of this lack of a labor force and of the deep-rooted racial prejudice that prevented Brazilian elites from fully absorbing ex-slaves as free workers (Martínez 2000).[2] Therefore, during most of the 19th century, immigrants were sought to work either as small farmers, first in the Northeast and afterwards in the South, or to become cheap labor in the coffee plantations of São Paulo (Oliveira 2001). Between 1884 and 1939 a huge influx of immigrants arrived in Brazil, including 1,412,263 Italians; 1,204,394 Portuguese; 581,718 Spaniards; 185,799 Japanese; and 98,962 Syrians and Lebanese (IBGE 2000).

The trend in Brazil's international migration has changed dramatically and quite recently, shifting Brazil from its earlier position as a target country for immigrants for more than a century. A host of factors that included extreme inflation, few possibilities of social mobility, and unemployment led to a wave of emigration in the second half of the 1980s (Jouët-Pastré, et al. 2004; Margolis 1994; Martes 2000; Sales 2003). According to data gathered in the 1980s by Brazilian Federal Police, 1.25 million or 1 percent of Brazil's total population emigrated, settling in a variety of countries that include the United States, Portugal, Italy, Paraguay and Japan.[3] In the most recent official data available, the Brazilian Ministry of Foreign Affairs (MRE) estimated in 2002 that these numbers reached 1.96 million, while unofficial data put estimates at over 3 million Brazilians living abroad.[4] For the most part economic refugees fleeing Latin America's deep economic recession during the late 1980s and early 1990s, many Brazilian immigrants chose the United States as their new home. The reasons for this choice parallel some of the same reasons that attract other immigrant groups to this country's borders, while other reasons are specific to Latin

America and to the context of Portuguese and Brazilian contact with the United States across the 20th century.

Within the broader context of immigration presented in the Prologue by Carola Suárez-Orozco, Brazilian immigration to—and the resulting communities in—the United States are continuously reshaped and redefined. In constructivist terms, "reality" does not exist independent of people's perceptions, which can come from community members (the "minority") and from non-members (the "majority"). Perceptions are also created through an interplay of the two categories, so that the majority's viewpoints influence the community's self-conception through a process of social mirroring (Suárez-Orozco and Suárez-Orozco 2001). In this way, not only can a person be perceived as *being* a Brazuca, the term commonly used in literature to describe (mostly undocumented) Brazilian immigrants in the United States (Margolis 1994; Meihy 2004; Tosta 2004; Vieira, this volume), but he or she can also be perceived of as *becoming* a Brazuca over time, as argued in recent literature (Braga 2007a and b; Margolis 2007).

Accordingly, many changes have occurred in these more than twenty years of Brazilian mass immigration to the United States, including changes in immigrants' demographic profile, projects of return, and methods of entry. In the 1980s, the majority of Brazilians tended to be young, male, middle or lower-middle class, more light-skinned, and more educated than the average population in Brazil; most of them came to the United States on regular tourist visas and, as they overstayed their time limit, they became undocumented immigrants (Margolis 1994, 2003; Martes 2000; Sales 2003; Siqueira 2006). In Brazil, Minas Gerais was the sending state par excellence, followed by Rio de Janeiro, São Paulo, Paraná, and Espírito Santo, while favorite destinations in the United States were New York City, New Jersey, Connecticut, Massachusetts, and Florida (Margolis 1994, 2003; Martes 2000). Data collected in hundreds of interviews testify that virtually all Brazilian immigrants had plans to make the largest amount of money possible while staying for the shortest amount of time possible prior to their return (Margolis 1994, 2003; Martes 2000; Sales 2003; Siqueira 2006). As posited in the remainder of this introduction and throughout this volume, this depiction of Brazilian immigrants, for the most part, does not hold true anymore.

Establishing a Research Agenda

How many Brazilian immigrants reside in the United States today? Due to the largely undocumented status of Brazucas, estimates range widely. One point of agreement by researchers is that U.S. Census data grossly underestimate this population; official estimates count approximately 170,000 undocumented Brazilians and fewer than 300,00 Brazilians in the country (Hoefner 2006; Margolis, this volume). Unofficially, estimates go as high as 1.5 million Brazilians in the United States, but the Brazilian government and the press generally accept the slightly more conservative figure of approximately 1 million Brazilians living here (Meihy 2004; Margolis, this volume). The ability to generate any estimates is partly due to the field research that has been conducted for over a decade.

Maxine Margolis published the first major study of Brazilian immigrants to the United States in 1994, detailing an ethnographic account of this population in New York City. Brazilians coming to this major pole of attraction for immigrants from all over the world created their own space within niche immigrant markets but, overall, blended into the complex fabric of foreigners who overstayed tourist visas to find their fortunes in the city. Margolis concluded that the Brazilian community in New York City at that time was not firmly established, and that most immigrants had plans to return to Brazil once they accumulated a certain amount of financial capital.

The ensuing researchers hailed from Brazil and focused on immigration to the Boston area, considered to be the second major area of settlement (behind New York City/New Jersey) for Brazilians in the United States (MRE 2002). Work by Martes (2000), Fleischer (2002) and Sales (2003), among others, advances some interesting hypotheses regarding the formation of the initial social networks that, though sparse, help to explain the emergence of Massachusetts as a major receiving state. Even though Martes (2000) deems further research is necessary to document the history of these important formative years, she speculates that at least six events triggered the first social networks: 1) During World War II, American engineers from the Boston area traveled to Governador Valadares, a city in the Southeastern state of Minas Gerais, to work on the region's mineral extraction and a railroad that linked the region to the coastal area. When they came back to the States, many of them brought their Brazilian domestic employees. 2) After the war, some Bostonians strengthened the relationship with Valadares via constant trips to buy semi-precious stones in the city and surroundings. 3) In the 1960s, newspapers from Rio and São Paulo published a number of ads offering jobs to Brazilian women interested in working as maids in the Boston area. 4) Also in that decade, a businessman from Lowell, Massachusetts, hired twenty soccer players from Belo Horizonte to form a soccer team. Apparently, most of them not only decided to stay permanently in the United States, but they also helped other family members to immigrate. 5) At the end of that decade, a group of more than ten young people from Governador Valadares decided to come to the States to spend some time on "an adventurous trip … in the country of theirs dreams" (p. 62). They ended up in the Boston area, where many settled permanently and helped family members make their journey to the United States. 6) Finally, several Brazilians came to study in Boston and decided not to return to Brazil. These episodes, and probably others, helped to forge links between Brazilian and American individuals, businesses and government organizations.[5] This also helps to explain why a majority of Brazilians in Massachusetts today still trace their origins to the same area: Governador Valadares.

Another facilitating factor was the attraction of an older, well established Portuguese community that offered immediate linguistic familiarity. The Boston area Brazuca scene comprises a dense settlement of immigrants with firmly established networks of families and friends that facilitate the search for employment and other information. An important consequence of having families versus only young adults coming to the United States is that a community—in the more traditional sense of the term—begins to take root, and the discourse of immigration shifts from just covering employment needs to one that includes the search for better educational opportunities than those possible (and affordable) in Brazil (see, for example, Souza 2005).

The main objective of these initial research projects was to paint a picture of the emerging Brazilian presence in the United States[6]; as argued above, this picture has been gradually changing. More Brazilians tend to postpone indefinitely their plans of returning (Jouët-Pastré 2004), the number of immigrants crossing the Mexican border has increased dramatically, and the population is almost evenly divided between males and females (Margolis 2003, and Siqueira 2006). This new reality is depicted in a film titled *A Fronteira* [The Frontier] (2002), which narrates the saga of two Brazilian families crossing the Mexican border under extreme hardship. *A Fronteira* also reveals another aspect of Brazilian immigration commonly experienced by other groups of immigrants: an increase in Brazilians coming from the lowest economic strata (Souza 2004). According to Piore (1979), this last trend is due to the fact that middle-class immigrants have the cultural and economic means to undertake the first journeys and establish a network of services that facilitate the immigration of poorer and less-educated populations. Although there is no updated data on the racial makeup of Brazilian immigrants, we could speculate that, as poorer Brazilians are making their journeys to the United States, the color spectrum of immigrants may be broadening to include more dark-skinned individuals. This speculation is based on the Brazilian history of racial inequalities that tends to confine Afro-descendants to the poorest ranks of society (Telles 2004).

A recent visit to Governador Valadares lent credence to these claims. The established middle-class neighborhoods built almost exclusively with remittances from the United States are still there and new ones are still appearing, though more slowly due to the poorer exchange rate of recent years. One can still be impressed by the mansions owned by those who truly become rich in this flow of people and money: the owners of construction businesses; the *doleiros* who, until a recent crackdown, openly exchanged *reais* for dollars in the center of town; and the *consuls*, affectionately named for the services they provide to residents wanting to migrate. Yet what is now clear to researchers and service providers is that the rural areas have become a key part of the migration flow. In many of these tiny towns almost no men remain and women are left to tend to the house and the children. In this region of valleys, one anecdote tells the story of groups of women who must climb a hill every afternoon so that they can have adequate cell phone reception, in order to check in with their husbands who are in the United States.[7]

As the Brazilian immigrant group continues to grow and begins to establish a second generation, the research agenda has understandably broadened to include a wider array of sending communities and U.S. destinations. Research in California (Beserra 2003; Ribeiro 1999) and Florida (Oliveira 2003; Resende 2003), for example, offers perspectives on settlement within established Hispanic communities. Furthermore, anecdotal evidence of a growing Brazilian presence in small communities within Northeastern and Southern states calls for greater attention to what might be considered secondary points of migration for immigrants who, by choice or necessity, leave the larger and more established areas of Brazilian settlement in the United States. Adding geographic variation to research leads to new findings, such as evidence that Brazilians living in Florida are more likely to identify as Hispanics in order to ally themselves with the most powerful ethnic population in the state (Oliveira 2003; Resende 2003). Yet just as important to the expanding research agenda—and to this volume—is a richer analysis of existing communities.

Becoming Brazuca

The three categories that divide the chapters in this book represent the latest concerns regarding Brazucas, offering perspectives on the past, present, and future of Brazilian immigration to the United States. Many of the chapters address methodological and theoretical gaps in research on Brazilian immigration as well as the broader questions of immigration research that Carola Suárez-Orozco presents in the Prologue. The variety of issues affecting Brazilian immigrants suggests that there are different perspectives to be considered and, therefore, there is a need for a national view of Brazilian immigration that encompasses interdisciplinary research. It is our hope, then, that the contributions in this volume serve to enrich the dialogue concerning the myriad questions facing researchers, practitioners, politicians, and other community members, whose roles as insiders or outsiders in new immigrant groups continuously shape the social landscape of the United States.

The Art of Seduction: Images of Brazil and the United States in the Twentieth Century

While the economic downturn of the 1980s was undoubtedly a major catalyst for emigration from Brazil, other factors must also be considered in order to understand why so many of those who left chose to come to the United States. As the title of this section implies, the twentieth century cemented a fascination with the United States by Brazilians, and vice-versa. One of the factors that greatly contributed to captivating the interest of Brazilians in all American "things" was the advent of cinema and the success of the Hollywood industry. Many leading companies in the highly profitable world of entertainment perceived Latin American countries, including Brazil, as a market to be explored on many different fronts. For example, in 1927 the Fox Company launched a contest in Brazil that sought new talents to take part in its movie productions. As Brazilian journalist Ruy Castro (2005) recounts in his biography of singer and actress Carmen Miranda, the offices of Fox in Rio de Janeiro were literally flooded with letters and photos of young aspiring actors and actresses from all over Brazil. This contest lasted several weeks and received ample coverage by the Brazilian media and, of course, generated great free publicity for Fox and for Hollywood in general. This attraction to American culture is blatant in the lyrics of numerous sambas composed in the 1930s and 1940s, including those by composer Noel Rosa in his samba "Não tem tradução" ("There Is No Translation"):

> The spoken cinema
> Is the main one to blame for the change
> ...

When the trickster gave up on dancing samba
He started dancing fox trot
In the samba club
...
And the rhymes of samba are not "I love you."

This early twentieth-century contact with the United States, at both individual and political levels, opened a dialogue that played an important role in artistic and intellectual movements in Brazil and less so in the United States. As Darién Davis describes in Chapter 1, a significant number of Brazilian performers traveled to the United States as early as the 1930s. This group of artists, which included Carmen Miranda and Ary Barroso, influenced and were influenced by American musical styles of the time, contributed to American's conceptions of Brazil by simultaneously distinguishing and blurring the lines between it and the rest of Latin America, and brought images of the United States back home with them. These exchanges were particularly salient during the Good Neighbor Policy instituted by the United States between 1933 and 1947, aimed at establishing political and economic ties between the United States and Latin America. Intellectual cross pollination also occurred: Gilberto Freyre, who studied under the anthropologist Franz Boas in the 1920s, used his experiences in the United States to shape his ideas, which brought forth a new wave of Brazilian scholarship that defended miscegenation and gave rise to the highly influential (and contested) idea of racial democracy in Brazil.

The consequences of these artistic, academic and political connections between the two countries are still felt by Brazucas today. The image of what the United States has to offer is only strengthened as more immigrants establish themselves and send tales of their successes back home, a process made almost instantaneous in this day and age with telephones and the Internet. And once Brazilians arrive, they often discover their "Brazilianness" in ways they never previously explored, either because they want to make a mark in defining their culture for themselves or because they see the need to feed into cultural expectations of what being Brazilian means. The image created of Brazilians can be perceived as positive and empowering or as negative and marginalizing. In Chapter 2 Bernadete Beserra analyzes the Brazilian community in Los Angeles, focusing on the ways women become aware of stereotypes held by non-Brazilians and their consequences. She describes how a false image of Brazil is consumed abroad and interrogates the role Brazilian women themselves have in subverting their culture into a commodity and into a potential for gaining power. Beserra argues that the exotic and differentiated image that non-Brazilians hold of them can both prevent discrimination by distinguishing them from other Latinos and reduce them to sexual objects. This chapter not only reflects upon the reception of a Brazilian community in Los Angeles but also asks provoking questions that ultimately lead to the future of relations between Brazilian and U.S. communities.

As the Brazilian communities in the States become older and larger, the number of Brazilian ethnic media grows exponentially. For example, Rede Globo, the main Brazilian TV network, is now broadcast in the main cable services throughout the United States and provides programs geared specifically towards the Brazilian community. This and other media are an important part of defining the immigrant community and how it is built within the context of interactions with non-Brazilians. Through the lens of the ethnic media, one can also pin down the social-ethnic-economic background of Brazilians who have been choosing the United States as a new home. In Chapter 3 Else Vieira shows, through an in-depth analysis of the Brazilian media in this country, that in the seventies there was a large contingent of émigrés who identified themselves as political exiles or as transnational entrepreneurs. Over time, this configuration has been changing and in the late eighties a new and larger group of émigrés emerged: the Brazuca or, in her own words, the "undocumented and precariously integrated Brazilian migrant." Vieira also explores the role that Brazilian publications on the East and West Coast play in defining the community for itself and for non-Brazilians. She focuses on two major newspapers: the New York-based *The Brazilians/The Brasilians* and the San Francisco-based *Brazil Today*, showing that the newspapers' agenda changed significantly over time to accompany the new configurations of the Brazilian communities. She also carefully analyzes the role that Portuguese and English languages play in articulating and reconstructing Brazilian identity abroad. Brazilians thus move from being foreigners to being immigrants who start building communities within established American contexts, a topic to which we turn in the next section.

(In)Visibility: Community and Belonging

The idea of community conjures up a critical mass of people who are established and visible to outsiders by means of commerce, political engagement, language, and a host of other factors. Yet numerous scholars have identified politics, ethnicity, lack of documentation, and the transient nature of Brazilian immigrants as factors leading to their invisibility in American society (as detailed in Jouët-Pastré and Braga 2005). As the community grows, the question of whether and why it is invisible must also be accompanied by the question of what the implications of invisibility are for the community, and whether such a status is passively or actively, inwardly or outwardly ascertained. Being invisible can connote nothingness or a lack of belonging, yet it has also been seen historically as strength and power (for example, through figures ranging from gods to superheroes). A critical factor is whether the person, entity or, in our case, the community feels in control of the process and outcomes of making invisibility a component of its identity.

One salient question is whether Brazilian immigration is a significant enough phenomenon to constitute an actual community in the United States. Using the size of the population as a measure of community is complicated given that a large proportion of Brazilians in the United States is undocumented. At the beginning of this wave of immigration, most undocumented Brazilians attained this status because they overstayed their visas. But as Carlos Eduardo Siqueira and Tiago Jansen detail in Chapter 4, there has been a significant recent increase in the much more dangerous and expensive entry through the U.S.-Mexico border, likely because of more stringent visa requirements. Siqueira and Jansen's chapter focuses on finding ways of establishing the number of Brazilians living in the United States. The authors use Massachusetts as a case study and propose combining a very creative data source with two more traditional ones: they analyze passport forms from the Brazilian Consulate in Boston along with the 2000 Census data, and the 2003 Immigration and Naturalization data. Finally, they argue that this study could be duplicated in other states and could offer a more accurate and rich picture of Brazilian demographics in the United States than the one we have currently.

Beyond numbers, other authors in this section present different measures of the presence of Brazilians in the United States. Ana Cristina Braga Martes (Chapter 5) contributes an in-depth study of remittances from the United States to Brazil. Her field research was conducted both in the United States and in Brazil. In addition to a survey targeting individuals who send remittances as well as owners of remittance agencies, she interviewed families and representatives of Non-Governmental Organizations that benefited from remittances in Brazil to resolve key questions that recent studies on remittances have raised. For example, she explores to what extent remittances contribute to local development and the reduction of poverty by discussing the impacts of the dollars sent by migrants to the people, families, and organizations that receive them. As Braga Martes indicates in her chapter, while they are still only 1% of the GDP, remittances already account for a larger product for Brazil than many exports. While sending money abroad might signal a lack of roots in the United States, the ability to earn enough money to send to family members in Brazil, who increasingly rely on this source of income, is also an indicator of the presence of Brazilians in the economic sphere at a significant level.

Remittances can be an indicator of transnationalism, which is discussed by Judith McDonnell and Cileine de Lourenço (Chapter 6) as it relates to the negotiation of race, gender, and class. The authors problematize the very concept of transnationalism and interrogate its meaning both through concrete examples drawn from a study they conducted with Brazilian immigrant women and through comparisons with studies conducted with other immigrant groups. They inquire whether it is possible to consider the existence of a transnational identity and the ways in which this identity is weaved vis-à-vis race, ethnicity, class, gender, and nation. In their analysis of narratives by Brazilian immigrant women, the authors examine how they perform Brazilianness as a way of maintaining personal and cultural connections between the United States and Brazil; for some Brazilian immigrant women transnationalism can act as a facilitator in defining one's place within the categories of race, gender, and ethnicity in the United States, rather than a barrier to fully investing in American society. Yet just as there are tales of success and of many immigrants who choose to make the United States their permanent home, there are immigrants who choose or are forced to return to Brazil.

In Chapter 7, Sueli Siqueira offers a perspective of return migrants in the most significant sending area of Brazil, Governador Valadares, in terms of numbers of people and of an established history of migration to the United States. She investigates the immigrants' projects and expectations about their return to Brazil and, conversely, she analyzes the difficulties of the immigrants who returned and did not adapt back. Siqueira asks important questions, such as the main reasons for the willingness to go back to Brazil and the causes for the lack of success of the ones who returned. Among her many interesting findings is that immigrants who plan to return tend to invest in real state and in businesses that offer services. According to her study, many Brazilian immigrants are already on their second stay in the United States. They could not adapt back home due to a range of factors, including failure of the businesses they opened in Brazil, urban violence, and difficulties in adapting to the Brazilian cultural and social life.

One of the first interactions that immigrant groups have with the American way of life is when learning how basic needs such as medical assistance and housing are fulfilled here. Clémence Jouët-Pastré, Branca Telles Ribeiro, Márcia Guimarães and Solange de Azambuja Lira (Chapter 8) narrate the experiences of Brazilian immigrant women in clinical settings as they seek medical attention. Basic barriers such as language need to be addressed and are increasingly being resolved through medical interpreters. However, there are more subtle impediments to the doctor-patient relationship that need to be understood, ranging from the more concrete trauma of the migratory experience that can necessitate psychological assistance to the more abstract cultural difference in the concept of time and how this affects expectations of the clinical encounter.

Within a turbulent political climate in which immigrant groups can be accused of terrorism or of robbing Americans' jobs, immigrants may take advantage of the American tendency towards pan-ethnic labels to gain a political voice as Latinos or as Asian Americans. In certain cases, alliances with Americans occur when citizens who are marginalized or who feel a loss of political power see engaging immigrant groups as a means towards empowering themselves. In the Boston area, for example, Josh Kirshner (Chapter 9) analyzes the conditions under which labor unions are reaching out to recruit Brazilian immigrant workers. His study demonstrates that labor unions are drawing Brazilians into their ranks by organizing and forging links to grassroots Brazilian immigrant organizations. Labor unions are also combining traditional organizing methods with more innovative ones, such as promoting both the long-established practice of hand billing outside plants and a new practice of visiting workers in their homes. Unions also hold citizenship workshops in grassroots community organizations, use the Brazilian ethnic media to raise awareness about their existence and interest in the community and, perhaps most importantly, they hire Brazilian immigrants as full-time organizers. Kirshner's chapter points out that as unions in the United States have experienced a lengthy decline, immigrants have the potential for changing the face of political engagement by creating new groups and supporting older voices that speak for marginalized populations.

Brazilians also engage in community formation by joining churches. Paul Freston (Chapter 10) begins to fill the gap in research on the role and demographics of religious participation for Brazilians in the United States by comparing this group to other immigrant groups in this country and to Brazilians in other countries. He argues that the Brazilian diaspora's religious affiliations cannot be simply understood as a transplant from Brazil, demonstrating, for example, that not all the religions present in Brazil migrate to the United States. In addition, the religions that migrate undergo profound transformations in the social roles they play in the life of the community. The minority religions either disappear in the diaspora or have a timid presence. On the other hand, the two most established religions in Brazil – Catholicism and varieties of Protestantism – are prevalent in the diaspora but clearly change vis-à-vis their importance in Brazil compared to their importance in the States. Here Protestantism has a relatively larger presence and, within the complexity and variety of the Protestant churches, the Pentecostal tendencies become stronger among the Brazilian émigrés.

A New Generation of People and Research

Studies of immigrant groups tend to start with the first generation of adults, though attention has also more recently been directed towards the second generation (e.g., Kasinitz et al. 2004; Portes and Rumbaut 2001; Portes and Zhou 1993; Waters 1999). Yet as Teresa Sales and Márcia Loureiro note in Chapter 12, there has been little to no research on the second generation of Brazilian immigration because of the recency of this migratory influx; research on youth in this community, therefore, has focused on immigrants born abroad instead of the children of immigrants born in the United States. The Brazilian immigrant group is already heavily comprised of adolescents who are encountering the United States for the first time through the school system rather than through the workplace.

While the focus on teenagers in the research agenda can be conceptualized as resulting from the lack of a true second generation, it is actually a critical step that must be included to understand immigrant adaptation. The "first" and "second" generational categories do not account for the particular experiences of adolescent immigrants and, as a result, sociologists introduced the "1.5 generation" category to better encapsulate the experience of newcomers who have been primarily socialized in their country of origin and enter the American educational system at the onset of adolescence. Recent studies support the argument that further subdividing and defining these generational cohorts may potentially reveal significant variation in adaptive outcomes within a particular national origin group (Rumbaut 2004).

At a cognitive-developmental level, these generational distinctions are important. One characteristic of immigrants is a dual frame of reference by which they constantly compare the "'here and now' with the 'there and then'" because of their exposure to multiple influences (Suárez-Orozco and Suárez-Orozco 2001, p. 87; see also Ogbu and Simons 1998). Adult immigrants may compare both cultures, but their identity is firmly grounded in their native country. Conversely, while second-generation youth might share the language and customs of their parents' background, their reference is not grounded in personal experience in their home country. The identities of youths who immigrate during late childhood or early adolescence, however, are forged in and by two cultural spheres of influence, which act as two mirrors refracting one perspective of what it means to be an immigrant. As Roberta, a Brazilian immigrant adolescent, says, "when I make a decision, with anything that I do here...I also think there, in Brazil, like 'Man, if I did this, there in Brazil, would I do the same thing?'" (Braga 2007a, p. 22).

Now twenty years into this wave of Brazilian immigration, a generation of American-born children of Brazilian immigrants has started to populate the community. As seen in the literature reviewed by Sales and Loureiro in Chapter 12, the second generation is often the ruler by which the success or failure of an immigrant group is measured in research. One basic but important difference between these children and their foreign-born siblings and parents is that they are all American citizens, while many of their family members may be undocumented. This division in documentation by generation carries serious implications for immigrant individuals, families, and communities, especially as immigration law reforms are discussed at the local and national level. Directly or not, variations in documentation status may influence and/or be influenced by levels of transnational practices, a topic that is now being incorporated into research on second-generation immigrants (Levitt and Waters 2002). Physical, virtual (electronic) and psychological connections to the sending country have implications for how youths are categorized generationally, for their educational goals, and for their self-identification in ethnic and/or transnational communities (Levitt and Waters 2002; Louie 2006 a and b). Emerging research suggests that second-generation Brazilians are more likely to embrace the pan-ethnic Hispanic label as an identity that provides access to the American practice of affirmative action in education (Menezes 2003). However, perceived discrimination in the current climate of raids and deportation could lead Brazilian immigrant youth to form a "reactive ethnicity" and identify more by national origin, as has occurred with other groups (Rumbaut 2004).

Ana Ramos-Zayas (Chapter 11) begins this section with an analysis of Brazilian immigrant adolescents in the working-class community of Newark, New Jersey. Issues of identity development, already prominent during adolescence, are heightened for immigrants who find themselves within a new context; this specific context becomes central in defining which classifications they will identify with, reject, transform or create. Ramos-Zayas explores how Brazilian adolescents in Newark negotiate their Brazilian identity to distinguish themselves from the substantial Portuguese community in the area. The adolescents draw on myths—like racial democracy—that they bring from Brazil, creating new identities of "cultural excess" that focus on the unique aspects of being Brazilian. These youths resist standard classification by emphasizing their culture and sustaining their racial invisibility, creating a category that is distinct from but compatible with the "Hispanic" and "American" categories associated with other groups in the area.

Teresa Sales and Márcia Loureiro (Chapter 12) compare data from consular and state sources to identify some characteristics of the second generation of Brazilian immigrants in Massachusetts. Certain patterns persist in that the majority of the population is concentrated in a few cities in the state, and most mothers still come from the state of Minas Gerais, the major sending hub of immigrants to this area. However, the data show an increase in sending states and receiving cities within Massachusetts, suggesting that this new generation will likely not be restricted to ethnic enclaves or to one manifestation of what it means to be Brazilian. Returning to the population of immigrant adolescents born abroad, the authors focused on their experience of work and how these experiences must be understood through the cultural frames that the recently arrived youngsters bring from Brazil. The authors also mention the language choices that adolescents make, which are influenced by dynamics such as location, age, and the relationship of those involved in the conversation.

In Chapter 13, Katia Mota explores the linguistic advantages that bilingualism offers Brazilian youth in the United States, from the questionable skill of controlling their parents' access to English-speaking authority figures to motivating career choices and the pursuit of further education. The discourses of return to Brazil or permanence in the United States vary among the families interviewed, leading to different reasons for parents' desires that their children maintain Portuguese fluency. The ability of these children to eventually achieve full bilingualism is intrinsically tied to the fluidity of their ethnic identities, which not only defines what it means to be a Brazilian immigrant but also contributes to a Brazilian national identity.

A pioneer in the research on Brazilian immigration to the United States, Maxine Margolis (Chapter 14) concludes this volume with an appraisal of the research agenda as it currently stands, and offers insights on important areas for research that need more breadth and depth of investigation in the years to come. Margolis also addresses an important event, the terrorist attacks of September 11th, which brought significant changes in global relationships that affect how immigration is conceived in the United States. At both the psychological and political levels, this event has both empowered xenophobic attitudes and promoted counterbalancing forces that call for the defense of human rights.

The consequences of 9/11 call for a more nuanced consideration of new immigration flows and of the pros and cons of visibility for immigrants in the United States. In the past five years, Brazilian immigrants started figuring prominently in the top ten source countries for unauthorized immigration, and showed the second greatest increase (70%) in such immigration to the United States between 2000–2005 (Hoefner 2006).[8] The number of Brazilians detained at the United States-Mexico border dropped by over 90% between 2005 and 2006 due to new automatic deportation measures and visa requirements for entry into Mexico, but those who continue to try face longer and more dangerous trips through Guatemala, for example (Maisonnave 2006). Furthermore, recent news is filled with examples of how the criminalization of immigrants has led to fear and upheaval in communities; many Brazilians have recently begun to return to their homeland. There is no consensus on the extent to which this flow of people is shifting, or how much of the shift is due to political climate (versus a poorer economy, for example), but headlines like "Brazilians giving up their American Dream" (Bernstein and Dwoskin 2007) and "Hardships in Mass. spur Brazilian exodus" (Ballou 2008) indicate that a significant number of people are leaving behind their hopes for a better life in the United States.

Another recent event, the destruction of the Gulf Coast region by hurricanes Katrina and Rita, should be considered in future directions of research with the U.S.-based Brazilian immigrant population. The storms attracted a new Latino population to work on reconstruction in the area, potentially shifting its established demographic landscape (Villegas-Muriel 2006). Brazilian immigrants in search of better wages and climates are playing a significant role in this migratory flow, with implications for the future look of New Orleans and of Brazilian immigration to the United States that have only begun to be studied (Mast and Frick 2006).

Brazuca: even the spelling of the word is representative of an immigrant group in the process of simultaneously forming its identity and feeling an identity imposed upon itself by the host society: should the "b" be capitalized if representative of nationality, as in English, or be a lower-case letter as in Portuguese? Is the root Brazil or Brasil? Whatever the choice, the word represents a combination that is at once both languages and neither one, echoing the sentiment of many Brazilians in the United States who struggle to define themselves; it should probably remain malleable in its spelling so that each person can foreground whichever part of her or his identity is most meaningful to them.

Notes

1. Researchers have long compared and contrasted the U.S. and Brazil on measures of race and racism, as Darién Davis explores in Chapter 1. The topic of racial versus class discrimination remains relevant and contested to this day, as seen by the success of recent publications such as Edward Telles' *Race in Another America* (2004), which received the top award in American Sociology for 2006, and the best-selling status of journalist Ali Kamel's *Não Somos Racistas* (We Are Not Racists, 2006).

2. In addition to the offer of free tickets, officials portrayed the country as a racial paradise, as exemplified by an official ad by the Brazilian government reproduced in an American newspaper: "A black man can become the president of Brazil and this fact would not draw further attention than the election of a white man here" (Ramos 1996, p. 63). This campaign attracted a number of young African Americans who proposed to buy land in Brazil to build the Brazilian American Colonization Syndicate; Brazilian diplomats denied visas to the young African Americans without acknowledging a racial issue, resorting instead to a nationalistic discourse that "denied to any government or foreign citizen the right to question the Brazilian immigration policy" (Lesser as cited in Ramos 1996, p. 64). Brazilian elites were not particularly enthusiastic about Japanese immigrants, either (Sakurai 2000; Lesser 2003). However, a carefully crafted negotiation between the two governments created the path for a long history of migration between Japan and Brazil. The negotiations were sustained by important subsidies from the Japanese government and by Brazilian interests to sell a vast array of products to the Japanese market (Lesser 2003).

3. Sales, T. (2003).

4. Meihy, J. (2004).

5. Research currently being done by Sueli Siqueira (a contributor to this volume) in Governador Valadares supports some of these hypotheses; narratives from some of the first migrants in the 1960s mention Americans who were drawn to the region by mining and established an English school attended by fairly affluent youth in the city. This exposure led to study and work abroad opportunities (albeit not necessarily in Boston) that likely influenced the flow of subsequent Brazilians from this area to the United States.

6. As the Brazilian experience is relatively new, there are still few publications available either in English or in Portuguese. In English there are five books that deal with the issue: *Little Brazil* (Maxine Margolis); *An Invisible Minority:*

Brazilians in New York City (Maxine Margolis); *Changing Gender Roles: Brazilian Immigrant Families in the U.S.* (Silvia DeBiaggi); *Brazilians Away from Home* (Teresa Sales); and *Brazilian Immigrants in the United States: Cultural Imperialism and Social Class* (Bernadete Beserra).

7. Leticia J. Braga would like to thank Sueli Siqueira for her hospitality and for this anecdote, provided during Leticia's research visit to Governador Valadares in May of 2007.
8. India showed the greatest increase during this period (133%).

References

A Fronteira. 2002. Dir. Roberto Carminatti. Motion Factory.

Alvim, Z. 2000. "O Brasil Italiano (1880–1920)." In *Fazer a América.* Ed. Boris Fausto. São Paulo: Editora da Universidade de São Paulo.

Ballou, B. R. 2008, January 8. Hardships in Mass. spur Brazilian exodus. *The Boston Globe.* Retrieved February 23, 2008, from http://www.boston.com/news/local/massachusetts/articles/2008/01/08/hardships_in_mass_spur_brazilian_exodus/

Bernstein, N. and E. Dwoskin. 2007, December 4. Brazilians Giving Up Their American Dream. *New York Times.* Retrieved December 4, 2007, from http://www.nytimes.com/2007/12/04/nyregion/04brazilians.html?ex=1197435600&en=601688a20e7559a0&ei=5070&emc=eta1

Beserra, B. 2003. *Brazilian Immigrants in the United States: Cultural Imperialism and Social Class.* New York: LFB Scholarly Publishing.

Braga, L. J. 2007a. "Understanding Context through Culture and Cognition: The Varied Experiences of Brazilian Immigrant Adolescents." Unpublished manuscript, Harvard University, Cambridge, MA.

———. 2007b (Spring). "Becoming Brazuca? A Tale of Two Teens." *ReVista.* Cambridge: David Rockefeller Center for Latin American Studies.

Castro, R. 2005. *Carmen: Uma biografia.* São Paulo: Companhia das Letras.

Fleischer, S. 2002. *Passando a América a Limpo: O Trabalho de Housecleaners Brasileiras em Boston, Massachusetts* [Cleaning America: The work of Brazilian housecleaners in Boston, Massachusetts]. São Paulo, Brazil: Annablume Editora.

Hoefner, M., N. Rytina and C. Campbell. 2006. *Estimates of the Unauthorized Immigrant Population Residing in the United States: January 2005.* Washington, DC: Office of Immigration Statistics.

IBGE. 2000. *Brasil—500 anos de povoamento.* Rio de Janeiro: IBGE.

Jouët-Pastré, C. 2004. "Tendências Contemporâneas nos Estudos da Emigração Brasileira para os Estados Unidos e Canadá." *Revista Brasileira de Ciências Sociais* 19(55): 186–190.

Jouët-Pastré, C. and L. J. Braga. 2005. "Community-based Learning: A Window into the Portuguese-speaking Communities of New England." *Hispania*, 88(4): 863–872.

Jouët-Pastré, C., M. Loveless and L. J. Braga. 2004. *Giving Voice to a Nascent Community: Exploring Brazilian Immigration to the US through Research and Practice.* Cambridge: David Rockefeller Center for Latin American Studies.

Kamel, A. 2006. *Não somos racistas: Uma reação aos que querem nos transformar numa nação bicolor* [We are not racists: A reaction to those who want to turn us into a bicolor nation]. Rio de Janeiro: Editora Nova Fronteira.

Kasinitz, P., J. H. Mollenkopf, and M. C. Waters. 2004. *Becoming New Yorkers: Ethnographies of the Second Generation.* New York: Russell Sage Foundation.

Lesser, J. 2003. *Searching for Home Abroad: Japanese Brazilians and Transnationalism.* Durham: Duke University Press.

Levitt, P. and M. Waters. 2002. Introduction. In *The Changing Face of Home: The Transnational Lives of the Second Generation,* pp. 1–32. Ed. Peggy Levitt and Mary C. Waters. New York: Russell Sage Foundation.

Louie, V. 2006a. "Second Generation Pessimism and Optimism: How Chinese and Dominicans Understand Education and Mobility Through Ethnic and Transnational Orientations." *International Migration Review* 40(3): 537–572.

———. 2006b. "Growing Up Ethnic in Transnational Worlds: Identities Among Second-Generation Chinese and Dominicans." *Identities* 13(3): 363–394. Special Issue on Global Spaces/Local Places: Diaspora, Transnational Practices, and the Meaning of Home.

Maisonnave, F. 2006, November 16. Brasileiros deixam de emigrar via México. *Folha de São Paulo.* Retrieved November 20, 2006, from http://www1.folha.uol.com.br/fsp/mundo/ft1611200601.htm

Margolis, M. 1994. *Little Brazil.* Princeton: Princeton University Press.

———. 2003. "Na virada do milênio: A emigração brasileira para os Estados Unidos." In *Fronteiras Cruzadas: etnicidade, gênero e redes sociais.* Ed. Ana Cristina Braga Martes and Soraya Fleischer. São Paulo: Paz e Terra.

———. 2008. "Becoming *Brazucas*: Brazilian Identity in the United States." In *The Other Latinos: Central and South Americans in the United States.* Ed. J. L. Falconi and J. A. Mazzotti. Cambridge, MA: Harvard University Press (DRCLAS Series on Latin American Studies).

Marrow, H. B. 2003. "To Be or Not to Be (Hispanic or Latino): Brazilian Racial and Ethnic Identity in the United States." *Ethnicities*, 3:427–464.

Martes, A. C. B. and S. Fleischer, eds. 2003. *Fronteiras Cruzadas: etnicidade, gênero e redes sociais.* São Paulo: Paz e Terra.

Martes, A. C. B. 2000. *Brasileiros nos Estados Unidos: Um estudo sobre imigrantes em Massachusetts.* São Paulo: Paz e Terra.

Martínez, E. 2000. "O Brasil como País de Destino para os Migrantes Espanhóis." In *Fazer a América*. Ed. Boris Fausto. São Paulo: Editora da Universidade de São Paulo.

Mast, R. and A. Frick. 2006. "Rebuilding a City, Rebuilding a Citizenry: Charting Immigration Growth and Patterns in post-Katrina New Orleans's Brazilian Demographic." Paper presented at the conference "Embracing Diversity: Latino immigration and the transformation of American society" at Harvard University, Cambridge, MA.

Meihy, J. C. 2004. *Brasil fora de si*. São Paulo: Editora Parábola.

Menezes, G. 2003. "Filhos da imigração: A segunda geração de brasileiros em Connecticut." In *Fronteiras Cruzadas: etnicidade, gênero e redes sociais*. Ed. Ana Cristina Braga Martes and Soraya Fleisher. São Paulo: Paz e Terra.

MRE (Ministério das Relações Exteriores). 2002. *Estimativa de brasileiros residentes no exterior*. Brasília: MRE (Divisão de Assistência Consular).

Ogbu, J. U. and H. D. Simons. 1998. "Voluntary and Involuntary Minorities: A Cultural-Ecological Theory of School Performance with Some Implications for Education." *Anthropology & Education Quarterly* 29(2): 155–188.

Oliveira, A. 2003. "O caminho sem volta—Classe social e etnicidade entre os brasileiros na Flórida." In *Fronteiras Cruzadas: etnicidade, gênero e redes sociais*. Ed. Ana Cristina Braga Martes and Soraya Fleischer. São Paulo: Paz e Terra.

Oliveira, L. L. 2001. *O Brasil dos imigrantes*. Rio de Janeiro: Jorge Zahar Editor.

Piore, M. 1979. *Birds of Passage: Migrant Labor and Industrial Societies*. New York: Cambridge University Press.

Portes, A. and R. G. Rumbaut. 2001. *Legacies: The Story of the Immigrant Second Generation*. Berkeley: University of California Press.

Portes, A. and M. Zhou. 1993. "The New Second Generation: Segmented Assimilation and Its Variants. *Annals of the American Academy of Political and Social Sciences* 530 (November): 74–96.

Ramos, J. 1996. "Dos males que vêm com o sangue: as representações raciais e a categoria do imigrante indesejável nas concepções sobre imigração da década de 20." In *Raça, Ciência e Sociedade*. Ed. Marcos Chor Maio and Ricardo Ventura Santos. Rio de Janeiro: Editora Fiocruz/Centro Cultural Banco do Brasil.

Resende, R. 2003. "Brasileiros no sul da Flórida—Relatos de uma pesquisa em andamento." In *Fronteiras Cruzadas: etnicidade, gênero e redes sociais*. Ed. Ana Cristina Braga Martes and Soraya Fleisher. São Paulo: Paz e Terra.

Ribeiro, G. 1999. "O Que Faz O Brasil, Brazil: Jogos Identitários em San Francisco." In *Cenas do Brasil Migrante*, pp. 45–85. Ed. Rosana Reis and Teresa Sales. São Paulo: Boitempo Editorial.

Rosa, N. 1993. "Não tem tradução." Retrieved June 2008 from http://muuziki.net/letras/noel-rosa/nao-tem-traducao.

Rumbaut, R. G. 2004. "Ages, Life Stages, and Generational Cohorts: Decomposing the Immigrant First and Second Generations in the United States." *International Migration Review* 38(3): 1160–1205.

Sakurai, C. 2000. "Imigração Japonesa para o Brasil: Um Exemplo de Imigração Tutelada." In *Fazer a América*. Org. Boris Fausto. São Paulo: Editora da Universidade de São Paulo.

Sales, T. 2003. *Brazilians Away from Home*. New York: Center for Migration Studies. (Originally published in Portuguese 1999).

Seyferth, G. 1996. "Construindo a nação: hierarquias raciais e o papel do racismo na política de imigração e colonização." In *Raça, Ciência e Sociedade*. Ed. Marcos Chor Maio and Ricardo Ventura Santos. Rio de Janeiro: Editora Fiocruz/Centro Cultural Banco do Brasil.

———. 2000. "A Colonização Alemã no Brasil: Etnicidade e Conflito." In *Fazer a América*. Org. Boris Fausto. São Paulo: Editora da Universidade de São Paulo.

Siqueira, S. 2006. "Migrantes e empreendedorismo na Microrregião de Governador Valadares: Sonhos e frustrações no retorno." Dissertation in Sociology, Universidade Federal de Minas Gerais, Brasil.

Souza (Galvão), H. 2004. "Brazilians in New England: A Changing Profile and the Consequences of 9/11." In *Giving Voice to a Nascent Community: Exploring Brazilian Immigration to the U.S. through Research and Practice*. Ed. Clémence Jouët-Pastré, Megwen Loveless and Leticia Braga. Working Paper no. 04/05-2. Cambridge: David Rockefeller Center for Latin American Studies.

Souza (Galvão), H. 2005. "An Oral History of Brazilian Women Immigrants in the Boston Area." In *Passing Lines: Sexuality and Immigration*. Ed. Brad Epps, Keja Valens, and Bill Johnson González. Cambridge, MA: David Rockefeller Center Series on Latin American Studies, Harvard University Press.

Suárez-Orozco, C. and M. M. Suárez-Orozco. 2001. *Children of Immigration*. Cambridge, MA: Harvard University Press.

Telles, E. E. 2004. *Race in Another America: The Significance of Skin Color in Brazil*. Princeton: Princeton University Press.

Tosta, A. 2004. "Latino, Eu? The Paradoxical Interplay of Identity in Brazuca Literature." *Hispania* 87(3): 576–585.

Villegas-Muriel, A. 2006. "Rebuilding New Orleans: Hurricane Katrina, Latinos, and Reconstruction." Paper presented at the conference "Embracing Diversity: Latino immigration and the transformation of American society" at Harvard University, Cambridge, MA.

Waters, M. C. 1999. *Black Identities: West Indian Immigrant Dreams and American Realities*. Cambridge, MA: Harvard University Press.

Part One

THE ART OF SEDUCTION: IMAGES OF BRAZIL AND THE UNITED STATES IN THE TWENTIETH CENTURY

1

Before We Called This Place Home: Precursors of the Brazilian Community in the United States

Darién J. Davis

The notion of home, or what the French call *chez moi,* takes on multiple levels of significance for immigrants, travelers, and exiles. Moreover, "away from home," the very notion of "home," takes on symbolic and psychological meanings that change and develop over time. These multiple meanings emerge or are "imagined," to borrow a term from Benedict Anderson, through complex negotiations among memory, desire, fantasy, and power relations inherent to the process of crossing borders. Early Brazilian travelers and immigrants who made their way to the United States often articulated their ideas of "home" in paradoxical ways. On the one hand, their reflections on life in the United States illustrated their relative privilege compared to the Brazilian population in general. To travel to the United States in the 1930s, for example, meant to go by boat or plane, both of which required either a certain level of income or sponsorship. On the other hand, North American society often limited the opportunities of Brazilians in a process that Jacques Derrida has shown to be violently hierarchical (Anderson 1983; Derrida 1977, 41).

This essay explores the early experiences of Brazilian travelers to the United States from the 1930s to the 1950s, before there was a *bona fide* Brazilian community. The majority of these traveler/immigrants were performers, that is, exporters of Brazilian culture to a largely uninformed North American audience. In this sense, they were *de facto* 'performing Brazil' outside of its organic context in which cultural practices were understood as part of an array of national rituals (whether it is *carnaval,* the *festas juninas* or June festivals, food, dancing, or clothing). These performances often allowed the North American media not only to engage in

Brazilian stereotyping, which reduced dynamic Brazilian cultural practices to a few static and essential characteristics, but also to fetishize Brazil in surprising ways (Freud 1977).

Contemporary theories on immigration and cultural studies can help us cast a critical lens on the historical experiences of the precursors of the Brazilian community in the United States prior to the 1960s. The historical crossing of borders by Brazilians involved distortion, or at the very least a transformation of perceptions or worldviews, particularly by the individual involved in crossing as s/he inserted himself or herself into a new social, political, and cultural reality. With few references to Brazilian culture in the United States prior to 1930, Brazilian precursors faced an interesting dilemma: What did "being a Brazilian" mean in North America? How did one "perform Brazil" and attain personal authenticity while living in the limited space of Brazilianness? Despite their position as performers rather than distributors or marketers of their cultural products, Brazilians expanded the North American national imagination and the sense of a Brazilian identity in the United States. That Brazilian identity often affirmed an essentialized identity and the cultural hegemony of Rio de Janeiro in all media, but particularly film. In addition, some performers often reinvented their pasts for the American gaze.

Brazilian performers should not be seen only as victims, however. Rather, it is essential to examine the ways in which individuals exercised agency in situations of unequal power or at the very least collaborated in the formulation of perceptions. How did these Brazilian pioneers in the United States accept, modify, contest, and manipulate stereotypes to maintain their sense of dignity? This process of engagement made the first etchings on the Brazilian community's *tabula rasa* that became reference points for Brazilian immigrants who would follow. Performers played and continue to play an important role in creating reference points since they occupy a unique position in any community's collective psyche. In general performers can often simultaneously reflect the cultural aesthetics of communities and become the depositories of a community's desires, hopes, and dreams. The list of Brazilian performers in the United States in the 1930s and 1940s included Raul Roulien, Lia Torá, Carmen Miranda, Aurora Miranda, Aloysio de Oliveira and other members of the Bando da Lua, Ary Barroso, the musical group Os Anjos do Inferno, Laurindo de Almeida, Elise Houston, Dick Farney, and Carmen Costa. Because of their status in Brazilian society, the print, radio, and film media back in Brazil also registered their impressions of lives in the

United States, providing memories and visions for future generations of Brazilian immigrants.

Brazilian immigrants prior to the 1960s, like immigrants today, cannot necessarily be neatly categorized by the length of time they spend in the United States. Influenced by political, cultural, and economic trends, the transnational flow of Brazilians meant that individuals may stay in the United States a year or an entire lifetime. Moreover, even short-term travelers play a role in the resident community. The experience of performers, however, may not necessarily be representative of the Brazilian experience in general, but the performer's visibility nonetheless affords others in the community an opportunity to place their personal interests, wishes, and desires into a collective or public forum. The examination of three issues helps us to understand the experience of Brazilians in the United States prior to the 1960s: Imbalance of Economic Opportunities; Race, Nationhood, and *Latinidad*; and the designation of Rio de Janeiro as a symbol of Brazilianness. All of these issues entail a degree of stereotyping in a process that, as Sander Gilman has argued, need not necessarily be a limiting experience. Indeed, some Brazilian performers sometimes used stereotypes to their advantage (Gilman 1985).

North American geopolitical policies affected how and when Brazilians in the United States constructed their stage identities and how they engaged with North American audiences. The 1904 Roosevelt Corollary, which historians view as a reiteration of the 1823 Monroe Doctrine that warned European powers to stay out of the Americas, set an ethnocentric and paternalistic tone that encouraged U.S. Americans to regard all of Latin America as their "backyard" (The Roosevelt Corollary 1904; Crickfield 1908; Wood 1961, 130; Rowland 1947). Although presidents Hoover and Roosevelt crafted foreign policy agendas aimed at fostering better ties with Latin America, the "Good Neighbor Policy" (1933–1947) cemented images of exotic, albeit fun-loving foreigners, while seeking to open Latin American markets to U.S. investors. Indeed, most U.S. audiences saw performers from Brazil as exotic foreigners who helped entertain them during the war in Europe. Although both Brazilian men and women traveled to the United States, feminine, unthreatening images of Brazil gained currency (Sandoval-Sanchez, 24–31). What could be less threatening in the 1940s, for example, than the ubiquitous image of Carmen Miranda, a white Brazilian woman with fruit on her head, moving her body to enchanting tunes? Such images penetrated the American consciousness and became reference points with which future generations of Brazilian immigrants would dialogue. Within the confined spaces where Brazilians performed, they nonetheless demonstrated a marked degree of creativity, often accepting, transforming, or subverting stereotypical images (Burton, 21–44; Mulvey, 19; Roberts 1993).

During World War II, while the Office of Inter-American Affairs along with important cultural centers such as Hollywood forged alliances with Brazil and other Latin American countries to galvanize support for the Allies, American institutions provided employment opportunities unavailable in Brazil and encouraged northbound migration. In her article on U.S. immigration policy toward Mexico, Saskia Sassen explains that immigration from underdeveloped countries such as Brazil to developed countries like the United States is not merely an arbitrary activity independent of larger global patterns. This is also true historically. The United States has played a crucial role in the expansion of the world economy, and this in turn has played an important role in what Sassen calls "the mobilization of people into migrations." Performers and other artists constitute a vibrant sector of the flow of human capital. In the case of Brazil, the performers of the 1930s, 1940s, and 1950s preceded the mass migration that followed beginning in the 1960s (Sassen 1990).

Bill Ong Hing, author of *Defining America through Immigration Policy*, and Roger Daniels, author of *Guarding the Golden Door: American Immigration Policy and Immigrants since 1882*, have shown how the United States encouraged some types of immigration while discouraging others. Daniels argues, for example, that the 1882 Chinese Exclusion Act began almost forty years of successive restrictive policies that would keep certain nations and ethnicities from entering the United States legally (Ong Hing 2004, Daniels 2004). The restrictive immigration policies were institutionalized during a period in American history when legalized racial segregation was a way of life across the South and was practiced widely on the East and West coasts and in the Midwest. Because non-whites faced routine discrimination, it is no surprise that the majority of Brazilians in the United States prior to the 1960s were white. U.S. segregation, based on the "one-drop rule," not only relegated blacks to the position of second-class citizens but also established social codes that would discourage if not make illegal the mixing of races in diverse venues, including nightclubs and in films. White Brazilians occupied an ambiguous social space during segregation, which gave rise to cultural conflict, particularly since these very performers had worked closely with black musicians in Brazil. Aloysio de Oliveira, director of the Bando da Lua, recalled, for example, how U.S. racial codes affected the composition of his band. Segregation also limited places where Brazilians of visible African ancestry could socialize (Oliveira 1981; Skidmore 1993).

Brazilian scholar Gilberto Freyre, who had traveled and studied in the United States in the 1920s, best articulated the conflict inherent to this ambiguous space as he wrote about Brazilian cultural identity using the United States as a counterpoint. Freyre studied at Baylor College in Texas (1918–1920) and at Columbia University (1920–1922) under the cultural anthropologist Franz Boas. More than any single scholar before him, Freyre challenged in international circles the theories of the inferiority of peoples of mixed racial background and pointed to the contributions of both Africans and Indians to the development of modern Brazil. The search for national unity coupled with his love for Brazil led him to attack the myth of the inferiority of the so called "mixed-blood," because he believed that Brazil was a *mestiço*, or racially mixed country. Freyre's experience in the United States was not only crucial to his scholarship but helped Brazilians understand themselves through the prism of North American segregation. According to Freyre, his desire to write about Brazil occurred when he was in New York. As Lewis Hanke tells us in *Gilberto Freyre: Vida y Obra, Bibliografía, Antología*, Freyre remembered "with bitterness the disrespectful phrase from two Anglo-Saxon tourists that spoke of the fearful Mongrel aspect of the Brazilian population." Freyre eventually led a new wave of Brazilian scholarship that defended miscegenation, which he believed had created a unique people in the tropics (Hanke 1939; Freyre 1971).

In *The Masters and the Slaves* (*Casa grande e senzala*), Freyre highlighted the importance of Brazil's cultural, sexual, spiritual, psychological, social, and racial mixing and intermingling. Given his stance as a fierce nationalist with an interest in promoting what he called *lusotropicalism*, or the Portuguese unique ability to adapt to the peoples and customs of the tropical regions and by extension the so-called darker races, Freyre's nostalgic and often idealized view of the Brazilian past was influenced by his life and travels in the United States. His ideas illustrate how Brazil's "imagined identity" was forged as a result of experiences in the United States during segregation. Indeed, intellectual explanations of Brazil's identity, like national identities everywhere, remain closely connected to the exchange of global capital and the power of the media (Freyre 1973).

The collective identities of the Brazilian communities in the United States emerged on the heels of the experience of a few individuals who articulated and propagated their sense of difference as a result of crossing national boundaries. One of these differences was related to

North American segregation and U.S. civil laws that privileged whiteness over blackness. Despite racial and class prejudices, official state-mandated segregation had been antithetical to the Latin American experience in general and the Brazilian experience in particular. Freyre's work would eventually challenge the *social* rules of segregation and force North American scholars such as Frank Tannenbaum and Samuel Elkins, writing in the 1940s and 1950s, to re-examine United States race relations in comparative terms. Both Tannenbaum and Elkins portrayed African slavery and race relations in Latin America in a rather positive light in comparison to slavery in the southern United States, for example (Tannenbaum 1946; Elkins 1959). At the same time, residents and immigrants from Latin America, the majority of them of Mexican and of mixed ancestry, understood the importance of claiming a white racial identity in a nation that treated blacks as second-class citizens. Jorge Chapa has explained that Mexican Americans objected to the 1930 use of the category "Mexican" in the U.S. Census, because it denied their American citizenship and precluded the possibility of being defined as white at a time when many privileges were defined only for whites (Chapa 2000).

The experience of Latin American populations in the United States would eventually challenge U.S. racial categories, although not until 1970 would the government census begin to continually gather information about Hispanics (or *Latinos*, a term that would be accepted much later, and not by all immigrant groups from Latin America). Since the 1970s, census takers have continually modified its terminology and conceptualization of race and ethnicity largely based on the experience of Latin American immigrants, many of whom come from more than one racial background and thus defy the traditional bipolar categories. This is not to say that miscegenation was negligible in the United States. Rather, for most of the country's history, U.S. officials failed to recognize individuals of mixed racial ancestry as a distinct social category for a host of political and social reasons. One needs only to consider the 1850 and 1890 census reports that included categories such as "mulatto," "quadroon," and "octoroon." Nevertheless, from the 1930s to the 1950s, "Latin" did not necessarily refer to U.S. residents but more often than not to an ambiguous exotic or foreign identity contrasted with the mainstream white American. Despite their low numbers, Brazilian performers played a disproportionately important role in shaping the early image of Latin-ness or *Latinidad* (Bureau of Census 1933, 350; Davis 1997, 8–15).

The so-called Good Neighbor Policy masked United States geopolitical *angst* caused by the Brazilian government's negotiations with Hitler's Nazi regime. Moreover, the astute governments of Getúlio Vargas (1930–1944) and Eurico Gaspar Dutra (1945–1950) were not as passive as Frank D. McMann claims in his *The Brazil-American Alliance, 1937–1945.* Diplomats in Washington and in Rio understood that the two nations needed each other and thus each engaged in a number of political, economic and cultural enterprises from which both nations would benefit. When President Dutra visited Washington and New York in 1949, for example, he was the first Brazilian head of state to do so since 1876, and he was treated like royalty. Dutra, who told Americans that he was a "good neighbor and friend," also met with Brazilians in the city and the business representatives from the Brazilian–American Alliance (Parke, 1949). Ten years earlier, Rockwell D. Hunt, dean of the graduate school at the University of Southern California, had noted the growing U.S. economic presence in Brazil and called for intellectual and spiritual reciprocity. Although intellectual exchange did occur, Brazilian performers who made their way to the United States, particularly popular performers, occupied a more important role in the media. These performers were not necessarily fleeing tyranny or escaping poverty, but they did find opportunities unavailable to them in Brazil. They would not have been able to travel to the United States, however, if American politicians had not understood the importance of strategic cultural exchanges and alliances with their South American neighbor (McMann 1973).

By examining the economic and cultural tensions inherent to the Brazilian performers' experience, the ability of performers to create new identities in the United States, and the rise of Rio de Janeiro as a symbol of Brazil prior to the 1960s, we are better able to understand the challenges facing Brazilians in the United States in general. Immigrants confront and respond in various ways to the tension between pull factors from the United States and what may be called "homeland pull factors," such as homesickness or longings for cultural products. Examining these historical experiences through the help of cultural and immigration theories allows us to understand more fully the forces and complications of constructing and living transnational identities

Imbalance of Power: Economic Opportunities versus *Saudade*

The story of Henrique Britto helps us to understand the multiple experiences of performers who made their way to the north in the 1930s. Britto had been a member of the pioneering popular *carioca* band, the Bando de Tangarás, comprised of musical luminaries such as Henrique Foréis Domingues (better known as Almirante), Noel Rosa, Lamartine Babo, and

Braquinha. With the disintegration of the band in 1932, Britto left Brazil to play in the Brazilian national band (led by Romeu Silva) at the Olympics in Los Angeles in July and August of that year. When the band was forced to return home because of lack of funds, Britto, a guitar player, stayed on for a year and played in various nightclubs. Before returning to Brazil, he learned how to adapt his playing to the amplifiers that he discovered for the first time in the United States. Consequently, Britto became one of the first Brazilian electric guitar players, utilizing an invention patented by the Dobro Corporation in San Francisco, a company that he came to represent when he returned to Brazil in 1933 (Didier and Máximo 1990, 218).

Britto's story reflects the sense of adventure with which many Brazilians often enter the United States. Fortunately for him, he had talent and connections that allowed him to travel and then to make a living, albeit temporarily, in the United States. Like many other Brazilians, Britto secured additional talents and expertise that he would take back with him to Brazil, allowing him to earn a living as a middleman between a U.S. corporation and Brazilian musicians. His particular story of enhanced opportunity contrasts, however, with that of guitarist Laurindo de Almeida.

Almeida left Brazil in 1946 as a result of a moralistic, anti-crime platform at the end of Getúlio Vargas's *Estado Novo* in 1945. Vargas's successor, President Eurico Gaspar Dutra, instituted a number of repressive measures including revoking the Communist party's legal standing and participation in labor unions. The government also launched an attack on immorality and began to crack down on prostitution, vagrancy, and gambling. The latter meant the closing of all casinos that had provided employment to hundreds of musicians and performers throughout the country, particularly in Rio de Janeiro. Scrambling to find new employment, many Brazilian musicians left the country. Almeida headed for the United States, where talented South American musicians could still find employment, especially those of his caliber (Didier and Máximo 1990, 218).

In many ways, Almeida's story is indicative of the classical "push-pull" factors associated with out-migration and brain drain. The United States continues to offer talented men and women from Latin America opportunities unavailable in their homelands today. In turn these immigrants contribute to the growth and vibrancy of the American economy. Almeida, who is considered by many to be the father of *bossa nova* and a pioneer of Brazilian-jazz cross-pollination because of the way he played his guitar finger-style, offered American audiences and musicians a new way of performing. Not surprisingly, invitations to perform allowed him to team up with a number of North American musicians, including Stan Kenton in Los Angeles in the 1950s and John Lewis at the 1963 Monterrey Jazz Festival. After 1950, he worked film scores for Twentieth Century Fox, such as *Rawhide* (1951), *The Godfather* (1971), *Unforgiven* (1992), and many others for which he was not credited. [1]

Despite his international success, however, Almeida's work was not well known in Brazil. Furthermore, when other Brazilian musicians gained success abroad before becoming well known in Brazil, the Brazilian press often menacingly compared them to Almeida, whom many accused of abandoning Brazil. This happened to Dori Caymmi, son of the Bahian Dorival Caymmi, who wrote the original song "O qué o que a Bahaina tem" that inspired Carmen Miranda's Bahiana persona. Dori had moved to Los Angeles in the 1980s, where he began to perform and record music. In an interview with Dori Caymmi in 1999, some fifty years after Almeida had moved to the United States, the *Folha de São Paulo* asked Caymmi if he was going down the same road as Almeida, who, in spite of his reputation abroad, was known to only a few in Brazil. A similar question plagued 50-year-old Brazilian percussionist Cyro Batista after he released his CD *Supergenerous* in the United States in 2000. The questions from the *Folha de São Paulo* indicate the importance of precursors as reference points for Brazilians who move abroad and for the memory of the Brazilian national psyche.[2]

At the same time, Batista's response illustrates how emotionally important the relationship to "the homeland" can be for Brazilian immigrants. Due to the influx and influence of immigrants from all over the world, the contemporary musical market in the United States has broadened significantly since the 1940s and the number and types of performers who have immigrated to the United States have multiplied. Many contemporary Brazilian performers who, like Almeida, struggle in Brazil to create a space to perform, decide to seek opportunities abroad. Unlike Britto, however, for many returning is not a viable option. Others, like Leny Andrade, an impressive jazz singer, have managed to become transnational artists with careers in both countries. When asked if he was afraid to repeat the trajectory of Almeida, Cyro Batista responded:

> "Before, I used to be very upset about this, thinking that Brazil didn't like me, but I feel that although my roots are Brazilian, today I am a musician of the world and to organize a show in Brazil with the type of music that I play, which is alternative, it is very expensive for people living in a delicate economic situation which the country is experiencing." (Bozzo Junior 2000)

Britto's and Almeida's stories illustrate the complex relation between the social and economic reality of Brazil that influenced their decisions to leave. Both he and Almeida were able to perform in the United States because of the expertise they had acquired in Brazil. Thus, in many ways, Brazilian musicians who leave Brazil are afforded opportunities because they are able to *perform* Brazilian culture abroad. Comparisons can be made with other performers, particularly Cubans from Ricky Ricardo to Celia Cruz, who celebrated their national traditions in exile.

The case of Ary Barroso, author of "Aquarela do Brasil" and perhaps one of Brazil's most well known popular composers and musicians, underscores the complex relationship between the Brazilian homeland and the American land of opportunity. Barroso moved to the United States to work for Walt Disney on a number of projects, but also ended up working for the now defunct Republic Films, in addition to collaborating on a number of different projects including a Broadway musical adaptation of Bertita Harding's *The Amazon Throne*. In addition, he came into contact with Brazilians working in the States, including Edmundo Santos, Alberto Soria, and Gilberto Souto, all of whom worked for Disney (Cabral 1992).

When he arrived in the United States, Barroso was elated and full of optimism. "It is a dream," he declared to the press. Furthermore, Barroso made explicit comparisons between his status as a musician in Brazil and his newly found success in the United States. In a letter to his wife back in Brazil dated January 15, 1944, Barroso claimed: "I am as popular here as I am in Brazil with one exception: here my name is admired, respected" (Cabral 1992, 209–213). Originally he intended to bring his wife and daughter to live with him in the United States to attain the so-called American Dream. In actuality, with business and family connections in Brazil, Barroso ended up living a transglobal life with stints in Brazil and the United States, a reality that has become common for many Brazilian performers, intellectuals, and film makers including Chico Buarque, Caetano Veloso, Leny Andrade, Karim Anouiz, Tânia Cypriano, and Helena Solberg. Like that of many other Brazilian musicians, Barroso's success abroad was tied to his celebration of Brazil and Brazilian culture as in his "Aquarela do Brasil." At one point there were six or seven different versions of his song in several different languages, including French. In *No tempo de Ari Barroso,* Sérgio Cabral reports that one of the English versions of the song recorded by Sidney Keith Russel, ends:

Now when twilight dims the sky
Above, recalling thrills of love,

I am certain of one thing:
Return I will to old Brazil.

The lyrics highlight the desire to return to an idealized Brazil in the waning years of the singer's life. Although Barroso was financially rewarded for his musical input in the United States, he eventually *did* return to Brazil. He had received numerous offers to continue his life in the United States, including one from Walt Disney. Sérgio Cabral recounts the exchange between Disney and Barroso that synthesizes one of the major challenges of the immigrant: coping with the longing for authentic and organic cultural practices. Barroso turned down Disney's offer to become one of his studio's musical directors. When asked why he would turn down such an opportunity, he expressed his reasons succinctly: "Because I don't have Flamengo here"—a reference to his Rio-based soccer club with which he would have a life-long association (Cabral 1992, 209–213).

While Flamengo fans may understand this loyalty, Barroso's answer symbolizes a development in his thoughts about Brazil. Barroso had clearly enjoyed his time in the United States and had succeeded economically but had somehow felt limited. Furthermore, "something" was missing, including a host of practices that he was not willing to discard. The number of Brazilians who lived in the United States was too few to allow for any meaningful attempt at *transculturation*, a term coined by the Cuban anthropologist Fernando Ortiz to describe the transfer of cultural practices from one place to another relatively *intact*. The celebration of "Brazil-ness" by Barroso and the other performers who remain in the United States for different lengths of time illustrates a number of important lessons. It indicates how important Brazilian culture and the symbols of Brazilian nationhood remain to the immigrant's *raison d'être*, and how immigrants continually dialogue with vital homeland history and symbols that often cannot be replicated abroad (food, ways of expressing affection, soccer, music, and many others).

It is also important to acknowledge a hierarchy of immigrant *needs*. As with immigrants today, it is impossible to ignore the economic and social influences that play a significant role in the so-called push factors that lead to migration. In Barroso's case, economic considerations did not play a major role in his return, although they may have played an important part in his decision to go to the United States. His move to the United States allowed him to take his career to a more lucrative level than he experienced in Brazil. Such opportunities are available to few immigrants. The tension between economic opportunity and cultural void remain constants in the lives of immigrants across the globe. The cases of Barroso, Almeida, and Britto reflect these concerns to different degrees.

Nationhood and *Latinidad:* A Historical Perspective

Immigrants adopt different strategies to navigate the maze of U.S. identity politics. The case of Carmen Miranda, perhaps Brazil's most famous immigrant-performer, is an important example. At one point, the American press reported that Carmen Miranda's father was a "coffee baron," presumably because audiences recognized Brazil as one of the largest producers of coffee, in a move to fit into U.S. expectations of glamour. Carmen, who grew up among the popular classes of downtown Rio de Janeiro, did not necessarily attempt to dispel such misconceptions. Like many other immigrant performers in the United States she adapted elements of North American culture to her performances, although the press back in Brazil criticized her for it. Few realized that she, like millions of immigrants, occupied a liminal space between American and Brazilian culture. Carmen along with her sister, Aurora Miranda, and Raul Gil and Lia Torá, two actors who preceded them, played critical roles in shaping *Latinidad* in the United States. Their experiences help us to understand the complex process of adapting to a cross-national identity before the creation of Brazilian communities in the United States.

In 1931, Raul Pepe Acolti Gil, better known as Raul Roulien, moved to the United States to star in two Hollywood films, *Delicious* and *Flying Down to Rio,* but would later appear in a string of others, including *Careless Lady* (Fox, 1932) set in Singapore, the detective thriller *State Attorney* (1931), and *It's Great To Be Alive* (1932), among others. Roulien was a white *carioca* child prodigy who began his artistic career at age eight. After a string of good movies for the era, Roulien returned to Brazil in 1936 to compose songs and to produce his own movies (see the 1937 *Grito da Mocidade*, for example). Allen Woll has argued that Roulien was reduced to playing the eternal Latin playboy or suave and handsome *galã,* as Brazilians call this character (Woll, 113).

Roulien, who spoke English, was well received in Hollywood, attaining an important place in the era of musicals in the 1930s. More importantly, he also played an important role in cementing the stereotype associated with *Latinidad.* He also appeared in a number of Hollywood films made for the Spanish-speaking audiences, a perceived market in which Latin American actors could find a place. Although the *carioca* Horácia Corrêa D'Avila, better known to her contemporaries as Lia Torá, also appeared in Spanish-speaking films, her time in the United States was considerably shorter and her path to Hollywood different. Hollywood studios often sponsored beauty contests in foreign countries to lure female talent to Hollywood. In 1927, Torá won a contest sponsored by Fox Film and landed a contract with the studio, which included appearances in a number of films including Emmett J. Flynn's *The Veiled Woman* (1929), Alfred Green's *Making the Grade,* and in Spanish-speaking movies such as Miguel Contreras Torres's 1932 *Soñadores de Gloria* (Dreamers of Glory) and George Crone's 1934 *Hollywood, Ciudad de ensueños* (Hollywood, City of Illusions).

Neither Torá nor Roulien officially settled in the United States. Instead, they became members of the broad transglobal professional community, a lifestyle that suited Roulien more than it did Torá. Like Roulien, Torá benefited from her experience in the United States and her international exposure. In 1929, she founded the Brazilian Southern Cross, an independent film production company, although some forty years would pass before she appeared in Braz Cediak's Brazilian production, *Confissões do Frei Abóbora* (1971), one year before her death. Torá, like many women in the performing arts in Brazil, abandoned her career after the birth of her children in the mid-1930s. Although she settled in Rio in relative tranquility while Roulien remained a prominent icon in the Brazilian press for most of his life, both had made contributions to North American film production, playing diverse 'foreign' roles. More importantly, however, both succeeded by playing exotic or foreign characters, and often as Spanish-speaking Latin Americans.

In *Hispanics in Hollywood: An Encyclopedia of Film and Television*, Luis Reyes and Peter Rubie erroneously conclude that Brazilian performers like Roulien and Torá, "who worked throughout Latin America," found the transition to Spanish easy. His statement undermines the fact that both actors worked diligently to attain fluency and credibility in Spanish. Furthermore, the crossovers to the Spanish-speaking market defy theories that continue to see assimilation as entrance into a unified monolithic (white) American culture. While we know little about the social interactions of Roulien or Torá outside of their movie careers, their employment opportunities illustrate that they had acquired sufficient skill and capital to be able to occupy a space within an industry that was limited and offered few possibilities to non-native English speakers. It is difficult to determine whether Brazilians like Roulien and Torá defined their identity in the United States in the 1930s as "Latin" or "Brazilian." Yet it is clear that Brazilians contributed to a sense of *Latinidad* whether one uses the official U.S. definition of "Hispanic" (designating a person from a Spanish-speaking country or their descendants) or Reyes's broader definition of "people living in the United States who can trace all or part of their background to Spain, Portugal, Latin America or the Philippines" (Reyes 1994, xx).

At the same time, North Americans felt comfortable working with Brazilian actors. Directors and producers called upon Roulien to play a variety of foreign roles, but he also served as consultant on South American cultural practices. Brazilians traveling to Los Angeles also felt comfortable calling upon him, and the society press in Brazil religiously covered his activities. In the United States Roulien became an official and unofficial consultant on issues related to Brazil. During the 1932 Los Angeles Olympics, for example, Maria Lenk, one of the members of the Brazilian delegation, recalled that Roulien invited her to the Hollywood studios and helped the Brazilian team with some of their expenses and translations into English. Link also confirmed the widespread ignorance of the general population about Brazil. When she tried to obtain a loan at a local bank to help with expenses, the bank official asked if Brazil was in Africa. Indeed, Roulien became a reference point and a contact for many Brazilians who traveled through Los Angeles as Carmen Miranda would become a decade later.[3]

Miranda's own quest for self-actualization conflicted with a growing demand for performing female Latin-ness, a role that she partly invented and manipulated. "I never sing if I'm not absolutely identified with the spirit of the music and the lyrics," she once said, reflecting more her desire for agency in a world in which she had attained unprecedented economic power but for which she paid a high price. Her *Bahiana* persona, inspired by the black women in the northeastern state of Bahia, gave her a platform to make a lot of money but also to remain close to Brazil in the same way that immigrants everywhere often invest in and festishize local or national icons (Davis 1997; Gil-Montero 1989, 31; Dunn 2001).

Allen Woll argues that Miranda's performance, which continued to represent the Brazilian experience, also came to represent "Latin-ness" *par excellence* as she added singing numbers in Spanish, Spanglish, Portañol, or Portuguese mixed with English. Other performers who followed in her footsteps included Aurora Miranda, Aloysio de Oliveira, Oswaldo Eboli (Vadeco), Helio Pereira, Afonso Osório, Stenio Osório, and Ivo Astolfi, Annibal Sardinha (O Garoto), and Nestor Amaral (the other members of the Bando da Lua). They adapted to a U.S. *gaze* that might have understood what Latin-ness meant in broad terms but certainly did not take the time to distinguish between national cultures, as they would, for example, if confronted with European immigrants. How many people mistake Germans for French or Spaniards for English, for example? Maxine Margolis has pointed out many of these contradictions in her ground-breaking work *Little Brazil: An Ethnography of Brazilian Immigrants in New York City* (Woll, 113; Margolis 1994).

In his 1939 review of the musical revue "The Streets of Paris" in the *New York Post*, Herbert Drake vividly illustrates how Brazilian performers come to represent "Latin-ness, "Tropical-ness," Carnival and "Fun! Fun! Fun!" After seeing Miranda perform on Broadway, Drake reported:

> "Miss Miranda is dark tan and shining with a personality apparently indigenous to Brazil. Whatever it is, she is wonderful to watch but the lady does not appear except once, when she sings a few monotonously fascinating chants, in Portuguese, perhaps. All the while she looks fabulously like a tropical Tallulah rampant against a costume-ball background, but very wicked around the eyes. She does serve as a particular symbol of the high-stepping, band-leading speed and glitter of the show." (Drake 1939, 16)

These stereotypes mesmerized many audiences, and have continued to dominate the press. Ironically, the maxim "bad press is better than no press," meant that this type of coverage increased the possibilities of further employment for Brazilian artists. At the same time, the American press reveled in the exoticism and often made fun of Carmen's accented English. When her sister Aurora came to join Carmen in the United States in 1941, for example, *The New York Post* and *The New York Telegraph* carried titles that spelled out English words according to Carmen's Brazilian pronunciation: "Hokay, Go Home Keed" and "Miranda Beelding Up Leetle Sister" (Wilson 1941, 9). Many of these jokes and images accentuate Brazilians' position as outsiders in U.S. society. At the same time, Miranda believed in the power of community, no matter how small, to preserving her integrity. She understood that the success of her act was dependent on performing with Brazilian musicians and she insisted on performing with them independently of the language in which she performed. She had insisted on it with Lee Shubert, agreeing to pay the Banda da Lua out of her own salary, and took "the Miranda boys," as the American press called them, with her to Hollywood (Davis 2000).

In late 1949, the William Morris Agency organized a tour of the United States and Canada for Miranda beginning in Las Vegas. This was during the time in which Miranda was working on *A Date with Judy* (1948) and *Nancy Goes to Rio* (1950). She and the newly constituted Banda da Lua, which now included members of the band Anjos do Inferno, performed "Aquarela de Brasil" and other Brazilian compositions (often without paying copyright) in addition to American-produced 'Latin' numbers. Although Miranda continued to perform Brazilian numbers, the longer she stayed in the United States, the more 'pan-Latin' her repertoire became as she began to relate to her new audience in the United States. This development did not represent, as Brazilian critics would claim, her losing her heritage and becoming Americanized (*americanizada*) but rather reflected the development of a musician and performer in a new cultural environment (Gil-Montero, 209). A similar process occurs with most immigrants as they adapt to their new environments.

For its part, the media in general, and newspapers in particular continued to present Carmen Miranda as their image of a "Latin lady," a "Latin dancer," "singing Latin lullabies," or as the "Brazilian bombshell." A number of American cultural interlocutors including Walt Disney and Orson Welles often took on didactic agendas in their work while also highlighting the exotic elements of Brazil performers. The recordings of the credits of Welles's *It's All True* and Disney's *Saludos Amigos* are two excellent examples. At the same time, Decca Records, a major international recording company, and Disney also hired Aurora Miranda and the Banda da Lua and others, for example, to highlight Brazilianness in recordings in Portuguese such as "A Jardineira," "Cidade Maravilhosa," "Aurora," "Pastorinhas," "Meu Limão," "Meu Limoneiro," and "Seu Condutor" (Oliveira 1981, 117; Garrod 1992).

That producers such as Disney and many others adhered to a given "Latin type-casting" is undeniable. At the same time, Disney allowed for the participation of Brazilians in creating many Latin icons including the yellow and green parrot Zé Carioca, the hybrid dance "Uncle Samba," and many others. Furthermore, given the opportunities available, Brazilians such as Aloysio de Oliveira and Aurora Miranda acknowledged their agency in an unprecedented period of cross-cultural collaborations. Artists such as Orson Welles and Genevieve Naylor understood how to utilize images for different purposes. Naylor and Welles, who were both Americans, worked for the State Department to take photographs and make films of the Brazilian reality as a way to promote friendly relations during the Good Neighbor Policy initiative. Naylor avoided exoticism when photographing her subjects. She also refused to depict extremes, whether of dire poverty or opulence. Welles made controversial films that documented the life of the underclass in Brazil. One film documented the black presence in Brazilian carnival, while another showed the plight of fishermen in the Northeast. Neither was released until 1992, in video format called *It's All True* (Levine, 1998; Oliveira, 1982). The fact that the Hollywood studios censored Welles's work illustrates the limits of individual agency, particularly when one's views clash with prevailing geopolitical interests.

In the United States, Brazilian artists often idealized their homeland, while also exaggerating their status and contribution to cultural production in the United States. Aloysio de Oliveira, for example, took pride in his consulting role in creating Disney films and in shaping characters such as Zé Carioca. Barroso wrote home about how popular he had become in the United States. Many Brazilian travelers to Los Angeles raved about how well Brazilians were being treated there, enforcing the notion that Latin Americans had 'conquered' Hollywood. On the other hand, some in the North American press (like their Brazilian counterparts) approached the new "Latin" presence critically. On January 28, 1940, Lucile Neville indicated that:

> "Any story with a plot about revolutions, tamale workers or the love of a marimba player for a beauteous senorita sounds fine to producers just now. But Hollywood can make a tremendous mistake, according to the comparatively few Latin-understanding movie people here." (Neville 1940)

Neville was well aware of the sensitivity and responses of the Latin American press to U.S. ethnocentrism and stereotyping. Nonetheless, she saw progress being made as "heads of studio foreign departments reported that directors and producers were beginning to ask for advice and sometimes take it."

Neville's article highlighted the principal challenge for Brazilian performing artists in the process of forging a new space in a foreign land. North Americans had constructed the space within which they were to perform. Some focused on the limits of the space while others viewed the potential, often transforming or expanding the outer boundaries. In most cases, however, it is important to underscore the dynamic nature of the exchanges among Brazilian performers and North American producers. Brazilian artists responded differently to different situations according to their own perceived interests. Miranda, for example, often played the "Latin bimbo," or pretended that she did not speak English when it suited her. When the federal government tried to collect back taxes, for example, she claimed ignorance of tax laws and the American system. Yet despite her ignorance and her unequal relationship with Lee Shubert, the American theater impresario who initially brought her to the United States, she was able to buy out her contract to allow her to participate in cinema. She fought to maintain an authentic Brazilian band, made her own costumes, and often lampooned herself. Furthermore, she borrowed from a number of cultures and participated in the forging of what North Americans would come to understand as "Latin" (Gil-Montero 1989).

The creation of a Latin type in the U.S. market did not only mean the assimilation of Brazilianness to a more ambiguous type that was more Spanish-speaking. In the Republic film *Brazil*, for example, Mexican actor Tito Guizar played the Brazilian lead Miguel, singing tunes in English and Portuguese composed by Ary Barroso. The historic construction of *Latinidad* often meant that Brazilian actors played Spanish-speaking Latin Americans, but it also allowed Mexicans such as Guizar and Dolores del Rio, who appeared in *Flying Down to Rio* (1933), to play Brazilian characters. How could Latin American artists like Miranda and the Bando da Lua not be influenced by the power, creativity, and harmonies of the American popular music of the 1940s? Many other popular North American musicians were certainly influenced by Brazil, creating adaptations and affecting the tone of global music from the 1940s and the *bossa nova* generation onward. Brazilian performers in the United States and abroad have likewise incorporated elements of jazz, hip hop, and a host of other genres that originated in the United States. Not surprisingly, six of Carmen's and the Bando da Lua's final recordings were with the Andrews Sisters, one of the most important North American trios of the time, and included songs such as "Cuanto Le Gusta," sung in Spanish. The Bando also performed and recorded standard Latin American songs in Spanish with Bing Crosby, who, in turn, recorded Latin-inspired songs such as "Copacabana," "Quizás Quizás," "Maria Bonita," and "Granada." While performers viewed these cross-cultural experiences as positive, Brazilian audiences and particularly the press often did not.

Brazilian performers such as Miranda, Roulien, and others understood the social system and abided by its rules in a process that was not always limiting. They saw learning and performing in Spanish as an opportunity to develop their knowledge and careers, although critics at home in Brazil often did not understand these motivations. Moreover, Brazilians often criticized Miranda and a host of others for their perceived assimilation into North American norms, often labeling them "americanizados/as." (Americanized). The tensions inherent in cultural adaptation constitute a crucial element of the immigrant's experience in the process of finding a space from which to engage in meaningful discourse. As M. Bakhtin has shown us, human beings do not engage with one another simply as human beings. Our perception of the world is ideological and dependent on various systems of knowledge including those informed by cultural artifacts and practices. Brazilians living in the United States prior to 1960 also had to reconcile themselves to a racial environment that not only saw them as Latin American and often Spanish-speaking, but also insisted on segregation between whites and blacks (Stam, 1989).

It is no coincidence that most of the Brazilian performers who made their way to the United States were white. What a conundrum for white performers who had lived in Brazil and had collaborated with black singers, song writers, and musicians and in many cases relied on the promotion of black Brazilian tunes, practices, and icons. Miranda's home in Beverly Hills became what some called the "unofficial Brazilian embassy," a place where Brazilians of all races often gathered to avoid the institutionalized racism in bars, clubs, and restaurants that barred blacks from fraternizing with whites. In Helena Solberg's documentary *Bananas Is My Business,* the Nichols brothers, two African American performers who knew and worked with Miranda, explain how public social policy turned Miranda's private space into a multicultural haven.

Ironically, performers such as Carmen Miranda had to confront the inequalities inherent to their own social and cultural backgrounds as they faced racism and ethnocentrism in the United States. These processes continue to occupy an important aspect of the Brazilian immigrant's experience in the United States, particularly when the American system and modes of identification conflict with their own construction of identity in Brazil. Many Brazilians living all over the United States today continue to dialogue with the initial impressions which have been passed on from generation to generation since the 1930s, as Bernadete Beserra so poignantly illustrates (31–49).

A Note on Black Brazilian Performers in the United States

Although white performers such as the Miranda sisters, Barroso, Oliveira, Roulien, and others were able to take advantage of the opportunities to perform and contribute to the emerging sense of *Latinidad*, many of them were uncomfortable with U.S. racial codes and etiquette that prescribed segregation. Carmen Miranda found ways to make her home a sanctuary where all of her friends of diverse backgrounds could mingle. Oliveira was forced to change the composition of the Bando da Lua because one of his white members was married to a black Brazilian woman, and he refused to travel with her to the United States. In his memoir *De Banda a Lua,* Oliveira also expressed his anxiety over the visit of his childhood Afro-Brazilian friend Haroldo Barbosa (Oliveira, 109). White Brazilian performers thus understood their relative privilege compared to their non-white Brazilian counterparts. On the other hand, the experiences of non-white Brazilian performers who traveled or immigrated to the United States before desegregation provide us with a different window on to issues of cross-national racial identities.

Afro-Brazilian Sinval Silva's visit to Carmen Miranda in 1951 is an interesting example of the black Brazilian experience in the United States in the era of segregation. In Brazil, Silva had worked as Miranda's chauffeur and had written and composed many tunes for her, including the classic "Adeus Batucada," before he went on to become a performer in his own right. In his biography *Carmen: A vida de Carmen Miranda a brasileira mais famosa do século XX,* Ruy Castro reports that during Silva's visit, Carmen had asked him to drive her automobile while she sat in the front seat. Apparently, Miranda had forgotten that a white woman did not sit in the front seat with a black man, a *faux pas* that was quickly pointed out to her by a passing motorist (Castro 2005, 486–487).

In Silva's discussions of his time in the United States, he never registered a complaint or noted any ill treatment while in the United States. Indeed, on his return to Rio he reported to the Brazilian press that his visit with Carmen had been an absolute success and that he himself had performed in a number of venues in Los Angeles, although it is difficult to verify whether Silva actually performed in the United States and whether it was in segregated clubs. Like Barroso and many other immigrants before and after him, Silva spoke about the United States in glowing terms that cast a positive light on Carmen's and his experience abroad. (Silva interview) This tendency is echoed in the experiences of the pioneering black actress Ruth de Souza and singer Carmen Costa, who provide additional insights into the experience of black Brazilians in the United States. De Souza, who was one of the co-founders of Rio's Teatro Experimental do Negro (TEN) in 1944, received a Rockefeller Foundation scholarship to study in the United States in 1951. Although De Souza would eventually spend two months in New York at the American National Theater and Academy and two months at Harvard, her base in the United States was the Karamu House in Cleveland, the oldest African American cultural arts institution in the country. Thus, in an era of segregation, De Souza's entrance into the American community could not have been like that of her white Brazilian counterparts. Even though De Souza was not a national celebrity, her status as a Rockefeller scholarship recipient meant that she entered into the American middle class, albeit through the highly regarded African American artistic community. On various occasions, De Souza has referred to her time in the United States as "a marvelous moment in her life" (De Jesus, 107; De Souza interview).

Carmen Costa's trajectory in the United States differed from the other Brazilians previously mentioned due to race and circumstance and provides another reference point and mode of entry into the United States: marriage. Costa, a young black vocal artist, met Miranda in Rio when she was working as a maid for Francisco Alves, one of Brazil's greatest popular male vocalists, before she made her debut on Ary Barroso's musical program at Radio Cruzeiro do Sul. In 1945, she married the American Hans van Koehler and one year later moved with him to New Jersey. Even though, according to one version, he abandoned her in the United States, she would continue to live between New York and Rio for the next three decades before returning to Brazil in the 1970s. While on the East Coast of the United States, she performed Brazilian, Spanish, and American standards. Her most acclaimed performance of this time was an appearance at New York's (Queens) Triboro Theater, a forum for many other performers including African Americans and Puerto Ricans. She also performed with Lionel Hampton and Dizzy Gillespie, two important African American musicians, and in the 1960s she participated in the *bossa-nova*-jazz exchanges in New York City. As happens with immigrants the world over, Costa also had to work at jobs that she did not quite anticipate. Ironically, she landed a job at RCA record factory pressing records. Like Silva, however, she highlighted her positive experience, her hard work, and her ability to persevere in the United States (Cardoso 2002, Costa interview).

Costa arrived in the United States the same year as Farnésio Dutra da Silva, better known as Dick Farney, a name that he choose because it sounded more American. Farney, who had an impressive musical education, gained an international reputation in Rio as the crooner for the Carlos Machado Orchestra and for performing at the Urca Casino in Rio. Like Carmen Miranda and unlike Carmen Costa, when he arrived in New York he was already well connected. He performed with a host of black and white musicians and entertainers, including Nat King Cole, and even performed American standards in English abroad. In 1947, he landed a recording contract with RCA and a lucrative performing contract at the Peacock Alley Bar at the Waldorf Astoria Hotel ten years later. Talent aside, such opportunities were hardly within the grasp of an immigrant woman without contacts, let alone a black woman (Shoof 2004).

Of all the Brazilian performers in the United States between 1930–1960, Elsie Houston's life was perhaps the most tragic (she committed suicide in 1943) and at the same time best represents the cross-national identity conflicts that Brazilians face who are "neither white nor black," to paraphrase the title of Carl Degler's now classic 1971 book. A trained lyrical singer with important musical and business connections, Houston was interested in performing Brazilian *haute culture* as well as Afro-Brazilian and Afro-Latin American popular and folk traditions. She was equally at ease at singing opera and at performing what would come to be called in the United States "voodoo numbers." Related to the Sam Houston family, Houston's father was an expatriate American living in Brazil. She, on the other hand, had married the French surrealist poet Benjamin Péret, and like him, became interested in Brazilian folkloric music, eventually publishing the book *Chants populaires du Brésil* in France and several other essays.

According to the *New York Times*, Houston, who performed regularly at New York's Rainbow Room, had become a mandatory act for any concert featuring South American music. At the same time, the American press made frequent reference to her dark skin and her "voodoo dances." While Olin Down wrote of her "voodoo incantations" in the *New York Times*, Grace Turner's May 1940 article on food recipes from Brazil that featured Houston began with a description of Houston's exotic looks:

> "Dark, slim to the point of thinness, vivid in every motion and the quick soft undertones of her Latin American speech, Elsie Houston, the internationally known Brazilian singer, is an exotic creature who you do not naturally associate with the household kitchen . . . Everything about Houston is colorful."[4]

Houston's exotic looks fascinated North Americans, no doubt enhanced her "voodoo performances," and certainly kept her in the press. Like the Miranda sisters, Houston was obliged to adjust her performances to the North American gaze. In Brazil, her *avant garde* performances and her research in African and indigenous folk culture, which had been a part of the growing debates and investigations of the modernist intellectuals and music aficionados such as Mário de Andrade, were transformed into performances that she herself called "voodoo dances" (Brazilian Music on the Air, 158).

As a Brazilian immigrant and performer in the United States prior to the creation of Brazilian communities, Houston exemplifies the difficulty of creating a space in a foreign land, and highlights the ways in which immigrants become reduced to a single one-dimensional identity. How could segregated North Americans make room for an upper-class Brazilian of mixed racial ancestry who grew up speaking French and performed in French nightclubs, but who was equally at home performing concert music and folk or popular forms? Houston grew up in privileged environments in Rio and Europe in which her skin color may not have played a restricting role. In the absence of a Brazilian community on the East Coast, she lived among the small French émigré community. Her life in the United States must be understood both as an individual experience and her choices must be placed into their proper historical context. Further work needs to be conducted to examine how her life in the United States contributed to her suicide. It is worthwhile reiterating, however, that less privileged performers such as De Souza and Costa took advantage of their varied opportunities in the United States before turning home to Brazil. Like Sinval Silva, they looked back on their experience in the United States as an important "conquest." Yet, their lives should also be carefully contextualized according to the choices available to them. At the same time, it is important to recognize that national identities continue to play defining roles on the experiences of immigrants of diverse backgrounds.

Brazilian immigrants have been forced to create, forge or otherwise navigate new and old identities within the American imagination, an imagination nourished by imperialistic notions of Manifest Destiny, political and economic interests and popular culture. While the aforementioned examples explore issues related to economic opportunities, race, nationhood and *Latinidad,* equally important were the geographical myths of Brazil-ness. In the formulation of Brazil in the United States, the city of Rio de Janeiro occupied a preeminent position.

Rio de Janeiro as a Symbol of Brazilianness

The political and cultural hegemony of Rio de Janeiro within Brazil was undisputed in the first half of the twentieth century. This was the place where media and mass community technologies began to flourish in the 1930s. As cultural and political capital for the first half of the twentieth century (until the move to Brasilia in the 1960s), Rio developed at a pace unlike many Brazilian cities. It helped that Rio was a coastal urban place full of natural and architectural beauty. From 1917 to the 1960s, most of the performers who went to the United States left from Rio. They took with them the symbols and imagery that would create lasting impressions for generations to come. These images were also propagated by the American media and by visitors to the city, including Welles and Disney and a host of Hollywood producers.

Many of the performers were native to Rio, among them the Miranda sisters and the members of the Banda da Lua, but even the others, such as

Barroso and Almeida, had worked and lived in Rio and associated with many of the city's symbols. Thus, it is not surprising that the first print and film images of Brazil were of Rio. Disney's 1943 *Saludos Amigos*, for example, takes viewers on a tour of Rio's major tourist spots, including the Pão de Açucar, the neighborhood of Copacabana, and the Corcovado. Donald Duck travels with his Brazilian parrot pal Zé Carioca (or Joe Carioca), whose name was inspired by the inhabitants of Rio de Janeiro, even though an actor from São Paulo played him. Zé, who dressed in the colors of the Brazilian flag and wore a straw hat, was a *malandro,* a street-smart hipster, yet suave character from the streets of Rio de Janeiro. His second name, "carioca," marked that he was from the city. He projected a laid back friendliness which continues to be associated with life in the tropical city by the ocean.

The first Hollywood productions with Brazilian themes focus on Rio. *Flying Down to Rio* (1933) featured Raul Roulien and showcased the talents of Ginger and Fred Rogers, who dance *the carioca*, a Hollywood-constructed Brazilian dance which even made its way into dance studios on the East Coast. Although Allen Woll has rightly pointed out that the studios tried to distinguish the various Latin American countries with their own films (*Flying Down to Rio, Weekend in Havana, Down Argentine Way*), these films treated complex Latin American countries as tourist destinations and Latin Americans as entertainers. Thus, Rio's tourist spots became logical images that many Americans and Brazilians would recognize as simply Brazilian rather than as a part of the southern *fluminense* state of Rio de Janeiro.

Even Carmen Miranda's Bahiana was a *carioca* invention associated with Rio's carnival and had little to do with the black women who carried their wares in a basket on their heads as many of their ancestors did for centuries all across Western Africa. In *The Three Caballeros* (1944), Zé Carioca accurately expresses the feelings that many *cariocas* had about Bahia, one of the states where African influences are most prevalent, when he nostalgically says "Aaah Bahia." "Have you ever been to Bahia, Donald?" he asks, as if Bahia were a magical land where all of one's dreams can be fulfilled. When Donald responds in the negative, Zé commands him to "Go!" Ironically, Disney's construction of Bahia had no black Brazilians. Brazilians from the South continue to regard the Northeast in general and Bahia in particular as the pristine unadulterated essence of Brazil. Meanwhile, Northeasterners face routine discrimination and are the butt of countless national jokes.

Over the decades, the figure of the *Bahiana* has remained a national symbol and one with which Brazilian immigrants must dialogue even though artists and symbols from the Northeast have found their own paths to the global market in recent decades. Brazilian women and men continue to dialogue with the fun-loving sensual image of Carmen Miranda and the dashing sensual male envisioned in actors such as Raul Roulien in the 1930s and Murilo Benicio and Rodrigo Santoro, two actors who have appeared in Hollywood films recently. (See Bernadete Beserra's essay in this volume.) Ironically, while some Brazilians categorically reject those images, others consciously embrace them for a host of reasons. For many North Americans and Brazilians these associations have often led to dramatic cultural conflicts and unrealistic expectations, particularly regarding Brazilian sexuality. A similar dynamics occurs in terms of the acceptability of Rio and its symbols as national. Many Brazilians from all over Brazil identify with them creatively, whether it is celebrating Rio-style carnivals or adopting the Corcovado as an emotional reference point. Others assert their *Mineiro*, *Bahiano* or *Paulista* identities, often stereotypically, often creatively, in a dynamic fashion depending on the situation. In the contemporary era Brazilian cultural and musical forms such as *axé* and *capoeira* have entered the United States directly from the Northeast, yet Rio remains and important national symbol and reference point for many immigrants and foreigners.

This process of nationalization of local symbols is not unique to Brazilians but relates to any national group abroad, including North Americans who nationalize the many symbols of New York, for example, when they are abroad. Nonetheless, the actions of Brazilian performers in the 1930s and 1940s must be placed in their proper historical context to appreciate their influence on the future generations of Brazilian immigrants and on North American attitudes towards Brazil. In the early years, Hollywood barred many minorities from depicting themselves, even if the roles were not complimentary. Most studios, for example, insisted on hiring white actors who used brown make-up to play South Americans whether they were performers, housewives or villains. Performers such as Roulien and the Miranda sisters were pioneers who represented oversimplified regional types, but they were pioneers! Others such as Houston and Costa may have received less publicity but they also helped in the construction of the Brazilian image, influenced by the wider sociopolitical environment of the time.

Conclusion

The American entertainment world is a multibillion-dollar industry that has an enormous impact on perceptions throughout the Western hemisphere. Film and musical producers have always been fascinated with the exotic. Unfortunately, more often than not this interest has not been a healthy desire to learn about *the other* but rather it has led to the appropriation and transformation of a foreign culture into static images for entertainment, without allowing it to serve as an example of that culture's dynamism. In many cases, even when foreign people are present, they serve as an exotic backdrop to the central plot. In other cases, performers participate in their own representations. In her essay on gender and empire, Ella Shohat has illustrated how Hollywood filmmakers often feminize foreign cultures to sanction the Western need for intervention and/or dominance. In the case of Brazilian performers, however, this view must also be supplemented by an analysis that recognizes the agency of well-established actors who not only took these images to the bank, so to speak, but also often subverted or creatively engaged them on and off stage (Shohat 1990). By the 1950s, the Latin American popular music boom in the United States initiated by Carmen and the Bando da Lua in 1939 was beginning to take other forms as the mambo craze reached its peak. Meanwhile, the invention of the television, which was quickly becoming an important forum for the mass distribution of entertainment, would give Miranda new life and an opportunity to once again adapt her act to a new milieu. Indeed, she died the day after recording a performance on the Jimmy Durante show for eager audiences in 1954. Brazilian performers were instrumental in preparing American audiences for the performers of the 1950s, including the "I Love Lucy" show that starred the Cuban conga player, Ricky Ricardo. It is no coincidence that in the third episode of "I Love Lucy" on October 22, 1951, Lucy wears the Bahiana outfit replete with fruit on her head in an episode in which she tried to rekindle her romance with her Cuban husband.

The North American and Brazilian imaginations are bound by the experiences of their performing predecessors from the 1930s to the 1950s, who had unprecedented access to the U.S. media, albeit within a confined space which limited their roles. Our options, immigrant or native, are never unlimited. Before Brazilian communities called the United States home, these precursors laid the foundation of symbols that relate to the imbalance of the economic and cultural power between the United States and Brazil. At the same time, they demonstrated an ingenuity and creativity in dealing with restrictive stereotypes. Sometimes this meant embracing stereotypes, but it also meant expanding the borders that encased Brazilian identity, assuming and taking on ever-present trappings of "Latin-ness."

Not all individuals find themselves as fortunate as Barroso, with the luxury to return and resume life and a vibrant career in Brazil or as Miranda, who became a wealthy star in Hollywood. Transnational residence, nonetheless, urges us to redefine immigration in terms of multiple crossings and loyalties across national borders. The experience of performers allows us to question our conceptualization of who an immigrant is. This is a question that becomes ever more important in a world of multiple cross-national residences. Still, there is the immigrant such as Britto, who gains technology and returns "home" to make a living and establish cross-national commercial identities. Like Laurindo de Almeida, many have stayed on and contributed to the eclectic American musical tradition. Others, such as Barroso and Torá, return for personal reasons. Still others do not have the choice of returning or staying. The experience of non-white performers adds another level of conceptualization and forces us to re-examine the meaning of "immigrant community" across racial and class boundaries. The cases explored here expose the ambiguity of the Brazilian immigrant experience and the complications of cross-national identities. These tensions often surface (and are resolved) emotionally, but they can also inhibit political and social engagement and the recognition of agency in one's new home.

The contribution of the relatively privileged Brazilian performers in the United States from the 1930s to the 1950s is better understood in relationship to global capitalism. Although these Brazilians played an important role in formulating the first reference points of *Brasilidade* (Brazilianness) and *Latinidad* in the United States, their experiences and the circumstances of their experiences must be distinguished from the more diverse types of emigration in recent years. This is particularly true for people with little access to the media and with few resources, who either idolize, dialogue, or consciously avoid the images of their predecessors. Both scholars of immigration as well as immigrants must continue to highlight the unequal balance of power between producers in receptor countries and immigrant performers who represent their nations *de facto*. At the same time, it is important to resist universalizing the immigrant experience and blur the power relations within immigrant communities. Moreover, we do well to recognize the problems of disjunctive immigrant narratives that discourage individuals from historicizing their own experiences.

Notes

1. "Obituaries," *The Guardian Online*, August 8, 1995. Almeida died on July 26, 1995. See webpage www.laurindoalmeida.com.
2. "Morando em Los Angeles há nove anos, Dori Caymmi vem ao Brasil para lançar seu novo disco: Dori traz sua 'música para pensar.'" *Folha de São Paulo*,

November 3, 1999 (http://www1.folha.uol.com.br/fsp/ilustrad/fq0311199914.htm). Accessed March 1, 2005. Carlos Bozzo Junior, "Supergenerous é o novo CD do percussionista brasileiro radicado nos EUA." *Folha de São Paulo,* November 8, 2000. http://www1.folha.uol.com.br/fsp/ilustrad/fq0811200014.htm. Accessed March 1, 2005.

3. "Los Angeles-1932: Sacas de café garantem pioneirismo em São Paulo," *Folha de São Paulo,* July 28, 2002. http://www1.folha.uol.com.br/fsp/dinheiro/fi2309200113.htm. Accessed March 17, 2005.

4. Olin Down, "Composers' Group in Concert Here: Elsie Houston Soloist," *New York Times* ProQuest Historical Newspapers (1851–2003), March 11, 1940, 17; Grace Turner, "Good-Will Recipes from Rio," *Los Angeles Times,* April 20, 1941; ProQuest Historical Newspapers *Los Angeles Times* (1881–1985), 118; Jack Gould, "News and Gossip of the Night Clubs," *New York Times,* March 6, 1938; ProQuest Historical Newspapers (1851–2003), 150.

References

Anderson, Benedict. 1983. *Imagined Communities.* New York, Verso.

Beserra, Bernadete. 2003. *Brazilian Immigrants in the United States: Cultural Imperialism and Social Class.* New York, LFB Scholarly Publishing.

Bozzo Junior, Carlos. 2000. "Supergenerous é o novo CD do percussionista brasileiro radicado nos EUA," *Folha de São Paulo,* November 8. http://www1.folha.uol.com.br/fsp/ilustrad/fq0811200014.htm. Accessed March 1, 2005.

"Brazilian Music on the Air." 1940. *New York Times,* November 10, 158.

Bureau of the Census, Social and Economic Statistics Administration, U.S. Department of Commerce. 1933. *15th Census of the US 1930 Population, Vol. 2-General Report.* Washington, D.C.: U.S. Department of Commerce.

Burton, Julianne. 1992. "Don Juanito Duck and the Imperial Patriarchal Unconscious: Disney Studios, the Good Neighbor Policy and the Packaging of Latin America." In *Nationalisms and Sexualities,* pp. 21–41. Ed. Andrew Parker et al. New York: Routledge.

Cabral, Sérgio. 1992. *No tempo de Ari Barroso.* Rio de Janeiro: Lumiar Editora.

Cardoso, Abel. 1978. *Carmen Miranda: A cantora do Brasil.* Rio de Janeiro.

Cardoso, Tom. "Carmen Costa, de arrumadeira a diva do canto colloquial." Agenda do Samba & Choro Jornal do valor Econômico. http://www.samba-choro.com.br/s-c/tribuna/samba-choro.0207/0287.html. Accessed March 3, 2005.

Castro, Ruy. 2005. *Carmen: A vida de Carmen Miranda a brasileira mais famosa do século XX.* São Paulo: Companhia da Letras.

Chapa, Jorge. 2000. "Hispanic/Latino Ethnicity and Identifiers." In *Encyclopedia of the U.S. Census,* pp. 243–246. Washington, D.C.: CQ Press.

Consejería de Cultura y Patrimonio De Extremadura (Spain). 1998. *La gráfica política del 98.* Cáceres, Spain: Centro Extremeño de Estudios y Cooperación con Iberoamérica.

Costa, Carmen. 1972. Recorded interview, Museum of Image and Sound. August 23.

Crickfield, George W. 1908. *The Rise and Progress of the Latin American Republics and Their Relations to the United States under the Monroe Doctrine*. New York: Brentano's.

Daniels, Roger. 2004. *Guarding the Golden Door: American Immigration Policy and Immigrants since 1882.* New York: Hill and Wang.

Davis, Darién. 2000. "To Be or Not to Be Brazilian: Carmen Miranda's Quest for Fame and 'Authenticity' in the United States." In *Strange Pilgrimages: Exile, Travel, and National Identity in Latin American, 1800–1990s Abroad.* Wilmington, Delaware: Scholarly Resources.

———. 1997. "The Brazilian-Americans: Demography and Identity of an Emerging Latino Minority." *Latino Review of Books* (Spring/Fall 1997): 8–15.

De Jesus, Maria Angela. 2004. *Ruth de Souza: Estrela Negra*. São Paulo: Imprensa Oficial de São Paulo.

Derrida, Jacques. 1972. *Positions.* Chicago: University of Chicago Press.

De Souza. 1990. Recorded Interview with author. July 16, 1990, Rio de Janeiro.

Didier, Carlos and João Máximo. 1990. *Noel Rosa: Uma Biografia*. Brasilia: Editora UnB.

Down, Olin. 1940. "Composers' Group in Concert Here: Elsie Houston Soloist." *New York Times,* March 11, 17.

Drake, Hubert. 1939. "The Theaters." *New York Post*, June 30, 16.

Dunn, Christopher. 2001. *Brutality Garden: Tropicália and the Emergence of a Brazilian Counterculture*. Chapel Hill: University of North Carolina Press.

Elkins, Stanley. 1959. *Slavery: A Problem in American Institutional and Intellectual Life*. Chicago: University of Chicago Press.

Freud, Sigmund. 1977. *On Sexuality: Pelican Freud Library 7.* Harmondsworth: Pelican.

Freyre, Gilberto. 1973. "O homen brasileiro: Formacão étnica e cultural." *Estudo de Problemas Brasileiros 167–178.* Recife: Universidade Federal de Pernambuco.

———. 1966–1970. *Casa Grande e Senzala. Casa-grande & senzala: formação da família brasileira sob o regime de economia patriarcal.* 2 vols. Recife: Imprensa Oficial.

Garrod, Charles. 1992. *Decca Los Angeles Master Numbers.* Vols. 1–3. Zephyrhills, Fla.: Joyce Record Club Publication.

Gilman, Sander L. 1985. *Difference and Pathology: Stereotypes of Sexuality, Race, and Madness*. Ithaca: Cornell University Press.

Gil-Montero, Martha. 1989. *The Brazilian Bombshell: The Biography of Carmen Miranda.* New York: Donald I. Fine.

Gould, Jack. 1938. "News and Gossip of the Night Clubs." *New York Times,* March 6, 150.

Hanke, Lewis. *1939. Gilberto Freyre: Vida y Obra. Bibliografía Antología.* New York: Instituto de las Españas en los Estados Unidos.

Hunt, Rockwell. 1939. "How We Can Help Brazil." *Los Angeles Times,* May 20, A4.

Levine, Robert. 1998. *The Brazilian Photographs of Genevieve Naylor, 1940–1942.* Durham: Duke University Press.

"Los Angeles-1932: Sacas de café garantem pioneirismo em São Paulo." 2002. *Folha de São Paulo,* July 28. http://www1.folha.uol.com.br/fsp/dinheiro/fi2309200113.htm. Accessed March 17, 2005.

Machado, Carlos. 1978. *Memórias sem maquiagem.* São Paulo: Livraria Cultura Editora.

Margolis, Maxine. 1994. *Little Brazil: An Ethnography of Brazilian Immigrants in New York City.* Princeton: Princeton University Press.

McMann, Frank D. 1973. *The Brazil-American Alliance, 1937–1945.* Princeton: Princeton University Press.

"Miranda Beelding Up Leetle Sister." *New York World Telegram,* August 13 (n.p.).

"Morando em Los Angeles há nove anos, Dori Caymmi vem ao Brasil para lançar seu novo disco: Dori traz sua 'música para pensar'." 1999. *Folha de São Paulo,* November 3. (http://www1.folha.uol.com.br/fsp/ilustrad/fq0311199914.htm). Accessed March 1, 2005.

Mulvey, Laura. 1989. *Visual and Other Pleasures.* Bloomington: Indiana University Press.

Neville, Lucile. 1940. "Now That Hollywood Has Discovered Latin America, Anything Can Happen." *Washington Post,* January 28.

Oliveira, Aloysio de. 1981. *De banda para a lua.* Rio de Janeiro: Editora Record.

Ong Hing, Bill. 2004. *Defining America through Immigration Policy.* Philadelphia: Temple University Press.

Parke, Richard. 1949. "City Pays Tribute to Brazil's Chief." *New York Times,* May 24, 1.

Reyes, Luis and Peter Rubie. 1994. *Hispanics in Hollywood: An Encyclopedia of Film and Television.* New York: Garland.

Roberts, John Storm. 1993. *The Latin Tinge: The Impact of Latin American Music on the United States.* New York: Oxford Univeristy Press.

Roland, Donald W. Org. 1947. *History of the Office of the Coordinator of Inter-American Affairs.* Washington, D.C.

Roosevelt Corollary, The. 1904. http://www.latinamericanstudies.org/us-relations/roosevelt-corollary.htm. Accessed January 6, 2006.

Sandoval-Sanchez, Alberto. 1999. *José Can You See? Latinos On and Off Broadway.* Madison: University of Wisconsin Press.

Sassen, Saskia. 1990. "U.S. Immigration Policy toward Mexico in a Global Economy." *Journal of International Affairs* 43(2): 369–381.

Shohat, Ella. 1990. "Gender and the Culture of Empire: Towards a Feminist Ethnography of the Cinema." *Quarterly Review of Film and Video* 13:45–84.

Shoof, Kees. 2004. "Brazil's Most American Crooner: (Review) Dick Farney no Palco CD." http://musicabrasileira.org/reviewsinterviews/dfpalco.html. September.

Silva, Sinval. 1967. Recorded Interview. Museu da Imagem e do Som, January 20.

Skidmore, Thomas. 1993. *Black into White: Race and Nationality in Brazilian Thought*. Durham: Duke University Press.

Solberg, Helena. 1994. *Carmen Miranda: Bananas Is My Business*. New York: Noon Pictures.

Stam, Robert. 1989. *Subversive Pleasures: Bakhtin, Cultural Criticism, and Film*. Baltimore: Johns Hopkins University Press.

Tannenbaum, Frank. 1946. *Slave and Citizen: The Negro in the Americas*. New York: Vintage Books.

Turner, Grace. 1941. "Good-Will Recipes from Rio." *Los Angeles Times*, April 20, I18.

Wilson, Earl. 1941. "'Hokay, Go Home Keed,' They Said to Aurora But Aurora, Carmen Miranda's Sister, Showed Hollywood Up." *New York Post*, October 13.

Woll, Allen L. 1983. *The Hollywood Musical Goes to War*. Chicago: Nelson-Hall.

Wood, Bryce. 1961. *The Making of the Good Neighbor Policy*. New York, Columbia University Press.

Movies

Butler, David. 1931. *Delicious*.

Cummings, Irving. 1940. *Down Argentine Way*.

Disney, Walt. 1944. *The Three Caballeros*.

Freeland, Thornton. 1933. *Flying Down to Rio*.

Green, Alfred. 1929. *Making the Grade*.

Lang, Walter. 1941. *Weekend in Havana*.

Werker, Alfred L. 1933. *It's Great to Be Alive*.

2

In the Shadow of Carmen Miranda and the Carnival: Brazilian Immigrant Women in Los Angeles

Bernadete Beserra

"Americans think that Brazil is only about good weather, revelry, and sex. Their collective fantasy is that Brazil is a big orgy: women are always topless, sex is everywhere, and we never stop partying." Curiously enough, there is no difference between what Ivan Becker—a 44-year-old Brazilian journalist whom I interviewed on April 14, 1999, in Los Angeles—describes as the U.S. fantasy about Brazil, and the common belief spread throughout seventeenth-century Europe according to which "there is no sin below the equatorial line." [1]

Brazil of today, like the tropical America of Europe's seventeenth-century imagination, is perceived as an earthly paradise with no laws, no suffering, no work, and no punishment: "the tropical Eden to which many of us at one time or another secretly longed to escape," confides Joseph Page in *The Brazilians.* Page also adds that things have changed lately, and from the 1990s on "mention of Brazil was evoking images of street children being preyed upon and slaughtered by private death squads composed of off-duty policemen, and chain saws and fires destroying the world's largest remaining rain forest" (1995, 1).

None of these images, whether that of the seventeenth-century or of today's Brazil, confirms the realities that inspire their construction, because exotic images or preferences are produced "exclusively by their relation to the observer" (Todorov 1993, 264). Thus, what matters are the desires, interests, and projections of the observer and his attraction for certain contents at the expense of others. In the case of the European exoticization of America, or U.S. exoticization of Brazil, the characteristics around which fantasy develops always converge on a primitivism already surpassed by the observer's *civilized* or *fully developed* societies. In this specific sense, although the most common, exoticization no longer represents a preference of otherness over likeness—as the etymology of the word suggests—but rather a deformed representation that facilitates and justifies domination. In other words, the relationship between the exoticizer and the exoticized as developed by the Western world is delimited by a broader one, that between the colonizer and the colonized (Said 1979; Memmi 1991; Fanon 1963). It is "a relation of domination, not of reciprocity" (Todorov, 315).

It is within the context of these meanings and relationships that immigrant integration occurs everywhere. Immigrants, and foreigners in general, always have to deal with images of themselves of which they were sometimes completely unaware before immigration. In fieldwork conducted in Los Angeles between 1997 and 1999, I observed that besides having to learn new ways of dealing with issues of class, race, nationality, gender, and language, Brazilian immigrant women still had to deal with the eroticization and all the consequences connected to it. All the Brazilian women whom I interviewed were aware of the stereotype. Some of them did believe that the stereotype restrains their movements, promotes the idea of prostitution, and has, consequently, a negative impact on Brazilian women in general and those living abroad in particular. Others, however, considered that the image is advantageously ambiguous, and it is up to each Brazilian woman to ratify or deny any connection with prostitution and submission. The aim of this paper is to discuss the strategies Brazilian women in Los Angeles use to negotiate such stereotyped images in their favor.[2]

The Research and the Context: Brazilians in Los Angeles

When in 1996 I decided to study Brazilian immigrants in Los Angeles, I knew already that it was not a typical region of settlement for Brazilian immigrants in the United States. Things have not changed much since, and today the Brazilian Foreign Ministry estimates that about 90% of the Brazilian immigrant population in the United States is concentrated on the East Coast (New York, 300,000; Miami, 200,000, and Boston, 150,000; MRE 2001).

The number of Brazilians in the Los Angeles metropolitan area is estimated at 33,000 (MRE 2001). Although smaller than its counterpart on the East Coast, this community has been significant in terms of spreading Brazilian culture abroad. The prime example of this is Carmen Miranda, through whom the Hollywood movie industry created and disseminated throughout the world the still dominant although contested stereotype of the Brazilian (and also *Latina*) woman (Beserra 2003, 42). Brazilians in Los Angeles have also been able to project the popularity of Brazilian music worldwide through the recording industry as well as through sophisticated marketing, distribution, promotion, and broadcasting services (Riedinger 1997).

The suggested connection between Los Angeles and the projection of Brazilian culture worldwide led me to include studying samba schools in my original research proposal since samba and carnival have been the most important ways of Brazilian immigrants diffusing Brazilian culture, not only in Los Angeles but also in many other cities all over the world (Torresan 1994; Ribeiro 1997; Machado 2004).

The other reason to do fieldwork among samba schools was because the two other groups I researched constantly questioned the eroticized image of Brazil diffused by those Brazilians connected to the so-called Brazilian cultural industry. Thus although they acknowledge that samba became a national symbol of Brazil, not all Brazilians agree that it should represent Brazilianness internationally. The Brazilian Women's Group, one of the associations that I studied, for instance, has as its main purpose to disconnect the representation of Brazil from the sexualized image of Brazilian women, created precisely through samba and carnival (Beserra 2005, 68). By observing samba schools I intended both to explore their specific influence in the construction of a Brazilian identity in Los Angeles and to understand the ways their members relate to Brazilians from other groups.

The data that support this chapter are based upon my observation of and participation in the regular meetings and other social gatherings of the Portuguese-speaking Seventh-Day Adventist Church of Chino and the Brazilian Women's Group, between November of 1997 and November of 1999, as part of a larger study entitled *Brazilians in Los Angeles: Imperialism, Immigration, and Social Class* (2000). During this period, I tape-recorded in-depth, open-ended interviews with fifteen members of each of the two associations and with ten other Brazilians connected to other associations and institutions, such as the Brazilian Consulate, the Brazil-California Chamber of Commerce, the Brazilian Sociocultural Committee, the Cultural Gaucho Center, the Brazilian Evangelic Community-Salvation Army, the MILA and the SambaLA samba schools, and the Hollywood Palladium Carnival. In conversations face to face or by telephone, I also collected socioeconomic data (age, time of immigration, state of birth in Brazil, level of education, type of job before and after immigration, marital status, etc.) of 195 people, most of them connected to the two researched groups.

Research and demographic information on the Brazilian population in the United States is still very limited. Since the U.S. Census does not provide a socioeconomic profile for the Brazilian immigrant population, scholars have used their research samples to create a variety of different profiles of this population in the United States. The profile I constructed from my sample reveals some differences from those of scholars studying the Brazilian population on the East Coast.[3] My sample of 195 Brazilian immigrants in the greater Los Angeles area was made up of women (65%); married individuals (73%), and adults between the ages of 30 and 45 (53%). They came from the Southeast, Brazil's most industrialized region, primarily from the states of Rio de Janeiro (27%) and São Paulo (20%), although there were also some immigrants from the Southern state of Rio Grande do Sul (14%), and the northeastern state of Bahia (7%). The great majority (76%) of the Brazilians I sampled immigrated to the United States over the last twenty years, and mostly between 1981 and 1999.

Coming generally from the Brazilian middle class, most of the people in my sample had attended college (52%) or at least finished high school (32%). There is a relative congruency between the educational level of the population I researched and the jobs they held, especially among those who have lived longer in the area. Sixty-three percent of those who were married had a Brazilian spouse, while 30% were married to U.S. citizens. The remaining 7% were married to Mexican, European, and other South American immigrants. It is interesting to note that most of the 40 Brazilians I interviewed in depth stated that they had come to the United States for reasons other than "making money." Thus, they came, for example, to work for Brazilian or U.S. companies, to study, to marry, or simply to have an adventure. They either arrived with their families or had them in Los Angeles, and although many dreamed of going back to Brazil, they nevertheless still struggled to integrate into U.S. society.

Becoming Aware of the Stereotype and Its Consequences

During my five-year-long stay in Riverside, California, between 1995 and 2000, I became acquainted with a version of myself that I totally ignored before living in the United States. It was quite an interesting revelation to learn about North Americans' attraction to Brazil: "Brazil? Wow!" But it also felt annoying to deal with exaggerated reactions such as the following: one day a cable repairman came to fix my television antenna. After noticing my accent, he (a young white American, about 25–30 years old) asked where I was from, and after I answered Brazil, he replied quite surprised: "Brazil?! I did not know that there were any Brazilians in Southern California!" He kept staring at me as though I was some sort of *rara avis*. After the shock, he even apologized and explained that this was his first time meeting a live Brazilian, and told me that he watches some cable channels that have special shows with Brazilian women. I did not feel encouraged to ask what kind of show it was, since I was already feeling embarrassed and I think he was, after all, a bit uncomfortable too.

Most of the time, however, I felt as if the word Brazil had the power to trigger day-dreaming. Innumerable times and in many different circumstances, I was told about peoples' dreams of visiting Brazil. Suzana, a Mexican American friend, told me that she learned to like Brazil because of her grandmother. She said that the old lady stuck to her dream of visiting Brazil during Carnival until the day she died.

Eventually I noticed that, different from the Latino stereotype, which evokes immigrant patterns and social stratification, the image of the eroticized/tropicalized other seemed more benign and, to some extent, more liberating too.[4] This understanding was not built overnight but homeopathically, by living and talking to other Brazilian women that I met and became friends with at graduate school or, later, when doing my fieldwork among Brazilian immigrants in Los Angeles.

My first "teacher" on the issue of colonial and neocolonial politics of labeling was Amélia, a Brazilian student that I met right after arriving in Riverside, for my Ph.D. studies. Very much aware of the games of power involved in the production of Latina women as primitive, submissive, sensual, desirable, and promiscuous, Amélia, nevertheless, would always dress like the *baiana* doll that she herself so strongly criticized. Like her, I quickly learned that a positive reaction to the word "Brazil" is mostly grounded on fantasies about Brazilian carnival, but it never really bothered me to the point where I felt I had to lie about my nationality as was the case of Elizabeth, 67, married to a white American and living in Los Angeles since 1985:

> "In a general way the idea that Americans have of Brazil is of Carnival. Carnival and the most beautiful women in the world. Carnival means you are always ready for fun. That is, to say you're Brazilian is already giving them a green light. It's an invitation to play around. The greatest advertisement of Brazil is the rear end . . . if it were a billboard Brazil would be an enormous rear end. Now tell me, why is it that Brazil must forever be represented by rear ends? If it is not only one behind it's thirty. The ad for the Hollywood Palladium Carnival was something horrible, I don't know how many *mulatas*' behinds were there. Until when will Brazil live off rear ends? Oh well, this is the market which Brazil offers here: rear ends, sexuality, carnival. That is, it is nothing serious. It's absurd! Many times I even say I am Portuguese. When I am among a more serious crowd I don't have the

courage to say that I'm from Brazil because of this reputation. Everybody looks at my face and sees a rear end. I can't stand the quantity of rear ends that comes together with the idea of Brazil, it's not possible! It's like a nightmare! So it's like this, all over, if there aren't some thirty behinds, preferably of *mulatas*, it seems as if the message doesn't get through, it doesn't sell. Even the Brazilian consulate promotes this."

Elizabeth's comment reveals that the construction of identities in foreign settings may become a rather dramatic enterprise when the image of the group to which one belongs is a composite of only a few characteristics with which one does not identify. Not only in the case of Brazil or colonized countries, but in general, the images through which people and countries are represented are almost impossible to identify with because they are always too broad and too shallow to really fit any concrete individual.[5] What Elizabeth explained is that she is left no room to claim her Brazilian identity because it is too loaded with meanings she does not want to deal with. Also she feels powerless to change it because, she says, "even the Brazilian consulate promotes it." In other words, what power does she have to question the version of Brazil divulged by its very government? If the image was only an exotic construction produced by the distant other—whether American or European—she would more easily question it than when it is the Brazilian government itself that reinforces exoticism. Thus instead of being a positive reference, her connection to Brazil works as a trap which she tries to avoid whenever she has the possibility of passing as a Portuguese.

Elizabeth's case shows, among several things, how difficult immigrant integration becomes when the immigrant group to which one belongs is portrayed in a way that so clearly interferes in their new lives. But it also demonstrates—considering that many Brazilians, including the Brazilian consulate, also promote the contested image—that the variety of images is the result of the diversity of worldviews of classes and groups in a historical society. The selection of features is usually processed in function of the interests of the hegemonic classes and have purposes historically defined by each new configuration of power (Larrain 1994).

There are thus two key aspects to take into account when considering the construction of an international Brazilian identity: one is related to internal political dynamics, as explained above, and the other is a function of the place of the nation in the international division of labor.

The rise of nationalism takes place in a world already globalized by the capitalist mode of production. Therefore national identities are forged in the context of submission or resistance to the expansion of the colonial regime. Anderson (1991, 53) explains that one of the reasons of the early nationalism in Latin America was the way Europe treated its Creoles. Europeans believed that Indians and Negroes had contaminated them, and the people thus afflicted should be treated as impure. The European discrimination against their children who had suffered the fatality of a transatlantic birth made these get closer to Indians and Negroes and look at them as part of a new and different community; their most important aim at that point was to get free from European dominion and exploitation.

Brazil shares with most of the nations the misfortune of having been formed under the control of imperialist powers. Brazilian national identity therefore will be constructed in relation to the dominant "others," but also in relation to its Latin American neighbors.

One of the bases of Brazilian national identity is the *myth of the three races* according to which the Brazilian people is a harmonious mixture of the Portuguese, Africans, and Native Brazilians (Freyre 1946; Da Matta 1981).[6] Despite the actual power socially given to these three groups of people, the cultural elements chosen to represent the country are those connected to that mixture, such as samba, carnival, and soccer. It is needless to say that these cultural elements are just some among many others that could have been chosen. Nowadays, however, it is hard to think of other symbols that would represent Brazil as well, since we have all learned to recognize them as part of our national soul.[7]

As it has already been pointed out, in the international division of labor Brazil is on the colonized side and, as such, its powers are very limited in terms of fabricating and changing images. Recently I had the opportunity to talk about international images of Brazil with a Brazilian diplomat serving in the Middle East. I asked him if the images of Brazil presented to Middle Easterners are the same ones as divulged in the United States and Europe. He answered that the Brazilian government can do nothing but start from what already exists. Therefore, instead of questioning universal stereotypes of Brazil, it uses them to attract people to Brazilian culture, and once they get closer to Brazil and Brazilians, it is more likely that people will go beyond stereotypes and change their perception. He admits that the only possible way to understand/interpret Brazil in an international context is by connecting it to whatever ideas have already been constructed, which suggests that we have to surrender to the stereotyped image.

For Brazilians in Los Angeles, however, there is a choice since they can choose between exoticization and latinization, as Ivan Becker explains:

> "The image that the world has of Brazil is that we are good with a ball, good at samba, good at fucking, good at everything, understand? It's exotic! Deep down they like it because they don't know much about us. So we aren't put in the same boat . . . you know? In a racist country such as this, the Brazilian even has a privileged position because we are not placed together with other Latinos. Brazilians are a separate category."

What this observation suggests is that if the context requires Brazilians to identify either with Latinos or with the Brazilian exoticized image, it is very likely that they will choose the latter because of the reasons presented above; that is, Brazil is too far away to allow U.S. residents to prove their own ideas right or wrong and, taking this into consideration, the exotic image is more appealing than that to which the term Latino is generally connected in Los Angeles, given the local patterns of immigration and social stratification. In this case, the exoticization of Brazilians, contested in many other circumstances, is seen as positive since it relativizes their inclusion into the Latino group which is so discriminated against (Oboler 1992; Beserra 2003 and 2005; Kearney and Beserra 2004).[8]

To accept a stereotyped image, nevertheless, is to surrender to the idea of remaining a creation of the colonizer other and have one's movements constrained within the narrow boundaries of his imagination. What to do then? Brazilian governmental agencies as well as Brazilian immigrants themselves seem to have little choice but to accept (at least temporarily) the international image of Brazil and to deal with it individually.

Regardless of how able they are to negotiate these images to their advantage in their process of integration, Brazilians generally feel misrepresented by the reduction of Brazil to three or four symbols. Gustavo Ribeiro, a Brazilian anthropologist who studied Brazilians in San Francisco, expresses his uneasiness about it. He says "it is a little anti-climactic for an anthropologist doing research abroad on people from his country to find that in the end national identity is reduced to its most stereotypical expressions: carnival, *feijoada* [the Brazilian national dish], *capoeira* [a mixture of martial art and dance], samba, soccer, and not the least g-string bikinis (also known as dental floss bikinis)" (Ribeiro 1997, 7).

Despite all nations being reduced to three or four stereotyped images, it is noteworthy to observe that the production of these images and consequently international immigrant integration is conditioned by the racist basis of imperialist expansion. Only Western European nations and peoples (and their "pure" children, United States and Canada) have the attributes to classify and exoticize the entire world. Only they "had the power to make their discourse of the Other come true globally" (Savigliano 1995, 9). Thus beyond the forever ongoing philosophical quest between us and them, exoticization has had always very practical purposes. It works, for instance, as a maneuver of the colonizer to keep the colonized in their place. Primitive, savage, lawless, and so forth, the exoticized is always put in a position that demands *civilized* intervention, aid, or domination (Aparicio and Chávez-Silverman 1997; Benz 1997; Urraca 1997). But exoticization works also as a means of commodifying the colonized and their "goods," whatever they may be. Music, dance, sex, and food, for instance, become commodities submitted to the same rules as other products in the capitalist market. And so do people.

By studying Brazilian immigrants in Portugal, Machado (2004) observes that by fitting in the Brazilian image as cultivated by Portugal—which, as expected, is not particularly different from the one existing in the United States—Brazilian immigrants acquire more value in a job market that works with the structural advantage of (exotic) Brazilians over other nationalities. In this particular case, which is also the case of the Brazilian cultural industry in Los Angeles, those Brazilians who are *more* Brazilian are better rewarded. Therefore, Brazilian immigrants soon face the challenge of turning into allegedly *real* Brazilians, which means, among other things, learning how to dance samba, making *feijoada*, dressing accordingly, playing soccer (for men), and so forth. Thus they deliberately work on their own exoticization and become "victims and agents of an active subordination" (Machado, 218). So they are victims in that they do not have the power to challenge the image of Brazil and Brazilians in the international world, but are agents in the sense that by giving in to the dominant image and negotiating it accordingly, they attain advantages over those who are *less* Brazilian or not Brazilian at all: they become the authentic representatives of Brazil and Brazilianness.

Elizabeth's comment also calls attention to the fact that the masculine cast of the colonizer tends to further exoticize the colonized along gendered lines. Memmi (1991), Fanon (1963; 1967), Sinha (1995), and others have discussed the feminization of colonized men in the depictions of the colonizing powers. In order to stress the power and the need of the intervention of the colonizer, colonized men are either out of the picture or feminized. Exoticization of Brazil, as pointed out by Elizabeth, is heavily concentrated on exoticization of Brazilian women, which explains why she suggests that they alone bear its burdens.[9]

I propose that Brazilian women have become a commodity in the international market of cultural and sexual exoticism ever since Hollywood used Carmen Miranda to create and diffuse the myth of Brazilian (and also Latin American) women's sensuality and grace. I know, however, that if today her image is so closely attached to Brazil and Brazilianness, her international fame came from performing a chummy, frivolous, and sensual Latin American character (Pérez 1997; Rodríguez 2004; Clark 2002). Despite her appearance in the movies as a stereotype of Latin American women, I argue that the connection of her image with Brazilianness prevailed and endured for two main reasons: she was a Brazilian (even though born in Portugal), and her stereotype of the Brazilian woman kept on being fed by the broadcast of the Brazilian Carnival, especially the samba schools' parade in Rio de Janeiro.

Old myths of the tropical paradise inspired and guided the creation of the new ones, which are now produced by Brazilians themselves to feed cultural and tourism industries.[10] The difference between now and the 17th century in Europe is that at that time exoticization was based on distance and ignorance; now, it is recreated with the input of Brazilians themselves. Therefore, the United States and the European distant colonizer are no longer the only ones to benefit from exoticization. Who are the Brazilians to feed the stereotyped images or, in Machado's terms, who are the agents and victims of exoticization?

Elizabeth suggests that cultural and tourism industries are the agents and beneficiaries, and women are the victims. But things are a bit more complicated. For now, despite Elizabeth's suggestion, let's hold on to the assumption that most Brazilians have become simultaneously victims and active agents of the construction of the Brazilian tropicalized image.

Hollywood transformed Carmen Miranda into a representation of the tropical woman: sexy, bubbly, entertaining, submissively sympathetic, and so on. Such an image was not immediately accepted by Brazilians or the other Latin American national groups that she represented. In fact, it was much contested by several groups of Brazilian society, and she was accused by sectors of the Brazilian media of not representing Brazil properly. Carmen Miranda tried to explain that the representation was *Americanized*. She even inspired the famous song *Disseram que eu voltei Americanizada* (They Said That I've Come Back Americanized), in which she argues that in spite of appearances she was still very Brazilian. The point, however, was not about her being Brazilian and keeping her Brazilianness to herself but rather her submission in embodying an *American* version of Brazilian women and culture. A São Paulo paper, *A Folha da Noite*, registered its disapproval in the following terms: "So that's how Brazil shines in the United States: with a Portuguese woman singing bad-taste black sambas. It is really like that! And so that's how it should be. Because there really aren't many people in this country who are worth as much as that Carmen, that great and excellent Carmen who left to sing nonsense abroad" (cited in Davis 1997, 13).

The fact is that the image of Brazilian women projected by Carmen Miranda was further developed and sophisticated with the broadcast of samba schools' parades in Rio de Janeiro. Indeed, the image of Brazilian women that Elizabeth contests is not Carmen Miranda's *baiana* doll, but the more sexualized representation promoted by carnival.[11]

However, linking the carnival to sex and prostitution exclusively is a misinterpretation of what effectively occurs. By interviewing U.S. citizens and other non-Brazilians at the 1999 Palladium Carnival in Los Angeles, I was led to challenge the predominant idea of sexuality related to the Brazilian carnival. One of my interviewees, a white American male, about 40 years old, said that he connects carnival with music, dance, festivities, and sexuality. He said, "Do you know, for me the whole thing is very sexual, but sexual in a very special way. It is like the celebration of the body with music and joy. It is a very positive way of bringing out sexuality to the public scene. The whole thing; music, freedom, costumes . . . all lead to a very special way of celebrating the body." He proposed much more than the easy connection of carnival with hardcore sex; that is, he included in his perception all the magic and poetry connected with the general idea of carnival to finally arrive to a fantasized sexuality, free from the burden of Protestant repression.

Thus, although highly sexualized, the image of Brazilian women also has elements that underscore their exoticism: mystery, wildness, innocence, and submission.

Negotiating Images: From Carmen Miranda to Gisele Bündchen

Sexy, bubbly, beautiful, submissive, and promiscuous: how do Brazilian women in Los Angeles live with these images?

I collected many stories from the Brazilian women I interviewed. A journalist friend told me that a Brazilian upper middle-class lady came to visit Los Angeles and when she was introduced to a white American male, his reaction was: "Huh, Brazil?!" She then turned to her Brazilian friend who had introduced them and said, in Portuguese, "Why is this guy so affected by learning that I am Brazilian? Is he assuming that we are all whores?"

Not all Brazilian immigrant women react so defensively to the manifestation of the stereotype. Paola, age 35, a university professor, explains:

"I'm not bothered in the least by Americans taking advantage of the fact that I'm a Brazilian to dream a little about the sensuality that they don't have, the poor guys. They look at me as if I held some secret they would give everything to discover. I feed this stereotype a little, of course. I think deep down inside I also believe it."

Paola, like Gisele Bündchen (a Brazilian supermodel recognized as being one of the most successful and highest-paid in the world), is not the best sample of the Brazilian advertised *mestizaje*. In fact, she fits the white American stereotype better than the Brazilian. Her explanation about how she deals with the Brazilian stereotype suggests that it merely adds some flavor in her life. Moreover, she has been convinced that there is indeed a strong correspondence between stereotype and reality: "I think deep down inside I also believe it." It is in fact a belief shared by both the exoticizer and the exoticized. By being constantly under the exoticizing gaze, the exoticized ends up embodying its perception. But things are not just as magic as Paola pictures them in the quote above. In several other conversations she told me about how hard she has to work in order to get the same respect and rewards as her colleagues. Her complaint, however, seems very similar to those made by feminists in general: when competing in traditionally male areas, women have to work harder since men are always suspicious about their resorting to unorthodox strategies. In regard to her academic job, she declares that she has problems both with her colleagues and their wives. They trust more in the efficiency of her beauty than of her intelligence and discipline. Yet, after all, besides confirming that she is as capable as are her male and female U.S. colleagues, she still has this additional Brazilian sex appeal which she can occasionally use as a trump card—one more asset to favorably negotiate her immigrant position in Los Angeles.

For Annie, age 36, things are a bit more complicated. Let us follow a dialogue between her and her husband, Ivan:

I: I know that the American has the greatest fascination with Brazilian women. The collective fantasy of Americans is that women in Brazil are all topless. Nobody goes to the beach in Brazil topless, it is very rare, but they have this idea. They also think that Brazil is a big orgy, a non-stop party. But, after all, it is a positive image they have of us.

A: No, but I think that this idea that the women are hot and this and that makes the image very distorted. When you say you are Brazilian, other Latinos look at you with such fascination: "Wow!"

And Americans too. But I think it is an unreal image, bad for us. It has not bothered me much because I have a very serious attitude, and I am not a person who gives much of a chance for this type of thing. And when I see that someone is going to say something, or see that he'll come up with some truncated idea I change it quickly. I don't let anyone bring up this subject with me, no. I don't give him a chance. I don't have this problem, normally. But I have friends who go through this. For example, it becomes much easier for them to flirt and to come on to you, you know how it is? Despite everything, I've been hit on. Every once in a while I hear something. When they ask me where I'm from and I tell them I am a Brazilian, people sometimes come on, and, apparently without pretensions, start "Ah, Brazilian, Ah the country of Carnival," then it starts. After Carnival there comes the question of whether you're married and such.

I: Ah, but all this is because you are pretty. I'm sure that if you were a hag it would matter little if you were from Transylvania or from Brussels.

A: Maybe, but I think that when they know we are Brazilian they become more fired up.

I: But it's because this sex thing here is very heavy. The way we do it in Brazil enchants them because we can deal with the body and sensuality without becoming a seven-headed monster. The women wear bikinis on the streets, but no one is self-conscious . . . American men go crazy because they don't know how to deal with the body as generously, and for them it always has to mean something else . . . The Brazilian uses the body as one more space for expressing the personality . . . She doesn't have to take off her clothes to get a boyfriend, she will get the boyfriend anyway. She wants to show off her body because her body is hers and that's it! They go nuts over this, because they are so stingy with their bodies and we are so rich in expression with this body, right?"

Annie and Ivan present different perspectives of the same subject. Annie insists on bringing up her discomfort with the signals she receives from men when they know that she is Brazilian. Even though Ivan argues that she attracts men's attention because of her beauty, she insists that her connection to Brazil is what increases men's attraction. And, of course, if beauty and sexual attraction are the goods on sale, it is obvious than being Brazilian spices it up a bit. If that is not the case, however, it is really bothersome to deal with what Annie calls the "distorted image" of Brazilian women in Los Angeles.

Like Elizabeth, Annie insists that the image leads straight to sex and permissiveness. Ivan, however, brings about other meanings, similar to the ones introduced to me at the Palladium Carnival in Los Angeles, which suggest that the fascination that Brazilian women exert over U.S. men is not only about sex but also about exotic fantasies. Ivan, like Paola, believes that Brazilians do have a very particular way of dealing with sexuality: "the way we do it in Brazil enchants them because we can deal with the body and sensuality without becoming a seven-headed monster . . . They go nuts over this, because they are so stingy with their bodies and we are so rich in expression with this body, right?"

Ivan's and Paola's perception seem to be shared worldwide. In an article called *Pleasure Principle* published by *Brazzil* (a magazine for English speakers interested in Brazil), Espinosa (1997, 13) affirms that "Club Med—a chain of more than 120 pleasure resorts spread all over the world—wanted to know from its annual 1.5 million well-to-do visitors which are the most sensual people on earth. Brazilian women and men came up on top as the hottest."

What is especially interesting in the discussion of this issue is that regardless of how Brazilian women interpret and deal with the sexualized stereotype, most of them, like Ivan and Paola, *truly* believe that Brazilian women are more erotically appealing than U.S. women. The following quotes are samples of this understanding:

> "I think it is very natural for Americans to be attracted to the image of Brazilian women that is divulged here. Of course, they are gorgeous women, with marvelous bodies, fantastic! And they think that Brazil has a sensuality that they don't have, and I sincerely think they are right about this. In fact, the Brazilian woman is very sensual, especially when compared to the American! Anyone of us here is more sensual than any American. I know this, everybody knows this. It's not only Americans who know this, understand? My point is that we have much more than pretty bodies and sensuality, understand? And we want space to show the other things." (Claudia, age 43)

> "It's an advantage for a Brazilian woman to marry an American. Now, it is a disadvantage for a Brazilian man to marry an American woman. I'll explain. The American is not used to a homey, affectionate wife, okay? And the Brazilian is. And the American woman is not homey, is

not affectionate, is not feminine, and they say that she is not good in bed. I know a Brazilian who married an American woman, and it was he who told me. But he got married mostly to stay in the country. He lived with her, would go out with her everywhere, and introduced her as his wife. But he says that the American women he met left much to be desired sexually speaking. I think they start with sex very early and then become like machines. You understand? There isn't the sensuality, the charisma, the seductiveness that we Brazilian women have." (Telma, age 46)

Whatever are the partial truths that exoticization spreads, they are shared by both the exoticizer and the exoticized. What is at first a truth from the limited perspective of the other slowly becomes a truth for everybody, and such a truth might be transformed into a trump card, depending on what is at stake. For those negotiating heightened sexual pleasures, there is no doubt about the value of exoticized Brazilianness.

But the above comments also suggest that those negotiating sexual pleasures are not the only ones to take advantage of exoticized Brazilianness. Therefore, most Brazilians interviewed do not support Elizabeth's interpretation of exoticization according to which women are the victims and cultural and tourism industries are its agents and beneficiaries. For instance, Telma does not question the veracity of the reputation of Brazilian women's sensuality. The attributes of the stereotype are already part of her assets. Claudia, for her part (like the Brazilian diplomat that I mentioned before), is not so much interested in the stereotype as in moving beyond it to show to the world that Brazilian women are far more than just beautiful bodies and sensuality.

What is common in their discourses is that the stereotype is positive because it attracts people to Brazil and Brazilians, but also because it is based on *reality*. In fact, Brazilian women (and men, according to Club Med) are the hottest, the sexiest, and the most sensual. But what is the use of these attributes when what is at stake is to find a husband, a job, or to get tenure? Many Brazilian women believe that for those looking for husbands, and not just casual or commercial sex, the exoticized image has a positive effect:

"My husband had this fixation for black women. He had a relationship with a black American whom he liked very much, but it was a very complicated relationship. He also felt very attracted to Brazil and all those fantasies related to carnival and mulatas. I think he was looking for this ideal mulata when he found me." (Jociclênia, age 42)

For its connection to colonialism and domination, it might be reasonable to suppose that attraction to Brazilian women leads more naturally to casual sex than to marriage, since the active exoticizer "always breaks off the relationship with exoticized women and invariably goes back where he came from" (see Todorov, 315). Getting closer to the exoticized other, however, always leaves some room for unpredictable results.[12] The proximity, though for a short time, might dissipate fantasies and dreams, but it might also deepen desires, contempt, or admiration for the other's fantasized or new revealed qualities, as proposed by Marta, age 45:

> "I don't know, I'm married to a Brazilian man, but I DO think that many foreigners feed this belief that Brazilian women can offer them the ultimate sexual pleasure, the wildest, the most beautiful, whatever. But I don't think that this is the only reason why many American men choose Brazilian wives. I think that they also believe that Brazilian women are more submissive and traditional than American women, which is generally true. I mean, it is more than just sex and fun. Hello? Are we supposed to believe that all those Mormon missionaries marrying Brazilian women are looking for ultimate sexual pleasure?"

As suggested by the comments discussed here, but also by what I observed in my own experience and fieldwork, the Brazilian stereotype as experienced by Brazilian women in Los Angeles is very flexible. Like any other stereotype, at first it limits the other, but, it does not do so forever. In other words, it seems that going beyond the stereotyped image is in the hands of the exoticized other and not the other way around. Let us focus a bit more on Paola's observation. Instead of feeling imprisoned into the stereotype, she plays with it. For her it is a game in which she apparently keeps all trump cards in her hands. As I interpret her reasoning, the exoticizing powers also become slaves of their own creations. But in her present situation the stereotype does not constrain her life as much as it would were she in a more vulnerable position.

I did not explore much further the issue during fieldwork, but I am led to believe that the efficiency of exoticization—especially in terms of keeping the other in its place—is a function of factors other than exoticization itself. The stereotype works more efficiently the better every exoticized individual fits its general characteristics.

Conclusion

Throughout the manuscript I discussed exoticization in two levels, an individual/group level, that of the Brazilian immigrant women in Los Angeles, and a national/international level, that of loose images of Brazil and Brazilians around the world. What I conclude is that, despite all the limitations imposed by colonialism, there is room for changes both at the individual and national levels. In other words, regardless of how powerful these images are and how much they effectively limit the exoticized other, to be (or to remain) a puppet in the hands of the colonizer is a choice. The question to ask now is, how much does this choice affect survival?

Paola, Ivan, Marta, and many other Brazilians who have proved themselves beyond exoticization believe that besides being good about "our exotic qualities," we can also be good at those more stereotypically connected to the colonizer, including intellectuality and politics. The stereotype itself does not prevent the exoticized from negotiating non-exotic goods like knowledge or politics. Thus, remaining within the limits of exoticization seems to depend on factors other than exoticization itself, such as physical appearance and social class, otherwise how to explain phenomena like Gisele Bündchen? In other words, are the chances of getting over exoticization similar for both black and white Brazilians? How does exoticization affect the life of Brazilian women of different social classes? More research is needed to answer these and other questions raised throughout the present study.

Notes

An early version of this paper was previously published in *Pagu* on Jan/Jun 2007 under the title "Sob a Sombra de Carmen Miranda e do Carnaval:Brasileiras em Los Angeles."

1. The exoticization of tropical lands and women is not new. Even before the Portuguese and Spaniards were adventuring through the unknown seas, the Europeans already dreamed of earthly paradises. For more on European mystification of the tropics, see Augras, 1991; Buarque de Holanda 2003 [1968]; Casalla 2003; Del Priore 1992; Deleneau 1992; Todorov 1993, and Turner 1990.
2. Latino Studies scholars have developed an interesting critique of exoticization, stereotyping, and other hegemonic representation of Latinos and Latinidad. Aparicio and Susana Chávez-Silverman's *Tropicalizations: Transcultural Representations of Latinidad* (1997), for instance, proposes challenging hegemonic interpretations that stop at colonial imperialist domination to focus also on Latinos and Latin Americans' agency. According to this perspective, not everything is in the hands of colonial and imperialist powers. Especially now

that Latino population is growing in the United States, it is possible to foresee hegemonic changes. See also Rodríguez 1997.

3. Margolis (1994:83–88), for example, found that Brazilians who live in New York, are nearly evenly divided between men and women; they are mostly single (60%); fairly young (79% of the sample are under forty); and have a high educational level (46% had attended college). Margolis also found that although they were educated, most of the Brazilian immigrants (around 90%) in her sample hold typical immigrant jobs. Over the years, other research samples have provided different kinds of profiles of Brazilians. But all the researchers agree that their profiles do not represent the totality of the reality for the Brazilian population in those cities. Still, they provide some idea of the composition of the immigrant population. As Martes (2000, 59–60) suggests, one should consider several profiles instead of just one. For more about the numbers of Brazilian immigration in the United States, see also Goza 1994; Margolis 1994 and 1995; Sales 1999; Davis 1997; Ribeiro 1997; Martes 2000; DeBiaggi 2002, and Beserra 2003.
4. Elsewhere (Beserra 2005), I discuss in detail the relationship between Brazilians and other Latinos. See also Martes 2003 and Tosta 2004.
5. Contrary to that, and for obvious reasons, Western men's stereotype seeks to enhance their dominant qualities. By studying exoticization of Asian women, Prasso writes, "in the bars of Bangkok and elsewhere in Asia, Western men who may find traditional notions of masculinity diminished by modern cultural expectations find restitution. In their perceptions of their interactions with Asian women and Asian culture, they can experience feelings of dominance, wealth, power, and masculinity—at least temporarily. Here any man can experience feeling attractive again—even loved. Old, fat, or ugly, by Western standards, it doesn't matter. Anyone can be the Alpha Male and Lord Jim" (Prasso 2005, 7).
6. Effectively, as says Ribeiro (1995, 19–20), we [the Brazilian people], "emerged from the confluence, the clash and the blending of the Portuguese invader with the Indians and the African Negroes—the last two subordinated as slaves. In this confluence, under the rule of the Portuguese, disparate racial origins, distinct cultural traditions, well-developed social formations confront each other and fuse to give way to a *new people* [which] rise as a national ethnicity, culturally differentiated from its formative sources, strongly mixed, dynamized by a syncretic culture and singularized by the redefinition of cultural traces from which it is derived." Ribeiro stresses two points in his description: the cultural and racial mixture and the rule of the Portuguese. It was the intense original mixture—more imposed by the circumstances than desired—that made almost mandatory the promotion of more miscegenation in the ensuing history.
7. Brazilians in general, even those closer to the national image, feel uneasy about its limits and political consequences. For an insightful interpretation of

Brazilian national identity in relation to the elements that are included or excluded in its composition, and from the perspective of a Brazilian born in Rio Grande do Sul, a state that does not fit the tropical stereotype, see Oliven (1996). For a brief appraisal of the negotiation of Brazilian identity among Brazilians in the United States, see also Ribeiro 1997; Beserra 1998, 2003, and 2005, and Sales 1999.

8. The choice Brazilians make between the Latino and the Brazilian exoticized sterotype also depends on religion. Resorting to the "carnavalesco" stereotype was not so much observed among the Brazilians Adventists as it was among other Brazilian groups in my research. (See also Beserra 2005: 192.)

9. Attaching exoticization to women, however, is not limited to Brazil. By studying Pierre Loti's works from the 19th century, Todorov (308–323) observes that the naval officer and writer reduces the countries which he visits to their women. Thus instead of a colonial relationship what he shows is a "strictly individual relationship." This dual relation, of man to woman and European to foreigner, is by no means symmetrical, nor could it be: an experience devoted to the search for impressions implies, as we have seen, that the traveler is the only human being elevated to the dignity of subject; the woman is only the foremost among his objects of perception. The male traveler is active; one day he arrives, another day he leaves. Between those two events we learn about his experiences and sensations. The woman and the foreign country (the woman because she is a foreigner, the country because it is eroticized) both allow themselves to be desired, governed, and abandoned (315). Todorov insists on the position of active subject of the European traveler. As said in the beginning of this paper, what counts for the exoticizer is solely his own perspective. Thus "it is always Loti who breaks off the relationship (since his ship is about to leave), whereas the woman remains, desolate, at home." Todorov concludes that "the two phases of this relationship—the infatuation with the incomprehensible foreigner and the final abandonment—translate perfectly the ambivalence of Loti's exoticism. The European male is attracted and seduced, but he invariably goes back where he came from. He thus gains on both fronts: he has the benefit of the exotic experience (a foreign woman and a foreign country) without ever really calling into question his own belonging or his own identity" (328).

10. In fact, Davis argues in this volume that since the beginning Brazilians contributed to the construction of the stereotype. As I do to an extent in this chapter, Davis claims that Brazilian performers—the group on which he focuses his attention—must not be seen as victims. Rather, he says, "it is essential to examine the ways in which individuals exercised agency in situations of unequal power or at the very least collaborated in the formulation of perceptions."

11. Using the Brazilian carnival as the main source of a Brazilian international representation is especially limited and problematic because it means basing a representation, the image of Brazil, upon another representation, carnival.

Besides, carnival is a very particular kind of representation itself. First, it happens in a determined space and time. That is, carnival is not a daily life event, but an exceptional event. Second, as a ritual of reversal, the Brazilian carnival's symbols and behaviors do not reflect reality as it is, but as Brazilians represent it for the purposes of the event. Third, the carnival of Rio de Janeiro is only one of several versions that take place countrywide in Brazil.

12. Despite the tendency "to go back to where he came from," marriages between European and U.S. men and "exotic other" women have become more common now that sectors of Western culture have questioned patriarchy, and society has stopped rewarding traditionally masculine roles. On the other hand, the percentage of Brazilian women married to U.S. citizens, as well as that of U.S. citizens (mostly Caucasian) married to other ethnic groups reveals, for instance, that U.S. and European men are considerably more likely to get married to "exotic" women than men from other nationalities, particularly Third World men, because the international marriage market also follows the general paths of colonialism, which determines that European and U.S. men are more valuable than the colonized.

References

Anderson, Benedict. 1983. *Imagined Communities*. New York: Verso.

Aparicio, Frances R. 2000. "Ethnifying Rhythms, Feminizing Cultures." In *Music and the Racial Imagination*. Ed. Ronald Radano and Philip Bohlman. Chicago: The University of Chicago Press.

Aparicio, Frances R. and Susana Chávez-Silverman. Eds. 1997. *Tropicalizations: Transcultural Representations of Latinidad*. Introduction. Hanover: University Press of New England.

Augras, Monique. 1991. "Imaginária França Antártica." *Estudos Históricos*, Rio de Janeiro, 4(7): 19–34.

Beserra, Bernadete. 1998. "Keeping the Flame: Brazilian Gauchos in Los Angeles." *Brazzil* 10(156): 26–27.

———. 1999. "Move Your Body! Brazilian Carnival Takes over the World." *Brazzil* 10(158): 19–24.

———. 2000. "Brazilians in Los Angeles: Imperialism, Immigration, and Social Class." Ph.D. Dissertation, University of California, Riverside.

———. 2003. *Brazilian Immigrants in the United States: Cultural Imperialism and Social Class*. New York: LFB Scholarly Publishing.

———. 2005a. "From Brazilians to Latinos? Racialization and Latinidad in the Making of Brazilian Carnival in Los Angeles." *Latino Studies* 3(1): 53–75.

———. 2005b. "Negotiating Latinidad in Los Angeles: The Case of Brazilian Immigrants." In *Latino LA: Transformations, Communities, and Activism*. Ed. Enrique C. Ochoa and Gilda L. Ochoa. Tucson: The University of Arizona Press.

Benz, Stephen. 1997. "Through the Tropical Looking Glass: The Motif of Resistance in U.S. Literature on Central America." In *Tropicalizations: Transcultural Representations of Latinidad.* Introduction. Ed. Aparicio, Frances R. and Susana Chávez-Silverman. Hanover: University Press of New England.

Buarque de Holanda, S. 2003. *Raízes do Brasil.* São Paulo: Companhia das Letras.

———. 2000. *Visão do Paraíso—Os Motivos Edênicos no Descobrimento e*

Colonização do Brasil. São Paulo: Folha de São Paulo/Brasiliense.

Casalla, Mario. 2003. *América Latina en Perspectiva: Dramas del pasado, huellas del presente.* Buenos Aires: Altamira.

Clark, Walter A. 2002. "Doing the Samba on Sunset Boulevard: Carmen Miranda and the Hollywoodization of Latin American Music." In *From Tejano to Tango: Essays on Latin American Popular Music.* Ed. Walter A Clark. New York: Routledge.

Collins, Patricia Hill. 1990. *Black Feminist Thought.* Boston: Unwin Hyman.

DaMatta, Roberto. 1981. *Relativizando: Uma Introdução à Antropologia Social.* Petrópolis: Vozes.

Davis, Darién. 1997a. "The Brazilian-Americans: Demography and Identity of an Emerging Latino Minority." *The Latino Review of Books* 3(1–2): 8–15.

———. 1997b. "To Be or Not to Be Brazilian: Carmen Miranda's Quest for Fame and 'Authenticity' in the United States." Paper presented at the IV Meeting of the Brazilian Studies Association, Washington, D.C.

DeBiaggi, Sylvia Duarte Dantas. 2002. *Changing Gender Roles: Brazilian Immigrant Families in the U.S.* New York: LFB Scholarly Publishing.

Del Priore, Mary L. M. 1992. "Retrato da América quando jovem: Imagem e representações sobre o novo continente entre os séculos XVI e XVII." *Estudos Históricos* 5(9). Rio de Janeiro: Fundação Banco do Brasil.

Deleneau, Jean. 1992. *Uma história do paraíso. O jardim das delícias.* Lisboa: Terramar.

Espinoza, Rodolfo. 1997. "Pleasure Principle." *Brazzil* 9(142): 13–21.

Fanon, Franz. 1963. *The Wretched of the Earth.* New York: Grove Press.

———. 1967. *Black Skin White Masks.* New York: Grove Press.

Freyre, Gilberto.1946. *The Masters and the Slaves.* Berkeley: University of California Press.

Goza, Franklin. 1994. "Brazilian Immigration to North America." *International Migration Review* 28: 136–152.

Kearney, Michael, and Bernadete Beserra. 2004. "Migration and Identities: A Class-Based Approach." *Latin American Perspectives* 31(5): 3–14.

Larrain, Jorge. 1994. *Ideology and Cultural Identity—Modernity and the Third World Presence.* Cambridge: Polity Press.

Machado, Igor J. R. 2004. "Estado-nação, identidade-para-o-mercado e representações de nação." *Revista de Antropologia* 47(1): 207–233.

Margolis, Maxine. 1994. *Little Brazil—An Ethnography of Brazilian Immigrants in New York City*. Princeton: Princeton University Press.

———.1995. "Brazilians and the 1990 United States Census: Immigrants, Ethnicity, and the Undercount." *Human Organization* 54(1): 52–59.

Martes, Ana C. B. 2000. *Brasileiros nos Estados Unidos: Um estudo sobre imigrantes em Massachusetts*. São Paulo: Paz e Terra.

———. 2003. "Raça e Etnicidade—Opções e Constrangimentos." In *Fronteiras Cruzadas: Etnicidade, Gênero e Redes*, pp. 73–98. Ed. Ana Cristina Braga Martes and Soraya Fleischer. Petropolis, R. J.: Editora Paz e Terra.

Memmi, Albert. 1991. *The Colonizer and the Colonized*. Boston: Beacon Press.

Oboler, Suzanne. 1992. "The Politics of Labeling: Latino/a Cultural Identities of Self and Others." *Latin American Perspectives* 19(4): 18–36.

Oliven, Ruben. 1996. *Tradition Matters: Modern Gaucho Identity in Brazil*. New York: Columbia University Press.

Page, Joseph. 1995. *The Brazilians*. New York: Addison-Wesley.

Pérez, Richie. 1997. "From Assimilation to Annihilation: Puerto Rican Images in US Films." In *Latin Looks: Images of Latinas and Latinos in the U.S. Media*. Ed. Clara E. Rodríguez. Boulder, CO: Westview Press.

Prasso, Sheridan. 2005. *The Asian Mystique—Dragon Ladies, Geisha Girls, and Our Fantasies of the Exotic Orient*. New York: Public Affairs.

Ribeiro, Darcy. 1999. *O Povo Brasileiro: A Formação e o Sentido do Brasil*. São Paulo: Companhia das Letras.

Ribeiro, Gustavo. 1997. "Street Samba: Carnaval and Transnational Identities in San Francisco." Paper presented at the IV Conference of Brazilian Studies Association, Washington, D.C.

Riedinger, E. 1997. "Brazilian Americans, an Emerging Hispanic Group in the United States." Paper presented at the IV Conference of Brazilian Studies Association, Washington, D.C.

Rodríguez, Clara E. 1997. *Latin Looks: Images of Latinas and Latinos in the U.S. Media*. Boulder, CO: Westview Press.

———. 2004. *Heroes, Lovers, and Others: The Story of Latinos in Hollywood*. Washington, D.C.: Smithsonian Books.

Said, Edward. 1979. *Orientalism*. New York: Vintage Books.

———. 1994. *Culture and Imperialism*. New York: Vintage Books.

Sales, Teresa. 1999. *Brasileiros Longe de Casa*. São Paulo: Cortez Editora.

Savigliano, Marta. 1995. *Tango and the Political Economy of Passion*. Boulder, CO: Westview Press.

Sinha, Mrinalini. 1995. *Colonial Masculinity: The 'Manly Englishman' and the Effeminate Bengali' in the Late Nineteenth Century.* Manchester: Manchester University Press.

Todorov, Tzvetan. 1993. *On Human Diversity—Nationalism, Racism, and Exoticism in French Thought*. Cambridge, MA: Harvard University Press.

Torresan, Angela. 1994. "Quem Parte, Quem Fica: Uma Etnografia sobre migrantes Brasileiros em Londres." Master's Thesis, Museu National, Universidade Federal do Rio de Janeiro.

Tosta, Antonio L. 2004. "Latino, *eu*? The Paradoxical Interplay of Identity in *Brazuca* Literature." *Hispania* 87(3): 576–585.

Turner, Frederik. 1990. *O espírito ocidental contra a natureza: mito, história e terras selvagens*. Rio de Janeiro: Campus.

Urraca, Beatriz. 1997. "A Textbook of Americanism: Richard Harding Davis's *Soldiers of Fortune*." In T*ropicalizations: Transcultural Representations of Latinidad*. Intro. Ed. Aparicio, Frances R. and Susana Chávez-Silverman. Hanover: University Press of New England.

3

The Formative Years of the Brazilian Communities of New York and San Francisco through the Print Media: *The Brazilians/The Brasilians* and *Brazil Today*

Else R. P. Vieira

> *"We must not merely change the narratives of histories, but transform our sense of what it means to live, to be in other times and different spaces, both human and historical."*
>
> —Homi Bhabha

The long-standing newspaper *The Brazilians/The Brasilians* (New York) and the more recent *Brazil Today* (San Francisco Bay Area)—amongst many others which redefine Brazilian media production as no longer co-extensive with a national territorial framing—provide a wealth of information and a complex picture of the phenomenon whereby Brazil, historically a predominantly immigration-receiving country, has become, in the last decades, a migrant-sending and labor-exporting one.

The survey of the monthly *The Brazilians/The Brasilians* (hereafter *TB*), presumably the first one produced outside the national territory, covers nearly three decades, from its launch in December 1972 to the end of 2000. By virtue of its seniority and regularity along the decades of its publication, it is crucial for the documentation of the emergence and consolidation of one of the earliest Brazilian communities abroad. At the outset, it depicts the emergence and the mutation across the decades of two Brazilian social types outside the national territory, the transnational entrepreneur and, on the opposite side of the social spectrum, the *Brazuca* (see below), initially the undocumented and precariously integrated Brazilian migrant who, like his/her national counterpart, the folkloric *malandro*, enters the transnational spaces and develops a series of survival strategies abroad. The regularity of *TB*'s publication over three decades further enables the coverage of three major initial stages of the migration process in correlation with three major moments of Brazil's political and economic history: (a) the post-Institutional Act V economic boom and the transnationalization of the Brazilian economy implemented via repression and coercion ; (b) the *Abertura* (transition to democracy) during the presidency of João Baptista de Figueiredo (03/79 to 03/85); (c) the *Nova República.* Evidence elicited from *TB* offers a disclaimer to the widespread misconception that Brazilian emigration and the emergence of national communities abroad started with *Abertura*'s escalating inflation and legitimacy crisis (see below). These may have boosted an ongoing process, but they were not the initiators of Brazilian emigration. It will thus be argued that these are by-products of the transnational policies introduced by the military dictatorship. Prior to the economic upheaval of the late 1980s and early 1990s, *The Brazilians* had already, in fact, pointed out the connection between the first flow(s) of Brazilian migration and the insertion of Brazil into the global economy. The revised editorial orientation of *TB* in 1975, signaled by the recasting of the name of the newspaper into a Brazilianized and, for that matter, more nationalistic spelling (*The Brasilians*), will be seen to expose major fractures in Brazil prior to *Abertura,* which also account for the motivation to migrate and to produce Brazilian newspapers abroad: the tools of repression and coercion used to implement the economic policies. *TB* thus becomes a channel for political expression and for denunciation abroad. A third stage begins with the country's redemocratization, when the need for *TB*'s contestatory role ceases to exist.

The focus of the analysis of *TB*-English will be thus on these main functions of print media: the creation of an economic and then of a political space; and the push to enable a community to develop its own cultural institutions within a dominant society. The use of two languages, English and Portuguese, in general featuring different contents, signals *TB*'s double orientation. *TB* in English perceives North Americans as the intended readership; its promotional bias confirms its initial function of creating commercial spaces and a cultural niche for Brazil in the economic center of New York and, conversely, of promoting tourism in Brazil. The use of Portuguese will otherwise define the Brazilian readership and reveal its partial function as a community newspaper.

Post-*Abertura TB* increasingly becomes a community newspaper, sharing a number of features with the co-terminous *Brazil Today* (hereafter *BT*).

Both will usually feature news and opinion pieces about events relevant to Brazil; social news; literature and literary criticism; essays on citizenship; political relationships involving the diaspora, Brazil and the United States. Yet they differ in that the New York community was already established when the San Francisco one emerged. It is the more recent community of San Francisco that seems to be an outgrowth of the late 1980s and early 1990s *Abertura* mood of disillusionment and hopelessness in Brazil arising from escalating inflation and corruption, the intractable external debt, unemployment and impoverishment resulting from diminished economic activity, as well as the instability bred by *Nova República*'s consecutive economic shocks during José Sarney's (1985–90) and Fernando Collor de Mello's (1990–92) governments. The formation of Brazilian communities does not start then, but the growth of migration flows was greatly facilitated by the *Abertura*- and globalization-related lifting of the compulsory loan embedded in the price of airline tickets and currency exchange. The illusion of quickly making large sums of money shared by rampant inflation and migratory movements cannot be ignored here. *BT* seems to pick up the political thread where *TB* has left off, but in distinctive ways: in the challenging attempt to articulate the Brazilian community and to preserve the national culture and language in a new conjuncture, when migration changes from the individual utopian search for an Eldorado to a generalized force in the global economy. This chapter then surveys four main functions of *BT*: serving a scattered population, establishing links between diaspora communities and the homeland, fostering ethnic solidarity, and maintaining and revitalizing the national culture.

This essay offers a chronological follow-up to the earlier Brazilian traveler-cum-immigrant case study of Chapter 1, while shifting the emphasis from named individuals to the collective. It further shows how the imaginary of a tropical paradise and of a sexual Mecca created about Brazil by performers in previous decades (see Chapter 2) is used for the promotion of large-scale tourism in Brazil by the travel agent Brazilian American Promotion Center, a partner of *TB*. In terms of identity-construction, it shows how female stereotypes of exoticism and sensuality created abroad by earlier celebrities such as Carmen Miranda (see Chapter 2) are politicized by *TB* after the newspaper's editorial shift, although, I shall suggest, not quite convincingly. Crucially, nationalized local symbols (see Chapter 2) are internationalized along two vectors by the print media: to project Brazil commercially to the host country and to articulate a sense of Brazilianness for an otherwise scattered community of nationals.

Illuminated by David Levinson (1994), Canclini (1995) and Jonathan Friedman (1994), this chapter outlines the major insights into Brazilian migration and constitution of communities abroad offered by these two newspapers, more specifically in terms of:

1. The way that Brazilian political, economic, and/or cultural spaces are articulated abroad;
2. How the collateral networking Brazilians develop with the mainstream population or with other ethnic groups;
3. The function of the print media and how this relates to the use of English, Portuguese or both;
4. The way that a Brazilian cultural identity and a national sentiment are reconstructed abroad and the symbols employed and/or relocated by the communities in this process;
5. The role the print media plays in the construction and enhancement of these symbols;
6. The community's primordial attachment (does Brazil remain its symbolic, emotional and material tie?) and degree of internal cohesion;
7. Transnational fluidity and the shifting fractures within Brazil of which the formation of these communities abroad may be symptomatic.

The Brazilians/The Brasilians (New York)

The creation of business and tourism niches for Brazil abroad.

The editorial of the first issue of *The Brazilians* (as it was initially called) situates the country's migration within the historical conjuncture of the transnationalization of its economy. Its original functions were to promote and publicize the potential and facilities of Brazil in terms of investments and tourism and to foster business liaisons between Brazil's emerging market and the United States. The launch date of this monthly publication, Christmas 1972, in itself emblematic of a new era, and its first editorial renders evident its uncritical embrace of the opening of the national economy to transnational capital exempt from taxation:

> "President G. Medici of Brazil signed a bill regulating the functions of export trading companies, establishing the basic fact that these companies will not pay internal revenue tax on their export profits, up to and including 1977. The Bill authorizes the National Monetary Council to affix the participation structure of foreign capital in the formation of companies, as well as determine the minimal capital." (Dec. 1972, 1)

The expression "Brazilian Miracle," which had started to gain currency in 1968 (Prado e Earp 2003, 207), relates to the country's economic boom, the government's political propaganda, an accelerated growth rate, and international integration. *The Brazilians'* initial objectives of "exporting Brazil" within this context are projected, still uncritically, by the same editorial:

> "Brazil's recognized economic boom has stimulated worldwide interest toward this vast country—its people and its economy . . . The widespread interest generated by this economic phenomenon has provoked an urgent need for information about Brazil. THE BRAZILIANS was created to meet this need . . . Brazil's industrial production rose by 80% between 1965 and 1971 . . . Brazil now exports everything from such standard industrial items as shoes and textiles to specialized machinery. Several billion dollars of domestic and foreign capital are invested in Brazilian shipyards and aircraft plants, a growing auto industry, and one of the most delightful natural resources—the tourist attractions . . . THE BRAZILIANS . . . hopes to provide an active record of events and a liaison between the American and the Brazilian peoples." (Dec. 1972, 1)

As early as 1973, the eminent sociologist Fernando Henrique Cardoso, in his landmark "Associated-Dependent Development: Theoretical and Practical Implications," one of the collected essays in *Authoritarian Brazil* (ed. Alfred Stepan, published by Yale University Press), had already highlighted the *aporias* of globalization, whose moving force, the multinational corporation, puts a dynamic element into operation in the peripheral economies through the investment of industrial capital; paradoxically, it breeds stagnation as it is based on dependence (Cardoso 1973, 149). Yet the editorial of *TB* of September 1974 issue carries on with the tone of euphoria and renders the conjuncture more explicit by reviewing Delfim Neto's *The Brazilian Miracle.* The stress is on the capitalist ethos of efficiency and modernization:

> "In today's Brazil, the fifth largest country in the world, the seventh in population size, the thirteenth word-power, those of common sense outnumber the trouble-makers, the efficient ones outnumber the incompetent, the studious overcome the lazy ones, the hard-workers take up the space of the negligent ones, those forward planners push the careless ones, and the meticulous triumph over the alienated ones." (Sept. 1974, 1)

The promotional bias reverberates in the November 1974 issue, which stresses Brazil's capacity to be aligned with the world powers (its car output, the eighth in the world, its metalworking industry, the inauguration of Brasília, its hydraulic potential) and, tellingly, reports on a new Varig terminal at Kennedy airport. While building up the image of the country's great potential for investments, *TB* also makes the United States attractive for Brazilian migrants by spelling out the superiority of the latter's educational system over the national one (Feb. 1973, 2).

A tone of achievement envelops the references, also in the first issues, to the Brazilian street in New York. Advertisements of its shops and services further reflect the establishment of an infrastructure for compatriots in New York: a Brazilian café-restaurant, a Portuguese-speaking salon, a Brazilian pharmacy, Rulane (whose pronunciation meaningfully emulates the chain Duhane-Reade in New York), an export center and an international removals company for Brazilians. Two years later, comparisons are established with the predecessors of the Brazilians in the conquest of transnational spaces (Italians in Brooklyn and Greenwich Village, Latinos in Queens and part of Long Island). There is national pride in the remark that a "green and yellow" commerce, reproducing the colors of the Brazilian flag, is burgeoning on West 46th Street (Dec. 1974). A chronicle by Kathryn Schulhoff, published in March 1981, strikes the keynote of a non-Brazilian's first perception of a Little Brazil on 46th West as "warm and friendly—a welcoming place." Even though there is no clearly defined neighborhood associated with Brazilians, this street is, in fact, the first place outside the national territory where the Brazilian presence makes a visible impact. Special supplements of the newspaper celebrate either its 20th anniversary or, specifically in 1995, a landmark victory when the mayor of the city, Rudolph Giuliani, declared 46th Street between Park Avenue and Times Square "the Street of the Brazilians." Even though many Brazilian nationals, often undocumented, remain an invisible segment of the population in the United States, the official name of the street has become a visible icon of the country's presence abroad. Attention is finally drawn to a most meaningful cover of *TB* in the August 1986 issue. Aligned with the skyscrapers that make up Manhattan's skyline, there looms the image of the Cristo Redentor. As seen in Chapter 2, Rio has been defined as a symbol of Brazilianness; it now becomes an icon for the internationalization of Rio and Brazil. In this postnational geography, this Brazilian icon merges with North American ones such as the Empire State Building, projecting an equality of power relations. Such triumphalist representation of equal footing is regretfully very distant from the reality of the asymmetrical integration of the world.

New social actors: the transnational entrepreneur and the Brazuca. The depiction of the two Brazilian social actors emerging on the international scene, as early as the first issue of the newspaper, bears evidence of the displacement of the polarized class system of Brazil across frontiers. One is the image of the successful entrepreneurs who opened shops and businesses on 46th Street, in the heart of Manhattan, very close to Times Square (two of them are partners and commercial directors of *The Brazilians*). In contrast, there emerges the figure of the Brazuca, a historically shifting undocumented immigrant from a lower class, reminiscent of the folkloric *malandro* (trickster), who, through ingenuity, finds his way abroad. Both Miracle entrepreneurs and early Brazucas may have projected the imaginary that has attracted so many to the North—of the United States as the country of open opportunities where obstacles either do not exist or may be overcome. They may also have planted the seeds for what over the decades became an intense migratory flow and the establishment of labor, commercial, and cultural sites associated with Brazil in New York. The comic section of *TB*-Portuguese, "The Adventures of Zé Brazuca," Jota Alves's witty depiction of the early Brazilian migrants, in fact gives currency to the neologism "Brazuca," a term that signals another dimension of transnational Brazil and which, over time, has acquired a broader significance, namely, that of the Brazilian migrant or the undocumented Brazilian who have migrated in search of a job. This fictional character in disguise creates through the years an image of the lower-class Brazilians finding their way abroad and taking on menial jobs. Interestingly enough, the Brazuca is an outcome of the same phenomenon that created the Brazilian entrepreneur abroad, the transnationalization of the national culture and economy, and, for that matter, the transplantation of the Brazilian sharp division of classes. A few strokes of the section throughout 1973 and 1974 are given here, in order to advance the view that the early Brazuca can be seen as an internationalized version of the folkloric *malandro*, swinging to-and-fro between order and disorder, as first studied by Antonio Candido (1970).

While still in Brazil, Zé Brazuca was a nice-looking shoe-shiner in Zona Sul who was born in Boca do Mato, state of Rio de Janeiro. He ended up meeting not only many tourists but also Martinho da Vila, who encouraged him to visit New York. He, who had only travelled from Boca do Mato to

Rio, managed a place on a ship and arrived in New York without a cent in his pocket. He looked for Kid Valadares, later Vadeco (suggestive of another early flow of immigration from Minas Gerais), but learned the Kid had not been in Manhattan since September 1972 because Tia Mimi (nickname for immigration authorities) wanted to interview him. But on his very first day Zé Brazuca managed to find work in a shoeshine shop on Broadway and to play football (meaning soccer, here and hereafter) in Central Park, where he made a pass at Susan, a well-travelled American with a particular preference for Latinos. He felt comfortable in her apartment, managed to get in at the Waldorf Astoria Ball and ended up dining with Brazilian celebrities. He had little money, his English was no good, but he was happy discovering the secrets of the "world's second Cidade Maravilhosa" (*The Brazilians*, spring 1973 issue). Other details of his adventures are provided in the summer issue of the same year: Zé coped well with the cosmopolitan life of New York and, in fact, on his first day of work, bought several gifts for his lovers back in Brazil. After his first experience with Susan, he met the serious Eunice, from Minas Gerais, who is well settled in a fashionable part of New York. But she used Zé for a dangerous Miami connection, his plane is hijacked, and Zé ends up in Cuba. He liked the unexpected adventure and wrote about it in several letters to his relatives in Rio. A year after his arrival, Zé's English was better and he was working for a Minister who was also a wealthy international businessman. It was then that he found out and denounced the fact that students, collectors and researchers had been stealing precious historic and artistic documents from Brazilian libraries and smuggling them into the United States. But, parallel to this, he acted as messenger for international gangsters. Like the folkloric *malandro*, the early Brazuca was also capable of some honorable gestures in defense of the exploited. Despite the new and often difficult circumstances, he, like his national counterpart, found his way and became exemplary of the survival strategy of those precariously integrated.

A decade and a half later, two issues of *TB* (May and June 1988) feature growing misery in Brazil and deconstruct the popular claim that God is Brazilian. A deterritorialized Carnival song is also reproduced illustrating another type of migrant. Zé Brazuca is no longer the adventurous *malandro* in the world's second Cidade Matavilhosa. He is now a poor, illegal migrant running away from Aunt Mimi or from imprisonment, on second thought maybe a blessing, given his penury:

Olha a Tia Mimi, olha a Tia Mimi
Não saia de casa que ela te leva

Embora daqui
Vou fazer igual ao urso polar

Eu vou preparar a minha hibernação
Cinco litros de cachaça
Não saio de casa nesta confusão
Tou longe da terra

E sempre fugindo da Imigração
Como eu existem milhares
Querendo sair desta situação
Olha Tia Mimi

Estribilho

Mais eu tou sem dinheiro no bolso
E aqui me conhecem como um ilegal
Estou andando atrás dessa gente
E com esse negócio a coisa vai mal
Se me pegam eu perco o meu emprego
Vão ter que me dar casa e comida
Ali o negócio melhora
E eu nunca mais eu vou sair dessa vida

Olha a Tia Mimi . . .

The *Brasilians* and the Attempts to Create a Political Space Abroad

A major change in the editorial policy of *The Brasilians* in 1975 set out to create an increasingly political channel of expression for Brazil in New York during the repression period, despite the difficult historical conjuncture of the early 1970s and the limited possibilities available at the time:

"What trajectory to follow? The easy or the hard way? We either promoted artists, with their contestatory exhibitions; with their songs to freedom, Carnival and football (then excellent), two great collective creations, of the Brazilian body and soul, things that are ours, above military regimes and systems; or we would publicize official Brazil, the one of the 'economic miracle.'" (Sept. 1993:2)

The radical shift in the agenda of *TB* took place in April 1975, when Jota Alves, previously studying International Law in Moscow, becomes the publisher and editor-in-chief of the newspaper. The new agenda is explained but, in my view, still somewhat euphemistically, in the editorial of the December 1976 issue: although the newspaper had been founded to publicize and foster the interests of the Brazilian American Promotion Center, an organization that led entrepreneurial, social, cultural and artistic events in New York, it could no longer continue to be a commercial tool for the interests of a travel agent. It is only years later, when *TB* celebrates its 15th anniversary, that the reason for the addition of *Brasilians* with an "s" in the name of the newspaper is accounted for (December 1987). *TB* becomes a forum for debate on political and social issues that increasingly fall under the watchful eye of the dictatorship back in Brazil.

In September 1993, Jota Alves sent to *TB* a long meditation on its evolution from a house organ disseminating the deals and events of a promotion center in the 1970s and 1980s, to a newspaper expressing opinions censored by the military regime. It became unwelcome in the embassies and consulates. It will be recalled that Cardoso had already stressed the perverse side of the integration of the Brazilian economy and the economies of the peripheral countries into the international capitalist system, a move that turned them into dependent and minor partners and that could be achieved only through coercion and suppression of expression (1973). Jota Alves also takes up the task of laying bare such a conjuncture, stressing the challenge of doing it in the country whose government supported the establishment and maintenance of the regime (Sept. 1993, 2). Such a courageous stance is clear in the October 1975 issue, in which *TB* reproduces an article by Bruce Handler, originally published in the *Washington Post*, the *New York Times,* and other American newspapers, with an invitation to debate it, which sparks off an interrogation of Handler's complimentary words to Brazil's authoritarian rule in the name of economic progress. Handler further affirms the ideology of globalization—an integrated world enjoying the benefits of high technology:

> "Brazil's economic miracle is based on harsh military rule and a daring program of indexing inflation, a formula that interests economists the world over . . . *When the generals took over in 1964 they let it be known that they would welcome foreign money and technical investment.* . . . No other country in the world has been able to get the multinationals to play its game as well as Brazil . . . *The overall economic boom has created more jobs, and more wives and daughters who live at home are working than ever before. Working-class families are buying TV sets, refrigerators, and even cars in record numbers.*" (October 1975, 3; emphasis mine)

Moreover, important political contributions (banned in Brazil) are published in *TB* by critics such as Paulo Freire, Darcy Ribeiro, and others. Interviews with Celso Furtado counter the ideology of globalization and feature the development of economic theories specific to Latin America or, later, bring out the need to accommodate lender nations. The contrast of a Brazil for export and the national reality is often brought under scrutiny. In January 1976 the building of the Transamazonas motorway is questioned. The smuggling of gold from the Amazon into the United States is denounced. Issues published in 1978 present a wide range of open debates on quite sensitive issues such as the problem of the abandoned minors in the large cities, the contradictions of a Brazil that exports labor when it most needs it (no. 56, March 1978), the myth of racial democracy and the role of money as a way of "whitening" racial discrimination against blacks in Brazil. An article on Glauber Rocha's quite political film *A Idade da Terra* (The Age of Earth) (no. 62, September 1978) appears in an issue that stresses poverty in Brazil (no. 65, December 1978). A review of the film *Bye Bye Brazil* (1979) stresses the disappearance of one Brazil and the emergence of another, inasmuch as the newspaper demands from General Pinochet an explanation for the disappearance of so many citizens. A discussion on human rights within the context of transnational capitalism opens the 1979 agenda (no. 67/69, March 1979).

If words were risky at the time of the editorial shift, Jota Alves's view was that another way to combat the dictatorship was through the creation of a positive image of Brazil. Even though this politicized view is not obvious without this background information, the fact is that it increasingly underlay two major Brazilian events abroad which he created: the Democracy Ball and Brazilian Day. But the early tensions between the desire for expression and the limited channels available seem to be reflected in the uneasy juxtaposition of images of the New York Carnival and the politically motivated articles.

The first issue of *TB*-English had announced the Carnival Ball at the Waldorf Astoria which, over the years, became the largest Brazilian Carnival outside the country. The rationale underlying the projection of Brazilian women celebrities during Carnival is later explained by Jota Alves who, using the pen name of Saci, argues that the Italians intelligently launched the image of their *bambinas* abroad. In Brazil one can see dozens of Cardinales and Lorens every day; his long experience abroad has shown that "The Girl from Ipanema" has created a positive universal image of the Brazilian woman and has sold more tickets to Brazil than all the tourist agencies put together; why not follow this up? ("A opinião do Saci," April 1982). Accordingly, such sexual symbols as Sônia Braga loom large. In order to reach the American imaginary, the not quite Brazilian Carmen Miranda is frequently projected as a symbol of Brazil for export (see Chapter 1): the one who brought the samba to North Americans and taught them about Rio, Carnival, and humor (August 1973, 3). These feminine icons share the space with other celebrities such as soccer star Pelé, photographed when he was given the keys of New York. The January 1984 issue surveys the history of Carnival in Brazil as part of its promotion. Texts by supposedly American contributors bear evidence that the explosion of this Carnival in the United States also projected images of a sexual paradise or a living dream of exoticism. Poems written by Gwen Leslie confirm this impact. Another writer, Louis Elton, is quoted on his view of Brazil as the heavenly dream of beautiful women, sexy music, inimitable beat, hell breaking loose when the tunes of Cidade Maravilhosa strike the beginning of Carnival (April 1977, 28). The uncomfortable fit of these sexualized images of hedonism (see below) with the daring political articles of *TB* seems to reach a climax in the issue of February 1985, in which pervasive nudity is out of harmony with the published list of torturers.

In 1986, the New York Carnival, which had been featured for a decade and a half as the largest Carnival outside Brazil, comes to an end. In its place Independence Day, also created by Jota Alves, in time became a major visible marker of Brazil for New Yorkers while enhancing a national sentiment that unites migrants. September 7th also became a forum for debates in *TB*, as when in 1980 Jota Alves invited New York-based Brazilians to meditate on the class division among them and on the meaning of independence in this context. In 1984, the mayor of New York proclaimed the first Sunday in September as The Brazilian Day, an evidence of Brazilian history defining a space abroad, and in 1986 thanked Brazilians for the celebration. Independence Day became a major celebration and the most visible unifying factor in the construction of a sense of Brazilianness abroad and for the expression of a relocated Brazil. In August 1986, when Jota Alves returned to Brazil, the BACC (Brazilian American Cultural Center), the tourism organization that for over three decades has specialized in promoting Brazil, took over the celebration of Independence Day and its affirmation of Brazilianness.

The Brasilians further claims, albeit without elaborating it, that the newspaper's intended platform against the dictatorship had an impact on Brazilian politics. The scholar José Bom Meihy has brought this possibility to my attention with particular reference to the section "A opinião do Saci" as the bearer of a subtext expressing an alternative political voice. Such discussion and analysis, however, lie beyond the scope of this chapter.

The Brasilians Responds to *Abertura* and to the *Nova República*

The lifting of censorship, first reported in issue no. 75 of October 1979 and taken up in subsequent ones, marks a change in the combative second stage of the newspaper. The tone now is more analytical, commenting on the effects of the dictatorship and the aftermath of the economic program it introduced by force: mentioned are those left out of the false economic miracle (the Indians and the landless people), the bitter land disputes, the growing *favelas* and problems of urban land use, supermarkets looted in Rio and the politics of hunger in Brazil (no. 103, April 1982). Discussions about the consequences of transnationalized capital and the hard-hitting economic packages, as well as the effects of conservative modernization, culminate with the more direct question as to whether the Brazilian economic model has failed (no. 118, July 1983).

In this context, the part of the newspaper intended for the Brazilian readership, *TB*-Portuguese, gains prominence. Its agenda increasingly includes issues now relevant to an already established community, such as the impact of American culture on the Brazilian migrant. It shares with *BT* (see below) the recurrent announcement and explanation of issues relevant to the Brazilian community such as changes in immigration laws, information on how to legalize the status of children of Brazilians, on the question of retirement abroad, on voting outside the national territory and on maintaining Brazilian citizenship. Warnings are also sounded about the difficulties of the illegal immigrants' experience. Important developments such as the emergence of religious services in Portuguese are reported.

Crucially, the April 1987 issue publishes the translation of a poem originally written in English ("A Spark of Imagination") by an 11-year-old Brazilian girl, Ana Patrícia Neves Tanaka, who had been living in New Jersey for four years. While stressing the undeniable achievement of the little girl, the winner of the 10th Annual New Jersey Poetry Contest, the text fails to name what may be the first instance of another unprecedented phenomenon in Brazilian literature: the production of creative writing in another territory. This production raises an important issue for Brazilian literary historiography: does literature produced in another language by a Brazilian-born qualify for categorization as Brazilian literature? Is Brazilian literature defined by the use of the mother tongue, by its locus of production, or by birthplace?

As do many other community newspapers, *TB* often quotes the well-known poem "Canção do Exílio" and similar works as a form of psychological emphasis of the sense of being cut off from the nation. An important related discussion focuses on the resentment of the Brazilians migrant over the pervasive indifference of most of their countrymen towards them (July 1988). It will be in the later 1990s that Walter Salles, Império Serrano and also Chico Buarque's "As Cidades" (The Cities) hit the average Brazilians' eyes and ears with images and sounds that made them aware that there is now a postnational Brazil. *Terra Estrangeira* (Foreign Land), it will be recalled, does not strike a note of triumphalism. It is a sad film, at a moment of profound political disillusionment, about the loss of a national image, the loss of a nation, and the migrant's loss of nationalist pride upon the realization that a Brazilian passport means very little abroad. In turn, the tone of Império Serrano's *Samba School* is neither glorifying nor disillusioned. It reveals tenderness towards those Brazilians abroad and offers a corrective to the long-standing reductionist view, fuelled by the dictatorship's fascist slogan, "Brasil, ame-o ou deixe-o." of the migrant as the one who betrays the country.

Two 1986 texts by Jota Alves on the Nova República's new symbols and the upsurge of a new nationalism bear evidence to major changes. Even though the February 1986 issue still features Carnival, the political voice had progressively pushed aside the promotional image of an eroticized nation for export. The following issues in fact foreground a major political item in the agenda of residents abroad, namely, the importance of their vote. *TB*, which had created a space for debate and political expression during the dictatorship, now claims to be also a space for decisions and for the maintenance of citizenship.

It is at this juncture that the landmark editor Jota Alves leaves New York and returns to a democratic but changed Brazil. As far back as 1981 he had already started meditating on the frame of mind of Brazilians abroad, with divided allegiances—body and head in the United States while the heart is in Brazil (July 1981). In 1988 the partnership is broken, and he writes an editorial on *TB* as 27 years of Brazilian history abroad. Jota Alves leaves behind an important legacy and a politicized view of what it means to be a Brazilian abroad.

***Brazil Today* (San Francisco Bay Area)**

This first Brazilian newspaper on the West Coast of the United States was founded in June 1991, in Los Angeles, and moved in 1992 to the San Francisco Bay Area. José Luiz Emerim and Sílvia Barandier, who had previously been publishers for *Brazil Today* (hereafter *BT*) in El Cerrito, became its San Francisco editors in May 1994. It is funded by advertisements and no official subsidies are received. *BT*'s biweekly print run of 7,000 copies is distributed in shops and pizza houses; Brazilians come for the issues and avidly read them from beginning to end seeking information on practical matters. Brazilians in the Bay Area are its main intended readership, but it also attempts networking with others across the United States and throughout the world (regular accounts are provided, for example, of the *dekasseguis* (Brazilian of Japanese origin returning to Japan), the second largest contingent of Brazilians abroad. It also stresses the need to address the large university population in the area.

BT's political orientation is manifest in its overriding function of cultural maintenance. The editorial of the first issue (when it was still produced in Los Angeles) strikes the keynote of the vitality of the Brazilian community in California, of which it intends to become a symbol. If dispersal, arising from the urban features of the city, and the distance factor have been obstacles to the recognition of the expressiveness of the third major Brazilian community in the United States (New York and Miami coming first and second), *BT* will articulate, integrate and render it visible, "emphatically giving expression to its grandeur." Also apparent in this editorial is the allegiance to Brazil of those who "from a distance, love the country and commit themselves to still contribute to it" (*BT*, year 1, no. 1, 1–2). The local Brazilian artist Bakari, who formerly worked in the Brazilian Consulate, is cast in the first issue as an emblem of such a role: he attempts to articulate the Brazilian community through its expressive culture and takes it to be his duty to promote Brazil and particularly to create a positive image of its people.

This function further relates to the distinctive role of the Brazilian Consulate in the area and its policy of disseminating the national culture (*BT* year 1, no. 2). The cultural agenda is broadened and takes on greater prominence as Emerim's and Barandier's contribution as editors of *BT* parallels the appointment of João Almino to the Consulate in San Francisco. A noticeable and immediate change was the greater space allotted to Brazilian music, including interviews with João Bosco and Milton Nascimento and articles on Gal Costa, Paulinho da Viola, João Gilberto, Egberto Gismonti, the Olodum Group and Tom Jobim upon his death in 1994.

Articulating a National Sentiment through Symbols.

BT features and interacts with landmark events in the area to create a national consciousness. A number of *BT* issues enable the perception that, among all the communities surveyed, San Francisco is the only one that stresses football as a symbol of Brazilianness. The 1994 World Cup, held locally, was a watershed in terms of a public expression of this sentiment. Until then to be a Brazilian tended to be mostly clandestine; it was to be cast in the inferior position of the socially marginalized; it was to be hidden.[1] The World Cup enabled this repressed sentiment of Brazilianness to find a public expression. The paper's title, as of mid 1993, incorporates green and yellow, the colors of the Brazilian flag. *BT*, which is quite didactic about the country's symbols, prints the words of the national anthem regularly. In the special year of the World Cup the history of the event was also featured in issue 60, which came out one day before the decisive game.[2] A large picture of Bill Clinton in a green and yellow shirt with a small tag in front meaningfully strikes a note of hospitality, "Welcome Brazilian Friends." In the shifting world of the diaspora, the editors claim, the flag and the national anthem take on greater value as immutable symbols of Brazilianness.

This enhanced sense of nation related to the World Cup also triggered the formation of groups of *capoeira*, samba schools, etc. *Capoeira* looms increasingly large as one of the markers of Brazilian identity in the Bay Area; its stardom is increasingly acknowledged (September 1993, August 1995; year 5, no. 81; year 8, no. 130). Samba schools also thrived in 1994 and a merge of all of them was proposed as a way of jointly overcoming the difficulties each one has individually (year 3, no. 53, p. 7). Film is also cast as an expression of Brazilianness, an enabling factor being the proximity of Los Angeles; a sense of national pride is strengthened by the nomination of Brazilian films for the Oscar. There is extensive coverage of Brazil and the Oscars with reference to *Central Station*, including two important interviews with Fernanda Montenegro and another with the director Walter Salles Jr. (year 8, nos. 135 and 138). The newspaper reports on an important Brazilian film festival in Berkeley, California, in 1998, *Cinema Novo and Beyond*, showing over 32 films (year 8, no. 135) and covers another, of 24 films, in Los Angeles in 1999 (year 8, no. 136).

The revitalization of the national culinary tradition and the creation of a forum for debate.

Print media and cuisine interact in the preservation of the national traditions abroad. Food, which impregnates our senses of taste, smell and sight throughout life, becomes in the diaspora a type of cultural transmission and a sign of belonging to a cultural community. Cuisine has in fact a visceral power and food has been claimed to share with music the strongest evocation of linkage as it relates to national and family traditions rooted in childhood. Advertisements for restaurants, recipes and information on how to get specific ingredients feature prominently in Brazilian newspapers abroad. In turn, some restaurants become sites of distribution of the newspapers, as both promote the encounter of an otherwise scattered community. The Brazilian communities in general, particularly in the United States, demarcate cultural identity through an emphasis on cuisine. *BT*'s goal of maintaining Brazilian culture is further evident in a section especially devoted to Brazilian cuisine; Christmas, for example, is the occasion to include more Brazilian recipes (*BT* year 9, no. 45, 1999).[3] Its advertisements for restaurants also disseminate orientation programs beginning with talks on emigration followed by *feijoada.*

Restaurants thus ally with *BT* in the attempt to develop an ethnic politics with emphasis on the rights and important issues for the émigrés. A major one, the question of children without a motherland, relates to the 1995 amendment to the Brazilian Constitution, which broadens the scope for Brazilian nationality to be granted to the children of Brazilians abroad when they are of age, by registering with the Consulate, but because of an only recently rectified lapse in defining "of age," the amendment leaves out those younger children who have to wait until they are 21 in order to be registered (year 4, no. 74, p. 8). An important constitutional move in Brazil (09-09-1995) is addressed at length, namely the possibility of dual citizenship, the emigrants' contribution to Brazilian Social Security as self-employed individuals and the rights to retirement and the opening of a savings account to buy a house and the ensuing obligation to pay income tax (year 5, no. 86, pp. 1; 11).[4] The program for the retirement of Brazilian émigrés under the auspices of Brazilian law makes up the headline of issue 115, year 7 (August 1997). The need for Brazilians to register with the consulate was stressed in preparation for the October 1994 elections—the latter also emblematic of the awareness that Brazilians in the Bay Area have a political weight and are important for Brazil as well. Conversely, Brazilians have an impact on American culture, as seen in the interview with Ana Dias Souto on the creation of Children's Day in the United States after the Brazilian model. Other topics include the serious risks involved in illegal crossings of borders, the clarification of legal issues such as deportation, how to get a visa; health plans for the immigrant; changes in immigration law; news on the Immigration Lottery and an account of the impact of the Immigration Reform Act '96; the growing number of Brazilian voters abroad (10,000 in the United States). As from October 1992 an international lawyer started a column with legal advice to the immigrant, for example, on what Brazilians should do in relation to the home country when there are changes in family circumstances such as divorce and child birth (year 7, no. 126).

Maintaining the mother tongue and the encounter of Portugal's former colonies in the diaspora.

The philosopher Jacques Derrida has elaborated the sense of nostalgia developed by displaced persons (exiles, those who are deported, expelled, rootless, nomads). They continue to recognize the mother tongue as their ultimate homeland, and even their last resting place. Language, in his view, is the first and last condition of belonging: we carry it with us but it also carries us from birth to death. Language, he goes on, resists all mobility because it moves about with us; it is our "auto-mobile of affection" (2000: 89–91). The use of the vernacular is also one of the several ways identified by Levinson in which the ethnic media preserve cultural identity and integrity: it increases its importance in day-to-day communication, provides a model for those who do not speak the local language, and serves as a marker that distinguishes members of the indigenous community from outsiders.

BT hopes to keep alive in the United States the national sentiment strongly connected to the Portuguese language. This policy is already shown by the words in the subscription form, "Mantenha a Língua Portuguesa Viva," under the title "Committed to keep the Portuguese language alive in the USA"; the history of the language is a related theme (year 9, no. 145). This goal is reaffirmed when the editors and the layout of the paper change in 1994. This entails the development of collateral solidarity with the Lusophone immigrants (Portuguese, Angolans, Mozambicans) whose total in California is between 1.1 and 1.3 million and who even have a TV channel created by an Angolan with the main purpose of preserving the language (year 1, no. 9, p. 16). This becomes evident in the allocation of a section to Portugal in the newspaper, *Espaço de Portugal*, which is doubled in 1994. Sections heavily stress language themes, such as the specificities of the Portuguese language, curiosities drawn from the *Guia do bem falar lisboeta* (year 1 no. 4), the differences between *Brasilês* and *Português* or between *Brasinglês* and *Portinglês,* the emergence of *Emigrês,* the geographical distribution of the Portuguese language in the world, etc. *BT* surveys the history of Portuguese immigration to the West Coast of America and examines the important economic, social and cultural contributions of Portuguese immigrants to the dairy industry, whaling, fishing and agriculture.

In 1993, on the occasion of the June celebrations of *Dia de Portugal, de Camões e das Comunidades Portuguesas/Portugal Day, Camões and the Portuguese Communities*, the Brazilian presence and its rhythms and institutions are acknowledged as part of the Portuguese communities. Yet this historic re-encounter of the two countries (year 3, no. 43, p. 11) is marked by certain ambivalence. Both Portuguese and Brazilian immigrants are perceived to be very industrious, but they do not work together; Brazilians, mostly from Goiás, remain in their pizza business with a staff of cooks, managers and delivery boys who are all Brazilians. Articles on topics such as Portuguese jokes (the Brazilians' second favorite sport) are not innocent; humor is in fact cast as an attempt to elaborate the tensions between the two groups (year 4, no. 75, p. 12). The celebration of present-day Portuguese customs stresses their strong adherence to mainland Portuguese traditions. Portugal's imperial past is brought to the fore in several discussions on East Timor's 20 years of struggle. Great prominence is also given to the growing diplomatic crisis related to the Brazilians in Portugal, epitomized by the dentists' issue in November 1991. The increasingly visible cultural presence of Brazil in Portugal, not only via reverse migration but also through the media such as Globo TV, which entered the country in 1992, implicitly features a shifting power relation between the two countries, again not without tensions.

Networking with the Brazilian consulate and the renowned universities in the area.

A distinctive trait of *BT* is its strong relationship with the Brazilian consulate. Consuls regularly contribute to the newspaper. This connection, aimed at the creation of a cultural space for Brazil, is particularly evident in the case of Consul João Almino, a diplomat in the Bay Area for 5 years. Endowed with the artistic sensibility of the writer, he is shown to have given great prominence to the Brazilian cultural life as featured by *BT*. His strategy of integrating the consulate, commerce and the universities in the Bay Area is highlighted by the then Ambassador Rubens Ricúpero as he explained the choice of San Francisco for the venue of the symposium *Trade and Investments Opportunities in Brazil* in April 1993. His view is that Northern California has a great potential because of the concentration of high-technology industries and of two universities with a strong tradition in Brazilian Studies and interest in things Brazilian. But the main reason, he stresses, is the presence of Consul João Almino "who has a strong sense of initiative, good outreach in the area and this shows how an individual can make a lot of difference" (no. 42, April 1993, p. 7).

The presence of a vibrant academic life in the area again connects the consulate to the press. The occasion is the inauguration of the Joaquim Nabuco Chair for Brazilian Studies at Stanford University during the 1996 visit of Brazil's President to San Francisco, a process initiated by Ambassador Paulo Tarso Flecha de Lima and boosted by João Almino as visiting fellow in the Department of Spanish and Portuguese and Consul-general in San Francisco. This is the first chair in any U.S. university dedicated to just one country in the Southern Hemisphere and enables Stanford to bring a prestigious Brazilian scholar to campus each year. An equivalent one, the Rio Branco chair, was created for Berkeley. Almino organized the Center for Brazilian Studies at the University of California in Santa Cruz and published with Michael Palmer an anthology of recent Brazilian poetry (year 6, no. 113, p. 11). His work with the public library in San Francisco was also intense in terms of building up a collection of Brazilian books, to be increased by donations, and organizing regular conferences. Libraries are in fact known to have played a major role in the process of integrating immigrants in the United States. The headline "A diplomat that made the difference" stresses the indelible print that João Almino left on the cultural and economic life of Brazil in the Bay Area, which *BT* covered and with which the newspaper is strongly associated.

BT's achievements in the articulation of the Brazilian community. On the first anniversary of the newspaper, *BT* assessed its achievements in articulating the Brazilian community. It had not been an easy task. The group lacked unity and cohesion (*BT*, year 2, no. 24). The Brazilian community had not yet reached a good level of organization; for example, no support was provided for newly arrived Brazilians in finding housing, buying a car, finding products in the supermarket, and coping with other everyday difficulties. At times the role of articulator is expressed as ethical criticism. The editorial in the 11th issue, for example, stands out for its heavy criticism of adventuresome Brazilians' individualism as they enter a highly competitive society and heedlessly cause harm to one another (year 1, no. 11). *BT's* strong emphasis on Brazilianness, in short, is not of an *ufanista*/celebratory type. The newspaper discusses Brazilian cordiality and the positive and negative aspects of being unconfrontational (year 1, no. 2). As a by-product of the disillusionment of *Nova República*, *BT* tries to recreate abroad a national sentiment, a culture of awareness of civil rights and of debate.

Notes

1. Prior to the World Cup, a gradual and less conspicuous shift from the private to the public expression of Brazilianness was already noticeable. Note *BT*'s coverage, for example, of Brazilians on mainland streets in 1992 publicly demanding President Collor's impeachment, or in their fervent participation in Independence Day celebrations, in which the National Anthem "vibrated in Union Square" (year 4, no. 65). The same issue acknowledges the greatest celebration that took place in New York, where half a million people celebrated Independence Day with national pride enhanced by the championship, labelling it *A festa do tetra.*
2. *BT* regularly provides historical information, such as on the Independence of Brazil.
3. A survey of Brazilian food cookbooks adjusted to life in America is provided in *Eat Smart in Brazil* (Gingko Press), *Delightful Brazilian Cooking* (Ambrosia Publications) and *Brazil: A Cook's Tour* (Clarkson Potter Press) (year 5, no. 86).
4. In March 1996 the President of Brazil visited San Francisco and inaugurated the Council of Citizens of the General Consulate of San Francisco, people who are expected to act as interlocutors formulating Brazilians' demands (year 5, no. 91). The new Program of Support for Brazilians Abroad was created by President Fernando Henrique Cardoso, with greater emphasis initially on Japan and the United States, where the largest contingents of Brazilian emigrants are now living (year 5, no. 87).

References

Bhabha, Homi. 1994. *The Location of Culture.* London: Routledge.

Brazil Today. San Francisco, California.

Canclini, Néstor García. 1995. *Consumidores y ciudadanos: Conflictos multiculturales de la globalización.* México, D.F.: Editorial Grijaldo.

Candido, Antonio. 1970. "Dialética da malandragem." In *Revista do Instituto de Estudos Brasileiros.* São Paulo: Universidade de São Paulo (8):67–89.

Cardoso, Fernando Henrique. 1973. "Associated-Dependent Development: Theoretical and Practical Implications." In *Authoritarian Brazil.* Ed. Alfred Stepan. New Haven: Yale University Press.

Cross, Malcolm. 1999. Editorial. *Journal of Ethnic and Migration Studies,* 25(2): 181–185.

Derrida, Jacques. *Of Hospitality.* 2000. Transl. Rachel Bowlby. Stanford: Stanford University Press.

Friedman, Jonathan. 1994. *Cultural Identities and Global Processes.* Thousand Oaks: Sage Publications.

Levinson, David. 1994. *Ethnic Relations: A Cross-Cultural Encyclopedia*. Santa Barbara: ABC-CLIO.

Palmer, R., Bonvicino, R., Ascher, N. 1997. Eds. *Nothing the Sun Could Not Explain: 20 Contemporary Brazilian Poets.* Los Angeles: Sun & Moon Press.

Poets Adrift, Brazil Within: First Anthology of Brazilian Diaspora Poetry/Poetas à deriva; primeira antologia poética da diáspora brasileira. Compiled and introduced by Else R. P. Vieira. Belo Horizonte: Editora UFMG, forthcoming.

Prado, Luiz Carlos Delorme & Earp, Fábio Sá. 2003. "O 'milagre' brasileiro: crescimento acelerado, integração internacional e concentração de renda (1967–1973)." In *O tempo da ditadura: regime militar e movimentos sociais em fins do século XX*, pp. 207–43. Ed. Jorge Ferreira and Lucília de Almeida Neves Delgado. Rio de Janeiro: Civilização Brasileira.

The Brazilians/The Brasilians. New York, New York.

Vieira, Else R. P. 2000. *Brazil Today:* Interview with José Luiz Emerim and Silvia Barandier. San Francisco. Unpublished.

Movies

Diegues, Carlos. 1979. *Bye Bye Brasil.* Embrafilme.

Rocha, Glauber. 1980. *A Idade da Terra.* Embrafilme.

Salles, Walter. 1996. *Terra Estrangeira.* Riofilme.

———. 1998. *Central do Brasil.* Vidoefilmes.

Part Two

(IN)VISIBILITY: COMMUNITY AND BELONGING

4

Updating Demographic, Geographic, and Occupational Data on Brazilians in Massachusetts

Carlos Eduardo Siqueira and Tiago Jansen

Brazilian immigration has been a frequent topic in the news media in the Boston area in the last few years. The news reports quite often reproduce the common perception that Brazilians who live in Massachusetts are mostly undocumented, come from the state of Minas Gerais, and are concentrated in a few cities in the state. A *Boston Globe* reporter recently wrote, "Immigrants from Brazil have made their mark here—so much so that they've created a little Brazil in the center of town [Framingham]" (Franco Ordoñez 2005). The idea that Framingham may be "the most Brazilian town in the United States" is based on a high percentage of Brazilian immigrant residents and the spatial concentration of Brazilian businesses in downtown Framingham.

The published literature on Brazilian immigration to Massachusetts has described it as determined by social networks originating historically in the state of Minas Gerais. Research conducted in the nineties identified Governador Valadares as the major city in this state from where emigrants left (Sales 2003). The study of other sending areas of Brazilian emigration to Massachusetts has been limited to Criciúma, a city in the state of Santa Catarina (Assis 2003). However, the authors of this chapter have lived in Massachusetts for years now and observe a wider spectrum of Brazilian immigrants in the state, especially from the South of Brazil.

There has been an ongoing debate amongst scholars, community leaders, and officials about the demographic characteristics of Brazilian immigration to the state. Scholars who analyzed official Census data have argued that there is a gross undercount of the Brazilian population in the United States and Massachusetts, but the debate continues on the magnitude of the undercount (Margolis 1994, 1995; Siqueira and Lourenço 2006). If the 2010 Census will include a specific option for Brazilians to choose their nationality in all its forms, there may be a reduction in the undercount and the official numbers may come closer to the estimates offered by Brazilian officials and community sources. Yet it will continue to be very difficult to ascertain the exact count of Brazilians as long as the proportion of undocumented Brazilians is high. Fear of deportation and retaliation will prevent most from participating in the Census.

The First Conference of Brazilian Immigration to the United States, held in Massachusetts in 2005, highlighted the most important issues in the research agenda on Brazilian immigration. Updated analysis of the geographic and demographic aspects of Brazilian residents in Massachusetts ranked high in the concerns of participants.

This chapter will contribute to the debate with analyses of rich data provided by three complementary sources of data on Brazilian immigrants to Massachusetts: 2003 passport forms from the Brazilian consulate in Boston, maybe the largest demographic data source available on Brazilians beyond official Census data; 2000 Census data, and the 2003 Immigration and Naturalization data. To our knowledge, our study is one of the few published either in Portuguese or English that analyzes large sources of demographic data on Brazilian immigrants in the United States. Though this particular effort emphasizes Massachusetts, it could be replicated in other states where there are large Brazilian immigrant populations served by Brazilian consulates, such as Florida, New York, California, and Texas, to provide a national study of Brazilian immigrants in the United States.

Data Sources

2003 Passport Forms and Census 2000 Data

The Consulate General of Brazil in Boston is located downtown and covers the five states of New England. The former Brazilian consul granted us permission to collect and analyze information from the 2003 passport request forms. The data presented in this chapter were collected from 8,623 passport forms filed in 2003. Brazilians request passports from the Brazilian consulate in Boston to renew expired passports, to replace a lost passport, or to obtain a first passport. The latter is likely to apply to children of a Brazilian parent born in the United States or undocumented immigrants that enter the country through the U.S.-Mexican border. Access to the consulate was determined by proximity to either its main office in Boston or the "Itinerant Consulate," which rotated through several areas in eastern Massachusetts (Lowell, Framingham, Hyannis, and Stoughton were common locations in 2003). Ninety-three percent of the respondents lived in

Massachusetts. No personal or confidential information was collected to preserve confidentiality rights established by Brazilian regulations. The following information was gathered: *year of birth, city of birth, state of birth, gender, marital status, occupation, current city of residency, and current state of residency*. The consulate does not have a computerized system to manage passports. We created a database with data from the original passport request forms. Descriptive data were compiled through statistical analysis.

The information collected in the passport forms is verified against original documents and is thus deemed to be very reliable. *City and state of birth, age, gender, and marital status* are confirmed by other Brazilian documents (or American documents in case of dual citizenship). We think that information on *current city and state of residency* is also reliable because passports were usually returned by mail to the declared mailing address. Brazilians knew that they had to provide accurate addresses to receive their passports. However, data on *occupation* are not as reliable because the field "occupation" in the passport form does not specify whether it refers to his/her occupation in Brazil or the United States. Since the consulate does not require documentation to prove the veracity of this information, it is likely that many undocumented respondents who work here reported their higher skill profession or occupation in Brazil, instead of their unskilled manual work in the United States (Braga Martes 1999; Fleischer 2002; Sales 2003).

To verify the reliability of the consulate data, we compare it with Census 2000 Summary File 4 data on 30,653 Brazilian residents in Massachusetts. The United States Census Bureau produces the Summary File 4 (SF4) database containing sample data compiled from the questions asked of a sample of all people and housing units in about one in six households. People who are included in this sample respond to the housing and population long form, also known as the "Sample Data" (U.S. Census Bureau). The Sample Data are presented in 213 population tables (matrices) and 110 housing tables, identified with "PCT" and "HCT," respectively. Each table is iterated for 336 population groups: the total population, 132 race groups, 78 American Indian and Alaska Native tribe categories (reflecting 39 individual tribes), 39 Hispanic or Latino groups, and 86 ancestry groups. We conducted analyses based on Brazilian ancestry tables of foreign-born Brazilians, generated by Census software available at the Census website. According to the U.S. Census, ancestry "refers to a person's ethnic origin or descent, their 'roots,' heritage, or country of birth of the person or the person's parents or ancestors before their arrival in the United States" (U.S Census Bureau a).

Immigration Yearbook 2003

The United States Office of Immigration Statistics (OIS) is part of the Management Directorate of the Department of Homeland Security (DHS). The OIS is responsible for developing, analyzing, and disseminating statistical information needed to assess the effects of immigration in the United States. Every year it publishes a *Yearbook of Immigration Statistics* that provides text, tables, and charts on foreign nationals who, during a fiscal year, were granted lawful permanent residence (as immigrants or legal permanent residents); were admitted into the United States on a temporary basis (tourists, students, or workers); applied for asylum or refugee status; or were naturalized. The *Yearbook* also presents data on immigration law enforcement actions, including alien apprehensions, removals, and prosecutions (DHS 2005). We review data on deportation, naturalization, and immigration of Brazilians from the 2003 *Yearbook* in this chapter.

Demographic Profile of Brazilians in Massachusetts

Fifty-three percent of Brazilians who requested passports in 2003 were male and 47% female. Fifty-three percent were married, while 38% were single and only 6% divorced or separated. In comparison, 51% of Brazilians who responded to the 2000 Census housing and population long form were male, and 49% female. Fifty-five percent were married, 35% single, and only 9% divorced or separated.

Figure 1a presents the age distribution of the population studied in five-year intervals. Sixty-two percent of Brazilians who requested passport from the Brazilian Consulate in Boston in 2003 were working-age adults between 21 and 50 years old. This finding confirms the results of previous ethnographic studies with smaller samples showing that most Brazilians emigrate to the United States to work. Our data detected a surprising 1,294 children younger than five (15% of total population). Almost 90% of those children lived in Massachusetts and 96% were born in the United States.

On the one hand, this high number of children may represent the growing number of second-generation Brazilians born in this country. On the other, there is an overrepresentation of children in the database because many Brazilian parents want to legalize their U.S.-born children as Brazilian citizens by requesting their passports. In addition, only 36 out of 8,623 people were over 70 years old, which confirms studies conducted by Sales (2003) and Braga Martes (1999) that also found a small number of elderly Brazilians in Massachusetts.

Figure 1b shows the age distribution of the 2000 Census population in five-year intervals. Seventy-one percent of Brazilians who responded to

Figure 1a: Age Distribution in Five-year Intervals

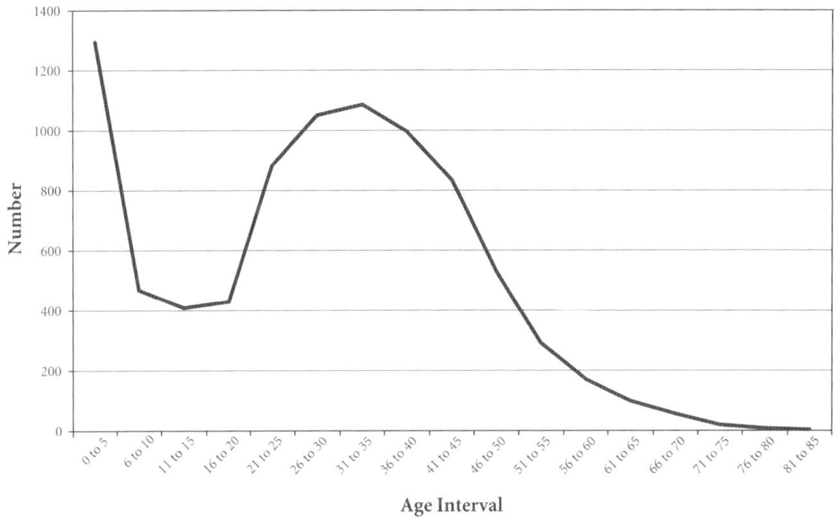

Source: 2003 Passport Forms, General Consulate of Brazil in Boston

Figure 1b: Age Distribution in Five-Year Intervals

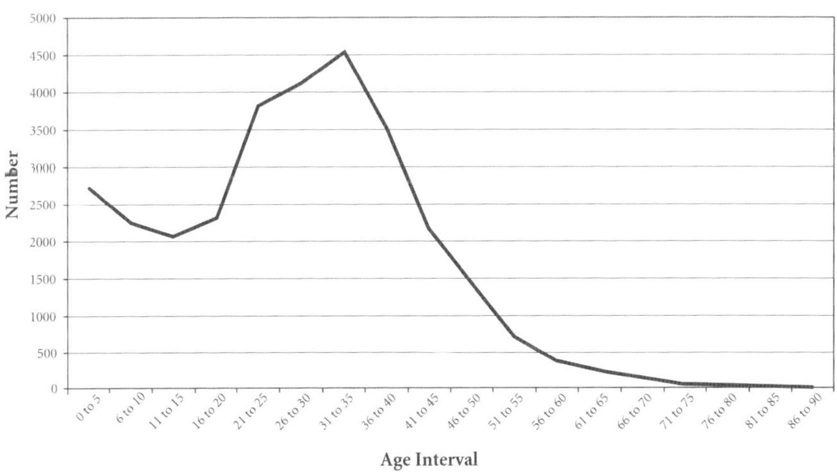

Source: Census 2000, Summary Form 4

the 2000 Census housing and population long form were working age adults between 21 and 50 years old, while ten percent were children under five, confirming the significant share of children under five in the Brazilian immigrant population. This pattern should be expected given the predominance of young adults in both data. Overall, there is much similarity between the consulate and Census age-distribution data, strengthening the validity of the former.

Geographic Distribution of Brazilian Immigration to Massachusetts

Sending Hubs

Consulate data indicates that the main sending states in descending order of relative number of emigrants were (Figure 2): Minas Gerais (45%), São Paulo (11%), Paraná (8%), Santa Catarina (7%), Rio de Janeiro (7%), Espírito Santo (6%), Goiás (4%), and Bahia (3%). Sixty-nine percent of Brazilian immigrants came from the Southeast and 17% came from the South, which are the wealthiest regions of Brazil. Yet the data included Brazilians from twenty-four states (out of twenty-six) and the Federal District (the capital Brasília and its surrounding satellite cities).

The predominance of Minas Gerais as the most common sending state, with almost half of the immigrants, may explain why prior studies and common perceptions portrayed Massachusetts as a land of "mineiros."[2] This portrayal, on the other hand, seems to be a reduction of a migratory phenomenon that is national, meaning that Brazilians have emigrated from everywhere in Brazil, not only from Minas Gerais.

When we weighted the same data by dividing the total population of immigrants from each sending state by the total population of each in Brazil and multiplying the result by a factor of 100, a different picture emerged (Figure 3). Espírito Santo, Santa Catarina, Paraná, and Goiás became more important as sending states, while São Paulo fell to eighth place. This new rank of less populated states such as Espírito Santo and Goiás suggests that immigration may be a much more visible issue there than in larger states such as São Paulo. The state of Minas Gerais remains as the most important sending state, but its relative contribution to emigration flows decreases.

The ten most common cities of birth of Brazilians who requested passports in 2003 are presented in Table 1.

Although this data does not link place of birth with place of residence in Brazil prior to emigration to Massachusetts, the cities listed above seem

Figure 2: Brazilian Immigrants by State of Birth

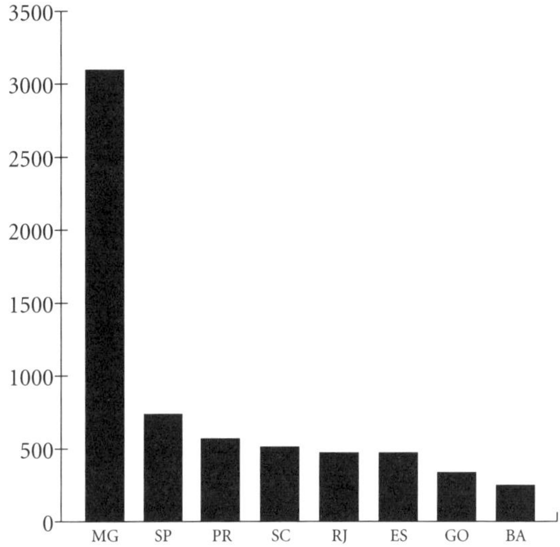

Source: 2003 Passport Forms, General Consulate of Brazil in Boston.
* index = number of Brazilians in the sample per state / 2000 state population × 2000 Brazilian population / 100.

Figure 3: Brazilian Immigration by State of Birth Weighted by State Population

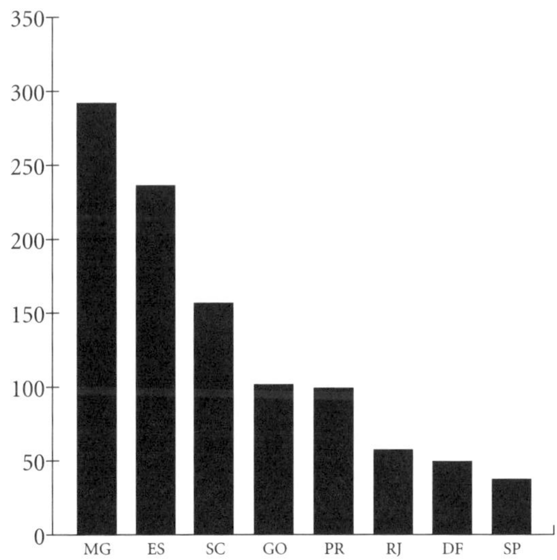

Source: 2003 Passport Forms, General Consulate of Brazil in Boston.
* index = number of Brazilians in the sample per state / 2000 state population × 2000 Brazilian population / 100.

Table 1. Ten Most Common Cities of Birth in Brazil

City of Birth	Number of People	Brazilian State
1. Governador Valadares	539	MG
2. São Paulo	366	SP
3. Belo Horizonte	341	MG
4. Rio de Janeiro	264	RJ
5. Criciúma	206	SC
6. Conselheiro Pena	194	MG
7. Mantena	136	MG
8. Vitória	125	ES
9. Curitiba	119	PR
10. Resplendor	111	MG

Source: 2003 Passport Forms, General Consulate of Brazil in Boston

to partially confirm previous ethnographic studies of Brazilian emigration to Massachusetts (Braga Martes 1999; Sales 2003).

In Chapter 7 of this volume, Sueli Siqueira discusses more recent evidence on the long-term flow of emigration from Governador Valadares to the United States. The characteristics of her sample confirm prior research that indicated that the emigration network of Valadares has supported mostly chain migration. Yet there are also cases of people whose stories suggest a weaker pattern of circular or "yo-yo" migration—when immigrants go back and forth between Brazil and the United States—that was more common during the 1990s under less stringent immigration policies (Margolis 1994; Fusco 2001).

Minas Gerais has five of the ten most common cities of birth of Brazilian immigrants to Massachusetts. Four of them are small and mid-size cities in the Vale do Rio Doce macro-region of the state (Governador Valadares, Conselheiro Pena, Mantenas, and Resplendor). São Paulo, Rio de Janeiro, Belo Horizonte, and Vitória are state capitals and the largest cities of the four Southeast states. Curitiba is the capital and largest city of the state of Paraná, one of the states in the South of Brazil. Criciúma is a mid-sized city located in the state of Santa Catarina, also in the South of Brazil.

Our analysis of Brazilian immigration at the level of city of birth also suggested an interesting pattern in the geographic distribution of sending cities. There are a few cities and counties that concentrate emigration within each sending state. These "sending hubs" are the geographic expression of emigration networks found by ethnographic studies of researchers (Braga Martes 1999; Assis 2003; Margolis 2003).

The capitals of the states of São Paulo and Rio de Janeiro seem to be the only relevant sending hubs of these states, with respectively 50% and 57%

of emigrants from the state. The capitals of the state of Paraná (Curitiba) and Espírito Santo (Vitória) are primary sending hubs of these states, with respectively 21%, and 39% of emigrants. Paraná also has five smaller sending hubs: Londrina, Maringá, Apucarana, Ponta Grossa, and Faxinal dos Guedes. Espírito Santo has four smaller sending hubs: Colatina, Pancas, Mantenópolis, and Barra do São Francisco. Goiás has a couple of equally important sending hubs, the capital Goiânia and Anápolis, which account for 53% of emigrants from the state. Criciúma is clearly the sending hub of the state of Santa Catarina, with 42% of emigrants from the state. Three other much smaller sending hubs are Araranguá, Florianópolis (the state capital), and Urussanga.

In the state of Minas Gerais, the Vale do Rio Doce macro-region of the state is the sending hub, with 67% of "mineiro" emigrants. Governador Valadares is the largest sending hub within this region with 17% of "mineiro" emigrants, but there are many other important sending cities in this state: Conselheiro Pena, Mantena, Resplendor, Ipatinga, Tarumirim, Coronel Fabriciano, Guanhães, and Engenheiro Caldas. The state capital, Belo Horizonte, is a sending hub of 11 % of "mineiro" emigrants to Massachusetts.

Children are a special case because the location where the births occurred is usually different from their actual place of residence. Almost 80% of the children younger than ten were born in Massachusetts (1,390). Twenty percent of those (271) were born in Cambridge, but only 19 of them live there. It is common knowledge amongst the Brazilian community in Massachusetts that the Cambridge Health Alliance is a good healthcare provider that offers good, culturally competent, free care services. This may explain why so many children who do not live in Cambridge were born in that city.

Receiving Hubs

Table 2 presents a list of nineteen cities where more than one percent (over ninety people) of the total population of Brazilians who requested passports in 2003 has lived.

These cities account for 64% of Brazilian residents in Massachusetts, who are concentrated in Eastern and Central Massachusetts.

While Framingham, Boston, and Somerville had already been acknowledged as receiving cities or hubs where Brazilians had settled in large numbers (Braga Martes 1999), this is not the case for Everett, Worcester, Lowell, Malden, or Fall River.

Our data also suggests that during the last decade Brazilians have continued to find new places to settle. They now live in 250 out of 350 cities

Table 2. Cities of Residence of Brazilians in Massachusetts, Consulate Data

City of Residence	Number of Residents
1. Framingham	847
2. Boston	656
3. Somerville	619
4. Everett	459
5. Marlborough	348
6. Worcester	313
7. Lowell	299
8. Hyannis	274
9. Malden	272
10. Medford	208
11. Revere	208
12. Milford	198
13. Brockton	157
14. Peabody	140
15. Cambridge	125
16. Fall River	117
17. Lynn	101
18. Hudson	91
19. Yarmouth	91

Source: 2003 Passport Forms, General Consulate of Brazil in Boston

and towns in the state. Thus, it is not an exaggeration to suggest that by 2005 Brazilians reside everywhere in Massachusetts. Receiving cities and towns in Massachusetts include many small places such as Tyngsboro, Leominster, and Littleton. This spatial dispersion seems to have occurred more recently and suggests that Brazilian networks have expanded beyond those already described in the literature.

It is likely that Brazilians first settle in major hubs (larger cities) in the state, moving to smaller suburbs as they become familiar with U.S. mainstream society and less dependent on the original ethnic migration network. This spreading trend was briefly discussed by Portes as "the spatial counterpart of cultural assimilation as foreign groups melt into the host society" (Portes and Rumbaut 1996).

Table 3 presents Census 2000 SF4 data on Brazilian residents of receiving cities in Massachusetts. The threshold for populations to be included in Summary File 4 is a minimum of 100 people. In addition, there must be at least 50 or more Brazilians in each location. Cities and towns that did not meet these criteria are not part of this dataset.

Table 3. Cities of Residence of Brazilians in Massachusetts, 2000 Census Data

City of Residence	Number of Residents
1. Somerville	3,870
2. Boston	3,594
3. Framingham	3,500
4. Lowell	1,820
5. Marlborough	1,388
6. Everett	1,278
7. Worcester	1,099
8. Malden	1,027
9. Barnstable	930
10. Revere	846
11. Cambridge	694
12. Fall River	595
13. Medford	520
14. Hudson	487
15. Brockton	441

Source: Census 2000 – SF4

All fifteen cities and towns listed in table 3 also appear in table 2. The ranking of the receiving cities are also similar, with a few noticeable changes: Framingham falls to third place and Somerville becomes the most populated. In addition, Lowell moves up three positions, becoming fourth, while Barnstable makes the top fifteen. Hyannis, which is the eighth in table 2, does not appear in table 3.

Despite the fact that consulate and Census data were collected at different times, 2003 and 2000 respectively, using very different methodologies, the important receiving cities are almost the same. Therefore, we are confident that the geographic distribution of Brazilians in Massachusetts is now well established.

The differences in the ranking order of cities in the two sources of data may be explained by, among others, the following factors: first, it is well known that recent immigrant populations are highly mobile and the data were collected three years apart. Second, local characteristics and/or circumstantial events may account for participation in the Census as well as access to the Brazilian consulate. For example, the legal status of Brazilian residents varies in different cities in the state and there are indications that Framingham has a higher percentage of undocumented Brazilians than Boston or Somerville.[3] We should expect less Census participation in places with a larger numbers of undocumented Brazilians because of their fear of deportation. Brazilian immigrant participation in the 2000 Census was also influenced by a campaign conducted by Brazilian ethnic press and media in Massachusetts to encourage the Brazilian community to respond to the Census surveys. This campaign provided information about the purpose and operation of the Census through public service announcements and advertisements, but may have had different impacts in the receiving cities and towns.

Occupational Profile of Brazilian Immigrant Workers in Massachusetts

There were 1,109 blank responses to occupation, out of a total of 6,296 adults (eighteen years old or older) who requested their passports. Eighty-four percent of all Brazilian males who responded to the Census housing and population long form worked in 1999. Ninety-one percent of those males who worked in 1999 usually worked thirty-five or more hours per week, and 69% of those worked between fifty and fifty two weeks in 1999. Sixty-nine percent of all Brazilian females who responded to the housing and population long form worked in 1999. Seventy-three percent of those females who worked in 1999 usually worked thirty or more hours per week, and 62% of them worked between fifty and fifty two weeks in 1999 (U.S. Census Bureau b). Five hundred respondents reported their occupation as students.

Table 4 presents the most common jobs held by the remaining 4,687 adult Brazilians who reported their occupation.

Table 4. Jobs Most Often Reported by Brazilian Immigrants

Job	Number	%
Cook	369	7.9%
Housecleaner	349	7.4%
Salesperson	327	7.0%
Housewife	294	6.3%
Teacher	255	5.4%
Painter	212	4.5%
Driver	162	3.5%

Source: 2003 Passport Forms, General Consulate of Brazil in Boston

Although we do not know the biases present in the information provided in table 4, we assume that figures for an occupation with higher social recognition in Brazil or Massachusetts, such as painter and teacher, may arguably have higher validity than those with lower social recognition, such as housewife. Our assumption about social recognition is based on qualitative data collected in interviews with many Brazilian immigrants, who tend to value more those occupations that enable them to earn higher incomes in the United States, as previously discussed by Braga Martes (1999) and Sales (2003). There may also be over-reporting of cooks because many food preparers or cook assistants may have chosen to report their occupations as cooks, which is a job with higher prestige. Thus, the limitations of the occupational data provided in the passport forms have to be carefully taken into account before drawing any solid conclusions.

Our experience as residents of Massachusetts for many years and the available literature on Brazilian immigration indicate that restaurant workers, housecleaners, painters, salespersons, and drivers are certainly amongst the most common jobs held by Brazilian immigrants in Massachusetts. We suspect that a significant number of people who reported their occupations as housewives may work as housecleaners in the United States, which would increase the number of housecleaners. Housewives and teachers may have actually reported their occupation in Brazil.

Table 5 shows Census 2000 information on the most prevalent occupational sectors of Brazilian immigrants in Massachusetts.

Table 5. Occupational Sectors for the Employed Brazilians Aged 16 Years and Older in Massachusetts

Occupational Sector	Massachusetts Total	%
Service occupations	8,147	47.7%
Production, transportation, and material-moving occupations	2,786	16.3%
Sales and office occupations	2,416	14.2%
Management, professional, and related occupations	1,855	10.9%
Construction, extraction, and maintenance occupations	1,846	10.8%
Farming, fishing, and forestry occupations	20	0.1%
Total	17,070	100.0%

Source: Census 2000 – Table PCT 86 - SF4

Brazilian immigration literature has already pointed out that recent immigrants to urban areas of the United States tend to find jobs in the service sector, construction trades, sales and office occupations, professional occupations, and production occupations (Margolis 1994; Braga Martes 1999). Seven hundred and ninety-eight Brazilian male workers reported that they were self-employed in their own, non-incorporated businesses. Those were probably informal construction contractors who own their painting or residential construction businesses. Over 1,700 Brazilian female workers also reported that they were self-employed in their own non-incorporated businesses in 1999. Those were probably the housecleaners who run their own informal cleaning business, though they did not incorporate it as a formal company or business.[4]

The predominance of service occupations, the absence of farming, fishing, and forestry occupations, and the close ranking of the other four most prevalent occupational sectors in table 5 seem to validate previous findings based on smaller samples and qualitative research (Siqueira and Lourenço, 2006; Margolis, 1994, 1995; Braga Martes, 1999). In fact, it would not take much effort to find Brazilians working as retail workers, customer service representatives, cashiers, or laborers in several neighborhoods in Boston or downtown Framingham.

Table 6 presents the thirteen most common occupations of Brazilians sixteen years and older in Massachusetts, which correspond to percentages equal or above two percent of respondents.

Table 6. Occupations of Employed Brazilians in Massachusetts

Occupational Sector	Massachusetts Total	%
Building and grounds cleaning and maintenance	4,347	25.5%
Cooks and food preparation workers	1,593	9.3%
Other food preparation and serving workers, including supervisors	800	4.7%
Painters and paperhangers	794	4.7%
Management	629	3.7%
Other production occupations, including supervisors	575	3.4%
Cashiers	556	3.3%
Driver/sales workers and truck drivers	520	3.0%
Construction laborers	444	2.6%
Waiters and waitresses	402	2.4%
Material-moving workers	401	2.4%
Retail sales workers, except cashiers	394	2.3%
Food processing workers	340	2.0%

Source: Census 2000 – SF4

The breakdown of the occupational sectors listed in table 6 specifies the principal occupations held by most Brazilian immigrants in Massachusetts. According to this data, Brazilians in Massachusetts worked in 1999 mainly as housecleaners and janitors, cooks and food preparers, other food workers (including busboys, bakers, and dishwashers), and painters. Table 6 suggests that the consulate data correctly identified cooks, housecleaners, retail workers, and painters amongst the most common Brazilian occupations in Massachusetts.

Trends in Legal Status and Deportation

Naturalization

The number of Brazilian immigrants who became American citizens increased significantly in the 1999 fiscal year (October 1998–September 1999), when it grew from 1,947 to 4,114, reaching a peak in the fiscal year 2000, when 4,524 Brazilians gained citizenship (*Immigration Yearbook*, 2003). According to table 32 of the *Yearbook*, 3,091 Brazilians were naturalized in the 2003 fiscal year (October 2002–September 2003), of whom 37% were males and 63% females. Based on data derived from the Profiles of Naturalized Citizens (OIS, 2005) we calculated that 24% were permanent residents of Florida, 17% resided in California, 11% in New York, 9% in New Jersey, 8% in Massachusetts, and 4% in Texas and Maryland.

Permanent Residents

According to our analysis of data from the Profile of Legal Residents (OIS, 2005), of the 6,331 Brazilians who became permanent residents in the 2003 fiscal year, 34% were males and 64% females; over 70% were between 18 and 44 years old, while 74% were married and 24% single. Twenty-one percent of those Brazilians settled in Florida, 16% in Massachusetts, 14% in California, 8% in New Jersey, and 7% in New York. Five percent or less of Brazilian permanent residents settled in Texas, Virginia, Washington, D.C., Illinois, Maryland, Georgia, among several other states.

Deportation

According to data from the 2003 *Yearbook* (table 36), there were 5,740 deportable Brazilians in 2003, about 55% of all deportable South Americans in that same year. Brazilians became the fifth largest country in number of deportable aliens, after Mexico, Honduras, El Salvador, and Guatemala. The number of Brazilians removed from the United States increased between the 1998 and 2003 fiscal years (table 43, October 1998-September 2003). While only 349 Brazilians were removed in the 1998 fiscal year, there were 3,797 in the 2003 fiscal year, an increase of over 1,000%. Starting in 2002, Brazil displaced Canada from the top ten countries whose nationals were removed from the United States. The former Immigration and Naturalization Service (INS), now Immigration and Customs Enforcement (ICE), classified most of the Brazilian removals as non-criminal removals, which means that most of them left voluntarily, after being apprehended by the Border Patrol or refused entry in the United States by an immigration inspector.

The Brazilian newspaper *Folha de São Paulo* recently reported that there were over 8,600 apprehensions of Brazilian immigrants at the U.S-Mexico border during the 2004 fiscal year (Maisonnave 2005). In addition, according to sources from the Brazilian Consulate in Mexico, there were 5,084 apprehensions in Mexico until October 2004: 1,212 of those were apprehended in Mexico and 3,872 were refused entry at the Mexico City airport (Maisonnave 2005).

Conclusion

The triangulation between the 2003 Consulate and the Census 2000 data adds validity to the former, which appears to be representative of the Brazilian immigrant population in Massachusetts. According to our data, Brazilian immigrants are for the most part a working-age population, evenly distributed between genders. The percentage of seniors is very small. Most adults were married and most children were born in the United States. This demographic profile is typical of a recent immigrant population, with a second generation in the making (Portes and Rumbaut, 1996, Chapa, 1998, Stalker, 2001). In addition, there is a significant group of Brazilians who emigrated as children and will grow up in the United States, the so-called generation one and a half. In contrast to children under the age of ten, the majority of teenagers in our database (11 to 17 years) were born in Brazil; the older the teenagers the more likely that Brazil was their birthplace.

We found new spatial patterns for the Brazilian immigration. In addition to the well-known dominance of Minas Gerais as the main sending state, we must also include São Paulo, Rio de Janeiro, Paraná, Santa Catarina, Espírito Santo, and Goiás in future descriptions of emigration from Brazil. Once we take into consideration the total population of sending states to measure the relative weight of emigration, it becomes clear that less populated states play an up to now hidden role in the overall emigration picture. Espírito Santo and Santa Catarina are very good examples of this scenario. Other states worth mentioning are Mato Grosso, Mato Grosso do Sul, Roraima, and the Federal District.

The Vale do Rio Doce macro-region of Minas Gerais should be emphasized as the major emigration hub from Brazil, not only the city or micro-region of Governador Valadares, which was reviewed in detail in Chapter 7. This macro-region also includes several counties of Espírito Santo and influences emigration from this state. To better understand emigration patterns from Vale do Rio Doce and Espírito Santo, we should focus on them as a combined emigration hub, beyond the rigid division established by state borders.

We also recognized new sending hubs in Brazil. Cities such as Goiânia, Anápolis, Criciúma, Brasília, and Curitiba must be part of the new places discussed from now on when Brazilian emigration is analyzed. Furthermore, there is plenty of evidence that Brazilian emigration is now a national phenomenon, gradually turning into a daily theme of conversation in the whole country. Brazilian media, government, and businesses have gradually incorporated Brazucas[5] into their worldview. By the same token, Brazilians have also settled in new states in the United States, such as Georgia, New Hampshire, Maryland, and Texas. National emigration also became national immigration. In Massachusetts, the receiving hubs include a larger number of cities and new areas of residence have developed, suggesting a process of decentralization.

The triangulation of Census and consulate data on occupation was essential to strengthen our evidence that the majority of Brazilian immigrants in Massachusetts work in the service and construction sectors. Although the standard industrial classification adopted in the Census may not parallel the lay understanding of occupational sectors, there is strong evidence that cleaning and food and restaurant services are the most important services provided by Brazilians workers, while painting is the most common construction trade. However, it is interesting to note that a significant number of Brazilians work in the retail industry as cashiers, clerks, and supervisors. Starting in the year 2005 the consulate passport form has a new field for occupation that requires the respondent to provide his/her occupation in the United States. Thus, future studies on the occupations of Brazilians could gather better occupational information than we were able to.

Recent trends in naturalization, legalization, and deportation emerged by the end of the nineties, especially after 2001. According to the most recent available data, there has been an increase in naturalization and legalization of Brazilians as permanent residents in the late nineties, followed by a decrease after the year 2001. In addition, as visas in Brazil became more difficult to obtain for those who lived in sending states, there has been a drastic growth of immigration through the Mexico-United States border. Data provided by the CIS on deportations highlight the growing number of arrests of Brazilians at the border. Newspaper stories of deportations and even death of Brazilians in border crossing have also increased in both Brazil and the United States. It is still unclear what impact these deportations will have on the future migration choices of Brazilians.

Considering that Brazil has about 40% of the population of Latin America, Brazilian emigration to the United States may reach a new scale if it continues unabated in the future. While it is far from clear what the main trend will be, there are warning signs that emigration could become part of Brazilian culture to an extent never seen before. Yet there are also indications of a reversal of this pattern. In any case, it will become even more important to conduct future studies to understand Brazilian migration. Finally, our experience convinced us that the existing infrastructure of Brazilian consulates in the United States is insufficient to provide the kind of data collected and analyzed in this study. There is no electronic database storing the information routinely collected by the Brazilian consulates, such as passport forms, birth certificates, and power of attorney documents. Our research team had to spend hundreds of working hours to manually transfer data from paper forms to a computer database. Therefore, we can not overemphasize the need for the Brazilian Ministry of Foreign Relations (Itamaraty) to update the technology used to collect and store such information. Electronic databases could improve consular services provided to Brazilian citizens in the United States as well as facilitate future research to analyze Brazilian migration patterns and trends in different cities, states, and regions of this country.

Notes

1. Grant Number 1 R25 ES 012588-1 from the National Institute of Environmental Health Sciences (NIEHS) partially supported the authors to write this chapter. Its contents are solely the responsibility of the authors and do not necessarily represent the official views of NIEHS.
2. *Mineiros* are Brazilians who are born in the state of Minas Gerais.
3. Data from the Framingham's "Centro Comunitário Bom Samaritano," available with the authors, show that over 3,500 Brazilians visited the organization during 2004. Three hundred and seventy-six of those were recent arrivals in the United States. This Centro helps Brazilians to find jobs in the area.
4. In addition, Census data not shown here reveal that Brazilian males did not work in the aircraft and traffic control, rail and water transportation, installation, maintenance and repair occupational, and government sectors in 1999.
5. For a discussion of this term, please see the introduction in this volume.

References

Assis, Gláucia de Oliveira. 2003. "De Criciúma para o mundo—Os novos fluxos da população brasileira: gênero e rearranjos familiares." In *Fronteiras Cruzadas: Etnicidade, Gênero e Redes Sociais*. Rio de Janeiro: Paz e Terra.

Braga Martes, Ana Cristina. 1999. *Brasileiros nos Estados Unidos: Um Estudo sobre Imigrantes em Massachusetts* (*Brazilians in the United States: A Study of Immigrants in Massachusetts*). Rio de Janeiro: Paz e Terra.

Chapa, Jorge. 1998. "The Burden of Interdependence: Demographic, Economic, and Social Prospects for Latinos in the Reconfigured U.S. Economy." In *Borderless Border: U.S Latinos, Latin Americans, and the Paradox of Interdependence.* Ed. Frank Bonilla, Edwin Meléndez, Rebecca Morales, and Maria de los Angeles Torres. Philadelphia: Temple University Press.

Department of Homeland Security. 2003. *Yearbook of Immigration Statistics.* Available from World Wide Web: http://uscis.gov/graphics/shared/statistics /yearbook/index.htm.

Department of Homeland Security. Office of Immigration Statistics (OIS) 2005. Available from World Wide Web: http://uscis.gov/graphics/shared/statistics /index.htm.

Fusco, Wilson. 2001. *Redes Sociais na Migração Internacional: O Caso de Governador Valadares (Social Networks in International Migration: The Case of Governador Valadares).* Campinas: Núcleo de Estudos de População, UNICAMP.

Fleischer, Soraya. 2002. *Passando a América a Limpo: O Trabalho de Housecleaners Brasileiras em Boston, Massachusetts*, São Paulo: AnnaBlume Editora.

Maisonnave, Fabiano. 2005a. "Estranhos no Paraíso." *Folha de São Paulo,* São Paulo.

———. 2005b. "Prisões também aumentam do lado mexicano." *Folha de São Paulo,* São Paulo.

Margolis, Maxine. 1994. *Little Brazil. An Etnography of Brazilian Immigrants in New York City*, Princeton: Princeton University Press.

———. 1995. "Brazilians and the 1990 United States Census: Immigrants, Ethnicity, and the Undercount." *Human Organization* 54:52–59.

———. 2003. "Na virada do milênio: A emigração brasileira para os Estados Unidos." In *Fronteiras Cruzadas: Etnicidade, Gênero e Redes Sociais.* Rio de Janeiro: Paz e Terra.

Ordoñez, Franco. 2005. "In Framingham, Brazilians have made themselves at home." *Boston Globe.*

Portes, Alejandro and Rumbaut, Rubén. 1996. *Immigrant America: A Portrait*, 2nd ed. Berkeley: University of California Press.

Sales, Teresa. 2003. *Brazilians Away from Home,* New York: Center for Migration Studies.

Siqueira, C. Eduardo and Lourenço, Cileine. 2006. "Brazilians in Massachusetts: Migration, Identity, and Work." In *Latinos in New England*. Ed. Andres Torres. Philadelphia: Temple University Press.

Stalker, Peter. 2001. *The No-Nonsense Guide to International Migration*, Toronto: New Internationalist.

U.S. Census Bureau. 2003. Census 2000 of Population and Housing, Summary File 4: Technical Documentation, Available from World Wide Web: http://www.census.gov/Press-Release/www/2003/SF4.html.

U.S. Census Bureau a. American Factfinder. Available at http://factfinder.census.gov/home/en/epss/ancestry.html.

U.S. Census Bureau b. Census 2000 of Population and Housing, Summary File 4. Data calculated from Table Pct82: Sex by Work Status in 1999 by Usual Hours Worked per Week in 1999. Bb Weeks Worked in 1999 for the Population 16 Years and over. Ancestry: Brazilian.

5

The Commitment of Return: Remittances of Brazilian Émigrés

Ana Cristina Braga Martes

The statement that globalization is an irreversible process, that it intensifies and expands the scope of social relations (Giddens 1990, Orozco 2004, Martine 2005), and that it is currently the principal motor of international migration has raised little controversy (Sassen 1996, Milanovic 1999). According to George Martine (2005), "migration [and I would add whether legal or not] is inevitable and has the potential to be quite positive in terms of development and reduction of poverty. The policies that have their origins in this principle will be more successful than those that attempt to oppose, intransigently, both globalization and the migration of people in space" (Martine 2005, 2). Here, indeed, we arrive at a point that is highly debatable: do current international migrations produce positive effects? Or are they merely the result of poverty and inequality among nations, in the face of which people find themselves forced to leave their homelands? The main objective of this chapter is to contribute to this discussion through an empirical study of the Brazilian case, which takes remittances as its focus. Thus, I identify those immigrants who send remittances from the United States to Brazil and ask to what ends the remittances are directed, who the beneficiaries are, and how the remittances affect the lives of the people who benefit from them. The research uses a microeconomic issues development approach and is based on a non-representative but in-depth sample from Boston and from Governador Valadares, the Brazilian city with the largest number of émigrés to the United States.

World leaders and representatives of multilateral organizations have emphasized, perhaps more than researchers, what we here call "positive effects of the migratory phenomenon." According to Kofi Annan (president of the United Nations in 2006), "poor countries can also benefit from emigration: in 2002, émigrés sent to developing countries remittances in the amount of at least 88 billion US dollars, that is, 54% more that what they received in development aid (57 billion US dollars) in the same period" (*Folha de São Paulo*, January 29, 2004). In the following year, Donald Terry (one of the directors of the Inter-American Development Bank-IDB) warned in a graver tone that, without these remittances, the economies of some countries could collapse (*Folha de São Paulo*, November 30, 2003). During the same period, the International Monetary Fund (IMF) advised governments to encourage the entrance of remittances, with the justification that in developing countries, this money acts as "a shock absorber during times of internal crisis," reduces the volatility of the growth of the Gross Domestic Product, and contributes to the reduction of poverty (Report "World Economic Perspectives").

In the case of Latin America and the Caribbean (LAC), remittances received totaled 45 billion US dollars in 2004, surpassing the total annual volume of Direct Foreign Investment (DFI) in the region (*Sending Money Home: Remittance to Latin America and the Caribbean-May, 2004;* IDB/IMF). Even when compared to the inflow of foreign capital, the amount from remittances was only exceeded by what tourism generated in this period. For some countries, remittances represent a considerable slice of the GDP, as, for example, in the Dominican Republic, 14% of whose GDP consisted of remittances in the year 2004 (*El Popular,* April 6, 2005: http://www.elpopular.com/news.php?nid=336)

Despite the increase in restrictions on the entrance of Brazilians into the United States since September 11, remittances sent to Brazil have been rising since the year 2001. Remittances reached the sum of 5.6 billion US dollars in 2004, coming not only from the United States, but also from Japan and Europe (IDB 2004). This amount represents 1% of the Brazilian GDP. However, a portion of these resources is sent by informal means, without being recorded by the Central Bank (CB), therefore, the CB accounted for merely 2.3 million US dollars in remittances in 2004. At the same time, calculations of the amount must take into account the fact that the average cost of a remittance to Brazil varies from around 8.9% of the sum sent, to as much as 20% in some cases. The IDB estimates that "the current rules make remittances and their accounting difficult, pushing the entrance of resources into the informal market." This possibly explains the difference between the data of the Central Bank of Brazil and that of the IDB with regard to the total amount of remittances.

When unrecorded, remittances represent one of the facets of the Brazilian "informal emigration industry." It is only one of the facets because, besides the resources that enter without any official record, Brazilians are among the 11 million illegal immigrants who currently reside in the United States. Thus, part of the "informal industry" is not motivated merely by opportunistic economic behavior, but also by restrictions imposed on the number of visas granted to Brazilians, principally those from the state of Minas Gerais, and people coming from cities considered focal points for the outflow of immigrants.[1] The restrictions of the U.S. government have contributed to increasing the "informal emigration industry," but not to reducing the migratory flow. In Mexico, illegal migrants with the goal of crossing the U.S. border put nearly 5 billion US dollars per year into circulation (*Folha de São Paulo*, May 11, 2003). The number of Brazilians detained on the Mexican border rose from 500 in 1999 to more than 8,616 in 2004 (Department of Homeland Security *Yearbook of Immigration Statistics*). At the same time, the first international accord was signed recognizing that immigration does not constitute a crime—this is the Palermo Protocol, which has as its goal combating the mafias that specialize in human trafficking—and it was later ratified by 40 countries in Geneva.

Obviously, the restrictive policies of the U.S. government are not aimed solely at Brazilians. Since September 11, 2001, a decline can be observed in the number of entrance visas from 6.9 million to 4.9 million, especially for the inhabitants of the countries of the Middle East (*Folha de São Paulo*, November 30, 2004). However, the number of illegal immigrants grew 23% in a period of four years. This signifies an increase of approximately 485,000 people every year between 2000 and 2004. The predictions indicate that, compared to the last two decades, the total number of immigrants into the United States will jump from 12 million in the 1990s to 14 million in the first decade of the twenty-first century (*The Sydney Morning Herald*, March 2005).

The emigration of Brazilians hasn't stopped either. Neither the economic stability that occurred in Brazil beginning in the mid 1990s, nor the increase in restrictions on the entrance of Brazilians into the United States (especially the denial of tourist visas), were sufficient to cause Brazilians to stop looking to that country for new opportunities. There are no exact numbers, but some information can be helpful in making some estimates. In the case of this study, which is focused on Massachusetts, some of the available data is furnished by the Brazilian Consulate in Boston itself: comparing the years from 2000 to 2004, the total number of principal documents emitted (notarized and recorded legal documents) increased by 26.8% from 2000 to 2001 and by 39.16% from 2001 to 2002.

Positive and Negative Factors, on Micro and Macro Levels

Do remittances contribute to local development and the reduction of poverty? What are the consequences of the dollars sent by the migrants to the people, families, and organizations that receive them in the cities of origin? These are the key questions that recent studies have raised. Some authors seek to understand the way in which remittances might positively affect the economies of the countries of origin of the immigrants.

Discussing the role and significance of these remittances thus implies a discussion involving the existence (or lack thereof) of a "set of positives" from the international migratory phenomenon (Martine 2005). Specifically in relation to Brazilian emigration, such an approach is unheard of, as the economic factors that push emigration always appear in reference to poverty, unemployment, economic instability, and the absence of social mobility (Martes 2000) resulting from the absence of economic expansion since the 1980s.

Approaching Brazilian emigration from the point of view of the positives generated by it does not mean leaving aside its negative aspects. Rather, it means posing the question: do remittances bring about positive effects, whether on the micro or macro level?

Because remittances are variable and difficult to measure or evaluate, their impact in the remitters' countries of origin is subject to debate (Wucker 2004). Some authors emphasize the problems that the remittances cause to local economies, since they are being preferentially channeled towards the acquisition of consumer goods rather than into productive investment, especially enterprises and projects that might stimulate local production and thus contribute to raising income levels and reducing unemployment. One of the roots of this problem may lie in the lack of available information for remitters and receivers, as well as the fact that there is no local "culture" capable of encouraging the employment of this money for the promotion of local development (United Nations DESA 2005). That is, the remittances are being preferentially directed towards consumption and, when directed towards investments, these tend not to be productive. Moreover, conflicts arise between families who receive and who do not receive remittances, and they are a cause of inflation, especially in the price of rural and urban real estate (Reichert 1981).

Scholars who highlight the positive aspects believe that local economies can benefit from the remittances, especially because they contribute to the reduction of poverty (Newland 2003). More specifically, the remittances promote improvements in life style and consumption—since the money is channeled towards education, healthcare, and the acquisition of family consumer goods. Thus, the remittances contribute to improving the quality of life in the domiciles that receive them in the communities of origin. Likewise, since most immigrants invest in their countries of origin, the remittances contribute to the opening and attraction of new businesses (Orozco 2004, Lowell and Garza 2000).[2] Independent of the national origin of the group studied, research studies provide evidence that remittances are principally being directed towards current day-to-day expenses. That is, the money is used to supplement the family budget of those who stayed, for the acquisition of home appliances, home improvements (remodeling and construction), and the acquisition of short-term consumer goods (Massey and Basem 1992; Taylor et al. 1996). This study also shows that Brazilians primarily direct their remittances to their families in Brazil in order to contribute to increasing the consumer power of the family members who did not emigrate. However, as Susan Eckestein points out "first, remittances that may be good for individuals are not necessarily unequivocally good for states . . . Second, while remittances benefit recipients, in the Third World individuals vary in access to transnational income-sharing networks. As a consequence, remittances are not a substitute for other sources of assistance. Third, remittances may generate consequences that recipients or the state do not envision or even desire" (Eckestein 2003, 1).

Among the Brazilians who emigrate, a great many plan to send remittances periodically. For this reason, the exchange policy is perhaps the factor that most directly encourages Brazilians to emigrate. As they are "target earners," the value of the dollar makes it possible for them to earn more in less time and, consequently, to return to Brazil having saved enough money to buy land, real estate, or to open a small business. From the beginning of Brazilian emigration in the 1980s, the exchange policy maintained the dollar substantially above the value of Brazilian currency, with the exception of the period from 1994 to 1999, corresponding to the first administration of Fernando Henrique Cardoso. In those years, the dollar and the *real* (the Brazilian currency) were equalized. The impact of the exchange policy in the city of Governador Valadares—the Brazilian city with the greatest number of émigrés—caused perceptible changes in the real estate market and in civil construction. In some of the city's neighborhoods, several apartment buildings awaited the infusion of a larger amount of dollars to be finished. At the same time, the construction of new buildings stagnated. Civil construction and the real estate market entered into recession.

Although there has been no research[3] on the effects of remittances in Governador Valadares after this period, according to the President of the Municipal Counsel on Food Supply, CONSEA, in an interview given for this study, the price of rural real estate has risen to the point of becoming inaccessible to local residents, as a function of the interest of émigrés in purchasing land. This occurred after the exchange rate became once again favorable to the dollar in the early years of the twenty first century: "the entrance of dollars into the rural sector has the effect of overvaluing real estate—if you take into account the profitability of the property, the price that rural real estate has acquired in the market makes no sense. Rural real estate does not have much importance for local production in productive terms, but it does as a reserve fund for émigrés. The entry of dollars is prejudicial for those who are trying to produce." The price of land became inflated and agricultural production fell once the émigrés began acquiring land for investment, with no intention of production in the short term.

While some economists and multilateral agencies believe that remittances represent a stable source of revenue and thus contribute to the stability of the domestic economy (Ratha, 2003), the case of Governador Valadares seems to show that remittances can cause other forms of instability. Dollars cause inflation in some sectors of the local economy and dependence on the continued influx of dollars, especially in the real estate market and civil construction. In both cases, the two factors are closely related to the domestic exchange policy, or rather, the fluctuation in the rate of exchange.

As we saw, the literature has emphasized that remittances contribute to the reduction of poverty when they are used to supplement income. Is this the case for Brazilians? Although, according to U.S. standards, Brazilian immigrants are in the category of "low wage family," according to Brazilian standards, these families are not considered poor. The poor in Brazil do not emigrate, if for no other reason than they have no way of financing the voyage. Even with regard to other groups, several authors have shown that immigrants do not belong to the poorest social strata of their countries of origin (Portes 1997). The relevant fact is that the majority of these families belong to the Brazilian lower middle class. It is a social sector that has been losing its consumer power over the past two decades and is threatened with poverty, that is, of entering into a process of downward social mobility. Under these conditions, the positive effect of remittances is evident and immediate, not for relieving poverty, but for avoiding it.

The effects of remittances are visible in cities and in families, but, from the macroeconomic point of view, they have gone unnoticed. The money is distributed throughout the émigrés' hundreds of cities of origin. However, according to the CEPAL, Brazil is the second largest recipient of remittances in Latin America; Mexico is ahead of it, and just after it is Colombia. In 2004, Mexicans remitted $16.62 billion US dollars, that is, 2.56% of the GDP (source: IDB and OCDE). Brazilians, on the other hand, sent $5.6 billion US dollars, or the equivalent of .93% of the GDP.[4] It is interesting to observe, however, that if we compare Brazil and Mexico, Mexicans send proportionally less money, given that the Mexican population in the United States is thirteen times larger than the Brazilian population residing there. However, Mexico receives only three times more remittances than Brazil.

Parallel to the discussion involving the impact of remittances, researchers have analyzed governmental policies relative to remittances. They have been the object of public policy in several Latin American countries. The Mexican government has established policies to direct remittances to productive investments (Torres 2001). In Cuba, government policies intended to attract and facilitate the influx of remittances have promoted changes in the country's entire financial system (Eckestein and Barberia 2001). In the case of Brazil, remittances have not yet been the object of government public policy. Since the year 2000, however, they have been the object of the interest of some public agencies (the Bank of Brazil and the Federal Savings Bank) and of agencies that encourage entrepreneurship (Brazilian Support Service for Micro and Small Businesses, or SEBRAE). SEBRAE, meanwhile, is developing a program directed exclusively at Brazilians who have emigrated to Japan. The Ministry of Social Welfare has also taken some initiatives to attract the contribution of Brazilian émigrés to the retirement fund, but has not yet put together any program with this objective. Brazil does not yet have a migratory policy, just as it does not have public policies directed at émigrés or their remittances.

Methodology

This article is based on field research carried out in two parts.[5] The first part was conducted in Boston, Massachusetts, and the second in Governador Valadares (state of Minas Gerais), in 2004. In Boston, the research had the following objectives: to identify the sociodemographic profile of Brazilian émigrés who send remittances, and to estimate the frequency, value, end use, and destination of these remittances. Questionnaires were administered to 252 Brazilian immigrants over 18 years of age in the cities of Cambridge and Somerville (located in the Boston metropolitan area) in May and July.[6] The interviewees were selected unsystematically in Brazilian stores. From the data obtained in the 252 interviews, a sample of 235 Brazilians was defined, after having eliminated 17 interviews that were outliers. The survey was carried out by means of a multiple choice questionnaire, although there was a final open-ended question in which the interviewee could add anything he or she wished; or something that had not been asked. We opted to conduct the survey among people who send remittances because they rarely receive the attention of researchers who, in general, direct their interviews towards the recipients (Orozco 2004). However, in order to increase the scope of the field research within a transnational perspective, we also interviewed families in Brazil who are beneficiaries of remittances, specifically in the city of Governador Valadares. Back in Boston, ten questionnaires were administered to Brazilian owners of remittance agencies in the month of July, with the objective of obtaining supplemental information about the profile of the remitters and their remittances. Thus, the sample from the field research is not representative and merely indicates possible tendencies.

The city of Governador Valadares was chosen because it is the city with the greatest number of émigrés in Brazil. The field research conducted in that city had the following goals: 1) To investigate the impact of remittances on three families through in-depth interviews (in May and July). The families were chosen because they had been pioneers in emigration to the United States. Twelve in-depth interviews were conducted with members of these families. 2) To identify Nongovernmental Organizations (secular or religious) that benefited from remittances and to analyze the manner in which the money is being sent and employed. Twenty-four questionnaires were administered to representatives of NGOs, after conducting fact-gathering in city hall and in the city's churches regarding occasional support sent by Brazilian émigrés (October to November).

Brazilian Immigrants: The General Population and Those Who Send Remittances

Relations between Brazil and the United States that indirectly supported Brazilian emigration were reported in the 1940s (Martes 2002). In the 1960s, the first record is made of Brazilians who emigrated to the United States. But it is in the 1980s that this movement acquires its mass character (Sales 1999 and Margolis 1994). Ten years after its explosion, that is, in the 1990s, the points of origin of emigration are spread throughout practically all of the states of Brazil, although the there is a concentration in Minas Gerais (Martes 2000).

According to the 2000 U.S. Census, there are currently 247,020 Brazilians living in this country. Note that in 1980 there were, according to the same source, 47,965. The number thus jumped from 98,089 in the first year of the decade to almost 250,000 in the following decade. About 20% of the Brazilians included in the census reside in the state of Florida, followed by Massachusetts with 17%, California with 12%, and New York with 10%, which is tied with New Jersey, which also has 10%. The notion that the number of Brazilians is underestimated has been heavily emphasized by scholars (Margolis 1997). If one observes professions, level of education, and English language skills, it is easily verified that the census data do not correspond to what the researchers have found. Note the following two examples: 34.5% state that they have completed higher education and 43% state that they speak English very well. Demographic profiles drawn from Massachusetts and Florida show that the level of education is concentrated at the high school level and that there are few Brazilians who admit to speaking English well (Martes 2000 and Capuano 2003).

In 2004, the Brazilian Ministry of Foreign Relations declared that 2.5 million Brazilians had emigrated, although officially only 1.8 million Brazilians were to be found outside the country:[7] "officially" because these are the people who emigrated and voluntarily registered with the Brazilian embassy or consulate (FSP, Ana Flor, July 4, 2004). Insofar as Brazilian emigration is not documented, technically it is unknown how many Brazilians currently reside in the United States. Whatever the number is, since Brazilian immigrants have been characterized as *target earners* (Margolis 1994, Martes 2000), we hoped to confirm our hypothesis that the vast majority of the interviewees would state that they send periodic remittances to their cities of origin.

In fact, according to the results of the survey, of the total number of interviewees, 78% send remittances to Brazil with some regularity, 8% sent them but currently no longer do, and 13% never sent them (1% did not respond).

The data show that there are no significant differences in the sociodemographic profile of those who send and those who don't send remittances, except with regard to gender, marital status, and having children or not. Of the 176 Brazilians who send remittances to Brazil, 64% are male and 36% are female. Of these, a little more than half (51%) are married; 41% are single, and the rest are divorced, widowed, or other. Having or not having children and the children's place of residence (Brazil or the United States) is the variable that most affects the decision regarding sending remittances. Over half of the interviewees have no children (52%), and of those who stated that they do have children (47%), approximately half of their children live in the United States and the other half in Brazil. However, if we consider only those who send remittances, more than half have children (52%), and approximately half of these children live in Brazil and the other half in the United States. This is not surprising, because the majority of those who send remittances to Brazil have as their goal helping with family expenses.

The remaining variables, including age and level of education, do not distinguish those who send remittances from the other Brazilians interviewed. There is also no significant difference with regard to the state in which they were born and the state in which they lived prior to emigrating. Minas Gerais is the Brazilian state that is home to the greatest number of émigrés (in both groups); 42% of those interviewed lived in that state prior to emigrating. The rates for the states that follow Minas Gerais with the highest numbers of émigrés also do not change in relation to the sample of those who send remittances: São Paulo (13%), Espirito Santo (9%), Paraná (5%), and Goiás (5%). What is most notable about this data is the finding that São Paulo ranks second. Because São Paulo is the richest state in Brazil, contributing 33.4% to the GDP in 2004, we would expect less need for remittances to that state (source: SEADE).

Note that there was no relationship between sending remittances and religion, be it Catholic or Protestant. This is because, among the total number of Brazilians interviewed, 89% stated they were religious, while 90% of those who sent remittances stated that they were religious.

Being a legal immigrant or not and the length of stay in the United States are variables that do not affect the decision to send remittances to Brazil either. This is because, among those who send remittances, 84% are undocumented, 15% are legal residents, and 1% did not answer. Among the total population interviewed, 83% stated that they were undocumented, 16% that they were legal residents, and 1% did not respond. This result is surprising, as we were working under the hypothesis that the longer the length of time in the United States and the closer to legal residency, the weaker would be the ties that Brazilians had with Brazil, and therefore the chances that they would be sending remittances would be lower.

Use of Remittances

According to the IDB, remittances are indispensable to the survival of millions of families and for the welfare of many developing economies. Almost two thirds of immigrants send money regularly to their family members who remained in the country of origin. Among Brazilians, the vast majority of those who send remittances have as their goal helping their families, following the previously confirmed tendency of other Latino immigrants. According to the IDB, more than 1.3 million Brazilians receive money from relatives who live abroad. The table below summarizes the results of the survey with regard to the purpose and use of remittances.

Table I. Purpose and Use of Remittances

In Brazil you have	Brazilians who send remittances	**City that receives remittances**	Brazilians who send remittances
Businesses	5%	Governador Valadares	9%
Financial Investments	16%	Ipatinga	3%
Debt	6%	Vitória	3%
Family Members You Help	76%	Goiânia	3%
Real Estate	25%	Curitiba	3%
Organizations	4%	São Paulo	3%
Other Commitments	2%	Belo Horizonte	2%
No Answer	5%	Sorocaba	2%
*Multiple Choice	N = 176	Other	38%
		No Answer	25%

The first conclusion from the data presented in this table is that the item "Family Members You Help" appears as the main object of remittances, including 76% of the respondents.[8]

The interviews conducted with the families in Governador Valadares offer us a broader understanding of the significance and use of the money remitted. The Silva family for example, consists of 11 siblings, most of whom live in the United States. A portion of the earnings of the émigré siblings is sent to the relatives who have remained in Governador Valadares, the father of the family being the main beneficiary. The money is principally sent for the monthly payment of current expenses such as healthcare, education, and the purchase of durable consumer goods, in addition to the purchase of real estate. These remittances, directly or indirectly, helped to purchase the father's house and that of one of the sisters. In addition, the remittances financed a small videogame store for one of the sisters. The business, however, was not successful due to lack of experience and operating capital. All of the siblings send some money periodically, except one who was arrested crossing the border into the United States through Mexico. Because he had to pay bail, he has not managed yet to earn enough income to send money to Brazil.

According to one of the sisters, "my father has been supported very well by his children. Because he is retired and his children send him money every month . . . Every month is sacred: the money comes. Can you imagine if he had to live on minimum wage alone? [NB: The minimum wage in Brazil was about $120 US dollars per month in 2006.] So, he has a health plan . . . He's now supported well by his children. If he needs anything, he has everything he needs from them. The house was remodeled. They pay for the health plan . . . And then they sent a car for him for when he needs to go out, to go to the doctor. So I think he's happy, he's very grateful." The other sister adds: "We all began from the bottom, but we always had a house to live in, which is very important. I was born on the farm, but then we moved to a small town, and then here because of our studies in the 1980s. There were eleven children in 4 rooms. It was all very crowded, with those full bunk beds. Then we made it here in Valadares. One worked in a pharmacy, another on the police force, another was a teacher."

The story of these two women leads toward one conclusion: they feel threatened by poverty and their siblings' emigration has made it possible for them and their father to maintain lower-middle class status. If it weren't for the remittances, they would have to pay rent, their father wouldn't have health insurance, they would have a lower monthly income, etc. In the following interview, the same family seems to make even clearer the difficulties faced by the Brazilian middle class in gaining access to education and thus gaining social mobility: "The only thing that bothers me is missing them. But we can keep in touch by telephone, by the emails that they send. Now with the computer it has become even better. There is nothing better than having a computer in the house. But there has also been a lot of progress because now each one has his own home. So, if they were still here, for example, let's say me, up to today I have only this house. And they [the ones who emigrated] are even the ones who pay my college tuition. If they were here, how would I get the 500 *reais* to pay my tuition each month?"

What this interviewee tells us is that part of the money that is sent is used to pay her monthly college tuition and that, for someone from the lower middle class like her, the biggest priority is to be free of the monthly rent for the house where she lives. It isn't by chance that the second most mentioned item in the survey conducted in Boston with regard to the use of remittances involves the acquisition of a home of one's own. The second family, the Mendes family, believes that buying real estate is the best investment they can make with the remittances: "If my family had not managed to go to the U.S.A., I would be worse off. . . . Because they went there, we were able to buy two houses. We have already sold one house and we opened a grocery shop. My other sister bought an apartment. My aunt and uncle also bought an apartment. Another aunt had a house here and now is working hard to buy a house there." So, "they invested in real estate; that is a desire that a person has, to buy real estate today, and tomorrow, or in the future, he knows that if he decides to sell it, he can. It is an investment that they are making so that the money doesn't stagnate."

According to the "patriarch" of the Monteiro family, "first my son-in-law went and nine months later . . . he brought my daughter. That was nine years ago. It was good because it enabled us to buy a little house and now we are opening a grocery shop. Now the young man has a son there. The only thing that she bought here was an apartment that cost 30,000 *reais* at the time. They have no desire to ever return here." Interviewer: "But if they don't intend to return, why did they buy an apartment here?" Answer: "To leave the money for me."

From these accounts, we can conclude that the purchase of real estate can have three objectives: to help those who stayed to be free of rent (the item that weighs most heavily on the income of the Brazilian middle class); as an investment for those who have emigrated and who wish to return, or to help supplement the income of those who stayed, by renting out the property. It is important to note that the acquisition of real estate in the city of origin shows everyone living there that "that guy made good."

Returning to the other items on the survey related to the use of remittances, "businesses" generally refers to the opening of a small commercial establishment or the acquisition of a small rural property used for production. The use of remittances to open businesses is illustrated by the Campos family. The first of the siblings emigrated and brought the rest. With the money that they managed to put away, they were able to open various businesses—a motel, a restaurant, and a bookstore—besides buying an apartment. They also helped buy property for the relatives who stayed in Brazil; remittances helped to buy a grocery shop and are used for supporting their mother.

According to one of the sisters interviewed who stayed in Governador Valadares, "one brother had some motels, restaurants, and also bought an apartment . . . later he lost it all. Another bought an apartment . . . I bought an apartment, too. In this family, some of the siblings emigrated to New York due to the difficulty of finding employment in Brazil, and now they send remittances of money to their relatives, especially to our mother, who stayed here."

This short passage calls attention to a frequent occurrence: those who managed to open a business in Brazil with the money they earned in the

United States rapidly lost everything. The failure of the businesses is easily explained by the lack of previous experience and interference by government agencies that could instead be encouraging the channeling of remittances into productive investments. Therefore, in the face of this situation, the most rational thing is to buy real estate and not to risk losing everything that they managed to earn.

The interviews suggest a more or less common routine. Within each family, the remittances are sent primarily for maintenance expenses. Secondly, they are sent for the purchase of real estate, especially homes, to "get out of paying rent." Thirdly, remittances are used to buy real estate as an investment or for income. In fourth place is the purchase of real estate to open a business and, finally, remittances are used to finance small businesses. Obviously, not all of the families follow this pattern or the order set out here.

Returning to the survey, the item "financial investments" refers above all to opening a savings account, and "debts" refers to the assistance received to finance the cost of emigration or debts incurred in Brazil because of the failure of a business that was opened prior to emigration. However, none of the families interviewed mentioned these items in the interviews that were conducted; rather, they only appeared in the survey carried out in Boston.

The last item to appear on the survey is "organizations" and, although it represents merely 4%, it is an important finding of this study because previously there was no record at all of any kind of organization in Brazil. This item will be revisited below when we present the data gathered in conjunction with the NGOs in Governador Valadares.

Destination of Remittances

The money remitted to Brazil by the émigrés is sent to various Brazilian municipalities. In the survey some concentration can be observed in the following cities: Governador Valadares (14%), Ipatinga (5%), São Paulo and Goiânia (4%), and Vitória and Belo Horizonte (3%). We believe this is a relevant finding of this study because, considering that the destination points are as spread out as they seem to be, it is possible that the impact of remittances is of little significance in the economic dynamic of these four municipalities, with the exception of the cities of Governador Valadares and Ipatinga in the state of Minas Gerais. This is because the other cities noted above are state capitals of the Brazilian federation and have high demographic density. The other cities that appear in this item and that have at least 2% representation in the sample are: Criciúma, in the state of Santa Catarina, Curitiba, in the state of Paraná, and Sorocaba in the state of São Paulo. Of these, only Curitiba is the seat of a state government. Thus, it is also possible that the economic dynamics of the cities of Criciúma and Sorocaba are being affected by remittances coming from international migration.

The remaining cities cover 56% of the interviewees, a finding that indicates that the destination points are spread out considerably throughout Brazil. On the one hand, this may mean that since there is little concentration, the effects of remittances on the local economic dynamic are not very significant. On the other hand, in the case of very small cities, the monetary dynamic may be affected by remittances, as is the case in Mantena, in the state of Minas Gerais, and other small cities in Brazil.

Amount: Possible Estimates

From the sample of 235 interviewees we calculate that the average remittance amount is $6,535 US dollars per interviewee per year, with an average number of 10.11 remittances per year and an average value of $646.10 US dollars per remittance, as the graph below shows.

Since there is no data regarding the exact number of Brazilians who live in the United States and considering that more than 80% of them are

Graph 1. Concentration of Amounts Sent

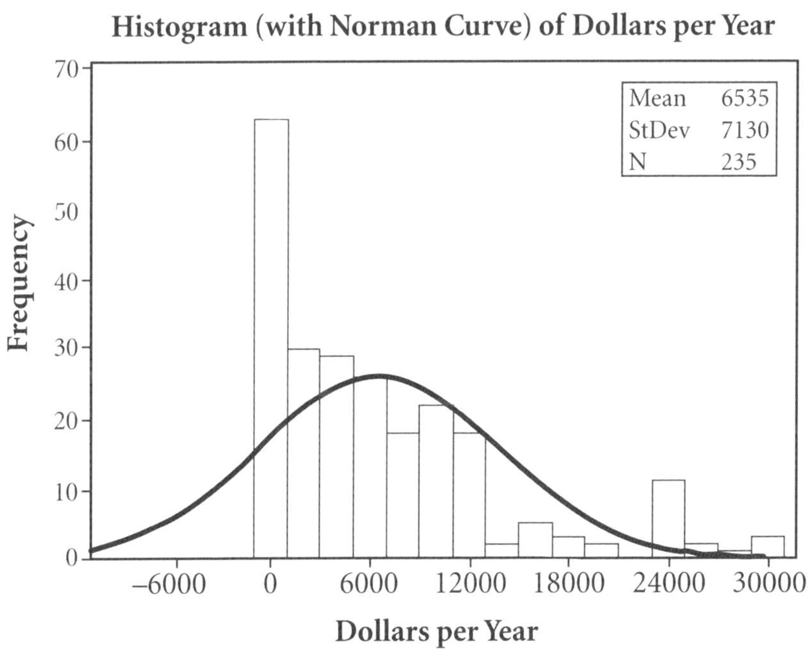

undocumented (Martes, 2000), we have opted not to define an exact value for remittances, but rather to work with possible scenarios as a function of the available data. The scenarios vary according to the statistic selected for number of Brazilians in the United States. Such fluctuation, in turn, depends on the source of data that supplies the number of Brazilian residents in the United States. Thus, the Brazilian Ministry of Foreign Relations estimated one million U.S. Brazilian residents in 2005; while the 2000 U.S. Census estimated about 213,000. Possible values of remittances sent according to the number of Brazilian residents in the United States can be seen in the graph below.

Remittance Agencies: Boston

According to scholars, remittances are primarily made by businesses, not by banks (Orozco 2004). This is also the case for Brazilians. The majority of remittances are sent by small Brazilian businesses. Officially, the agencies that make remittances to Brazil are the Bank of Brazil and Western Union (a partnership), the Federal Savings Bank, and VIGO. Note that there are no credit unions.

The owners of 10 Brazilian remittance firms in Somerville and Cambridge were interviewed. No business deals exclusively in remittances: three are variety stores, and the rest deal in clothing or groceries, are travel agencies, or sell cellular phones and credit cards. None of the businesses has been opened for less than three years, and none for more than eight

Graph 2. Amounts Sent x Brazilian Population

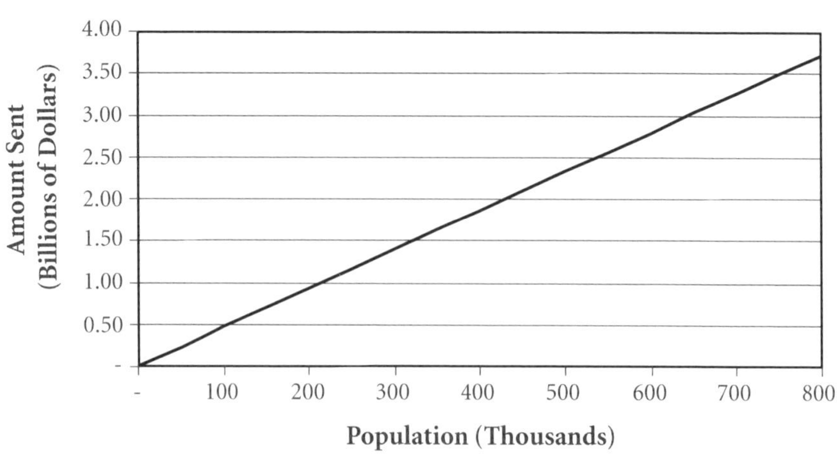

years. Only four owners gave information about the amounts of remittances that their establishments send: $400,000 US dollars, 7,500 US dollars, $20,000 US dollars and $100,000 US dollars. The money is sent, in descending order, to the following cities: Governador Valadares, Vitória and Belo Horizonte, Jaurú: Mantenópolis, Criciúma and Conselheiro Pena; São Paulo and Ipatinga, Goiânia, Porto Alegre, Florianópolis, Rio de Janeiro, Coperac, Resplendor, Barra do São Francisco, Curitiba, Anápolis, Engenheiro Caldas, and Sobrália. When asked about the frequency with which most senders make remittances to Brazil, five agency owners said every fifteen days, and five said monthly. With regard to the fees charged, the majority said that they charged ten dollars plus 4% of the amount sent, if it was sent in dollars.

The cost to the immigrants of making remittances underwent a reduction from 14% to 8%. This was because multilateral agencies have encouraged the reduction of fees due to the increase in competition between agencies and banks. However, the cost of sending remittances is greater for immigrants who send money to Latin America and the Caribbean than to other parts of the world, given the low level of competition between financial institutions (IDB—*Sending Money Home*). Some Brazilian banks began, in 2003 and 2004, to enter into partnerships with American institutions that send remittances: Itaú Bank with MoneyGram, Bradesco with Bank of America, etc. The IDB and IMF have played an important role in Brazil in opening the discussion of encouraging the formalization of remittances (through institutionally formalized agencies and not through informal market dollar sellers), and of encouraging the participation of other agencies to increase competition and reduce the fees charged to effect the transfer of funds.

Remittances and Community Support

The role of remittances in community organizations in the émigrés' cities of origin has been little explored as yet (Garza and Lowell 2002). The importance of this dimension does not involve merely a possible economic impact that the money can offer to the organizations, but also the formation of *transnational communities.* In the opinion of some authors, the remittances will have a fundamental role in the creation of networks capable of linking the two ends of the migratory flow: origin and destination (Portes, Guarnizo, and Landolt 1999). In this regard, the major research efforts have concerned primarily communities in the Dominican Republic (Itzigsohn 1999, Levitt 2001), Mexico (de la Garza and Szekely 1997), and Central America. The geographic propinquity of these regions to the

United States and long-established migration networks raise questions concerning the applicability of this model to more remote and recent communities of origin.

In the survey conducted in the first part of this research in Boston, we found with certain surprise that 4% of the total number of interviewees had declared that a part of the remittances sent were destined to help some organization in their cities of origin. Would the remittances be playing an important role in the financing of the organizations that receive them, especially in the nonprofit sector? What type of assistance would they effectively be receiving? With the objective of clarifying these questions, we carried out research in Governador Valadares and were able to identify 24 institutions as potential recipients. Of this total, nine stated that they had never received any type of assistance from Brazilian émigrés, and 13 stated that they had received assistance at least once. The results are not conclusive, that is, they merely permit us to have an approximate idea of the kind of support that Brazilian émigrés have given to philanthropic and sociocultural organizations in Brazil. Since there are different types of assistance, we opted to classify them as follows: 1) occasional and sporadic contributions, 2) occasional but significant contributions, and 3) regular contributions of determined amounts.

1. Occasional and Sporadic Contributions. The five organizations that receive occasional remittances were not able to specify either the amount or the date received. With the exception of one organization, which is a nursing home, all of the others provide social assistance to children and adolescents. Without exception, all are connected to the Catholic Church. The contributions did not come only from the United States, but also from Italy and Switzerland. Only one organization received support for two years from a Brazilian NGO in Boston, the Brazilian Children's Foundation (BCF). According to the representative interviewed: "BCF sent $1,000 US dollars monthly. With this money, a car, a refrigerator, a washing machine, and some beds were purchased. However, the BCF practically closed its doors after September 11."

2. Occasional but Significant Contributions. Two organizations are included in this category: one Catholic and one Spiritist.[9] The first is a childcare center and the second a nursing home. According to the official interviewed, "Everything began when the priest from here contacted the priest from Framingham (MA). He organized a campaign to raise funds for our organization. Two campaigns were

organized, one in 1997 and one in 2004: the first to buy the lot, which cost $8000 US dollars, and the second in 2004 raised $6,000 US dollars. Without this money we wouldn't have our own center." The second organization received donations from Brazilians residing abroad who were relatives of the directors of the organization. Two donations were made: "the first of $2,000 US dollars and the second of $3,000 US dollars. The first donation was applied to the construction of the addition to the institute, a structure of 3,600 square meters. The money from the second donation was used to re-roof the nursing home. The institution does not depend on these resources for its operation."

3. Regular and Fixed Amounts. Of the four organizations that fall into this category, one is connected to the Assembly of God Church, two are Catholic, and the last is Spiritist. The first received monthly remittances. According to its representative, "It all began when a Brazilian called the United States and asked his brother, who is an Assembly of God pastor, to raise some money for the organization. Since then, $300 US dollars per month has been sent. Once, we received $15,000 US dollars when we needed to finish building the center. The $3,600 US dollars received annually are used to cover the following expenses: employee salaries, food, and transportation." According to the representative of the second organization: "we always receive help from Brazilians who live abroad. They contact us by telephone or they bring it when they come here on vacation. For three years clothing, canes, toys, walkers, wheelchairs, etc. have arrived from the United States. Some people bring cameras, DVD players, and other items that are given as prizes for the Bingo games that we organize to raise funds. There is one person who sends clothing every 4 months. They send from $500 to $1,000 dollars at least once a year." The third organization received financial support from immigrants who live in Boston and in Portugal: "The donations began in 2003 when I wrote to the Catholic communities of Boston. I asked for funds to remodel the temple and for social assistance work. The Brazilian priests from there helped us to promote the campaign during Christmas of 2003, sending $12,000 US dollars." The fourth organization is connected to a Brazilian organization headquartered in Framingham. In Valadares, the group conducts computer courses for young people and consciousness-raising campaigns in the schools dealing with citizenship and transition. The

money is sent monthly, in the amount of $1,300 *reais*. According to the interviewee, the group attempts to "copy" acts of American civic responsibility because it is based on the "idea that the main problem with Brazilians is a lack of civic consciousness."

In addition to these groups, it is necessary to mention the existence of the Sister Cities Program between Governador Valadares and Framingham (Massachusetts).[10] The initiatives towards the signing of the agreement began in the late 1990s. Although it has great potential for exchange, the program today basically exists only on paper.

Conclusion: What Is the Impact of the Remittances?

To summarize the data presented, the research concludes that almost 80% of the Brazilians interviewed send remittances to Brazil with some regularity. The sociodemographic profile of the Brazilian population of Boston is quite close to the sociodemographic profile of the Brazilians who send remittances, except with regard to the variable of children. Although the results of this research are merely indicative (because we did not work with a representative sample), Brazilians who have children are more likely to send money to Brazil. This data is consistent with the fact that the majority of those who send remittances to Brazil (76%) have the goal of assisting with expenses and helping family members. The other goals are: financing the purchase of real estate in Brazil (25%), application to financial investments (16%), payment of debt (6%), and assisting organizations (4%).[11]

The qualitative interviews conducted with families in Governador Valadares reinforce the importance of money sent with the goal of helping relatives who stayed, especially supplementing retirement income, payment of tuition, remodeling or buying a home, and supplementing income. Assisting organizations, although it represents 4% of the answers to the survey, was not shown to be significant in the findings of the field research carried out in Governador Valadares. The majority of the organizations studied stated that they received sporadic help, although the interviewees were unable to state with clarity either the exact amounts or the frequency with which remittances are sent. Only one organization stated that it depended on the remittances that were sent for its operation. Also note that groups connected to churches have a greater chance of receiving help from Brazilians abroad, because they can already count on an institutionally organized network, principally through specific campaigns of limited duration and purpose, such as, for example, for the construction or remodeling of a center.

With regard to the locations to which the remittances are being sent, some concentration is observed in the cities of Governador Valadares, Ipatinga; São Paulo; Goiânia; Vitória; Belo Horizonte; Criciúma, Curitiba, and Sorocaba. Given that remittances are not concentrated but rather spread out throughout different municipalities, it becomes difficult to calculate the impact of the money sent on local economies.

The research suggests that the average amount of money sent is $6,535 per interviewee per year, with an average frequency of 10.11 remittances per year and an average value of $646.10 per remittance.[12] In calculating the total amount of remittances, it should be emphasized that it is subject to the variation in the estimates of the number of Brazilians who live in the United States; the numbers vary from 1 million (Brazilian Ministry of Foreign Relations) to 213,000 (2000 U.S. Census).

Since Brazilian émigrés belong to the lower middle class, there is nothing to lead one to believe that remittances are contributing to reducing poverty in their cities of origin, as researchers have observed for other Latin American immigrants. In general, the American literature identifies the recipients of remittances as low-income families. Here, perhaps, there is an important difference. Brazilian immigrants are considered poor in the United States (according to U.S. standards), but their families are not considered poor according to Brazilian standards. If we use minimum wage as a criterion of classification of monetary poverty (Hoffmann, 2001), those who receive up to one quarter of the minimum wage are considered below the poverty line (indigent), and those who receive up to half are considered poor. This is not the case of Brazilian émigrés and their families, whose incomes are higher, independent of remittances (Martes 2000). Other factors can also be considered: Brazilian émigrés, in their majority, are not illiterate, they did not come primarily from rural areas, they were not unemployed when they emigrated, and they did not leave the poorest region of Brazil, which is the Northeast. Thus, this research suggests that the impact of remittances should be sought in the lower middle class, just as understanding the causes and effects of emigration in Brazil means questioning what is happening with the middle class of that country.

The main motivation of Brazilians who emigrate is not to help the family, but rather, and above all, to acquire goods in Brazil with the money they save while working in the United States. It is a matter of a medium to long-term objective. This does not mean that they do not help their relatives who stayed in Brazil. In other words, the major impact of remittances can be observed in the family budget, as the results of the survey show, even though this is not the major goal of those who emigrate. Helping is a short-term and relatively easy goal given the difference between the value of the dollar and the Brazilian currency. One hundred dollars is not difficult to obtain for someone who works in the United States, but it represents precious aid to the family budget of the lower middle class in Brazil. It is like climbing a staircase, in which helping the family may be the first step, but not the final destination.

The remittances sent to improve the lives of those who stayed behind are also a sort of compensation for absence. The commitment to send them periodically can be understood—within the interpersonal universe of this macro-phenomenon called migration—as "Penelope's task." Remitting and receiving the money that is sent from so far away means maintaining ties, so as to negate the disconnection that the distance threatens to impose. From time to time the money reaffirms the commitment of return—be it physical or symbolic.

Acknowledgements

I am extremely grateful to Beth Ransdell Vinkler of Benedictine University in Lisle, Illinois, for her work in translating this article, and to the Getúlio Vargas Research Center (GV Pesquisa), the research arm of the School of Management of the Getúlio Vargas Foundation in São Paulo (Escola de Administração de Empresas de São Paulo, Fundação Getúlio Vargas) for its support in financing my research and the translation of the text.

I thank George Martine, Weber Soares, and Lorena Barberia for their contributions to this text.

Notes

1. Beginning in the second half of 2004, even stricter rules for the acquisition of visas were put into force, except for children under 16 years old and people over age 60, affecting the departure of skilled professionals, business people, and executives.
2. This topic is dealt with in "*Lições Fora de Casa—Emigração de Retorno e Empreendedorismo*" ["Lessons Away from Home—Emigration of Return and Entrepreneurialism"], Martes, Ana Cristina Braga 2006 (working paper, GV Pesquisa, Janeiro, 2006).
3. A very interesting study by Weber Soares includes the impact of dollars on the local economy in 1994.
4. At this writing the Brazilian economy was the twelfth largest in the world ($605 billion US dollars), despite having previously occupied eighth place. Brazilian industrial production in 2004 constituted 38.93% of the GDP (source: Ipeadata). Brazil received more money from remittances than from

international sources, which accounted for merely 0.7% of the GDP, or 4.32 billion US dollars in 2004 (source: Embratur).

5. I thank Tania Christopoulos and Leonardo Barone, the assistant researchers of this work.
6. The interviewees were selected randomly in Brazilian stores in the city of Somerville, and in Cambridge in the two public parks in the Boston metropolitan area.
7. Our goal here is to analyze only Brazilian emigration to the United States. According to Itamaraty, Brazilian emigration, calculated at 1.96 million, is distributed as follows: 784 thousand in the United States, 378 thousand in Paraguay, 274 thousand in Japan, 86 thousand in Portugal, 67 thousand in Italy, 45 thousand in Switzerland, 45 thousand in Germany, 44 thousand in Argentina, 30 thousand in England, 26 thousand in Surinam, 21 thousand in Spain, 20 thousand in France, 16 thousand in French Guiana, 15 thousand in Canada, 11 thousand in Israel, 10 thousand in Holland, 10 thousand in Bolivia, 9.7 thousand in Uruguay, 8.7 thousand in Belgium, 8.5 thousand in Venezuela, 7 thousand in Sweden, 6.7 thousand in Australia, and 5.9 thousand in Lebanon. The Itamaraty data was published in the newspaper *Folha de São Paulo*, August 15, 2003.
8. The goal of helping family members was also the use most often mentioned in Goza's (1998) research on remittances. See also Siqueira 2006.
9. For more details on the distinction between the various Protestant denominations, see the chapter by Paul Freston in this volume.
10. The Sister Cities Program was inaugurated in the United States in 1956 with the goal of promoting cultural, economic, education, scientific, and social exchange among municipalities all over the world. Currently, thousands of cities in 120 countries participate in this program.
11. Note: a multiple choice item.
12. This average value per remittance of $646.10 US dollars contrasts with the amounts presented by the IDB (Bendixen, "Studies of the Recipients of Remittances in Brazil, April-May 2004"). According to their figures, there are 1.3 million Brazilians who receive 9.7 remittances per year, with an average unit value of $428 US dollars, which make up a total of $5.4 billion US dollars, 50% of this amount coming from the United States, that is, $2.7 billion US dollars.

References

Barberia, Lorena. 2004. "Remittances to Cuba: An Evaluation of Cuban and U.S. Government Policy Measures." In *The Cuban Economy at the Start of the Twenty-first Century*. Ed. Jorge I. Dominguez, Omar Everleny Perez Villanueva, and Lorena Barberia. Cambridge: Harvard University Press.

Bendixen & Associates. 2004. "*Estudos sobre os destinatários de remessas no Brasil, abril-maio 2004.*"

Capuano, Adriana. 2003. "O caminho sem volta—classe social e etnicidade entre os brasileiros na Flórida." In *Fronteiras cruzadas: etnicidade, gênero e redes sociais*. Ed. A. C. B. Martes and S. Fleischer. São Paulo: Paz e Terra.

Cohen, Jeffrey H. 2005. "Remittance Outcomes and Migration: Theoretical Contests, Real Opportunities." *Studies in Comparative International Development* 40(1): 88–112.

De la Garza, Rodolfo O. and Szekely, Gabriel. 1997. "Policy, Politics, and Emigration: Reexamining the Mexican Experience." In *At the Crossroads: Mexican Migration and U.S. Policy*. Ed. Frank Bean, Rodolfo de la Garza, Bryan R. Roberts, and Sidney Weintraub. Lanham: Rowman and Littlefield.

De Sipio, Louis. 2000. *Sending Money Home . . . For Now: Remittances and Immigrant Adaptation in the United States*. Washington, D.C.: InterAmerican Dialogue and the Tomás Rivera Policy Institute.

Dominguez, Jorge I.; Villanueva, Omar Everleny Pérez; Barberia, Lorena. Eds. 2004. *The Cuban Economy at the Start of the Twenty-First Century*. Cambridge: Harvard University Press.

Eckestein, Susan and Lorena Barberia. 2001. "Cuban-American Cuba Visits: Public Policy, Private Practices." A Report of the Mellon-MIT Inter-University Program on Non-Governmental Organizations (NGOs).

Eckestein, Susan. 2003. "Diasporas and Dollars: Transnational Ties and the Transformation of Cuba." Cambridge: MIT Working Paper # 16, February.

Fleischer, Soraya. 2002. *Passando a América a limpo—o trabalho de housecleaners brasilerias em Boston, Massachucetts*. São Paulo: Annablume.

Giddens, Anthony. 1990. *The Consequences of Modernity*. Stanford: Stanford University Press.

Goza, Franklin. 1998. "An Examination of Remittance Activity Among Brazilian Immigrants in the U.S. and Canada." Anais do XI Encontro Nacional de Estudos Populacionais da ABEP. Caxambu.

Hoffmann, Rodolfo. 2001. *A distribuição de renda no Brasil no período 93–99*. Campinas: Unicamp, IE.

Itzigsohn, José. 2004. "Dominicans in Providence: The Formation of a Transnational Community in a Secondary City." In *Dominican Migration: Transnational Perspectives*. Ed. Ernesto Sagás and S. E. Molina. Gainesville: University of Florida Press.

———. 1999. "Mapping Dominican Transnationalism: Narrow and Broad Transnational Practices." *Ethnic and Racial Studies* 22(2): 316–339.

Kapur, Devesh and John McHale. 2003. "Migration's New Payoff." *Foreign Policy.*

Levitt, Peggy. 2001. *The Transnational Villagers*. Berkeley: University of California Press.

Lowell, Lindsay and de la Garza, Rodolfo. 2000. "The Developmental Role of Remittances in U.S. Communities and in Latin American Countries: An Examination of Remittance Activity among Brazilian Immigrants in the U.S. and Canada." Final Report.

Margolis, Maxine. 1993. *Little Brazil.* Princeton: Princeton University Press.

———. 1997. *Invisible Minority: Brazilians in New York City.* Boston: Allyn and Bacon.

Martes, Ana Cristina B. 2000. *Brasileiros Nos Estados Unidos– um estudo sobre imigrantes em Massachusetts.* São Paulo: Editora Paz e Terra.

———. 2001, 2003. "Empresários Brasileiros em Cambridge e East Boston. Relatório de Pesquisa Nos. 45/2001 and 54/2003." São Paulo: Núcleo de Pesquisas e Publicações da Escola de Administração de Empresas da Fundação Getulio Vargas (NPP/ EAESP/ FGV).

———. 2006. "Lições Fora de Casa—Emigração de Retorno e Empreendedorismo," (forthcoming).

———. 2008. "Neither Hispanic, Nor Black: We're Brazilians." In *The Other Latinos: Central and South Americans in the United States.* Ed. José Luis Falconi and José Antonio Mazzotti. Cambridge, Harvard University Press.

Martes, Ana Cristina Braga and Fleischer, Soraya. 2003. *Fronteiras Cruzadas—Etnicidade, Gênero e redes sociais.* São Paulo: Paz e Terra.

Martes, Ana Cristina Braga and Rodriguez, Carlos. 2003. "Church-Membership, Social Capital, and Entrepreneurship in Brazilian Communities in the U.S." In Curt H. Stiles, *Ethnic Entrepreneurship.*

Martine, George. 2005. "Population, Development, Environment Trends in a Globalized Context: Challenges for the 21st Century." In *International Conference on Trends and Problems of the World Population in the 21st Century: 50 Years since Rome 1954.* Rome.

Massey, Douglas S. and Basem, Lawrence C. 1992. "Determinants of Savings, Remittances, and Spending Patterns among U.S. Migrants in Four Mexican Communities." *Sociological Inquiry* 62(2): 185–207.

Meyers, Deborah Waller. 1998. "Migrant Remittances to Latin America: Reviewing the Literature." Washington, D.C.: Inter-American Dialogue and the Tomás Rivera Institute.

Newland, Kathleen. 2003. "Migration as a Factor in Development and Poverty Reduction." Migration Information Source, Migration Policy Institute (1 June).

Orozco, Manuel. 2001. "Globalization and Migration." *Journal of Inte- American Studies and World Affairs.*

———. 2004. "The Remittance Marketplace: Prices, Policy and Financial Institutions." PEW Reports.

Portes, Alejandro. 1997. "Globalization from Below: The Rise of Transnational Communities." Princeton University Report.

Portes, Alejandro, Guarnizo, Luis E. and Landolt, Patricia. 1999. "The Study of Transnationalism: Pitfalls and Promise of an Emergent Research Field." *Ethnic and Racial Studies* 22(2): 217–237.

Ratha, See Dilip. 2003. "Workers' Remittances: An Important and Stable Source of External Development Finance." Global Development Finance. Washington, D.C.: World Bank.

Reichert, Joshua. 1981. "The Migrant Syndrome: Seasonal U.S. Wage Labor and Rural Development in Central Mexico." *Human Organization* 40(1): 56–66.

Reis, Rossana and Sales, Teresa. 1999. *Cenas do Brasil Migrante*. São Paulo: Boitempo.

Saskia, Sassen. 1996. *Losing Control? Sovereignty in the Age of Globalization*. New York: Columbia University Press.

Siqueira, Sueli. 2006. "Migrantes empreendedores na Microrregião de Governador Valadares—Sonhos e frustrações no retorno." Tese Doutorado em Ciências Humanas–Sociologia e Política, Faculdade de Filosofia e Ciências Humanas. Universidade Federal de Minas Gerais. Belo Horizonte.

Soares, Weber. 1995. "Imigrantes e Investidores: Redefinindo a Dinâmica Imobiliária na Economia Valadarense." Tese de Mestrado, IPPUR da UFRJ.

Taylor, Edward J. 2000. "Do Government Programs 'Crowd In' Remittances?" Washington D.C.: Inter-American Dialogue and the Tomás Rivera Policy Institute.

Torres, Federico. 2001. "Migrants' Capital for Small-Scale Infrastructure and Small Enterprise Development in Mexico." Draft presented on October 9. Washington D.C.: World Bank.

United Nations. 2005. "World Economic and Social Survey 2004: International Migration." UN Department of Economics and Social Affairs.

Wucker, Michele. 2004. "Remittances: The Perpetual Migration Machine." *World Policy Journal* 21(2).

6

Brazilian Immigrant Women: Race, Ethnicity, Gender, and Transnationalism

Judith McDonnell and Cileine de Lourenço

Our intention is to explore critically the extent to which the concept of "transnational" enhances our understanding of the lives of Brazilian immigrant women in the Boston area. Even while they maintain simultaneously a significant investment in Brazil and in the United States, some of the women we interviewed find that participating in two worlds leads to feeling split and alienated from both. Therefore, being transnational can be problematic, especially as it is experienced through race, ethnicity, and gender. Our analysis highlights the connection between transnationalism, belonging and not belonging, liminality, and (in)visibility. To these ends, we examine excerpts of narratives from Brazilian immigrant women while providing general commentary on the concept of transnationalism. We also comment on the different dimensions of everyday practices of Brazilian immigrant women who live, work, mother, and nurture in the Boston area, mostly in Framingham. In this chapter we focus on the stories that Brazilian women have shared with us, as they examine and describe themselves and each other.

Methodology

This work, based on thirty fully translated and transcribed interviews, is part of a larger and on-going examination of identity negotiation among these first-generation Brazilian immigrant women living and/or working in the Boston, Massachusetts, area, mostly in Framingham. Our main interview period was June 2004 through June 2005. Each interview is about 1½ hours long, taped, in Portuguese. The interviews were conducted at the time and place most convenient to the women who generously gave their time and shared their stories. Each woman signed an informed consent attesting to her understanding of our project and completed a questionnaire about basic demographic information. Each woman is anonymous; pseudonyms are used. Because the sample is small and many of the people with whom we talked about our project could possibly know some of the respondents, we have eliminated all references to specific home locations, places of work and any other feature that might identify anyone inadvertently. The pseudonyms and oblique references, at times, seem clumsy; however, confidentiality of our informants is essential particularly during the post-9/11 era. Our interviewees were selected using modified snowball sampling. Some of the women that we contacted were willing to participate and to provide us with additional names of women among their own work and social networks. Nevertheless, given the length of time needed to complete the interview and the general difficulties of scheduling, including the reluctance of some women to talk to us out of fear, the process of building our target group of thirty respondents was long and arduous. To the extent possible, we were careful to represent a range of ages and occupations.

The thirty women we interviewed exhibit a wide range of demographic characteristics. They range in age[1] from 20 to 61, with the average being around age 36. Nine of the women are in their 20s, ten in their 30s, eight are in their 40s, two are in their 50s, and one in her 60s. Their years of experience in the United States vary from a low of 2 months (but this person had been here as a child so this was her second trip) to 22 years, with an average of about seven years. Most of the women with whom we talked are employed, with a significant number in gender-segregated occupations. Two women own small businesses and a few of them are students. Although we are purposefully vague about who works where, the jobs include cleaning homes and offices, working in retail, a variety of professional and semi-professional jobs, including in health care, and jobs related to churches. Therefore, although some of the women, as global workers, may be underemployed given their abilities, skills, and intelligence, and some of them may be discouraged workers, almost all of the women are in the paid labor force. Almost all of the women also work in the unpaid labor force in some capacity, in the "second shift" (Ehrenreich and Hochschild 2002), inadvertently reproducing U.S. patriarchal gender roles.

The issue of racial identity is explored in greater detail below, but a preliminary description here will help situate the women in the varied racial identifications that exist. Racial self-identification is complex, and most of the interviewees immediately recognized that complexity in the form of the responses that they provided to our questions about their racial identity, both in Brazil and in the United States. Most of the women gave somewhat long answers to this question but arrived at a one-word racial identification that was consistent with how they thought North Americans define them. Twelve of the women self-identified in the United States as white, and all women, except for one, identified the nuances and layers that often define racialized experiences. For example, Helena said that she was white in Brazil and that it was "hard to give up being white here." Helena's teenage child had pressured her to adopt a black identity. Several women responded that they were white in Brazil and Brazilian in the United States. Renata said she was white but a different kind of white. Lúcia said she was white in Brazil, and an immigrant or alien here. Of the nineteen women who said that in Brazil they were white, most of them saw their racial identity as being more complicated in the United States. Ten women who said they were white in Brazil thought they were categorized differently in the United States. Five of that group said that here in the United States they are non-white or some version of non-white. Many of the women recognized that once in the United States, racial identity was no longer solely a matter of self-identification or skin color. If they talked with an accent, if they were of color, if they participated in cultural events associated with Brazil, if they faced the myriad forms on which they had to check their identities, they became something else. Sometimes they had the freedom to be Brazilian, sometimes they were Hispanic, sometimes non-white, and sometimes they were immigrants. In one case, our interviewee would not or could not respond at all.

Each of the women has a different story to tell about why she came to the United States, the circumstances of her journey, with whom she traveled and what and whom she left behind. As first-generation immigrants, whom they leave behind and for whom they are still caring may make a transnational status complex and contradictory. Some of the details about their journeys will be described below as part of their stories on transnationalism.

Transnationalism

Scholars from a variety of disciplines for some time now have employed the concept "transnational" as a theoretical tool of analysis regarding immigration.[2] This concept is often held up as a corrective to assimilation, the more traditional lens for viewing the integration of immigrants (Smith 2006). In comparison to earlier waves of immigrants to the United States, people migrating now in the context of transnational possibilities have an opportunity to maintain close ties with family and friends back home, which is a different narrative from the traditional assimilation model that posited a "clean break" with the home country (Smith 2006). For women in particular, ties with the home country are necessary as they continue their gendered work of caring for others. A clean break, a tenet of the assimilation model, is neither possible nor desired. In this context, transnationalism allows for an additive model of belonging with the potential of membership in two or more societies simultaneously.

Transnationalism is also used as a lens through which to examine institutions, individual actors and agency, communities and cultural practices. There have been many studies exploring everything from the definition of the concept, its various forms and usages, the practices and elements of transnational connections and networks, the nature of the connections, such as going "back and forth," monetary remittances, and religion, the counterhegemonic and transgressive aspects, the potentially liberating character of being transnational and the degree of transnationalism among the second generation. (See, for example, Garcia 2004; Hondagneu-Sotelo 2003; Levitt 2001, Levitt 2003; Levitt and Glick Schiller 2003; Margolis 1995, 2001; Martes 2004; Mitchell 2003; Portes 2001; Sánchez 2001; Smith 2006; Smith and Guarnizo 1998). Although scholars apply the idea of the transnational, with an emphasis on human agency, to the group for whom the label "immigrant" (or emigrant) is relevant, scholars debate whether all immigrants or emigrants are transnational or occupy a transnational space. Levitt (2003, 4) asserts simply: "Transnational migrants are individuals who live aspects of their social, economic and political lives in at least two settings." To Mitchell (2003) transnationalism is a set of activities, including periodic travel, that connect Brazilians in the United States to Brazil. Transnational research also examines the degree to which living in two settings can actually happen, how this phenomenon compares to past immigration settlement, the ease of movement of people, ideas, communication (Margolis 2001) and the reality that although individuals may have settled in one country, they can be of two or more countries and simultaneously affect and be affected by both.

Scholars have looked at Latin American immigrants as an example of transnational migrants. Still others examine Brazilians specifically or Brazilians as one of several groups of "transmigrants." For example, Christopher Mitchell investigates whether or not Brazilians are creating transnational ties by comparing the Brazilian experience in the United States to those of Mexicans, Guatemalans, Salvadorans, Haitians and Dominicans. Mitchell traces these experiences by examining some aspects of immigration he finds fundamental in determining what is transnational, such as per capita income, community size, legal status, time since immigration started, and assistance received in the United States by interest groups. Mitchell maintains that being undocumented is a great obstacle for Brazilians in the United States. He also asserts that lack of legal status interferes with transnationalism in that immigrants remain excluded from participation in social and political activities and traveling home becomes very difficult. Consequently, immigrants are not only exposed to denunciations and fear deportation but are also deprived of easy travel from host country to home. He concludes that "Brazilians communities seem to be developing in directions that will support the development of transnational ties within the next decade" (46).

Arguably, the implied emphasis in some work on the benefits of being transnational is the most contested aspect of the concept. The "liberating" possibility of this identity on migrants is one such benefit. One point is that transnational people have more options for the ways in which they identify and for casting off unwanted or irrelevant identity categories. Levitt et al. (2003) and Hondagneu-Sotelo and Avila (2003) note that the idea of liberation is common to this area of research. Some analysts suggest that living aspects of their lives in more than one place provides immigrants with the incentive, the need and the opportunity to overthrow ethno-racial hierarchies. This process was also seen as counterhegemonic and transgressive, full of the reality of resistance and change. However, migrancy can lead to a variety of liminal positionings, including invisibility and lack of community or belonging. The mixed blessing of migrancy for women has been explored in a number of recent studies (Kurien 2003). However, as Hondagneu-Sotelo and Avila (2003) suggest, the costs of transnational migration are often overlooked. Many immigrants, both in our study and in others (see Smith 2006) find themselves not fitting well into the available ethno-racial categories, which may be complicated by the possibility of connections both to home and to the host country.

Women are one such group for whom the problems of a transnational experience may be intensified (Hondagneu-Sotelo and Avila 2003; Webster 2006). Our work and Chapter 8 of this collection (Jouët-Pastré et al.) both reveal women's constant struggle for power, whether in a medical encounter or in negotiating identity in the transnational era. Several of our interviewees confirm that economic and social imperatives place a lot of responsibility on women to contribute financially to their families and socially and politically to their communities. On the one hand, this imperative can be experienced as increased autonomy, especially in comparison to their lives in Brazil. On the other hand, some experiences of deeply gendered employment are based on somewhat traditional sex-segregated occupations. Ehrenreich and Hochschild (2002, 3) call the "female underside of globalization" the significant demand of wealthier countries for workers, typically women, do to "women's work" in what has become the "care sector" (20). The high level of mobility relative to other immigration eras may be a signal feature of transnationalism.

This pattern resembles what Salazar Parreñas (2001) has called "reproductive labor," in that transnational women end up reproducing patriarchal gendered roles in the "host country" as they tend to work in domestic spaces and earn money to care for family back home. Moreover, the weight of motherhood and care-giving may increase in the women's transnational experience as they experience it in two countries. Furthermore, in addition to family care-giving connecting women to the home country, family responsibilities also connect them to powerful U.S. institutions. For example, as the authors of Chapter 8 note, women are also more likely to establish the first family contact with the health care system both for themselves and their children.

Thirteen of the women in our study are employed in cleaning or domestic service, in low-level nursing positions, child- or elder-care positions. Another three women list cleaning as one of several jobs, and several more women are employed in low-skilled service sector jobs, all of which are highly sex-segregated. Some of the women we interviewed either left their children in Brazil or brought them along. In either case, the women still comply with gendered duties that become more difficult as they face all the problems that immigrants do, plus rearing their children and caring for family here and making sure their children and family are cared for there. These tensions are experienced more acutely now, during the era of transnational possibilities, than they were during earlier times of immigration, when assimilation seemed to be the goal of many immigrants and the motor of the American Dream.

During the era of transnational possibilities, even with so many restrictions, immigrants plan to and do return home. Among our group, sixteen did not plan to stay in the United States permanently, seven were unsure, but six said that they planned to remain here permanently. For a variety of social, racial and economic reasons, a core group of women took jobs they probably never would have taken in Brazil to make money for themselves and their family, with the belief that their income here would help them get back to Brazil and to a better life for their families. This is another aspect of the gendered nature of transnationalism. Women find themselves experiencing downward mobility in terms of any status that may be attached to their occupations, as they work to maintain status as good mothers, wives, siblings and adult children, which some of them do across multiple borders.

Going Back and Forth: (Not) Belonging?

Making sense of the transnational phenomenon and its potential consequences requires an examination of the ways in which going back and forth might lead to (not) belonging. We start from the proposition that in Western society identity formation is a dynamic but unstable process, which may be affected by journeys home or the process of going back and forth. In addition to the actual physical movement across borders, sometimes at great peril, "back and forth" may also be construed by the women considering their identity as a place on the continuum of identity positionings. In other words, one does not actually have to travel back and forth to think of oneself as this type of sojourner. In this section, we focus on what the women said about their identities when they had gone back and forth and when they had not. Of the thirty women interviewed, fourteen have been back to Brazil. The following are narrative excerpts from several women who have been back to Brazil, even if only for a visit, and a glimpse of the consequences of traveling to Brazil, and back again.

For example, Isabel, 38 years old, here for eight years: "I used to think that I was in a country that did not belong to me (referring to the United States). I just wanted to work. I came here thinking that I would stay for 2 years. And didn't want to invest in anything in this country. But as time went by, I began to change my mind. When you first get here you don't know. It takes time to define yourself. You don't know if you want to stay or go home, you know? I think I began to define myself when I went back to Brazil."

For Isabel, going back and forth was key to her self, and going home allowed her to feel better about where she belonged. We might view this as an irony: Isabel began to define herself when she went back to Brazil, only to come back to the United States, a country that did not belong to her, to continue this process. This process might also be thought of as a grand possibility of the transnational era: one might go home again, taking advantage of an important role of "home," gaining confidence to create an additional home "here." On the other hand, Ana, quoted below, seems to have broken with Brazil as home and community. Given Ana's relatively extensive experience in the United States, her sense of not belonging anywhere, despite going back and forth, is profound.

Ana, 42 years old, here for 22 years, said the following: "I expected to stay here for two years to save money to buy a ticket to go to Australia. [She was here for two years before she went back to Brazil.] I did not stay for very long, 15 or 20 days . . . I would like to go back but I don't know how to live in Brazil anymore. Really, really I don't know how to live anymore in Brazil. I don't know if I have what is needed to relearn. [Ana talks about a tension Brazilian women experience.] There are a lot of things you keep inside and you don't tell. . . . we ignore our own selves and we end up simply surviving You don't think about yourself. You don't think about your own needs. You end up becoming numb. You are no longer Brazilian; you are not American. There are many who end up not even learning English. They are no longer Brazilian. You forget Portuguese and don't learn English. So the pain women feel here is the lack of consciousness about 'Who am I?'" Although Ana has traveled back and forth quite a bit, her insight on the experience of here versus there seems quite different from Isabel's. Ana highlights the transnational dilemma of not belonging anywhere, which may be exacerbated by going back and forth. This is one of the costs of "being transnational." Reading Ana's excerpt, one is struck by her unequivocal voice and her insight about the gendered nature of this dilemma.

Sônia (40 years old, here this time for two months) says: "I left Brazil exactly two months ago, this time . . . I returned after 2 years. . . . this time I came with a different purpose. This time I came here because I didn't want to be there. [Sônia later says:] I don't intend to make my life here. I intend to go back, though I'm going to stay here for a little while, but it is not forever. [And in response to a previous question about her racial identity in Brazil:] At times I would stop to ask myself this question: 'You're Brazilian, right? Who are you descended from?' . . . It's funny. I've never talked about this with anyone, but I've asked myself before, 'What kind of Brazilian are you?' I would ask myself 'What kind of Brazilian race are we?'" Sônia poses the challenge of going back and forth, which she had done at least once, when she experienced one of the dilemmas of identity construction illustrated by her rhetorical question: What kind of Brazilian are you? Each of these women, although around the same age, has been in the United States for various lengths of time; Ana the longest and Sônia the shortest, even considering her cumulative time in the United States. Yet within each narrative we see the juxtaposition of here and there; the sense of belonging and yet not. For example, Sônia posed the three versions of her question, or three different questions, when she was still in Brazil. But here, she says, she has never asked herself these questions. Later in the interview, Sônia insists that she will not stay in "their country" forever and that sometimes she feels uncomfortable "here" (United States) and sometimes she doesn't even think about it. On coming to the United States for the first time, Sônia says, "on the one hand I wanted to be there (Brazil) on the other hand I didn't want to be there." Both of her statements imply a sense of not belonging and double invisibility in that in the first instance she feels nowhere geographically and in the second she is nowhere racially.

Perhaps Helena, 35 years old, who has lived in the United States for fifteen years and has been back and forth several times, gets to the heart of the dilemma of not belonging. Although Helena has traveled back and forth more frequently than the majority of the women we interviewed, being home regularly is not a relief: "It's like I lost my place in the world." Helena, prior to that comment, said that living in Brazil again would be culture shock. She likes the United States and feels at home, yet still feels alone.

In our sample fifteen women have not been back to Brazil. None of them has been in the United States for more than seven years, with the range being from nine months. They have not been back to Brazil for a variety of reasons: lack of documentation;[3] waiting for documentation; financial reasons; no specific reason to go back. Most of the women had more than one reason for not returning to Brazil. Mitchell finds that indeterminate legal status can be a major impediment to both feeling and being a part of the host community and being able to go back and forth. Without a doubt, being somewhere in the documentation process but not fully legal affected some women's ability to go home and their sense of belonging in the United States. However, most of their reasons were layered. There were just a couple of women that thought of themselves as "illegal." Most of the women that have not been back identified something about Brazil that had to change for them to return, or something about themselves that had to change for them to change their minds about returning. Without the documentation that makes Brazilian women "legal," their transnational possibilities are limited and they must be careful about the expressions of visibility. They cannot go back and forth, they may be reluctant to make the type of work or community connections here that meet their needs, and they may find that they have to negotiate their identity relative to their illegality. We argue that transnationalism has always been a matter of degree and, in the post-9/11 era, this is all the more true.

Other women have not gone home for reasons that have most to do with their perceptions of themselves relative to whether they would fit in back in Brazil.

Vilma, 39, here for seven years, says: "I don't think I can get used to living in Brazil anymore. . . . Brazil is violent. The quality of life is much better here."

Renata, 44 years old, in the United States for six years, says: "To be honest, I moved here for good. You adapt and you change in order to get along. As the years go by you get a little harder and more experienced, but as the wounds come, you develop a shield to protect yourself from the difficulties. And so I came. Just as others have done it, I did it."

Renata was one of the six women who planned to stay permanently in the United States from the beginning. Although Renata would like to visit, she still does not want to return to Brazil for good. Her situation is different from many of the other women. Renata came to the United States with her husband and children. They had help in Brazil and help and contacts in the United States, giving them a higher level of social capital than many other Brazilians had. Several women made the difficult decision to leave their children in Brazil. For them, the conflict of belonging is heightened. Staying here does not automatically preclude a transnational status, because, with children in Brazil, these women have the most obvious of transnational experiences: motherhood across national borders. Each of them talked about the strong and regular connections they have with their children. Roberta (38 years old) has only been in the United States for nine months. Her motivation for being here is to improve the life of the family she left there, her children in particular. Yet even women who do not go back and forth or have children often still realize a transnational status, as they stay in regular contact with other family members, send money to relatives, are connected to Brazilian politics and culture and have general life experiences to which Brazil, rather than the United States, is the point of reference. For example, Flávia (22 years old, here a bit over two years) said that she is in the United States so that she can earn enough money to enable her to go back to Brazil to study at a university.

In summary, as Mitchell (2003) notes, a variety of activities connect Brazilians in the United States to Brazil. There are of course border crossings, or the comings and goings, but there are also political, social and cultural connections that would not be possible if the globe had not shrunk a bit. Each of the women that we have talked to maintains at least family ties to Brazil. Twenty women had parents and/or siblings in Brazil. All women seemed to have a significant amount of current information on the families they left behind. The assimilation model against which many scholars of transnationalism argue suggests that immigrant assimilation meant a break with the past. Although that was not necessarily true of assimilating people, for Flávia and Roberta at least, the era of transnationalism provides an opportunity and a necessity to maintain strong connections to home and to the past. However, the transnational aspect of life holds little uniformity even for the women that have gone back and forth. The degree of transnational possibility varies, particularly in "transnational households" (Salazar Parreñas 2001). Many of the women are primary income earners and support the children and family members left "back home." This degree of transnationalism adds to the traditional burden of women as mothers, nurturers and as the family member responsible for keeping the family together.[4]

Liminality: Being Neither Here Nor There

There are obvious difficulties associated with transnationalism, including the ways in which an immigrant is viewed by residents in the host country, which contribute to the possibility of liminality, or stage of indeterminacy. This shakiness seems to come from a momentary sense of loss or by a clear understanding of the immigrant's place in a hierarchical bipolar paradigm fashioned by how "they" see "us" as inferior. Immigrants experiencing a transnational status may find that liminality is further complicated by racialization, which we construe as a process of attaching racial meaning to a variety of experiences and phenomena. Smith (2006) in his study of Mexicans in New York City, also found that racialization was a profound force in the lives of the subset of people that he studied. Gender intersects with the racialization process. Women, some of them mothers and care-givers, cannot afford emotionally to succumb to the role conflict inevitable in care-giving across multiple borders.

Some of the excerpts below illustrate the link between racialization and liminality that occurs as women try to establish an identity. Racialization exists when immigrants speak with an accent, admit to holding jobs that have traditionally been occupied by people of color, or for something that may occur just walking down the street. There is an additional layer of tension on all immigrant populations since 9/11, especially on the groups that have a relatively high proportion of people without the documentation necessary to allow them to work and live legally and to be seen with some legitimacy by the rest of U.S. society. In the last several years, more and more Brazilians came into the United States via Mexico. It is not that many women in our sample have come to the Boston area via Mexico; in fact, that we know of, only two have, but all Brazilians live in a climate of rigid anti-immigrant ideology, which was made worse by 9/11 and, more recently, by the stories of some Brazilians' illegal border crossings.[5] The excerpts below illustrate not only the women's sense of loss and loneliness but also the discomfort of becoming aware of the marginal position to which they have been relegated. On the other hand, some of the stories suggest that although it is hard to know to where one belongs, people can still be content in that indefinite state.

Leticia (20 years old, here for five years) has noticed that her immigrant status is reinforced when she is in certain social contexts speaking English. She says "I know I am not from here. I'm an immigrant and I'm learning English." Leticia, however, is somewhat sanguine about what this means. Although her immigrant identity is reinforced when she speaks English, and she describes situations in which she is silent because of that, she talks about it as her choice. She later notes that although when she speaks she feels like she is "not from here," she has not noticed any discrimination because she is an immigrant. To Leticia the feeling of not belonging is not connected to mistreatment.

Marta, 55, has been in the United States for 15 years and has a professional job: "I think that the message they send you is that you do not belong and not necessarily because of the shade of your skin. Rather, it's because you speak with an accent, don't speak English well, or don't behave according to the norms of this society."

Lúcia (here 1½ years, in her late 20s) talks about being seen as an invader and the racialization that occurs with her immigrant status: "I consider myself just an immigrant who arrived in this country and feels like an alien. We try to get involved with the American society, as we improve our English. They (Americans) look at me like if I were black. It's prejudice against the immigrants. All immigrants came here searching for something better but it wasn't what Americans wanted. You are here kind of occupying their space in the job market. The difference is that there are some tasks they don't want to do."

A variety of factors contribute to the exacerbation of liminality. Among these, language and linguistic differences will always contribute to the difficulty of feeling a part of "here." Instead of being given "good citizen" credit for learning English, many immigrants are automatically racialized and reduced to a lower place in the hierarchy. It is also certainly likely that anyone speaking English is also going to speak with an accent. Marta's insights about the problematic aspects of accents, learning English, and learning culture speak to the complexity of the experience of trying to fit in, or being "here." Having an accent gives someone away, and the consequences can silence women even when they do have the language. Being silent reduces the likelihood of challenges to the ethno-racial hierarchy and to the very liminality that Brazilian women experience. However, when some of the women tried to establish their right to be here, they inadvertently recreated the racial hierarchy. For example, Lúcia's perception of "self" intertwines with that generated by the dominant ideology—a phenomenon common to other immigrants from Latin America. Moreover, upon constructing her self she is also forging an "other," in this case blacks. Her statement clearly recognizes a racial hierarchy in which she feels inferior or "like an alien" to the dominant social group but superior to blacks. In that sense, occupying a transnational space, made obvious by her accent, leads her to distance herself from the black other, making her feel better about being here. Waters (1999), discussing this phenomenon, finds that many West Indian immigrants would rather be identified as "immigrant" or "foreigner" than as black, which is an identity associated with "downward social mobility" (93).

On the other hand, earlier in the interview, Lúcia comments on why she is in the United States: "when you get here you find out that America is not only a country to make money but you can also find a more peaceful and tranquil lifestyle." She also says, "I loved it here, sure we have a better quality of life here but in Brazil people enjoy life better."

Lúcia's comment illustrates the constant shifts that are so telling of liminality. The ambivalence resulting from the movement "back and forth" that makes her assess "here" as better, but "there" as better too, clearly reinforces the state of liminality at the foundation of her transnational experiences and the identities she is trying to negotiate. This indecision reflects the very heart of a contemporary transnational status: one can experience a state of liminality even in both countries, or cultures, as these are defined as better in some way. Furthermore, negotiating identity between two places defined as better may make liminality more acute.

Maria's (38 years old, here 17 years) observations also suggest that although she has met some of her own expectations for her life in the United States, she understands very well that she has been racialized and consequently also excluded: "I believe that in general as a whole blacks and immigrants have been looked down upon, despite the fact that I have never experienced this kind of discrimination. I think that blacks and immigrants have been looked upon differently by the rest of society. Especially now in the case of immigrants because of terrorism. . . . In terms of comparison the immigrant is seen as invader. We came here, took it over without being invited, and immigrants take the jobs away from other people."

Sônia says: "I had a sensation that I would call bad but it was a feeling that was not pleasing. . . . The other day I was in a store and I thought to myself, 'My goodness, I'm not from here . . . It suddenly clicked. I'm in a foreign land. I'm a pilgrim . . . so this was the first time I really felt that I'm not from here.'"

The above examples suggest that a transnational status involves a complex array of memories, cognitive schemas including juxtaposing "there" with "here." One problem with this process is in the inevitable comparison of here and there. The comparison seems to induce a sentiment of marginalization and generate an ill-formed sense of belonging. Yet these experiences rarely occur without some aspect of their counterpart. Consider some of the terms used to describe everyday life experiences and feelings: *lost, invader, happy, pilgrim,* and *peaceful lifestyle.* Some of the other women, whose comments are not included in this part, also used some of the same words to frame their transnational experience.

(In)visibility: Racial and Ethnic Identity

An analysis of the consequences of transnationalism leads to the additional issues of racial and ethnic identity negotiation in general, and the ways in which "Brazilian" and "Latina" are constructed in the face of the ethno-racial hierarchy that exists in particular places. These issues are salient in the transnational era as the pace of immigration to the United States is high; Latin America has been sending large numbers of people to the United States for years, and the Latino/Hispanic population is the largest "minority" in this country. Thus there is an increased emphasis on Latino ethnicity. The authors of Chapter 8 discuss Brazilian women learning "the cultural language of the time" as being as important as learning a foreign language. In our study, we find that learning the language of racial and ethnic identity goes well beyond learning English. Brazilians, because they don't fit nicely or neatly into any of the bureaucratic or government-derived ethnic subpopulations, might have an even more tenuous hold on their right to self-identify than other Latinos. This lack of fit is experienced on the micro-level on a daily basis. The way Brazilians negotiate their Brazilian-ness here in the United States in part responds to North Americans' inability or unwillingness to consider the possibility that there is not one single Brazilian identity. It also responds to the identity transformation that takes place as one leaves home and moves to a different country. The categories Latina, Latin American, and Hispanic and black and white are problematic, as are American and Brazilian. Brazilians often negotiate an identity with obvious social and cultural distance from these categories. Often they lay claim to a "fourth space" that teeters closely to the space of "other" because Brazilians often do not see themselves in the racialized categories of Latina, Latin American, and certainly not Hispanic.[6] Some of the women we interviewed would rather identify with "other" than with the racial and ethnic identification categories offered to them, which are often neither familiar or appropriate. Beserra (2003) in her study of Brazilians in Los Angeles also explores this issue. She notes that in the United States Brazilians have to contend with the imposed identity of Latin American. She notes that to others "Brazilians only make sense to the extent in which they are seen as Latinos." However, in several instances, women demonstrate easiness with Latin American identity and use Latin American, Latina, and even Latin as labels that allow them to fit in but not compromise away too much. The complexity of the transnational situation is so great that many women are contemplative about both the good and the bad of being in a situation where, because of their ethnicity, race, gender, class, national status, they have to lay claim to categories that are unfamiliar to them. Vilma's words describe the identity transformation that occurs in a transnational setting.

In response to a question about whether she sees herself as a Latina and if she thought of herself as a Latina when she was in Brazil, Vilma responded: "I learned that here, because in Brazil you don't approach things from that perspective." She said that in the United States she sees herself as Latina rather than Latin American or Brazilian. She also notes that Americans see her as an immigrant rather than Latina because of her additional ancestries, but when she speaks they believe she is Hispanic.

This example also illustrates how Brazilians see North Americans "othering" them. This process is peculiar because it presents many layers of identity, all negatively charged. Because Vilma assumes that Americans are ignorant and therefore are not able to place her correctly, she chooses the Latina category, perhaps to disconnect herself from even more disagreeable associations of terms such as immigrant and Hispanic. To the extent that this type of conflation and misreading of the race/ethnicity/nation complex occurs on a regular basis, Vilma and many other Brazilian women find themselves constantly explaining and (re)defining themselves and negotiating their identities with relatively unappreciative audiences.

The belief that Brazilians can go back home whenever they want, that the United States is not their home and that their stay here is not permanent, nor should it be—hallmarks of the transnational era—complicates the positioning of identity. Being neither here nor there is coupled with the myth of "up and out" once immigrants make enough money. There is little incentive for people of the host country to understand the depth of Brazilian identity here in the United States, if those same people believe that Brazilians should not be here, will not stay here, and will go back home. While North Americans' unwillingness or inability to comprehend Brazilian identity in its many manifestations presents obvious difficulties to some of the women we interviewed, there is an additional problem that surfaced in several of the interviews. Many women are ill prepared for identity categories that are imposed on them.

For example, Marta speaks about the imposition of a racial identity inconsistent with Brazilian racial classifications.

> **I:** When you used to live in Brazil, what race did you think you belonged to?
> **Marta:** White
> **I:** When you first came to the U.S. what race did you think you belonged to?
> **Marta:** Brazilian. Brazilian race.
> **I:** Nowadays?
> **Marta:** I am not seen as white . . . Because of the color of my skin in Brazil I am white. I never questioned my race. . . . But here, when I first got here I found out in no time that I was not considered white because I come from Latin America . . . if I don't open my mouth perhaps I pass for white. If I remain quiet. I think I was much more mistreated because of my English. My accent. Because of my origin, for being Brazilian."

Later in the interview Marta is asked if she is seen as Brazilian or Latin American. "As something that does not belong here. Yes, something that comes from a country they are not even interested in."

Márcia, (22 years old, here for 1½ years) is resolute about her Brazilian identity as complete and complex. She also discusses the cultural characteristics of the typical Brazilian in juxtaposition to other racial/ethnic subpopulations in the United States:

"Well, I'm completely Brazilian. To be honest. To be hardworking. To love and respect your family, this is very important to me. That's it, I think, to be Brazilian. . . . Yesterday I went with a friend to one of her neighbor's home where the woman is Indian . . . she asked my friend if she was Brazilian, and my friend said we both were. And the woman looked at me and said, really, I though you looked like an American."

As much as Márcia insisted on her Brazilian-ness, in this situation at least she has little influence over the identity that someone imposed on her. Marta, in the United States much longer, understands that it is not completely up to her. The above examples illustrate convincingly that many of the women have identities that are not fixed in time or place and that they "resist established forms of belonging" (Croucher 2004, 92). Yet with this resistance comes the likelihood of not belonging anywhere—not Brazilian, not American and now not necessarily Latin American or Latina. Having a transnational status may allow more options for identity, in theory, including resistance, but it has potential costs as well.

Ana, who is black, discussed many aspects related to her identity including the prejudice she has experienced and how she sees herself as Brazilian rather than Latina: "I see myself as Brazilian . . . Even because I no longer have much to do with that which is Latino. I was more of a mixture and what is still inside of me, it is still Brazilian. I don't believe that Americans see me as Brazilian."

Ana's way of thinking about her identity is anchored in the reality that, at least in the United States, she is considered black. She also views her Brazilian-ness as something disconnected from activities that she defines as Latino. Ana's identity rests on both the presence and the absence of specific features: feeling Brazilian and not participating in Latino affairs. For Elza (41 years old, here 14 years), racial identity constitutes a sense of belonging or not belonging. In response to a question about her race, she says that Americans do not see her as white. "They see me as a strange class. I'm not one and I'm not the other." Marianna (22 years old, here one year) says that she is not as white as Americans are and that they (Americans) see her "as something less."

Maria talks about the connections and disconnections between Latin American, Latina, and Brazilian identity in Brazil and in the United States. Although Maria claims a lack of connection to Spanish-speaking Latinas, she claims to have become a Latina only since being in the United States. "We are totally different (Spanish-speaking Latinas). They are a different people. Another culture. Yes I am Latin American. But I consider myself more Brazilian."

> **I:** So in the first place Brazilian or first *mineira*? (identity linked to the state of Minas Gerais).
> **Maria:** No, Brazilian.
> **I:** Why do you feel that you are Latin American?
> **Maria:** Because we have that certain passion for life, that happiness that Latino people have.
> **I:** So this type of consciousness grew here?
> **Maria:** Yes, it grew here.

Fabiana (34 years old, here four years) says, with a laugh, that she never thought of herself as Latin when she was in Brazil, and, until the question, has not thought of herself as Latin American since she has been in the United States. She defines herself as a "white Brazilian" and acknowledged that she was not treated as well as white Americans.

Renata discusses the same issues, reaching the most concrete conclusion about her identity. She first responds to a question about tension between Brazilians and Hispanics. "I think it exists, yes. Soon after I arrived people told me that Hispanics were this and that, and they put them down. But since then I have had wonderful conversations with Hispanics. I don't see myself as Hispanic. I see myself as Brazilian. Even this term Hispanic. I had never heard this term back in Brazil. What is Hispanic? Well it is someone that speaks Spanish."

> **I:** Do you think of yourself as a Latina?
> **Renata:** I do.
> **I:** What does it mean to be a Latina? How do you see yourself as Latina?
> **Renata:** I think of myself as Latina because I'm from Latin America.

Conclusion

There is no doubt that the concept of "transnational" is contested and problematic. However, there is also no doubt that some of its components are important lenses through which to view Brazilian immigrant women. The narratives provide evidence that using this concept enhances our understanding of the experiences of the women with whom we spoke. This approach reveals the ideas of back and forth, being neither here nor there, invisibility, and the link between liminality and racialization that occurs with women's immigrant status. Clearly, it has provided an important angle on deciphering immigrant Brazilian women's narratives as they correspond to their daily struggles in crossing racial, ethnic and gender borders.

Applying the concept of transnational to their lives prompted us to look at the number of women that have gone back and forth, the reasons for doing so, or not, and the various ways this affected their lives. Our analysis also led to an examination of the nature of the ties that exist between the home and the host country, providing us a glance at the ways the women live in both worlds but not necessarily physically. Brazilian women do lead transnational lives, with all the variations we might expect from such a diverse group and with the complexities involved in transnational experiences. Although only about half of them cross and re-cross borders physically, and some of them never intended to go back to Brazil, almost all of them engage in practices that are considered transnational. Despite commonalities, we should not assume that just because of the myriad connections the women have with Brazil, they are living in both worlds. On the other hand, we should also not assume that the women who have not gone back and forth are not living in both worlds. Connections to home were realized through the self-defined changes women experienced in their journeys to the United States. Several women described some version of finding themselves or of redefining themselves as someone different. The juxtaposition of "here" and "there" also reflects the gendered and racial positions available to the women in their transnational experiences. Moreover, for some women, the state of being transnational held certain benefits, even if in their imaginations, including a sense of comfort that Brazil will always be home and enjoyment of a quality of life in the United States that they believe they would not have had if they had stayed in Brazil.

We discovered that almost all our interviewees must on the everyday level deal with a consequence of being transnational: the state of liminality or being neither here nor there. Applying this aspect of the concept of transnational to the women's lives, we now better understand the potential crisis. One woman talked about the experience of being a Brazilian woman in the United States. The self becomes subsumed within responsibility and that which was Brazilian is now not even American. This suggests to us the possibility of profound costs to a transnational identity as well as profound possibilities to which these lives are witness. Not many women expressed the burden in quite this way, but Marta's, Helena's and Ana's voices capture the dilemma of not being "here" nor "there" but somewhere in between. Several women talked about the complexity of being undocumented, either because they cannot be or because they have not yet completed the process. Thus the celebratory or liberating nature of this status might be inextricably linked to another status, that of legality. We suggest that an additional cost to some of the women with whom we talked is the stigma of "illegal alien" that gets applied to many immigrants whether they are legal or not. For them, it is difficult to impossible to resolve the tension of liminality or to feel empowered to cast off misperceptions of their motives or identity categories. Brazilian women's lives are often racialized, imposing on some a double burden of being neither here nor there and not belonging anywhere and the reality of being seen as inferior.

Using transnationalism as an analytical tool led us to an examination of Brazilian women's degree of resistance to U.S. ethno-racial categories. We conclude that qualifying this resistance as liberating and celebratory would be misleading. The narratives the women shared with us also provide evidence of the constraints in transnational identity formation. The issue that we explored is transnationalism as a form of resistance and its twin costs of liminality and wider marginalization. There is some evidence to suggest that being transnational carries with it a form of resistance to a hegemonic categorization. Many do resist *a priori* U.S. ethno-racial categories of identity: some because the categories are not accurate, others because the groups they feel are more representative of the category are not groups they identify with or simply dislike. When the women resist a racial categorization or ethnic label, they seem to do so less out of principle or resistance and more because of the inaccuracies of the categories that are being imposed. So we do find that women resist, transgress, and negotiate their transnational identities, but they do so at great cost. If they do not accept the categories they become, through no negotiation on their part, just "other." On the other hand, as Smith (2006) points out in his study of Mexicans in New York City, accepting or rejecting these categories does not prevent the inevitable racialization that occurs to transnational groups concurrently with their identity negotiation.

Our analysis suggests that a transnational status is clearly gendered as it exerts pressure on women to resume traditional gender roles, sometimes across multiple borders. Furthermore, women occupy a place in a patriarchal structure and, although they may have more autonomy than they had at home, their social status and even income may be lower here, thus reinforcing the structure itself. This situation may exacerbate their sense of not belonging because, , whichever way they look, there is a possibility that life could be better.

These stories suggest that using a transnational lens to view Brazilian women's lives adds valuable texture to their stories. It provides an important contextualization of their everyday cultural, social and political realities. In many ways, the Brazilian women with whom we spoke are transnational immigrants, with their heads and their hearts in both worlds. However, we cannot conclude that all is well in Brazilians' transnational existence, because some of them cannot seem to find a place in either society. Some of them are not permitted a place and hence do not belong and may be invisible. For some, being Brazilian in the United States may be a form of transgression or resistance, but many are also aware that holding on to Brazilian as a part of their identity may exacerbate their exclusion from U.S. culture. Thus it is with great ambivalence, we think, that they hold on to a Brazilian identity. In that identity there is both pride and fear, but not necessarily a great resolve to subvert the categories imposed on them by the host nation-state.

Notes

1. Each of the demographic characteristics is relevant at the time of the interview. The total size of the group is thirty; however, not all women answered all of the questions. Therefore the numbers do not always add up to thirty.
2. We acknowledge that in most disciplines the theoretical construct "transnational" is still contested. The scholarship is fascinating on a number of levels, not the least of them is whether the use of this concept aids our understanding of what it means to migrate, settle and resettle and assimilate, or if it operates as a neologism, or something in between. In this paper we relax what should be conceptual precision. For example, there is a difference between transnationalism and transmigration (Levitt) but here we use transnationalism. Our goal is not the further interrogation of "transnational" and everything associated with it. Rather, we use issues that emerge from the body of scholarship on this concept as a device or a lens through which to view and understand certain aspects of Brazilian immigrant women's lives.
3. At the outset of this project, we both committed to deemphasizing legal status, deciding that we would not ask directly about documentation. In response to some of our questions, some of the women identified their status. In other cases, it became obvious to us. However, as a matter of personal imperative, we wanted the women with whom we spoke to leave the interview never having to wonder about what our purpose was. Our efforts were directed at trust both during the interview and afterward. It may be that we lost an opportunity to comment specifically about connections between legal status and transnationalism, but, if this is a compromise, and we don't believe it is given the rich narratives that we have, we are certainly willing to live with it.
4. In her studies of Filipina immigrants, Salazar Parreñas refers to transnational households as "families whose core members are in at least two nation states" (80).
5. In the past few years there have been several news reports of Brazilians coming into the United States through Mexico. One article by Jerry Kramer in *The San Diego Union-Tribune* (June 4, 2005, internet version), entitled "Loophole to America: Migrants Exploiting Border Law for Non-Mexicans" reports on Brazilians taking advantage of a loophole in the law, avoiding being detained and arrested. However, Mexico is once again requiring visas for Brazilians so the number of Brazilians coming to the United States via Mexico could decrease significantly.
6. The *Providence Journal* (January 18, 2005) published an article in the local news section (internet version) by Paul Edward Parker, a staff writer for the paper, entitled "Latinos Organize Forum to Better Lives of Immigrants: They discuss the need for immigrant communities in the United States to link with their home governments to exert political pressure on behalf of immigrants here." This article is relevant to this paper for two reasons. First, the subheading suggests quite clearly a transnational theme. Second, this article describes

100 immigrants coming together to discuss with four officials from their home countries how they can improve the lives of Latin Americans. One participant commented that efforts must go beyond the four countries represented at the forum to include the entire Latin American community, "a community united by a common language." Needless to say, with Latin America constituted along language/linguistic lines, Brazilians are once again marginalized at best and excluded completely at worst.

References

Beserra, Bernadete. 2003. *Brazilian Immigrants in the United States: Cultural Imperialism and Social Class.* New York: LFB.

Croucher, Sheila. 2004. *Globalization and Belonging: The Politics of Identity in a Changing World.* Baltimore: Rowman and Littlefield.

Ehrenreich, Barbara and Arlie Russell Hochschild. 2002. *Global Women: Nannies, Maids, and Sex Workers in the New Economy.* New York: Henry Holt.

Garcia, Alma A. 2004. *Narratives of Mexican American Women: Emergent Identities of the 2nd Generation.* Baltimore: AltaMira Press.

Hondagneu-Sotelo, Pierrette, ed. 2003. *Gender and U.S. Immigration: Contemporary Trends.* Berkeley: University of California Press.

Hondagneu-Sotelo, Pierrette and Ernestine Avila. 2003. "I'm Here, but I'm There: The Meanings of Latina Transnational Motherhood." In *Gender and U.S. Immigration: Contemporary Trends.* Ed. Pierrette Hondagneu-Sotelo, pp. 317–340. Berkeley: University of California Press.

Kurien, Prema. 2003. "Gendered Ethnicity: Creating a Hindu Identity in the United States." In *Gender and U.S. Immigration: Contemporary Trends* Ed. Pierrette Hondagneu-Sotelo, pp. 151–173. Berkeley: University of California Press.

Levitt, Peggy. 2001a. *Transnational Villagers.* Berkeley: University of California Press.

———. 2001b. "Transnational Migration: Taking Stock and Future Directions." *Global Networks* 1(3): 195–216.

———. 2003. "You Know Abraham Was Really the First Immigrant: Religion and Transnational Migration." *The International Migration Review* 37(3): 847–973.

Levitt, Peggy, Josh DeWind and Steven Vertovec. 2003. "International Perspectives in Transnational Migration: An Introduction." *The International Migration Review*, 37(3): 565 (proquest version).

Levitt, Peggy and Nina Glick Schiller. 2003. "Conceptualizing Simultaneity: A Transnational Social Field Perspective on Society." *The International Migration Review*, 38(3): 1002–1040 (proquest version).

Margolis, Maxine. 1998. *An Invisible Minority: Brazilians in New York City.* Boston: Allyn and Bacon.

———. 1995. "Transnationalism and Popular Culture: The Case of Brazilian Immigrants in the United States." *Journal of Popular Culture* 29(1): 29–42 (proquest).

———. 2001. "Notes on Transnational Migration: The Case of Brazilian Immigrants." In *Negotiating Transnationalism: Selected Papers on Refugees and Immigrants.* Vol. 9: 202–222.

Martes, Ana Cristina B. 2004. "Transnational Institutions and Ethnic Entreprenuership." Paper prepared for "The Business Association of Latin American Studies" Conference at Wellesley, MA.

Mitchell, Christopher. 2003. "Perspectiva Comparada sobre Transnacionalismo entre Imigrantes Brasileiros nos Estados Unidos." In *Fronteiras Cruzadas Etnicidade, Gênero e Redes Sociais.* Ed. Ana Cristina Braga Martes and Soraya Fleischer, pp. 33–50. São Paulo: Editora Paz e Terra.

Portes, Alejandro. 2001. "Introduction and Conclusion." *Global Networks*, 1(3): 181–193.

Salazar Parreñas, Rhacel. 2001. *Servants of Globalization. Women, Immigration and Domestic Work.* Stanford: Stanford University Press.

Sánchez, Patricia. 2001. "Adopting Transnationalism Theory and Discourse: Making Space for a Transnational Chicana." *Discourse: Studies in the Cultural Politics of Education* 22(3): 375–381.

Smith, Michael Peter and Luis Guarnizo. 1998. *Transnationalism from Below: Comparative Urban and Community Research.* Vol. 6. New York: Transaction Publishers.

Smith, Robert Courtney. 2006. *Mexican New York: Transnational Lives of New Immigrants.* Berkeley: University of California Press.

Waters, Mary C. 1999. *Black Identities: West Indian Immigrant Dreams and American Realities.* Cambridge MA: Harvard University Press.

Webster, Wendy. 2006. "Transnational Journeys and Domestic Histories." *Journal of Social History* 39(3): 651–666.

7

Emigrants from Governador Valadares: Projects of Return and Investment

Sueli Siqueira

International emigration from Brazil has been taking place since the 1960s and is linked to the history of the Governador Valadares micro-region.[1] During the 1980s, the migration flow to foreign countries, which began in the 1960s, showed a marked increase. The destination country of these emigrants was mainly the United States and, to a lesser degree, Canada and (more recently) Portugal.

These emigrants keep a close relationship with their hometown. They share their families' everyday life through letters, the Internet, and especially phone calls. G. Assis (1994), for example, studied immigration to the United States through letters exchanged between friends and relatives that documented their hardships, successes, and failures. Further evidence of this close relationship is the continuous influx of foreign currency sent to this region. Most of this flow takes place unofficially. For most migrants, the migration project is closely linked to an economic dimension involving the purchase of durable and nondurable goods for themselves and their families. This effort produces a certain dynamism in the local economy. A great part of this migration process is also closely linked to the migrants' hopes of returning and establishing themselves in their homeland by starting a business in their region of origin that would bring them enough profit to live on.

The "dream of return" is an important element for understanding that from the immigrant's perspective his or her stay in the United States is temporary. As this dream becomes gradually more distant or frustrated by failure to achieve it, the search for North American society materializes. In chapter four of this volume, Siqueira and Jansen show data which display the increase in the tendency to establish a permanent residence in this country, based on the increase in the number of Brazilians who became American citizens. In 1999 they numbered 1,947 compared to 4,114 in 2000.

This chapter opens a discussion about the projects, life, and work conditions of the immigrants residing in New England and their intention to return to their country and invest in the Governador Valadares microregion. It also examines those who have returned and, for some reason, have not been successful in their investments and then re-emigrated back to the United States. In order to study this phenomenon, 141 interviews were carried out with immigrants whose hometown in Brazil is Governador Valadares.

To put the topic in focus, an overview of Brazil in the context of international migrations is provided, along with a description of the emergence of Governador Valadares in this scenario. Subsequently, I will discuss the data concerning my research conducted in the United States.

Brazil in the Context of International Migrations

Since the arrival of the Portuguese, Brazil has been an important stage for the phenomenon of international migrations. This movement came to be the foundation of Brazilian culture and population, and a fundamental variant in the history of Brazil's economy. First, the Portuguese came, with the aim of taking possession of the land. Later, from 1550 to 1850, with the beginning of massive agricultural production, about three million Africans were brought to Brazil (Camargo 1981). This forced migration characterized a stage of an economic development based on sugar cane cultivation.

In the second half of the 19th century, large-scale European immigration once more changed the face of the country. The first immigrant groups arrived between 1880 and 1903, with the influx of about 1,850,985 European immigrants (Camargo 1981).[2] Up to the 1950s, Brazil was recognized as a receiver country of international migrants. "In 1920 it [number of immigrants] corresponded to 5.11% of Brazil's residing population, while in 1980 this participation decreased significantly to 0.77%" (Patarra and Baeninger 1995, p. 80). The 1960s mark the start of a shift in status from a receiver to a sender country of manpower to more industrialized countries.

Immigrants tend to take unskilled market positions in global cities of developed countries. This is one of the aspects that have shaped new migration trends. Most Brazilians go to the United States mainly for work opportunities. A network of relations disseminates information about job opportunities and creates mechanisms that facilitate the emigration process (see Fusco 2005 and Soares 2002 for more information on these social networks).

The region of Governador Valadares contributes the largest number of migrants. It is important to note that, while the immigration "boom" from the Governador Valadares region to the United States occurred in the 1980s, Soares (1995) found that 1.7% of her sample emigrated in the 1960s, while 43.6% came between 1985 and 1990. According to some studies (e.g., Sales 1999), nearly 6% of the population of Governador Valadares emigrated to the United States, residing in and around Boston, Miami and New York. These emigrants are always in touch with their hometowns and keep sending regular sums of dollars. As discussed in Chapter 5 of this volume, these remittances influence the local economy of hometowns (especially in the areas of commerce and civil construction areas), promoting a new local lifestyle.

The local economies of areas of destination can also be affected by the influx of immigrants. In the Boston metropolitan region, downtown Framingham is a good illustration of how immigrants affect their destinations. In the 1980s the region went through a process of industrial decentralization which depleted businesses in the city, transforming the downtown into a degraded area of marginal activities (prostitution and drugs). The region was eventually revitalized, regaining its economic strength through the opening of several ethnic businesses, mainly Brazilian; work by Sales (1999) and Almeida (2003) highlights the impact that Brazilian immigrants have had in this area.

International Migration in the Micro-Region of Governador Valadares

In 1997, a survey performed by researchers from UNICAMP[3] estimated that 18% of homes in Governador Valadares had at least one family member who was an international migrant. This corresponds to 6.7% of the total population out of 210,000 inhabitants of the county[4] of Governador Valadares. Many of these emigrants headed to the Boston region. As mentioned in Chapter 4 of this volume, Siqueira and Jansen's research in 2003 found that the region of Governador Valadares is the one that sends the highest number of emigrants to Massachusetts.

Why emigrate? Why go to the United States? To answer these questions, it is necessary to examine the historic links between the city of Governador Valadares and this country. The phenomenon of Valadarian emigration can be understood by unveiling the connections between these two spaces (Assis 1994). Emigration began in the 1960s, increasing greatly in the 1980s and 1990s. Today, all families in Governador Valadares have a relative or friend who is, was, or wants to be an emigrant to the United States.

Assis (1994) describes three moments of this connection with the United States. The first moment was in the 1940s, during World War II, with the economic cycle of mica extraction. During this time, the city received many Americans who coordinated both mica extraction and development work. These activities produced many jobs that energized the local economic profile. Moreover, in this period, SESP (Special Service of Public Health) came into existence, financed by the American government with the purpose of treating the malaria that tormented the region's inhabitants.

The contact that residents had with the dollar, which was received as payment for jobs or favors performed and which was much higher in value than the Brazilian currency, painted a picture of American wealth and abundance. With the end of the mica economic cycle, the vision of the United States as El Dorado remained in the minds of the local people.

A great many of the Governador Valadares' population were already migrants, since they came from different parts of Brazil in search of better life conditions. This experience, coupled with long-standing, close relations with the United States in the 1940s, facilitated the birth of an international migration culture (Assis, 1999).

The perception that international migration was possible and relatively easy to execute explains the departure of the first Valadarians to the United States in the 1960s. They were young, adventurous people from middle-class families. Interviews with emigrants from that time show that the desire they had to "to make América,"[5] or to make money and return for economic independence, was not determined by financial needs, since they belonged to the middle class (Siqueira 2002).

> "I went for the first time in 1962 through an exchange program. I studied English in a school whose owner was an American who had come to Valadares in the 1940s and ended up staying here. When I came back, I started thinking about going back again, I thought it would be cool to get some money. . . . Things were easier there, I could get some money, have my own business here and be independent. My family has always been economically well, but all the time, I felt like going back. I ended up joining a friend and then we left . . . I stayed

> there for three years, then I returned. I started my own business and today I don't regret . . . I always go there three times a year on business."[6] (Pedro)

When questioned about why and where the idea of emigrating came from, no one could explain it clearly. The explanation most people gave was their desire for the unknown and belief in the possibilities offered by the land of "Uncle Sam." Reports of their experiences show how the culture of migration permeated an entire generation.

These first emigrants reported their experiences in their letters or upon their return. Their economic success was translated into investments made in the city. This instigated and motivated the desires of others to go and experience the same adventure. Relatives and friends were invited to emigrate. After some time, a significant group of Brazilians was in the United States, "making America." It was these first migrants who established a network of relations, supporting a large-scale emigration in the 1980s. "Economic factors are important for the decision of migrating, but information about opportunities is, in the same way, crucial to the decision to migrate" (Margolis 1999, p. 157).

In the 1980s, the successful emigration of those who left in the 1960s, the view of the United States as a symbol of progress and development where it was possible to make a large amount of money, the establishment of a network of information about all aspects of emigration, all of the above associated with the Brazilian economic crisis and the city's economic inertia, caused a boom in the flux of Valadarians to the United States.

At the time of defining the project of emigration, the future emigrant has at his or her disposal a series of services and information that facilitate its accomplishment. With the help of networks, Valadarians go through all phases of the process with a certain ease. If entrance to the United States is by legal means through tourist visas, some travel agencies make arrangements to take groups to the American Consulate in São Paulo. They provide information about required documents, what to wear and what to say. The migration process is generally financed by relatives or friends, who also lend dollars to the migrant so that he can enter the country. If the migrant does not obtain a visa by legal means, there are two other possibilities: a false passport or entrance through Mexico. For these mechanisms, there is also an information network accessible to those who decide to migrate. At times, an individual's desire to enter the United States is so strong that he may try all of these alternatives before he obtains a successful entry.

> "I applied for a visa five times; I couldn't obtain it. I compiled all the documents, my aunt transferred her store to my name, my father transferred his savings to my bank account, I had my papers as a legal worker for almost a year and when I got there, the Consul didn't ask me for anything, he just said: 'try again.' I had everything right . . . Now, I will pay three thousand dollars for a false passport. If I can't get it, the only way out is going through Mexico. . . . It is very dangerous and more expensive, but, it will be the only alternative." (Eloiza, 28 years old); (Siqueira 2002)

In the last few years, the difficulties Governador Valadares residents have experienced in obtaining tourist visas have increased the use of illegal means. False document services and illegal ways to enter the United States have been offered by clandestine agencies expert in these alternatives, and it is not hard to contact them.

Regardless of the method of entry into the United States, when Valadarians go through the emigration process, they have already made arrangements for where to live, which is generally in homes of relatives or friends, and where to work. All this has been established by the existing networks in the city, which are closely connected with those in the United States.

The Immigrant and the Project of Return

Methodological aspects of the field research.

A process of multi-methodological data collection was used in the field research. The use of quantitative and qualitative data allowed me not only to collect concrete information, but to also detect feelings, sensations and values which configure the complex social matrix that characterizes the life of an immigrant who aims at becoming an entrepreneur. This methodology also allowed me to unveil data which favored a broader and complete analysis of the web of social relations that permeates the migrants' everyday lives, work, projects and expectations.

What motivates the project of return? What are the reasons for the failure of those who returned? In order to answer these questions interviews were performed with immigrants whose hometowns in Brazil are located in the micro-region of Governador Valadares. The sample contained two groups:

> Group I. Emigrants who returned between 1980 and 2002 and became entrepreneurs with micro, small and medium businesses; subsequently, however, they closed their businesses and went back to the United States.

Group II. The emigrants in the United States who never returned to Brazil, but who plan to do so and become entrepreneurs of micro, small and medium businesses in the region of Governador Valadares.

This study focuses on the desire to return and the failure of this life project. Additionally, there is a third group of emigrants who were successful in returning and becoming entrepreneurs in the region. Even though this is a significant group that has revitalized the economy of the Governador Valadares region, it is not the focus of study here.[7]

The interviewees from the first two groups reside in the United States. Most of them are undocumented, and consequently (as discussed in the introduction of this volume) invisible to the public institutions. For these reasons, the most practical way of finding them was to stay for a couple of days during work hours at workplaces and ethnic establishments such as snack bars, beauty salons, laundries, restaurants, bakeries and supermarkets. The immigrants provided information concerning the most visited places by Brazilians from the micro-region of Governador Valadares. These formal interviews were conducted in the cities of Boston, Framingham, Somerville, Bridgeport, Newark, Danbury, and Fairfield. For the interviewees who accepted to participate in an in-depth interview, an appointment was made at their homes and, if allowed, the interview was taped. The research was conducted in the fall of 2004. In total, 141 formal interview questionnaires were administered. Besides the formal interviews, 20 in-depth interviews were completed, resulting in the reports presented in this work.

Immigrant profile and the emigrant condition

In the data from my field research, conducted in the cities of Boston, Framingham, Somerville, Bridgeport, Newark, Danbury, and Fairfield, the immigrants are 48.9% men and 51.1% women. Of the sample, 61% are married, 58% are between 20 to 40 years old, and 45% have graduated from high school.

It is important to mention that only 4.3% of interviewees were unemployed when they emigrated; 76.6% had engaged in some kind of professional activity prior to emigrating. Most (53%) had an income of up to three minimum wages when living in Brazil (in 2004, the minimum wage was 260 *reais*, approximately 85 dollars). According to this research, the main reason given by (former) inhabitants of the Governador Valadares micro-region for immigrating to the United States is the economic factor, the desire to make money to acquire properties in Brazil and build a better life (58%). Furthermore, 28% of the sample declared that they emigrated to meet their children, spouses, and/or parents; of these, 84% emigrated starting in 1990. These data show that the reasons for migrating were no longer solely economic but, rather, to reunite with family members in the United States. Some consider postponing their return or defining the United States as their country of residence. The following interview excerpt is from the daughter of a woman who emigrated in 1988 and brought her three children to this country starting in 1998, when she became an American citizen.

> "As soon as I finished my high school, I came here to meet my mother and two brothers who were here . . . My mother has a home cleaning schedule and she needed a reliable person to help her, so I decided to come . . ." (Ana, 21 years old)

The trip may be financed by relatives or friends in the United States (39%) or in Brazil (23%). It is noteworthy that 38% state they used their own resources to finance their migration. Most often they used savings accounts or sold property such as cars or motorcycles, land, and homes, or borrowed money from financial services companies or banks.

Most of the sample came with a tourist visa (52%), while 32% entered through the Mexican border. For 48%, the cost of the trip ranged from $800 to $2,000 for immigrants who entered with a tourist visa, and whose expenses included travels to the American Consulate in order to obtain the visa, tickets, and lodging in the United States. Some made hotel reservations to guarantee their entrance to the country while going through customs, but ended up staying with relatives or friends. For those entering through the Mexican border, expenses range from $5,000 to $9,000.

These data indicate that most of these immigrants are employed and have a certain financial flexibility since the migration process is expensive. They are not seeking to fulfill basic needs but to improve their life conditions or maintain their life standards.

As the immigrant settles definitively in the United States, he/she changes his or her perspectives and participates more effectively in the everyday life of the community. The immigrant's concern is no longer just to earn money to send to Brazil, but to improve the family's social status. When the immigrant is no longer worried about his or her legal documentation, he/she starts to take part in the associations and institutions of the community.

> "I am campaigning for this politician since he defends the immigrants' interests. . . . I arrived here in 1980 and worked really hard, I gave my contributions for this city to be what it is today, that's why I think the immigrant should be respected." (Carlos, 42 years old)

Work

Most emigrants in the sample are undocumented (57.4%); yet 20.6% have a green card, and 14.9% are already American citizens. Of those who are undocumented, most (52.4%) have been in the United States two to four years; of those who are documented, 33.3% have resided in the United States between 11 and 17 years and 28.3% have resided in the United States between 18 and 24 years. Those who have been here longer are less likely to be undocumented. In other words, the Brazilians searching for legalization are exactly those who have been living here longer. Even if immigrants enter with a legal visa, their status becomes illegal when they begin to work, as a tourist visa does not allow them to hold any kind of job.

The professional activities performed by these immigrants are regarded as belonging to a secondary market. As discussed by Siqueira and Jansen in chapter 4 of this volume, these activities have low social status and pay low wages when compared to the broader American society. The immigrants in this sample work in civil construction (27%), housecleaning (16.3%), babysitting (12.1%) and delivery services (9.5%). Most work from 6 to 10 hours a day (58.9%), and 33% keep two jobs. It is interesting to note that 22.7% own some kind of business. These include construction, remodeling, gardening, or ethnic retail businesses. Some women who work in housecleaning have a "schedule," that is, a number of houses they clean on a regular basis. These women often hire two or three helpers, and these are usually newcomers who neither own a vehicle nor communicate in English.[8]

> "I have a schedule (client base) of 20 houses and I have three helpers, whom I pick up at their places of residence. We perform the job together. . . . I spend an average of three hours in each house. I can make from $3,000 to $3,500 per week. After paying the helpers, I retain about $2,000." (Alzira, August, 2004)
>
> "The helpers earn between $50 and $80 dollars per day, but it all depends: if she is a fast worker, she may earn even more. As soon as they learn the job and start speaking some English, they get their own clients and leave us hanging." (Elza, August, 2004)

The immigrants' weekly wage is, at a minimum, about $300 dollars. Nevertheless, many stated that they (36.9 %) earn between $500 to $1,000 dollars per week. Business owners earn more than $2,000 dollars a week (12.8%).

Savings and investment in Governador Valadares

The main goal of emigration, as presented by interviewees, is to earn money to improve their lifestyle. Saving money is the emigrant's ultimate objective. The amount of money earned each month varies according to the seasons of the year, which also determine the monthly savings. For instance, construction, landscaping, and painting jobs decrease in the winter. For those who work in housecleaning, school vacation is the time of least work opportunities, since it is then that families often travel and don't have a demand for housecleaning services. Only 5.7% of interviewees stated that they do not save money. Most are newcomer emigrants who do not make enough money to be able to save, or they are still paying their trip to the United States. Among the 93.4% who affirm they have a savings strategy, many (45.4%) save an average of over $1,000 per month.

> "I have not been able to accumulate much money yet; I am still paying for money loaned by my brother so I could come. I'll finish paying that this year, and then I'll start saving." (Jerônimo, August 2004—2 years here)
>
> "The money I earn is enough for my expenses, only after August, when the job offers increase, I will start retaining more." (Meire, August 2004—2 years here)
>
> "I believe coming here and not saving money is foolish; every month I save at least $500 . . . my goal is to save $1,000 a month, but I haven't got a good client base (schedule) yet." (Jorgiana, December 2004—5 years here)

Interestingly, 36.2% of those interviewed had acquired property in Brazil, while 63.8% had not. Of those who had acquired property, many (47%) have been in the United States between two and four years, while most (77%) of those who had not acquired property have been in the United States between 11 and 24 years. These data show that, as time of residence in the United States increases, the acquisition of property in Brazil tends to decrease. In changing their original goals, many emigrants postpone their return indefinitely or define the United States as their permanent place of residence.[9] The property that is acquired is mostly in the form of houses (38.3%), rural properties (24%), and plots of land (10.9%).

The longer the permanence in the United States, resulting in better income and adaptation to the local society, the lower the percentage of people acquiring properties in Brazil. The in-depth interviews revealed that those who obtain legal status are especially likely to choose to acquire properties (mainly houses) in the United States.

> "In the beginning, I bought a house, lots, even a ranch in Brazil, but I ended up selling everything and investing the money here. I opened this restaurant . . . , I always send money to help my sister . . . pay for my godchild's college . . . I go to Brazil every two years to see my friends and relatives, and recharge the batteries." (Nilcéia–August 2004)

The connection between immigrants and their hometown can be seen through the monthly amount of money orders sent to Brazil. Among interviewees, 36% do not send monthly financial support for their relatives' expenses. Among the 64% who do, many (46%) send money orders ranging from $100 to $400 each month, while others (11.3%) send over $400 to $700 a month.

Project of returning to Brazil

Concerning their return to Brazil, 50.4% of interviewees have never returned; of those, 69.1% are still undocumented. On the other hand, 49.6% of interviewees have returned to Brazil at least once; of those within this group who are undocumented, 24.7% state that they have returned between one and four times, while a minority (6.2%) has returned between 5 and 10 times. The first return is always made with the intention of staying. The interviewees reported that after some time, for varied reasons, they decided to emigrate back through the Mexican border.

> "I have gone to Brazil five times, I always return through Mexico . . . I already know the way and I don't need a coyote. I've grown used to it, I don't find it dangerous and when I return I always bring someone along." (Mário, November 2004)
>
> "The first time I went with no intentions of returning, but I had problems . . . I came back through Mexico again. The second time I did not have plans to come back either . . . I ended up coming back, and now, when I am really homesick or when I need to take care of any matter I already know the way." (Eliseu, August 2004)

Those who are legally in the United States frequently return to Brazil; 26.7% affirm that they have returned from 5 to 10 times, and 18.3% more than 10 times. These data illustrate that there is a strong relationship with Brazil because even those with legal status continue to keep connections with their hometowns.

Among those who returned at least once to Brazil, 50% intended to stay. The main reason most people gave for returning to the United States (48.6%) is that they invested the money in some kind of business which was not successful; others (31.4%) reported it was because they could not re-adapt to the Brazilian lifestyle; and still others (17.1%) believed their investment was not profitable enough to support their families.

These immigrants invested in businesses (51.4%), industry (17.1%), and services (31.4%). They did no research on the market nor asked for help from public bureaus (SEBRAE, the City Hall, etc.) to become acquainted with market demands and the prospects of success in the business they chose. The majority of interviewees (51.4%) reported that they decided on what to invest based on information and advice from friends and relatives; others (31.4%) based their decisions on a "by chance" opportunity related to the chosen business, and only a minority (17.1%)

Chart 1. Reasons for Not Remaining in Brazil (percentages)

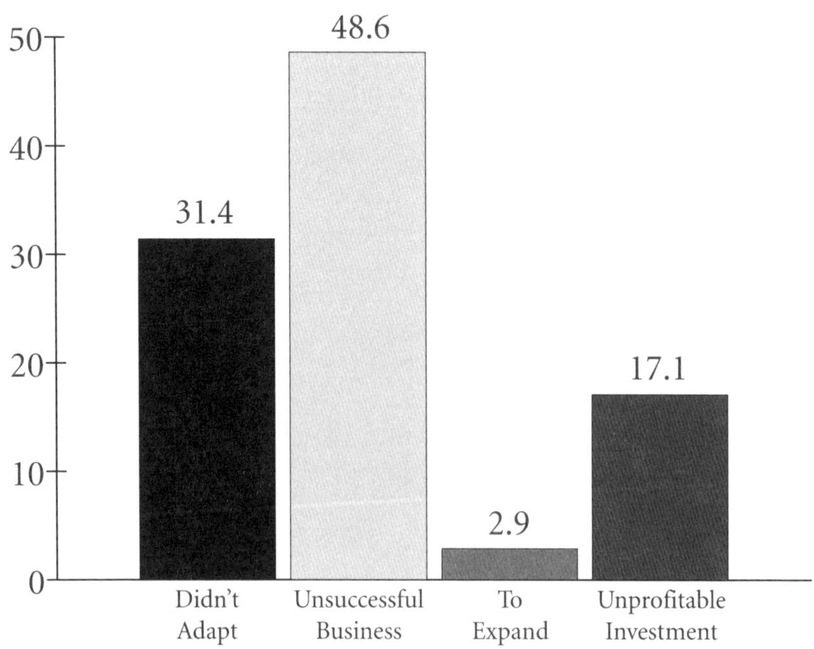

chose a specific business based on the experience they had previously in the field.

> "I bought the grocery store because I thought it was a good business . . . no, I had never worked in commerce before. . . . Now I know it would never work out, there was a big supermarket in the area and I could never compete with them. (Mateus, December 2004)

These data show that the majority of immigrants built their businesses without any guidance and with very limited knowledge about the type of business and the economic context, eventually being forced to close their businesses or maintain them with low profits.

Regarding their permanence in the United States, 38% of interviewees had already defined this country as their permanent residence; they have made investments and organized their lives there. Among those, 5.3% have financed the purchase of their homes and have sold or intend to sell their commodities in Brazil. They go to Brazil only on vacation to visit friends and relatives.

> "No, I do not have the intention to return to Brazil and live there; my life is already here, my children are here, my grandchild and my business are here. It is here that I make money. If I could earn there what I earn here . . . I would be already there . . . I sold my ranch, the house and two lots to buy this one. . . . Brazil is only for vacation." (Nilcéia, August 2004)

Concerning the return to Brazil, 62% of the interviewees state that they intend to return and live in Brazil. Among these (Table 1), 65% intend to return within a short time frame. They have a definite project of returning in the next two years, and they have investments in progress to make their living in the region possible. The investments include real estate (houses and apartments) for rental (15%), setting up businesses (45%), making a living from the income earned from rural properties (15%), or making a living with retirement money (Social Security) from the United States (12%). Others (35%) intend to return later, planning to stay more than four years in the United States. They plan to invest (or are already investing) in properties (13%) in order to live from a rental income, establish businesses (27%), buy rural properties (10%), or live on retirement income they will receive from the United States (10%). However, some of the interviewees with long-term plans of return (23%) have not defined a project yet.

"Thinking of going back one day is what gives me support to live and work here . . . here, I can make a lot of money, but the goal is to live in Brazil, where my family is, my house, my friends. . . . I don't want to bring up my children here . . . many of them go back and don't succeed . . . I have my garage operating there . . . I am going in December and I will stay till February to organize my garage, buy some equipment and take a training course . . . I also have rental income that will help me to support my family." (Robson, August 2004)

"During these years I invested in those apartments, [he built a building with six flats] . . . I must finish the last floor . . . the income will be enough to have a good life in Brazil." (Geilton, December 2004)

Table 1. Project of Return

Investment	Short period (65%)	Long period (35%)
Rental	15%	13%
Commerce	45%	27%
Rural property	15%	10%
Self-employed	4%	-
Civil construction	5%	7%
Retirement income	12%	10%
No project	2%	23%
Others	2%	10%

Chart 2 illustrates the main difficulties that interviewees indicated affect their return to Brazil. Responses include issues related to the economy (43%), such as instability, high interest rates, high taxes, unemployment, and low salaries. Another 16% said that having established a life in the United States makes returning to Brazil hard. Finally, it is significant to note that 20% state there isn't any difficulty in returning and living permanently in Brazil.

These data indicate that some Brazilian immigrants see themselves as being part of American society, in which they have become legalized and visible. It is interesting to note that this shift in the perception of belonging happens both to immigrants who have been in the United States for a long period of time and to those who have been unsuccessful in their return to Brazil.

Conclusion

Brazil is a nation that has traditionally received immigrants. In Governador Valadares, the trend stared to shift in the 1960s, and today Brazil has

Chart 2. Return Difficulties (percentages)

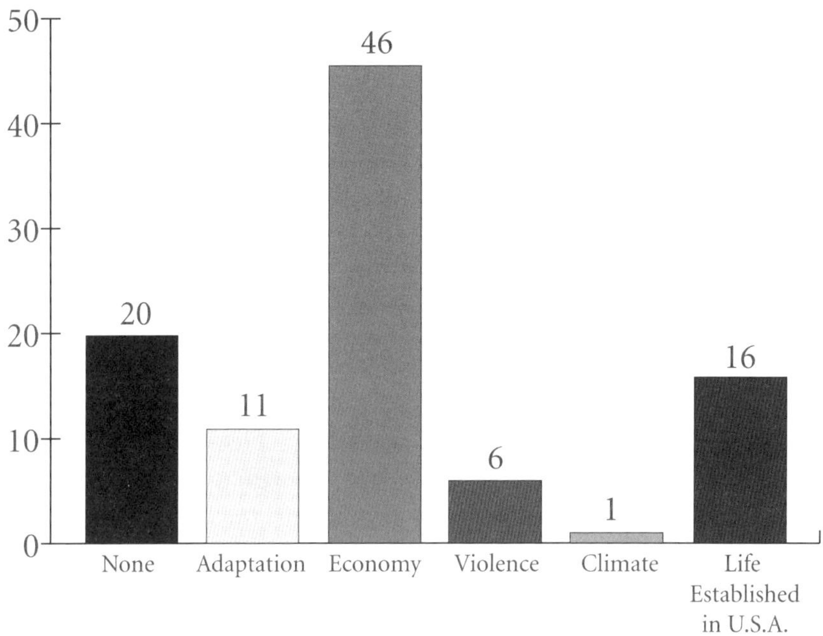

changed from being a country of immigrant reception to a country of emigrant exodus. This change is caused by a new dynamic of capitalism based especially on the economic reorganization marked by the globalization of capital (see Harvey 1993 and Sassen 1988). In this sense, currently, the phenomenon of international migration displays new characteristics. New migrants do not seek mere survival but also aim to maintain or raise their standard of living.

In Governador Valadares, the route to the United States started from a specific historical context, which gave its citizens the notion that there is a place where you can earn money and accumulate wealth in a short amount of time. The social networks then established allow new migrants to establish a web of social relationships[10] between the two countries. As discussed in Chapter 6 of this volume, migrants become trans-migrants, living in two countries with distinct values and customs (Assis 2004; Portes 1995; Siqueira 2006).

The prospect of buying their own house, car, or business in a short amount of time motivates more and more Valadarians to venture out. Interviewees affirmed that the main reason to emigrate was the desire to accumulate capital to purchase properties in Brazil and improve their lifestyle. Since the 1990s another significant reason has been to reunite with their relatives. This is a fact worth noting, because some of them decide not to return to Brazil but reunite their families again in the United States.

The aim to return to their homeland is always with them. The ones who want to return within the next two or three years invest in businesses that they believe will give them financial stability and a good standard of living in Brazil. They invest, or intend to invest, mainly in shops (bakeries, stores, drugstores, supermarkets, etc), real estate for rental purposes, and farms. Those who have already made investments hire people from their family to help manage their business. Most interviewees did not research the market to see the potential profits of these enterprises.

Since the start of this wave of emigration, many individuals succeeded in entering the United States and were able to save money and return to become small and medium local entrepreneurs, stimulating the flux continuously. Many others did not experience success when they returned as a result of business failure or lack of re-adaptation to their previous life, so they returned to the United States as immigrants once again. Today they say they have learned from their mistakes, and most of them maintain the goal of returning to their hometown. However, it is a project that each day becomes more remote as they settle, establish bonds, and get involved in the community.

We can consider that the dream of returning "home" is always present, in spite of all difficulties. Like the interviewees who returned and didn't succeed in their enterprises, those now in the United States who definitely plan to return in two or three years still have no strategic plans, previous business knowledge, or professional guidance. Thus it is likely that they will make the same mistakes. Even those who have established themselves in the United States (they are legal, have their own house, a good business or job) are sure that some day they will go back to Brazil. However, the idea of returning is always postponed until they retire, become incapable of working, or when their children become independent.

For this reason, it is important that both the public and private sectors provide mechanisms that can assist migrants as they return and seek to re-establish their lives in their homelands. There is a great lack of policies and initiatives to guide these emigrants in growing and managing their enterprises and investments. Better guidance could help them to generate the income necessary to help them re-adapt to life in their homeland, thus preventing them from leaving the country as migrants again. Civil society has begun to delineate some measures. In November of 2005, for example, relatives of emigrants created the Association of Emigrants and Family Members in Governador Valadares. In July of 2006, the União Operária (Worker's League) and Banco do Brasil (Brazil Bank) inaugurated the Centro de Informação, Apoio e Amparo à Família e ao Trabalhador no Exterior (Center for Information, Support and Aid to Families and Workers Abroad, which has as its main objective the support of emigrants who return, offering them and their family members financial counseling and psychological support).

Notes

1. Governador Valadares and its region are formed by the cities: Alpercata, Campanário, Capitão Andrade, Coroaci, Divino das Laranjeiras, Engenheiro Caldas, Fernandes Tourinho, Frei Inocêncio, Galiléia, Itambacuri, Itanhomi, Jampruca, Marilac, Matias Lobato, Nacip Haiddain, Nova Módica, Pescador, São Geraldo da Piedade, São José do Safira, São José do Divino, Sobrália, Tumiritinga, Governador Valadares.
2. The Prenetti Decree forbade free immigration fees to Brazil. São Paulo and the southern states financed the process of immigration of the European workers, mainly Italians.
3. The data of this research are presented in the articles found in the bibliography: Scudeler (1999) and Sales (1999).
4. IBGE, 1996—Preliminary data of population count.
5. Terminology used by immigrants that means to work a lot and save as much as possible to come back.
6. Interview for the research, carried out on December 11, 2000.
7. A detailed study of this third group is presented by Siqueira (2006).
8. Sales (1999), Scudeler (1999), and Martes (2000) provide a good analysis of the insertion of Brazilian workers into the informal work sector. For research on housecleaning specifically, see Martes (1999), Fleischer (2002) and Assis (2004).
9. See Sayad (1998) and Hall (2003) for a discussion of the difficulties of return and the re-elaboration of the project of temporary migration.
10. It consists of a group of connections established through social relationships and networking both in the countries of origin and destination.

References

Almeida, Zenólia Maria de. 2003. "Fazer a América. Inserção e mobilidade do imigrante brasileiro em uma economia étnica." Coronel Fabriciano (MG): Unileste.

Assis, Gláucia de Oliveira. 1994. "Fazer a América. A imigração de Governador Valadares para os Estados Unidos." Dissertação mestrado. Florianópolis: Universidade Federal de Santa Catarina.

———.2004. "De Criciúma para o mundo. Rearranjos familiares de gênero nas vivências dos novos migrantes brasileiros." 325 f. Tese (Doutorado em Ciências Sociais), Instituto de Filosofia Ciências Humanas, Universidade Estadual de Campinas, Campinas.

Camargo, J. F. 1981. "Crescimento da população no Estado de São Paulo e seus aspectos econômicos." *Ensaios Econômicos. IPE-USP,* 14. São Paulo.

Fleischer, Soraya R. 2002. *Passando a América a limpo: o trabalho de housecleaners brasileiras em Boston, Massachusetts.* São Paulo, Anablume.

Fusco, Wilson. 2005. "Capital Cordial: a reciprocidade entre os migrantes brasileiros nos Estados Unidos." 138 f. Tese (Doutorado em Demografia), Instituto de Filosofia Ciências Humanas, Universidade Estadual de Campinas, Campinas.

Hall, Stuart. 2003. *Da diáspora: Identidades e mediações culturais.* Belo Horizonte.

Harvey, David. 1993. *A condição pós-moderna.* 2nd ed. São Paulo: Loyola.

Margolis, Maxine L. 1999. *Little Brazil: An Ethnography of Brazilian Immigrants in New York City.* Princeton: Princeton University Press.

Martes, Ana Cristina Braga. 2000. *Brasileiros nos Estados Unidos. Um estudo sobre imigrantes em Massachusetts.* São Paulo: Paz e Terra.

Patarra, Neide L. and Baeninger, Rosana. 1995. "Migrações internacionais recentes: o caso do Brasil." In *Emigração e Imigração Internacionais no Brasil Contemporâneo,* pp. 79–87. Org. Neide Patarra. São Paulo: FNUAP.

Portes, Alejandro. 1995. *The Economic Sociology of Immigration—Essays on Networks, Ethnicity and Entrepreneurship.* New York: Russell Sage Foundation.

Sales, Tereza. 1999. *Brasileiros longe de casa.* São Paulo: Cortez.

Sassen, Saskia. 1988. *The Mobility of Labor and Capital. A Study in International Investment and Labor Flow.* New York: Cambridge University Press.

Sayad, Abdelmalek. 1998. "O retorno: elementos constitutivos da condição do imigrante." *Travessia,* número especial.

Scudeler, Cristina. 1999. "Imigrantes Valadarenses no Mercado de Trabalho dos EUA." In *Cenas do Brasil Migrante,* pp. 193–233. Ed. Reis, Rosana Rocha, Sales, Teresa. São Paulo: Boitempo.

Siqueira, Sueli. 2006. "Migrantes empreendedores na Microrregião de Governador Valadares—Sonhos e frustrações no retorno." 193f. Tese (Doutorado em Ciências Humanas, Sociologia e Política) Faculdade de Filosofia e Ciências Humanas. Universidade Federal de Minas Gerais, Belo Horizonte.

———. 2002. "Migração internacional e seus efeitos na configuração do desenvolvimento da cidade de Governador Valadares." *Caderno do Neder.* Universidade Vale do Rio Doce. www.editora.univale.br.

Soares, Weber. 2002. "Da Metáfora à Substância: Redes Sociais, Redes Migratórias e Migração Nacional e Internacional em Governador Valadares e Ipatinga." 344 f. Tese (Doutorado em Demografia), Centro de desenvolvimento e Planejamento Regional, Universidade Federal de Minas Gerais, Belo Horizonte.

———. 2005. "Emigrants e investidores: Redefinindo a dinâmica imobiliána na economia valaderense." 174f. Dissertação (Mestrado em Demografia) Universidade Federal do Rio de Janeiro, Rio de Janeiro.

8

The Concept of Time and Conflicting Expectations of Brazilian Women in Clinical Settings

Clémence Jouët-Pastré, Branca Telles Ribeiro, Márcia Guimarães, Solange de Azambuja Lira

Elena

> **E:** Then I tell Ricardo "the **time** (of consultation) for an American doctor is **fifteen** minutes." Clémence=
> **C:** =Uh huh=
> **E:** If it goes over that (pause) if you ask more questions=
> **C:** =Uh huh=
> **E:** =than the fifteen minutes (pause) they start getting upset.[1]

Denise

> **D:** Here there's no, there's no real dialogue=
> **S:** =//Uh huh//=
> **D:** =They hardly look at you, right?

This chapter discusses Brazilian women's narratives about their health-related experiences in the United States, specifically in Boston. The discussion focuses on what constitutes, for these women, different understandings of the clinical encounter as it takes place here and in Brazil; differences that trigger moments of discomfort regarding well-being and access to treatment. Specifically, we will discuss a key theme that emerged in our research interviews—the issue of time and how time affects the patient's relationship with a healthcare provider: how these women conceptualize time; how time is contrasted when compared to healthcare in Brazil; what expectations they have regarding attention and duration in the clinical encounter.

This study derives from an ongoing research project on *Brazilian Immigrant Women: Analyzing conflicting needs and expectations in clinical settings.* It includes professionals from Harvard and Lesley universities. We are an interdisciplinary team of Brazilian linguists and a psychologist living in the Boston area. Our concern derives from studies in doctor/patient communication attesting to the complexities of the clinical encounter (Mishler 1986; Sarangi and Roberts 1999, among others). Given the inherent linguistic and sociolinguistic differences for immigrant populations, this situation gets further complicated when added to the traumatic circumstances often related to migration. For example, the research presented in Chapter 6 of this book reveals that many Brazilian women have to rethink their racial identity in the United States and face other transnational dilemmas; in other words, they feel that they do not belong either to the sending or the receiving country. The aim of our project is to attend to the Brazilian community and its needs, specifically related to women, investigating first *the voices of the community*. Later we will research *the voices of the clinic* as well (as to what actually happens in the clinical encounter between patients, interpreters, and healthcare providers).

Immigration and Access to Information

Researchers such as Jack (1991), Nava (2001), Messias (2002), DeBiaggi (2002), De Fina (2003) among others, have pointed out that experiences of displacement, such as arriving, placing, and integrating oneself into a new society, are complex experiences often related to traumatic circumstances. They also pointed out that women particularly bear a heavier burden in these processes as they perform several roles in the family, in the community, and in the workplace.

Following narrative studies by Bruner (1986, 1990), Mishler (1986), Linde (1993), the questions we investigate focus on how Brazilian women make meaning of their everyday experiences in healthcare-related matters in the United States. What do they say about what they do as how they interact with doctors or healthcare providers? What key themes emerge in their narratives of health and illness? To address such issues, we need to turn briefly to the broad context that informs our research.

Brazilians in the Boston Area

The immigration of Portuguese speakers to Massachusetts is not a new phenomenon. Since the nineteenth century, immigrants came from mainland Portugal, from the Azores, and from Cape Verde. Brazilians came much later to Massachusetts and benefited from services and a large social network initially established by and for the Portuguese.

In the 1990s, the Brazilian immigrant population drastically increased and new services became quickly available. Recent organizations emerged to attend to the different needs of the community, such as the Brazilian Women's Group, the Center for Brazilian Immigrants, the Center for Brazilian Workers, and the Brazilian Community Center at the Parish of St. Anthony in Allston-Brighton. Also, the local Brazilian media include fourteen newspapers, two monthly magazines, and two websites entirely produced and circulated in the metropolitan Boston area.

As a research group, we decided that one of our first tasks was to map the multiple services and social networks in healthcare that attend to the Brazilian community. In 2003 we visited two community-based clinics and two major hospitals. All of them provide Brazilian immigrants with some type of special services, such as interpreters, written materials, and bilingual health care providers.

The first clinic we visited had treated 18,000 Brazilian patients in 2002—which meant that 30% of their clients were Brazilian. The second clinic is part of a large consortium of three hospitals and twenty clinics. In 2002, 64,000 patients went through health services provided by this consortium: 22% were Portuguese speakers, 14% Spanish speakers, and 7% were speakers of other languages.

The hospitals we visited also cater to a large Brazilian population. We were able to collect data related to their interpreter services. One of the hospitals had a team of fourteen interpreters just to serve the Portuguese-speaking patients. The other hospital presented figures on medical encounters mediated by interpreters. The data indicated that patient encounters for which Portuguese interpreters were used increased 750% in five years. Specifically, in 1998 there were 882 encounters mediated by Portuguese interpreters and 6,682 in 2003.

Voices from the Community

Eight research interviews were developed as part of our study. These interviews lasted for about an hour to an hour and half. We interviewed two groups of women: 1) high-school graduates, who generally have working-class jobs in the United States; they use free care or health services on an emergency basis; 2) college graduates, who hold professional jobs in the United States; as such, they have health insurance and are generally cared for in major clinics or hospitals as is the general American population.

Our research is based on qualitative in-depth interviews. As we wanted to elicit narratives, and didn't want to interrupt the on-going conversation, we mostly stayed within the topics that were brought up by the interviewees.[2] Most of all, we did not bring an *a priori* topic agenda. Following Linde (1993), Mishler (1986), among others, we stayed within story frames on issues of health and illness proposed by the interviewee and tried to probe further to learn more about narratives that were meaningful to the speaker.

Why Women?

A health assessment performed with thirteen healthcare providers in Greater Boston identified women as the most likely link to the family (Guimaraes 2003). Through pediatrician and obstetrician services, women establish their first contact with healthcare providers, and then bridge it to the health system. Women, thus, establish a link to the healthcare system earlier and more frequently as compared to men.

Gender roles also shed some light on what drives these women to the health system. Different cultures have different expectations regarding women and men's behavior. In Brazil, regardless of class and regional differences, women and men are still largely regarded as responsible for distinct spheres of life. Women are viewed as the family caretakers, often solely responsible for household tasks and child rearing (DeBiaggi 2003; DeBiaggi 2002; Beserra 2003). These roles expand as the woman emigrates. In the words of an interviewee, "giving birth in the U.S. is a way to be indirectly accepted by the receiving society: the new baby becomes a member of the new society." DeBiaggi (2002) emphasizes the importance of changing gender roles once the woman immigrates to the United States. Brazilian families face new patterns of gender role behavior and attitudes which affect their adjustment to the new society. Women become more independent, more self-assured and take more initiative. DeBiaggi's research states that 30% of the wives who emigrated to the United States entered the labor force for the first time, a social change that triggered more independence, power and autonomy.

Discussing a Salient Theme—Why Is Time of the Essence?

Issues related to time are one of the most salient themes in the interviews. Regardless of social and educational background and time spent outside Brazil, all the women indicated that healthcare providers in the United States have a radically different take on time than their counterparts in Brazil. Time—and associated topics such as attention and posture—constitute a recurrent theme for all these women.

The concept of time has been investigated extensively. Given our interest in language and culture, we followed researchers such as Munn (1992), Sapir (1968), and Thornton (1980) on how distinct cultures perceive, value, and pattern time. American anthropologist Hall (1983) argues that learning how cultures deal with time is as important as learning any spoken language: "A complicating factor in intercultural relations is that each culture has its own time frames in which the patterns are unique. This means that to function effectively abroad it is just as necessary to learn the language of time as it is to learn the spoken language" (1983, 3).

Brislin and Kim (2003) also point to complex ways of conceptualizing time in different cultures. Particularly interesting to us are the distinctions between "clock time" and "event time" (do people follow a set schedule or do they allow the event to take its natural course?) and "polychronic time" versus "monochronic time" (are people attending to one activity at a time or several activities at once). In alerting us that these are broad generalizations, Levine and Norenzayan (1999) state that clock time is usually found in North America, Western Europe, East Asia, Australia, and New Zealand. Event time is often found in South America, South Asia, and Africa (as cited in Brislin and Kim 2003). Our interviewees often contrast the time of the clinical encounter (the official, formal clock time) with the expected time of the personal encounter with the doctor or healthcare provider (the event time of the encounter). These differences often lead to misunderstandings. It also gets a bit more complicated when the American official time is said to be limited to fifteen minutes (clock time), which conflicts with the Brazilian expectation (of thirty minutes) as voiced by the interviewees. Closely related to the perception of "event time" is attention, more specifically attending to the patient as the unique focus of interest. In the doctor-patient encounter, conflicting expectations emerge when doctors are required to multi-task (ask questions, sit at the computer, write notes) while patients expect a conversational encounter (a face-to-face interaction). In such instances, these patients expect to have the doctor's constant attention (a single focus of attention) while clinicians are required to shift in participation structure (Goffman 1981) and attend to more than one activity at a time.[3]

Our data indicate that time may be captured in many different ways. It may be reflected in how fast interactions take place, for example, or how fast the healthcare provider speaks, or how much attention is given to the patient. Attention is often captured by different ways of speaking related to participants' use of language, as well as his/her posture, positioning, and eye gaze, as the following excerpts illustrate.

The Language of Time

The following excerpt from one of our interviews is a revealing example of how the language of time is, if not more important than, at least as important as any spoken language.

Excerpt (1), *Ilana*

> **C:** Do you **recommend** doctors?
> **I:** I do. Just like I recommended my doctor that I told you about=
> **C:** =uh huh=
> **I:** =Doctor Henrique.
> **C:** Ah:
> **I:** So-
> **C:** This Chilean?
> **I:** Right:::
> **C:** Uh huh=
> **I:** =That I had two friends that also had babies and at that time I told them "wow, look for him _'cause **he's really good!**"=
> **C:** =Uh huh=
> **I:** =Y'know? I **really** liked him.
> **C:** Uh huh.=
> **I:** =**Very kind**, you know?=
> **C:** =Uh huh.=
> **I:** =Like really attentive with us.=
> **C:** =Uh huh.
> **I:** But they couldn't, couldn't get an appointment with him, that he's very . . .
> **C:** Uh.
> **I:** He is very .. y' know? Exactly 'cause he knows- (pause) how to speak **our language a little** [laughs]. Y' know what I mean?=
> **C:** =Uh huh=
> **I:** =Everybody **wants to see him,** y' know?
> **C:** Ah:::
> **I:** So it's it's it's (pause) it's really very- (pause) very difficult to get an appointment with him. So they weren't able to get one. (pause) So I was the only privileged one. [laughs]
> **C:** What luck huh? And so he- he speaks a little bit of Portuguese too like this or-
> **I: No he doesn't speak Portuguese,** like I told you, he speaks, he speaks Chilean, but it's it's not that kind of Spanish that (pause) confuses you, y' know what I mean?=

C: =Uh huh
I: But sometimes he he tries- I think that (with) him- (pause) **I can understand his language, y'know?**=
C: =Uh huh=
I: =It's- confusing but you can understand well=
C: =Uh huh=
I: =He also has a lot of patience of- y'know?
C: Uh huh=
I: =Sometimes if you didn't understand, you w'd say "I didn't understand," y' know?
C: Uh huh
I: So he was **patient with you**, he'd say, y'know?

There are several points to address here. First, in looking at *the interview situation*, we see a fast-paced interaction between interviewer and interviewee (turns latch into one another). The interviewer assumes the position of the listener of a story (providing what linguists call "backchannels"—"uhm, uhm"). In rhythm, this interaction follows a conversational pace rather than a standard interview (in standard interviews, we would have a context of an inquiry with a Question/Answer/Question/Answer sequence). Here, both participants co-construct this encounter in a similar pace. Both participants use what Tannen (1989) calls *involvement strategies* indicated by 1) the joint pace of talk, 2) the constant ratification by the interviewer, signaling attention, and 3) a series of repetitive markers ('yknow, y'know what I mean) that attest to a conversation. Setting the interactional context as a conversation rather than an inquiry is important for a successful research interview, as pointed out by Mishler (1986), so that the interviewee will convey more interesting information that is relevant to her—and, most of all, is not likely to be interrupted.

Second, Ilana, the interviewee, makes statements that have implications for talk and communication in clinical settings. At the opening of this segment, in addressing the interviewer's questions, Ilana mentions that she recommended her doctor, from Chile, to two other Brazilian friends. She makes a series of evaluative statements "he's really good," "I really liked him," "he's great," and then explains why: "he's very kind," "really attentive with us." Then she adds: "Exactly 'cause he knows (pause) how to speak our language a little." The interviewer picks up on that a few turns later: "And so he- he speaks a little bit of Portuguese too?" to which Ilana answers emphatically "No, he doesn't speak Portuguese. . . . He speaks Chilean, but it's not that kind of Spanish that (pause) confuses you." The intriguing point in this interaction is that the doctor is Chilean, speaks

Spanish and not Portuguese. However, he is quite popular among Brazilian patients. And then she states: "I can understand his language." And restates it another time: "It's—confusing (his language) but you can understand well."

What is interesting about this data is that our interviewee actually states that speaking the same language may not be the only key issue in communication. What seems to be important (and equally valued) is the quality of the interaction. In clinical encounters, Ilana points to a doctor who actually listens to her ("who has a lot of patience," a statement that is repeated twice), to someone who is "very kind," and who is "really attentive." All the adjectives are marked by intensifiers ("very," "really," "a lot"). These evaluations qualify the interaction and create possibilities for communication beyond the linguistic realm. Regarding language *per se*, we also see that this doctor—in the eyes of this patient—makes an effort to be clear ("it's not that kind of Spanish that confuses you"), possibly speaking very slowly, attentive to the patient's feedback, and checking that he is being understood. As Ilana points out, "sometimes if you didn't understand, you'd say 'I didn't understand.'"

Research points to how critical communication is in clinical settings (Fisher and Todd 1983; Mishler 1986; Ribeiro 1994; Hyden and Mishler 1999; Sarangi and Roberts 1999, among others). It gets even more complex in interactions with speakers from different and yet related linguistic backgrounds. Portuguese and Spanish are two different languages derived from Latin. Given that some Spanish dialects may seem accessible to Portuguese speakers, serious misunderstandings may take place.[4] However, what Ilana seems to be highlighting here is that if the clinician takes the time to be really concerned about communication and its inherent complexities (which in this case involves also bridging the linguistic gap between a Spanish dialect speaker and a Brazilian-Portuguese speaker), the interlocutors may achieve shared understandings.

A serious word of caution is appropriate here. Often two related languages such as Spanish and Portuguese may seem to outsiders close enough to allow for straight communication. Yet intonation (stress patterns, for example) and prosody constitute serious impediments, along with many "false friends" on the way (seemingly closely related words which have quite different meanings and uses) that could provide enough damage in a complex communicative context such as a medical encounter. Thus to assume similarity and shared understanding between these two languages is very dangerous in professional clinical settings.

This excerpt contrasts with the following from the same speaker:

Excerpt (2)

C: And are they **Brazilian**, these interpreters=
I: =Yes. Most of them are.
C: They are- And what do you prefer to have, Brazilian interpreters or:::=
I: =Oh, Brazilian, of course.
C: 'Cause- sometimes who do you see **most** as interpreters besides Brazilians?
I: We don't- y'mean (pause) **No,** we are Brazilians, we ask for Brazilians, they have the habit of sending some Portuguese (interpreters), that sometimes we don't really understand, y'know.= [laughs]
C: =Uh, huh=
I: = Then you mix up everything. 'Cause sometimes there are some Portuguese, that speak fast, in a confusing way that sometimes we do not understand.
C: Uh, huh.

Ilana reports on another complex face-to-face encounter: a clinical encounter mediated by an interpreter. These professionals often see their roles as "culture brokers" who convey linguistic and sociolinguistic information. They play key roles in facilitating common understanding between patients and doctors. Such encounters portray a complex participation structure (Erickson & Shultz, 1982; Goffman, 1981), where both the healthcare provider and the patient rely on the interpreter to capture the message (what is said) and the metamessage (how it is said)—and where time, once more, is of the essence.

Ilana discusses some problems related to an interpreter's style and Portuguese dialects. On the one hand, Brazilians and Portuguese speak the same language. On the other hand, Brazilian Portuguese and European Portuguese are actually different dialects, often presenting a few barriers in a loaded communicative context (such as a clinical encounter). The differences are wider than those of British and American English. So we face an interesting sociolinguistic situation here, where Ilana, our interviewee, actually states that Portuguese interpreters and the use of European Portuguese may trigger miscommunication: "sometimes we don't really understand," "then you mix up everything." She explains the confusion as "they speak too fast," "in a confusing way," which ultimately results in lack of understanding. Of course, this contrasts with the prior situation where the doctor has "lots of patience," the language is "confusing but you can understand."

This leaves us with a discussion of language, communication, and most of all, shared understandings. In inserting language in a theory of communication, Hymes (1974) and Gumperz (1982) have discussed how participants engaged in conversation actually share (or don't) norms of production and interpretation (speaking and listening) in a given interaction—how participants actually share what they call "ways of speaking." This seems to be what Ilana is most attentive to here—it goes beyond sharing a language, which is crucial, of course, but is only a first step. What she is pointing to—which may lead to very serious problems in clinical environments—is the need to attend not only to language, but more importantly to how communication is shared in interaction, how participants actually capture and value time, attention, and care. In describing the Chilean doctor, Ilana captures in a nutshell key strategies in communication for a successful clinical encounter (to be attentive, to be kind, to be good at one's job). These two segments illustrate how the doctor's (or healthcare provider's) orientation, attention, and time in the interview situation convey a language of its own.

Time is a complex concept that covers multiple and sometimes conflicting layers of meaning. In classical Greek, time is referred to as *ora*, *aion*, *chronos*, and *kairos*. Two of these terms, *chronos* and *kairos*, interest us more closely. *Chronos* relates to a world view in which time can be measured, reckoned, segmented, and sequencialized. *Kairos* is "the time not of measurement but of human activity . . . *Kairos* relates to its close cousin *kainos,* which signifies new, newly invented or novel; *kainos* in turn connects with *kinein*, to move, from which comes kinesis" (Jaques 1982, 15). These two concepts apply in interesting ways in how our interviewees interpret their interactions with U.S. healthcare providers and compare them to their prior experiences in Brazil.

The women also described several moments of discomfort. These were triggered by what they perceive as a mismatch in interpretation between them and their U.S. health care providers relating to time. They display what Tannen and Wallat (1993) have described as a conflict in expectations or conflicting knowledge schemas—in this case, differences regarding what is considered "enough time."

We will discuss five instances that illustrate such mismatch in expectations (or uncomfortable moments) as identified by our interviewees: 1) perceptions of chronological time; 2) perceptions of discrete units of time; 3) attention and posture in the interview situation; 4) body orientation and gaze; and finally 5) the doctor's agenda.

1) Perceptions of chronological time

Excerpt (3), *Elena*

E: Then I tell Ricardo thus "the **time** (of consultation) for an American doctor is **fifteen** minutes Clémence=
C: =Uh, huh=
E: If it goes over that (pause) if you ask more questions=
C: =Uh, huh=
E: =than the fifteen minutes (pause) they start getting upset.

Excerpt (4), Rosa

R: I .. can tell you that from the appointment time=
M: =Uh, huh=
R: =I think, I think that I have **never** had an **appointment** in Brazil::: (pause) I know that there are people that talk more other less and I am one of these people that talk more [laughs-rapid speech] but::: (pause) I think I have never had an appointment which lasted less than thirty minutes (pause) maybe even forty minutes, I don't know.

Elena refers to a discrete chronological time (fifteen minutes) as the expected time for a clinical encounter in the United States. As a patient she has also inferred that beyond this time frame, the clinician would "start getting upset." It is interesting to note that healthcare web sites in the United States inform patients that time is limited. The number of questions a patient would raise in the clinical encounter is also limited (three questions). Elena's perception of time in the United States contrasts with Rosa's perception of time for the clinical encounter in Brazil: "I had never had an appointment in Brazil which lasted less than thirty minutes."

2) Perceptions of discrete units of time and topic

One of our interviewees carefully elaborated on this mismatch and actually uncovered what the expectation of the American health care provider is:

Excerpt (5), *Rosa*

R: The impression that I have is that she (American nurse) had, they have a quota per **day** that they have to **fill** or for **every** appointment you have:: to call and you have to tell what (pause) you call and in the telephone you have to tell the reception- receptionist **the reason** for the appointment. Then:: I imagine that after that (after the receptionist finds the reason for the appointment) they calculate a a (pause) specific time for that appointment (pause) and they have to follow that time. I imagine that that day she must have been **very late**=

M: =Uh:::=

R: =I had more than one question **for her** but I didn't know about that and it was at that moment that I understood how the system worked=

M: =Uh, huh=

R: So if you have three questions, you have to have three appointments, that's the impression I have.

This woman's perception is confirmed by a Brazilian female doctor who has been living and practicing in the Boston area for more than twenty years. She explicitly mentions what it means for Brazilians to perceive time as *kairos*, how one experience can lead to a completely different interpretation than the one previously expected:

Excerpt (6), *Marly*

M: The time that we have for an appointment is very **limited,** so we are encouraged to see the patient more often, y'know? Because an appointment is about fifteen minutes:::. And how can we in fifteen minutes (pause). It's like I told you, when a Brazilian comes, he/she doesn't come only saying "I have a headache." Generally it is like this, "By the way (laughs), this is also hurting, there is something else" (pause) because it is a different concept of health.=

M: =Uh huh=

Marly: =Do you understand? And I **understand** this, that it is not only one thing, y'know? But then with **tact** we have to say "Look, today we have to pay more attention to this (pause) you have to come back, when can you come back, in two weeks or in a month? What is more **urgent**?" Then I think that the people start little by **little** to::: prioritize, y'know? To prioritize, "today I'm here for **this** reason" (pause) y'know (pause) little by little this develops this type of selection because there is no other way with our health system, there is no other way, y'know, there is no appointment, a longer appointment is::: half an hour, forty-five minutes but it is check-up, a physical, you know, but generally an average appointment is very brief.

The Brazilian healthcare provider explains step by step what the expectation is for a clinical encounter: it is short and focused on a specific concern that the patient has. If there are other concerns, the patient has to return for another appointment later on. This mapping of a new script for a clinical encounter is important. It constitutes a schema (Bruner 1986, 1990) for interactions attesting to time and specificity/objectivity. Marly contrasts such a script (one that Brazilians need to understand) with the expectations that Brazilian patients have for the encounter: bringing up more than one concern: "By the way (laughs), this is also hurting, there is something else" and expressing a different understanding, "it is a different concept of health."

3) Attention and posture in the interview situation

Several metaphors about, and references to, attention and body positioning are related to *chronos* and *kairos*:

Excerpt (7), *Denise*

> **D:** No. I have never had a doctor that would really (pause) sit:: with me (pause)
> **S:** It is something very cold=
> **D:** =a **dialogue** (have) something more personal, y' know, no never (pause) it is always the same thing, the data the data are these.

Excerpt (8), *Elena*

> **E:** He he was sitting **there** he was at the computer taking notes on Vanessa's health answering the questions, but this way is not that thing=
> **C:** = uh=
> **E:** =of **stopping** (pause)
> **C:** uh, huh=
> **E:** =**sitting** and giving you some attention.

Excerpt (9), *Elena*

> **E:** Then that situation of you **sitting,** the doctor is there in front of you and he really (pause) **gives** you a special attention.

A series of cues captures how these women narrate their interactions with healthcare providers. Gumperz (1982) calls these signals "contextualization cues" that capture how we mean what we say. They may be paralinguistic and prosodic features of speech (lengthening of vowels, emphasis, pace, etc.), or they may be nonverbal cues (Scheflen 1973; Kendon 1981).

These cues signal how the speaker relates to what she is saying, how she creates a context for the interaction being depicted ("I never had a doctor that would really [pause] sit::: with me [pause]")—the pace is slow capturing the moment and the request for attention from the other; such an evaluation contrasts with a sense of being perceived as an object: "it is always the same thing, the data, the data are these."

Among the nonverbal cues, postural configurations appear to play a central role as embodiments of context in interaction (Erickson and Shultz 1977, 6). The segments above capture how body orientation constitutes interactional contexts of communication, "he was sitting **there**, he was at the computer taking notes," "but this way is not that thing of **stopping** (pause), **sitting** and giving you some attention." Thus Denise and Elena attest to a sense of disconnection, an orientation to the other "as data," and a brief time for interaction.

A major cue in analyzing nonverbal behavior is eye gaze. It signals participants' orientation towards one another in focused interactions (Goffman 1974). The following captures differences in perceptions:

4) Eye gaze

Excerpt (10), *Rosa*

> **R:** The way the doctor [in Brazil] **looks** at you, the way the doctor::: uhm:: listens to what you are asking, it seems to me that he is more **caring**, he is more **attentive**, I can't say that all of them, of course=

Excerpt (11), Rosa

> **R:** I think it is starts (pause) from the way the doctor looks at you, looks at your **face**, at your **eyes** and (pause) //a specific example? (pause) Let me see// (pause) I can't think of any right now (pause) I I I can tell you by the **length** of the appointment, I .. I can tell you by the **length** of the appointment=
> **M:** Uh, uhm=
> **R:** I think I have **never** had an appointment in Brazil::: (pause) I know that there are some people that talk more, other less, I am one of these people that speak more [laughs-rapid speech] but uh . . . I think I had never had an appointment that lasted less than half an hour (pause) maybe even .. forty minutes, I don't know=
> **M:** =In Brazil?
> **R:** no Brazil.

M: uh huh=
R: =and .. here (pause) let's say that I must have gone to the doctor or nurse here (pause), right?=
M: =( ) different=
R: =It is not different here, I mean, you (pause) I must have gone about:: ten times (pause) twelve times ( ) (pause) being here for **two** years (pause) two and half years, (pause) I mean=
M: =You have been here for two and half years?=
R: =Two and half years (pause) it will be three years now in August actually. Let's say that I have gone to the doctor **for myself** not considering the the ones for my son (pause) around **twelve** times. I must have had **two a**ppointments that lasted forty minutes.=
M: =uh, uhm.=
R: and (pause) finally, I think that the doctor explores more uh::: in Brazil, .. more **facets** of your illness, or of the questions you are asking (pause), right, it seems that he **understands**, it could be only my impression (pause) but that:: your physical illness might have other factors, uh::: it seems that he looks at the expression in your **face**, uh::: if you are **tense**, if you are not **tense**,=
M: =uh, uhm=
R: =if:: in conclusion:: if **you are happy**, if you are not happy, what is happening, **here** they are:::
M: Straightforward.
R: [laughs] they are straightforward, objective (pause) and you (pause) it seems that it is an American quality to be the most objective, (it's) possible (pause) and not **waste any time**. I have the impression that **anything** beyond your physical complaint [hitting the table as she speaks] is a waste of time, and he can't waste any time.
M: Uh, huh.

Rosa describes different ways of gazing that seem to be related to a sense of time as *kairos*: "the ways the doctor looks at you," "I can tell you by the length of the appointment." Rosa also describes contrastive differences; she points out that a Brazilian doctor would investigate the patient's health problems in a rather holistic way: "he understands . . . that your physical illness might have other factors, uh::: it seems that he looks at the expression in your **face**, uh::: if you are **tense**, . . . if **you are happy**, if you are not happy, what is happening." Such treatment of the patient as a whole (the person and the body, the self, mind, and body) encompasses a different sense of time, not chronological and discrete. It contrasts sharply with the

American system being "straightforward, objective," with its corollary that "**anything** beyond your physical complaint is a waste of time."

In each of these segments, we see how much the interviewees value location and positioning (expressed in how one sits). Body posture conveys an opening for a conversation to unfold. Also interrupting or suspending chronological time is pointed out as important to signal attention in the interview situation. Recurrent in our data is the relevance of eye gaze. All the above segments indicate how much these women value particularities (posture, sitting arrangements, gaze) in their interaction with healthcare providers.

5) The doctor's agenda.

The last two segments capture the way some of these women report specifically about the doctor's agenda.

Excerpt (12), *Eva*

M: Would you like a longer appointment?
E: Nao (pause)
M: No?
E: No .. [laugh] unless there is a problem I like I have always enjoyed **having my** time but my time I I always had (time) with the nurses=
M: uhm,uhm, but how is this this time?
E: Well the time that I mentioned like uh::: have::: one doesn't like to feel that the person is (pause) in a hurry (pause) in a hurry, y'know? He is ( ) nothing, I like that the person **listens,** I don't like feeling that the person is (pause) you explain your problem, when there is:: of course when there is:: when it is a regular check-up even you .. knew that it is a quick thing (pause) you want to go away.
M: What makes you notice that the person is in a hurry?
E: By a problem that happened, y'know? But for me to feel like (pause), ah::: when you complain about something .. uh.::: "I have already read this all here, do you have news? " It is the **way** of expressing, y'know? "Do you have any news?"[rapid speech] He doesn't treat you like a person, he treats you like::: business, that is all, the thing is all very fast. I don't know how to tell you that [laughs] tchau!
M: /uh, huh/
E: =It is like, as I am telling you, "Do you have any news? No, then sign here fast, it is all okay, you are all set" [rapid speech] You feel a (pause) you don't feel a smile, don't feel a:: "speak::: I want to listen to you,"

y'know, we like this (pause) it is a very (pause) **objective** thing very **fast.**

Eva uses reported speech to capture the doctor's sense of time and orientation towards the encounter. In speaking as if she were the doctor, she says that one must report a newsworthy complaint: "I've already read this all here, do you have news?" Paralinguistic cues signal a fast paced interaction as indicating a fast transaction, also captured in her evaluation "it's all very fast." It signals an orientation to the patient as "business" "he treats you like::: business," "it's all okay, you're all set."

Excerpt (13), *Rosa*

R: She (her female primary care physician) is **attentive**, she considers (pause) finally, you (pause) as I told you, I have the impression that **I** have adjusted, then I don't bring her questions that (pause) uh, that are not the first questions of the **appointment**,=
M: =uh. huh.
R: = unless I feel that she can- that she can **answer**, she is very **calm**, she isn't hurrying in **her** voice, she is not asking one question after the other without breathing [laughs]=
M: =She is a doctor, right?
R: =She is a doctor, this one is a doctor. If I feel that and if I really have an urgent question, I will **ask.**
M: She doesn't speak very fast, she speaks slowly, did you say.=
R: =This is important. You notice when the doctor, at least I notice when the doctor **is late.**
M: =uh. huh=
R: =He asks one question after another and you haven't even breathed to answer and he is already asking another question.
M: And how do you feel in this moment?
R: It is uncomfortable because::: you have gone there to talk about yourself::: I mean, I don't think (pause), I don't think it is, it isn't the most agreeable think to do in the world! You are exposing yourself to a **person**, you have to tell him that you feel pain **here and there**, you are not feeling well and the person is following a **protocol**, **running**, you have the sensation that you (pause) are **not being heard**! That (pause) uhm, he is going to **skip** something, he is not going to **pay attention** to me, he is not taking this into account, when he prescribes something to me, will he consider what I am **telling** him, what I consider **important?**=

Rosa first states that she now understands the doctor's agenda and set of expectations. She says "I have adjusted," "I don't bring her questions . . . that are not the first questions of the appointment." She learned to socially construct the encounter according to the doctor's expectations and therefore attempted to be communicatively competent in the new culture. As a person, Rosa also voices her own expectations regarding the doctor's attention in the encounter: this doctor is "attentive," "she can answer," "she is very calm." A posture that sharply contrasts with that of another MD: "when the doctor is late," and turn-taking is reported to be very fast ("you haven't even breathed to answer and he is already asking another question"). Here Rosa refers to how keeping time chronologically (being late, running, skipping) actually impedes good listening on the doctor's part ("it is uncomfortable," "you are not being heard."), which would require quality *(kairos)* time.

Conclusion: Making Sense of Health-related Experiences in the United States

The segments presented illustrate differences in expectations that are prevalent in our interviews, where time is considered of the essence by both participants (healthcare provider and patient) as reported by our interviewees. We had two groups of women/patients—Brazilian high-school and college graduates. We were expecting different perceptions within the two groups. Surprisingly, our participants displayed similar understandings of their clinical encounters. Our interviewees discussed the constraints of chronological time (the typical fifteen minutes meeting). They often contrasted the American time to an idealized time back in Brazil (where a doctor/patient encounter would last at least thirty minutes). In establishing these contrasting points, they discussed the relevance of the time frame to the quality of the interaction, of "being together" as opposed to "doing" or "going through itemized topics" in the interview situation. Time was conceptualized as "being," "feeling," "paying attention," "being treated as a person," "a talk that invites listening."

Learning the cultural language of time may be as important as learning a foreign language. This conclusion derives from broader cultural underpinnings, specific to Brazil and Brazilian women. It has implications for cross-cultural communication in clinical settings. Our findings corroborate Messias, who advocates that, "Despite the current trend in US health care that equates time with higher costs, the benefits of spending time with immigrants and making the best use of that time must be considered and documented through practice and research" (2002, 198).

One of the key issues in this discussion is how to make the best use of such a crucial and scare resource as time in clinical encounters. We certainly acknowledge that problems with time constraints are not limited to the Brazilian immigrant community. It is a problem that has a heavy impact on the larger American population and, consequently, it is an issue constantly present on the agenda of healthcare providers, administrators, the media, and the general public. However, we want to stress that Brazilian immigrants face the additional problem of "cultural miscommunication" when dealing with time and its implied meanings, which may lead to misinterpretations regarding the healthcare provider's positioning, posture, and alignment in the clinical encounter. Such misunderstanding may have serious implications related to the patient's acceptance and adherence to treatment. We hope that this chapter can shed some light on the many caveats present in multicultural clinical encounters and spark some dialogue about inherent difficulties and possible solutions.

Appendix—Excerpts of Original Interviews in Portuguese

(All interview excerpts were translated by the authors.)

Elena

E: Então eu falo pro Ricardo assim "o **tempo** do médico americano é **quinze** minutos"
Clémence=
C: =Hum=
E: Passou disso (pausa) se você faz mais pergunta=
C: =Hum=
E: =do que quinze minutos (pausa) eles começam a ficar irritados.

Denise

D: Aqui nun nun tem diálogo mesmo=
S: =//Hum hum//=
D: =Mal olha na cara né?

Excerpt (1)

Ilana

C: E você **dá** referência?
I: Dô igual eu dei do meu médico que eu gostei muito que eu te falei=
C: =Hum hum=

I: =Doutor Henrique.
C: Ah:
I: Aí-
C: Esse chileno?
I: É:::
C: Hum hum.=
I: =Que eu tive duas amigas também que ganhou neném:: que eu até na época eu falei "nossa, procura ele que **ele é ótimo!**"=
C: =Hum hum=
I: =Sabe gostei **muito** dele,
C: Hum hum.=
I: =**Muito carinhoso,** sabe?=
C: =Hum hum.=
I: =Assim atencioso com a gente.=
C: =Hum hum.
I: Mas num num conseguia achar horário com ele, que é bem...
C: Hum.
I: Ele é muito .. sabe? Justamente por isso por ele saber a- (pausa) ele falar um pouquinho **a língua da gente** [risos] entendeu?=
C: =Hum hum=
I: =Todo mundo **quer ele**, né?
C: Ah:::
I: Então num num num (pausa) é muito- (pausa) muito difícil apontamento com ele. Aí elas não conseguiram. (pausa) Aí acho que foi só eu a privilegiada mesmo. [risos]
C: Que sorte né? E aí ele- ele fala um pouquinho de português também assim ou-
I: Não ele num fala o português, igual eu te falei ele fala ele fala o chileno mas aqu- aquele num é aquele espanhol assim (pause) que te enrola entendeu?=
C: =Hum hum
I: Mas às vezes ele ele consegue- eu acho que ele- (pause) **dá pro cê entender a língua dele, entendeu?**=
C: =Hum hum=
I: =É aquele- enrolado mas que você entende bem=
C: =Hum hum=
I: =E ele tinha muita paciência também de- sabe?
C: Hum hum=
I: =Às vezes cê num entendia, cê falava assim "eu não entendi," sabe?

C: Hum hum
I: Aí ele tinha **paciência com você**, falava, sabe?

Excerpt (2)

Ilana

C: E são **brasileiros**, esses intérpretes=
I: =São a maioria são.
C: Tem- e o que que você prefere ter, um intérprete brasilei: ro ou::=
I: =Ah brasileiro, né.
C: Por que- às vêzes o que que **tem** mais além de brasileiro?
I: Não tem- cê fala assim [pausa] **Não** geralmente a gente é brasileiro, a gente pede os- os brasileiros, costuma vir uns portugueses que a gente não entende muito bem, entendeu.= [risos]
C: =Hum hum=
I: =Aí cê enrola tudo. Que às vezes tem uns portugueses, que fala, meio rápido, meio enrolado, que às vezes cê num entende direito.
C: Hum hum.

Excerpt (3)

Elena

E: então eu falo pro Ricardo assim "o **tempo** do médico americano é **quinze** minutos" Clémence=
C: =Hum=
E: passou disso (pausa) se você faz mais pergunta=
C: =Hum=
E: =do que quinze minutos (pausa) eles começam a ficar irritados

Excerpt (4)

Rosa

R: Eu .. eu posso dizer pelo **tempo** da consulta=
M: =hum hum.=
R: =Acho acho que eu **nunca** tive uma **consulta** no Brasil::: (pausa) eu sei que tem algumas pessoas que falam mais outras menos e eu sou uma dessas pessoas que falam mais [risos-fala rápida] mas é::: (pausa) acho que eu nunca tive uma consulta com menos de meia hora (pausa) talvez até 40 minutos não sei.

Excerpt (5)

Rosa

R: a impressão que eu tenho é que ela [enfermeira americana] tinha, eles têm uma produção por **dia** que eles têm que **cumprir** ou ou **cada** consulta tem um:: você liga e você tem que dizer o que (pausa) você liga e ao telefone você tem que dizer pra recepcion- recepcionista o **motivo** da consulta. Então::: eu imagino que diante disso eles calcule um um (pausa) um tempo limite pra essa consulta (pausa) e que eles têm que cumprir. Eu imagino que naquele dia ela devia tá **muito atrasada**=
M: =hum:::=
R: =eu trouxe mais de uma questão **pra ela** mas eu não tinha idéia disso e foi nesse momento que eu entendi como é que o esquema funcionava=
M: =hum hum=
R: =então, se você tiver três questões, são três consultas, essa é a impressão que eu tenho.

Excerpt (6)

Marly:

M: o tempo que a gente tem pra consulta é muito **limitado**, então praticamente a gente é encorajado a ver o paciente mais freqüentemente, entendeu? Porque uma consulta é praticamente quinze minutos:::. E como é que se pode em quinze minutos (pausa) é como eu te disse, quando chega um brasileiro não chega só dizendo "Eu tô com uma dor de cabeça." Geralmente é assim, "By the way [risos] porque isso também tá doendo," tem outra coisa (pausa) porque é é um **conceito** diferente de saúde.=
M: =hum hum=
Marly: =Entendeu? E eu **entendo** isso, que não é só aquela coisa, entende? Mas aí com **jeito** a gente tem que dizer "Olha, hoje a gente tem que ver mais isso aqui (pausa) cê vai precisar voltar, quando pode voltar, em duas semanas ou um mês? O que que é mais **urgente?**" Então nesse sentido também eu acho que o pessoal começa pouco a **pouco** a::: fazer a prioridade, entende? A prioritarizar, "hoje eu tô aqui por **esse** motivo" (pausa) entende (pausa) pouco a pouco isso se desenvolve esse tipo de discernimento porque não tem jeito com

nosso sistema de saúde, não tem jeito, entende, não tem uma consulta, uma consulta mais **longa** é::: meia hora, quarenta e cinco minutos mas é tudo um check-up, um physical, entende, mas normalmente uma consulta normal é muito breve.

Excerpt (7)

Denise

D: Não nun nunca tive um médico que realmente (pausa) senta:: sse comigo (pausa)
S: É um negócio bem assim frio=
D: =um **diálogo** uma coisa mais, entendeu, pessoal não nunca (pausa) é sempre aquela coisa são os dados os dados são estes.

Excerpt (8)

Elena

E: ele ele tá sentado **ali** ele tava no computador anotando os dados da Vanessa respondendo, mas assim num é assim aquela coisa=
C: =Hum=
E: =de eu **parar** (pausa)
C: Hum hum=
E: =**sentar** e te dar uma atenção.

Excerpt (9)

Elena

E: então assim essa história assim de você **sentar,** o médico tá ali na tua frente e assim ele realmente (pausa) te **dedicar** uma atenção especial.

Excerpt (10)

Rosa

R: A maneira como o médico [no Brasil] te **olha**, a maneira como médico::: é::: **considera** o que você tá trazendo como questão, parece que é mais **cuidadoso**, é mais **atencioso**, não posso dizer **todos,** é claro=

Excerpt (11)

Rosa

C: começa—(pausa) a maneira como o médico olha pra você olha pro seu **rosto**, olha nos seus **olhos** e (pausa) //uma experiência particular? (pausa) deixa eu ver// (pausa) não tô conseguindo recordar nenhuma agora (pausa) eu eu posso dizer pelo **tempo** da consulta eu.. eu posso dizer pelo **tempo** da consulta=
M: Hum hum.=
R: Acho acho que eu **nunca** tive uma **consulta** no Brasil::: (pausa) eu sei que tem algumas pessoas que falam mais, outras menos, e eu sou uma dessas pessoas que falam mais [risos-fala rápida] mas é....acho que eu nunca tive uma consulta com menos de meia hora (pausa) talvez até.. 40 minutos não sei=
M: =no Brasil?
R: no Brasil.
M: hum hum.=
R: =e .. aqui (pausa) digamos que eu tenha ido ao médico aqui (pausa) médico ou enfermeira né? =
M: =( ) diferente=
R: =não é diferente aqui, quer dizer, você (pausa) eu devo ter ido umas:: dez vezes (pausa) doze vezes (pausa) ( ) 'tando aqui dois anos (pausa) dois anos e meio, (pausa) quer dizer=
M: = você tá aqui há dois anos e meio?=
R: = dois anos e meio (pausa) fazem três anos agora em agosto na verdade. Digamos que eu tenha ido ao médico **pra mim** não considerando as- as- com meu filho (pausa) em torno de **doze** vezes. Eu devo ter tido **duas** consultas em torno de quarenta minutos.=
M: =hum hum.=
R: =e (pausa) enfim, eu acho que o médico **explora** mais é::: no Brasil, .. mais **aspectos** da sua doença, ou do que você tá trazendo (pausa) né, parece que ele **entende,** pode ser só impressão minha (pausa) mas que:: o seu quadro **físico**, pode ter outros fatores, é::: parece que olha a sua expressão no **rosto**, é::: se você tá **tensa**, se você não tá **tensa**,=
M: =hum hum =
R: =se:: enfim:: se **tá feliz**, se você não tá feliz, o que tá acontecendo, **aqui**, eles são:::
M: Straight forward.

R: [risos] eles são diretos, objetivos (pausa) e você (pausa) parece que é uma é uma qualidade do americano (pausa) ser o mais objetivo possível (pausa) **e não perder tempo**. Eu tenho a impressão que **qualquer coisa** além da sua queixa clínica [batendo na mesa acompanhando a fala] é perda de tempo, e ele não pode perder tempo.
M: hum hum.

Excerpt (12)

Eva

M: Você gostaria que fosse mais longa?
E: Nao (pausa)
M: Não?
E: Não [risos] a não ser um problema eu gostasse eu sempre gostei de **ter meu tempo** mas o meu tempo eu tinha mais com as enfermeiras.=
M: Uhm,uhm, como que é esse esse tempo?
E: Bom o tempo que eu disse assim é::: dispor::: a gente não gosta de sentir que a pessoa tá (pausa) correndo (pausa) tá **correndo**, né? Tá te ( ) nada, eu gosto que a pessoa **ouve,** não gosta de sentir que a pessoa tá (pausa) você expor seu problema, quando há:: lógico quando há:: quando é exame de rotina mesmo você .. ia sabia que era coisa rápida (pausa) você quer ir embora.
M: O que faz você perceber que a pessoa tá com pressa?
E: Pelo um problema que ocorreu, né? Mas pra eu se sentir assim (pausa), ah::: quando faz umas queixa (pausa) é::: "Eu já li tudo aqui, tem alguma novidade?" É a **forma** de expressar, né? "Tem alguma novidade?"[fala rápida] Num te trata como uma pessoa, te trata como::: business só é ali, a coisa assim, bem rápida. Num sei como expor pra você [risos] tchau!
M: /Hum hum/
E: =E tipo né, como eu tô te falando, "Tem alguma novidade?" "A não, então assina rápido, tá tudo ok, you all set" [fala acelerada] você sente um (pausa) num senti um sorriso, num senti uma um "fala::: eu quero te ouvir" né, a gente gosta disso (pausa) é uma coisa bem (pausa) **prática**, bem **rápida**.

Excerpt (13)

Rosa

R: ela (her female primare care physician) é **atenciosa**, ela considera (pause) enfim, você (pause) é o que eu te disse, eu tenho impressão que **eu** me ajustei, então eu não trago pra ela questões que (pause) enfim, que não são a a primeira questão da **consulta,**=
M: =hum hum=
R: = a menos que eu sinta que ela teje- que ela teje com condição de **responder**, ela tá muito **tranqüila**, não tá correndo na fala **dela**, não tá perguntando **uma pergunta atrás da outra** sem **respirar** [risos]=
M: =ela é médica mesmo, né?
R: =ela é médica, essa é médica. Se eu sentir isso e se eu realmente tiver uma questão premente, eu vou **perguntar**.
M: Não correr na fala, falar devagar, você disse?=
R: =isso é importante. Você percebe quando o médico, pelo menos eu percebo quando o médico **tá atrasado**.
M: =hum hum=
R: =Faz uma pergunta emendada na **outra** e você **nem respirou** pra responder e ele já tá te perguntando a outra.
M: E como você se sente neste momento?
R: é **desagradável** porque::: você tá indo lá pra falar de você::: quer dizer, já não (pausa) não acho que seja, não é a coisa mais agradável do mundo! Você se expor para uma outra **pessoa,** você ter que dizer que tá sentindo dor **aqui ou ali**, não tá se sentindo bem e tal e a pessoa tá ali, cumprindo um **protocolo**, **correndo**, você fica com a sensação de que você não tá (pausa) **sendo ouvida**! Que (pausa) enfim, ela vai **pular** isso, ela não vai me **dar atenção**, não tá considerando isso, será que quando ela tá medicando ela tá considerando isso que eu tô **falando,** que eu considero **importante?**=

Notes

1. Transcription Conventions:

..	short pause, not measured in seconds
(pause)	slightly longer pause, not measured in seconds
-	marks an abrupt cutting off of sound
/ /	spoken softly
// //	spoken very softly
=	between two turns indicate that turns latch
|	indicate overlap
talk	bold indicates emphasis
TALK	caps indicate stronger emphasis
:	indicate lengthening of vowel (extra colons indicate greater lengthening)
[laughs]	indicate comments
( )	indicate transcription impossible.

2. The fifteen minutes allotted to clinical encounters is a specific reference provided by our interviewees. This time reference is also provided on Internet sites. We want to point out that differences in expectations regarding time in the clinical encounter may not be specific to Brazilians and may be present among other groups of people.

3. It is interesting to note that such orientations in clinical settings seem to contradict broader trends of behavior as noted by researchers (Hall, 1983), where Latin Americans would be described as being polychronic (often engaged in more than one activity at a time) while North Americans have been traditionally described as M-types (monochronic—one activity at a time). Recent research indicates that U.S. inhabitants seem to be moving toward P-time given the fast pace of life (and its related demands) in urban settings (Brislin and Kim 2003).

4. Indeed, false cognates may be quite troublesome in clinical encounters with a Spanish-speaking health provider. An advocate of the Brazilian community mentions that in Spanish the word "embarazada" means "pregnant," and in Portuguese "embaraçada" means "embarrassed." This Brazilian advocate recounts that during a clinical encounter mediated by a Spanish-speaking interpreter, she was asked if she was "embarazada." She replied that she was not, believing the doctor had inquired if she was embarrassed. The doctor performed a Pap smear procedure, which could represent a threat to a fetus if she was indeed pregnant (Guimarães 2003).

References

Allen, A. 2003. "Meanings of 'Sadness' and the Use of Religious Beliefs and Practices by Brazilian Women in the Boston Area." Boston: Boston Healing Landscape Project.

Assis, G. 2003. "De Criciúma para o mundo—Os novos fluxos da população brasileira: gênero e rearranjos familiares." In *Fronteiras Cruzadas: Etnicidade, Gênero e Redes Sociais.* Ed. Ana Cristina Braga Martes and Soraya Fleischer. São Paulo: Editora Paz e Terra.

Beserra, B. 2003. *Brazilian Immigrants in the United States: Cultural Imperialism and Social Class.* New York: LFB Scholarly Publishing.

Brislin, R. and E. Kim. 2003. "Cultural Diversity in People's Understanding and Uses of Time." *Applied Psychology: An International Review* 53(3): 363–382.

Bruner, J. 1986. *Actual Minds, Possible Worlds.* Cambridge, MA: Harvard University Press.

———. 1990. *Acts of Meaning.* Cambridge, MA: Harvard University Press.

DeBiaggi, S.D.D. 2002. *Changing Gender Roles: Recent Immigration and American Society.* New York: LFB Scholarly Publishing.

———. 2003. "Famílias brasileiras em um novo contexto." In *Fronteiras Cruzadas: Etnicidade, Gênero e Redes Sociais*, pp. 175–197. Ed. Ana Cristina Martes Braga and Soraya Fleischer. São Paulo: Editora Paz e Terra.

De Fina, A. 2003. *Identity in Narrative: A Study of Immigrant Discourse.* Amsterdam: John Benjamins.

Erickson, F. and J. Shultz. 1982. *The Counselor as Gatekeeper.* New York: Academic Press.

———. 1977. "When Is a Context?" *The Quarterly Newsletter of the Institute for Comparative Human Development* 1(2): 5–10.

Fisher, S. and A. Todd. 1983. *The Social Organization of Doctor-Patient Communication.* Washington, D.C.: Center for Applied Linguistics.

Goffman, E. 1974. *Frame Analysis.* New York: Harper and Row.

———. 1981. "Footing." In *Forms of Talk* (Goffman), pp. 124–59. Philadelphia: University of Pennsylvania Press.

Guimarães, M. 2003. "Brazilian Immigrant Health Needs Assessment." M.A. thesis. Cambridge, MA: Lesley University.

Gumperz, J. 1982. *Discourse Strategies.* Cambridge: Cambridge University Press.

Hall, E., 1983. *The Dance of Life: The Other Dimension of Time.* New York: Anchor Books.

Hyden, L-C and E. Mishler. 1999. "Language and Medicine." *Annual Review of Applied Linguistics* 19:174–192.

Hymes, D. 1974. "Ways of Speaking." In *Exploration in the Ethnography of Speaking*, pp. 433–51. Ed. R. Bauman and J. Sherzer. Cambridge: Cambridge University Press.

Jack, D. 1991. *Silencing the Self: Women and Depression.* Cambridge, MA: Harvard University Press.

Jaques, E. 1982. *The Form of Time.* London: Heinemann.

Kendon, A. 1990. *Conducting Interaction. Patterns of Behavior in Focused Encounters*. Cambridge: Cambridge University Press.

Levine, R. and Norenzayan, A. 1999. "The Pace of Life in 31 Countries. *Journal of Cross-Cultural Psychology* 30:178–205.

Linde, C. 1993. *Life Stories*. Oxford: Oxford University Press.

Messias, D. 2002. "Transnational Health Resources, Practices, and Perspectives: Brazilian Immigrant Women's Narratives." *Journal of Immigrant Health* 4(5): 183–200.

Mishler, E. 1986. *Research Interviewing. Context and Narrative*. Cambridge, MA: Harvard University Press.

Munn, N. 1992. "The Cultural Anthropology of Time: A Critical Essay." *Annual Review of Anthropology* 21:93–123.

Nava, A. 2001. "Acculturation to Psychotherapy: The Experience of Brazilian and Portuguese and Immigrant Women in the USA." Ph.D. dissertation. Boston: Simmons College.

Ribeiro, B. T. 1994. *Coherence in Psychotic Discourse*. Oxford: Oxford University Press.

Sapir, E. 1968. *Time Perspective in Aboriginal American Culture: A Study in Method*. New York: Johnson Reprint.

Sarangi, S. and C. Roberts. 1999. *Talk, Work, and the Institutional Order*. New York: Mouton de Gruyter.

Scheflen, A. E. 1972. *Body Language and the Social Order*. Englewood Cliffs, N.J.: Prentice-Hall.

Tannen, D. 1989. *Talking Voices*. Cambridge: Cambridge University Press.

Tannen, D. and C. Wallat. 1993. "Interactive Frames and Knowledge Schemas in Interaction: Examples from a Medical Examination/Interview." In *Framing in Discourse*, pp. 57–76. Ed. D. Tannen. Cambridge: Cambridge University Press.

Thornton, R. 1980. *Space, Time, and Culture among the Iraqw of Tanzania*. New York: Academic Press.

9

A União Tem Força? Three Labor Unions' Outreach to Brazilian Immigrant Workers in Boston

Joshua Kirshner

It would be difficult not to notice the presence of Brazilian immigrants in certain sectors of Boston's economy today. Everywhere, from Dunkin' Donuts to pizzerias to housecleaning services, Brazilians are moving into specific job niches. Many of these jobs feature high turnover, few fringe benefits, little job security, and lack of representation from labor unions. In the past several years, however, three Boston-area union locals hired Brazilian-born staff members to work more closely with members of this community. In addition, the Brazilian Immigrant Center, in Allston, Massachusetts, has jointly hosted workshops (offered in English and Portuguese) with several labor unions on workers' rights, and on skills such as obtaining a commercial driver's license.

Curiously, these events are occurring in a broader context in which unions have experienced a lengthy decline, and in which only one out of ten workers in the U.S. private sector is currently covered by collectively bargained labor contracts. Labor activists and scholars are increasingly concerned with how unions can reinvigorate themselves by being responsive to a changing global economy. Since 2000, when the American Federation of Labor-Congress of Industrial Organizations (AFL-CIO) issued a new policy statement on immigration, this has explicitly included reaching out to immigrant workers as potential new members.[1]

This study analyzes the ways in which Boston-area labor unions are reaching out to and recruiting Brazilian immigrant workers. In the process, it seeks to address the following questions: are labor unions that represent jobs with growing numbers of Brazilian immigrants targeting these workers as new recruits? What are the barriers to joining U.S. labor unions for Brazilian workers? Does union membership help Brazilian workers improve their position in the U.S. workforce? Finally, what are the implications of Brazilians' lack of visibility in U.S. society—an issue that is debated in the chapters of this section—for their evolving relationship to the U.S. labor movement?

The Brazilian community in the Boston metropolitan area has grown steadily since the mid 1980s. Eastern Massachusetts is now home to the second largest concentration of Brazilians in the United States, estimated at 150,000, after New York City, at 230,000 (Margolis 2003, 53). Brazil ranked as the tenth leading source country for foreign-born residents in Massachusetts arriving in the 1980s, and it ranked second for those arriving the 1990s (Current Population Survey, cited in Sum and Fogg 1999). Although there have been several recent studies on unionization among Latinos, and to a lesser extent Asian immigrants, primarily in California, there has been little or no scholarly research on Brazilian immigrants and unions.

Two Brazilian scholars who investigated this immigrant community in Massachusetts during the 1994–2003 period note that most Brazilian migrants face downward mobility in the U.S. labor market. Many leave behind white-collar positions such as secretary, accountant, or schoolteacher in Brazil for jobs as dishwashers, housecleaners, janitors, painters, and construction workers in the United States (Sales 1999; Martes 2000). In addition, many of the Brazilian migrants in Boston are undocumented, arriving on a tourist visa and remaining illegally (ibid; Margolis 2003).

The Brazilian Immigrant Center, a community-based organization in Allston, Massachusetts, has identified several problems associated with the unprotected status of many of these workers: they often work long hours, in dangerous and unhygienic conditions, many do not receive wages or are paid less than agreed upon, and are frequently fired without due notice. Given the difficult conditions many Brazilian workers face, union membership could serve as a vehicle for wage increases and other workplace improvements. Meanwhile, Brazilian workers may contribute valuable strength and ideas to the U.S. labor movement that is struggling to redefine itself for the 21st century. This chapter will compare the approaches of three unions that seek to recruit Brazilian immigrants in the Boston area: the Painters Union, the United Food and Commercial Workers, and the Teamsters. The first two unions are drawing Brazilians into their ranks by organizing and forging links to Brazilian immigrant organizations, while the third has begun to form such links, but it is not yet actively working to organize Brazilians.

Methodology

I began this research by volunteering for two weeks in January 2004 at the Brazilian Immigrant Center (BIC). This community-based organization of 300 dues-paying members provides support and advocacy to Brazilian immigrants by offering English-language courses, community education, leadership training, and legal and social services. Several staff members help workers resolve workplace problems, with assistance from the state Attorney General's Office. Volunteering at BIC introduced me to some of the workplace issues affecting Brazilian immigrants.

For my selection of cases I used U.S. Census data and secondary literature to determine the sectors and occupations that have large numbers of Brazilian workers in Massachusetts. These occupations include residential and commercial cleaning, residential and commercial painting, restaurants, bakeries, and to a lesser extent freight transport and retail. I then conducted a telephone survey with representatives of six organizations and two churches that serve the Brazilian community, investigating their ties with U.S. labor unions. Of these, the Brazilian Immigrant Center and the Brazilian Workers Center have direct contact with labor unions, and these include the SEIU (Service Employees International Union) Local 615, the Painters Union District Council 35, UFCW (United Food and Commercial Workers) Local 1445, the Teamsters Union Local 25, and the Carpenters Local 33.

This study compares the approaches of the Painters Union, UFCW, and the Teamsters, all likely to organize Brazilians. Each of these unions is based in Boston and covers industries with growing numbers of Brazilian immigrants in the workforce. The research design therefore holds union and firm location and immigrants' country of origin constant. The information comes from eight in-depth interviews with union organizers and staff, combined with observations in Brazilian community organizations, churches, and an informal day labor site where Brazilian workers often congregate. I also accompanied union organizers on home visits and to file an unfair labor practice charge with the state Labor Relations Board.

Brazilian Immigration to Massachusetts and Labor Market Participation

While increasing arrivals of Mexicans and Central and South Americans in many regions of the United States have been widely documented, migration from Brazil has attracted much less attention. Since the 1980s, however, New York, Boston, Miami, and Chicago have all seen growing numbers of Brazilian newcomers (Margolis 1998, 2). The U.S. Census recorded 24,079 foreign-born Brazilians in the Boston metropolitan area in 2000, more than double the 1990 figure of 10,461.[2] Most observers agree this is an underestimate, as large numbers of Brazilians are undocumented and may avoid census surveys.[3] The Brazilian Ministry of External Affairs estimates 150,000 Brazilians in Massachusetts in 2000, and the Brazilian Consulate in Boston and other immigrant organizations also cite this figure, suggesting that the U.S. Census underestimates the size of the Brazilian population by one fourth (Margolis 2003, 53). According to a recent Citizens Bank publication, Brazilians make up the second largest population of recently arrived immigrant workers in the state, after Puerto Ricans, making Brazil the largest source of immigrants from *outside* the United States to Massachusetts in the 1990s (Sum and Fogg 1999).

This rise in migration has stimulated growing academic research on the subject, mostly coming out of Brazil. Margolis (1994) has written the first English-language book on Brazilian immigrants in the United States, based on her research in New York City. Part of her study looks at employment and labor markets, and she finds that Brazilians mostly work in "low-paid, low-status, unskilled jobs that Americans try to avoid" (1994, 109). She notes that jobs in this sector, such as restaurant work, have high turnover, few, if any, fringe benefits, little opportunity for advancement, and "are non-unionized."

Brazilian sociologist Sales (1999) and political scientist Martes (2000) have each written books in Portuguese focusing on Brazilians in the Boston area.[4] Both authors use ethnographic methods to offer baseline descriptions of this growing community. Along with profiles of immigrants, levels of education, and regions of origin in Brazil, these studies address motivations for emigration, social networks, insertion into the host-country labor market, and questions of social identity and assimilation.

Sales and Martes both find that emigration to the United States became an important trend in the mid 1980s, coinciding with a severe recession and job loss in the Brazilian economy. Although neither author claims a causal link, they both emphasize blocked social and occupational mobility in Brazil as a catalyst for emigration, especially for members of the middle class. Using a survey of 300 Brazilian immigrants, Martes compares jobs held in Brazil with those in Massachusetts, where she finds a paradox: while Brazilians come here to improve their quality of life, they often face a sharp decline in terms of occupational status. Many of her informants abandoned jobs as teachers, accountants, secretaries and the like in Brazil to become dishwashers, gardeners, cooks, busboys and housecleaners in the Boston area.[5]

Martes argues that differences in earnings are important, but not the only factor in explaining this pattern. She finds that being a housecleaner, for instance, carries a different meaning in the United States than it does in Brazil for these immigrants: it is more formalized and treated as a small business. Her survey data suggest that the majority of Brazilians working in Massachusetts are concentrated in the service sector, including jobs in restaurants, small businesses, domestic cleaning, nursing homes, and in civil construction. Sales has similar findings, and notes that several of her informants who worked as cleaners in nursing homes quickly moved up to positions as nursing assistants within the same place of employment (1999, 219). This observation reveals that many Brazilians are concerned with job mobility in the United States, but neither author examines how these immigrants upgrade their job skills and status, or how they seek workplace protections, such as through collective bargaining.

A recent Portuguese-language volume edited by Martes and Fleischer (2003) examines Brazilian migration dynamics from an interdisciplinary perspective. Several researchers explore questions of ethnic and national identity, social networks, gender relations, work and community among Brazilians in New York City, Boston, Connecticut, and South Florida. In a piece comparing transnational networks among Latin American immigrants, Mitchell argues that in contrast to Salvadorans who have allied with U.S. labor unions such as SEIU to gain wage increases and protections at work, Brazilians have yet to form links to what he calls "organized interest groups," with the exception of churches (2003, 43). Martes (2000) and Margolis (2003) concur that Brazilian immigrants in Boston show a lack of collective organization, and that churches serve as the main institutions for "mutual support and solidarity" (2003, 59).

Despite this view of Brazilians' lack of civic participation in the host society, their position in the Boston regional labor market suggests they may be good targets for union organizing. Using the 2000 U.S. Census to examine the occupations of foreign-born Brazilians in Massachusetts reveals several clear patterns that underscore Sales' and Martes' findings on Brazilians' employment in this country.[6] The data suggest Brazilians are clustering in specific low-wage jobs and industries, rather than scattering across the regional economy. For example, the most frequent occupation is "Cleaning—maids and housekeeping," with 36 cases out of a sample of 396.[7] A similar occupation, and one more likely to be unionized, is "Janitors and building cleaners," with nine cases.

Furthermore, Brazilians do not appear to be entering supervisory positions in large numbers. The job with one code up from "Cleaning—maids and housekeeping" is the more managerial "First line supervisors, managers of landscaping and grounds keeping," which has only one case in the sample. In construction, "painters, construction and maintenance" stands out with 14 cases for Brazilians. Several construction jobs have one case, such as "glazier" and "helper," and many jobs such as "roofer" and "pipe layer" do not appear in the sample. In manufacturing, the only occupation that stands out among Brazilians is "baker," with seven cases. In transportation, "laborers, and freight, stock, and material movers" has five cases, but no other job in this industry exceeds one case.

These data point to specific industries and occupations where Boston-area labor unions must increasingly recruit Brazilians in order to build membership. The data also contradict claims that Brazilians are mostly confined to informal and nonunionized sectors of the economy. Despite the lack of attention in the Brazilian immigration literature, one might expect Brazilian workers in the United States to be favorable to unions, given their concentration in unskilled and semi-skilled jobs, frequent lack of job mobility and security, as well as a strong labor union tradition in Brazil.[8]

The Challenge of Organizing Immigrants, Past and Present

Several points emphasized in the literature on immigrants and unionism offer a useful framework for this study. First, labor activists and scholars agree that in the past decade successful union revitalization efforts have focused on organizing unrepresented workers, often in services and light manufacturing industries previously untouched by union activity. In the postwar period, U.S. trade unions declined in membership, organizing capacity, level of strike activity, and political effectiveness. Union density (the percentage of the labor force in unions) fell gradually from a high of 37% in 1946 to 21% in 1980, and then plummeted below 15% by 1995 (Bronfenbrenner et al. 1998). Activists and scholars dispute the reasons for this decline, and these range from employer hostility, restructuring of industry, to inaction by unions themselves.[9]

The AFL-CIO "New Voice" leadership elected in 1995, headed by John Sweeney, has actively sought to reverse these trends and to transform the labor movement. New Voice has critiqued the previous two decades of labor's failures and holds that the U.S. labor movement is "irrelevant to the vast majority of unorganized workers in our country" (Sweeney cited in Brecher and Costello 1999, 11). Since taking office, this new leadership has created a separate organizing department and committed 30% of its overall budget to support new organizing drives (Bronfenbrenner et al. 1998). Many union affiliates met these changes by shifting resources toward organizing, and in some cases creating new organizing departments. This reemphasis on organizing has sparked the interest of academics and practitioners in new union organizing strategies.

A second point is that immigrants are key actors in many recent union victories due at least in part to their strong social networks and the shared travails of the immigrant experience itself. Parallels can be found in the historical literature on immigrants and unionization, which documents instances during early U.S. industrialization where immigrants helped build powerful unions by organizing along ethnic lines in such industries as apparel manufacture and coal mining.[10]

Many observers emphasize the continuing importance of shared ethnicity and social networks for union organizing, despite changes stemming from economic restructuring and the post-1965 growth of mass immigration. In an edited volume on immigrant organizing in California's new service-dominated economy (Milkman 2000), Wells describes variation in workers' receptivity to unions by national background and by occupations in San Francisco's hotel industry. She suggests that Asians, with the exception of Filipinos, often have a less positive view of unions than Latinos, particularly Central Americans, given the "dangerous authority-challenging struggles" they experienced as immigrants (2000, 119).[11]

Fine (2003) contends that in many cases unions are not doing enough to tap into the strong social ties found in immigrant communities. She argues that in instances where unions are failing to mobilize low-wage workers, certain grassroots organizations, often ethnically based, are "jumping into the breach."[12] Calling these organizations "community unions," Fine explains that they combine features of labor unions, ethnic associations and community groups to engage in local-level organizing to address work and wage issues. Although the community unions studied by Fine thus far lack the economic clout to make changes in industries employing immigrant workers, they have been politically effective at bringing about legislative protections in the workplace.

Milkman (2000) notes that one difference between current immigrant organizing and that of the earlier periods is the presence of large numbers of undocumented immigrants, a category that did not exist before immigration restrictions took effect in 1924. One might expect undocumented workers to be more wary of union organizing than other immigrants, because they are vulnerable to being deported. In a study of a successful mid-1980s union drive among mostly undocumented Latino workers in a waterbed factory in Los Angeles, however, Delgado finds that undocumented workers "seem to be neither more nor less organizable because of their citizenship status than other workers in the secondary sector" (1993, 147). The author suggests these workers had lost fear of both INS reprisals and employer threats as immigration officials rarely appeared, similar jobs were plentiful, and only immigrants were willing to take them.

Despite changes in the political and legal climate since Delgado's research, the flow of illegal immigrants has continued. A 2004 *New York Times* article notes that as union membership has dwindled nationwide, immigrant-heavy unions such as SEIU have added new members since 2000.[13] In some parts of the country, illegal immigrants dominate entire occupations, such as janitorial services and construction. Regardless of whether foreign-born workers are more or less favorable toward unions than their native-born counterparts, if organized labor were to maintain its earlier position against illegal immigrants in the workforce, it would be isolated from growing segments of the economy.

Some recent studies on transnational migration draw a less favorable picture with respect to immigrants and unionization. In an influential study of Dominicans in Boston, for instance, Levitt suggests that migrants often use their community of origin as a "reference group against which to gauge their status" (2001, 11). These migrants frequently play a critical role in the economies of sending communities, such as by sending cash remittances. Unionization may be less appealing to "target earners," who are part of circular migration streams and prioritize ties with home communities to which they plan to return. This may be true especially in cases where organizing involves short-term sacrifices, such as going on strike.

An important difference between current and previous waves of immigration, however, is that migrants increasingly work in the services or light-manufacturing sector, as opposed to heavy manufacturing. With large numbers of immigrants concentrating in manual factory and service jobs, and in the informal sector characterized by below-minimum wages, homework, as well as illegal practices, even temporary sojourners may in some circumstances support unionization as a means of job protection. The key point is that understanding the social context of migration is crucial for assessing the possibilities of unionization among immigrants.

Milkman (2000) and colleagues suggest that in California, perhaps more than elsewhere in the United States, breathing new life into unions is increasingly linked with efforts to reach out to the growing population of working-class immigrants. With its striking janitors, tortilla makers, *drywalleros,* racing wheel makers, and bus rider unionists, all overwhelmingly immigrants, Los Angeles has become what one writer has called "the major R&D [research and development] center for 21st Century trade unionism" (Davis 2000, 145).

Can this relationship between union vitality and immigrant organizing translate to urban regions with smaller but still important foreign-born populations, such as Boston? Can Brazilians bring new energy to unions as Salvadorans and Mexicans have done in some cases, despite smaller numbers and distinct immigration experiences? Or do employers hire Brazilian immigrants as a way to avoid unionization? Are unions integrating issues of specific concern to Brazilian immigrants into their campaigns, and if so, how? Probing these questions can shed light on the relationship between immigrants' social and political backgrounds and their receptivity to unions, and on whether Brazilians have different workplace concerns than other immigrants or native-born workers, and if so, how unions are responding to these concerns.

Painters Union District Council 35

The Painters Union is one of the Boston-area unions with the largest number of Brazilian members. This stems both from Brazilian immigrants' recent entry into the painting industry in large numbers and an effective approach by the union to maintain its influence on the regional labor market and to gain new members in the process.

The Painters Union District Council 35 is an affiliate of the International Union of Painters and Allied Trades (AFL-CIO), whose jurisdiction covers Massachusetts and northern New England. The union represents construction industry painters, wall coverers, glaziers, drywall finishers, residential painters, glassworkers, sign painters and erectors, and maintenance workers. District Council 35 has 4,000 members, and appears to be growing. Its website notes that DC 35's membership has increased 20% annually in the past few years, showing "[its] commitment to organizing, diversity, and [its] obligation to recruit and train skilled manpower for employers."[14] Currently, DC 35 has contracts with 340 companies, and 80 new companies have signed contracts since 1999. While the union's presence in residential painting in Boston is minuscule, it has an important market share in commercial and industrial painting, although the exact percentage is not known. The union belongs to the Boston Building Trades Council, which includes Ironworkers Local 7 and the International Brotherhood of Electrical Workers (IBEW) Local 103 and several other unions.

The Painters Union's efforts to gain new members and increase union density should be viewed in the context of the recent history of building trades unions. By the 1980s, a question facing all building trades unions was "how to successfully organize a constantly changing, on-the-move workforce employed by numerous local and national employers" (Lewis and Mirand 1998, 300).[15] Under these conditions, the model of organizing a workforce employed at a fixed location using NLRB elections does not fit, since construction jobs are often completed and the workers dispersed before elections can be held. In the face of employers' increasing avoidance of organized labor, unions such as IBEW and the Carpenters began to focus on one aspect of the market over which they have influence: the hiring process (ibid). They do this by organizing individual employees in order to influence the available skilled-labor pool, while applying economic pressure on nonunion contractors to sign the union's construction agreement for the jurisdiction.

Following this approach, the Painters Union DC 35 has attempted to increase its membership in the past decade by using both "top down" organizing (focusing on employers and customers) and "bottom up" organizing (focusing on employees). The top-down approach emphasizes training, regional bargaining agreements, and aggressive confrontation and litigation against nonunion contractors. First, the union uses its highly trained membership to attract employers to sign union contracts, despite paying higher wages and benefits. Union members can upgrade from apprentice to journey level in painting, glazing, and drywalling; they learn specialized techniques in these fields and receive mandatory occupational safety (OSHA) courses, cardiopulmonary resuscitation (CPR), and scaffold safety training.

Second, DC 35 uses a regional contract, which offers varying wage rates for different parts of New England depending on local conditions. This requires contractors to use union labor on all projects, regardless of location.[16] The union itself operates on a regional scale, with the District Council playing a more central role than the 14 local affiliates under its direction. Job training, organizing and negotiation activities are based at the District Council office, while the locals hold monthly informational meetings for members who live nearby.

Third, DC 35 applies pressure to nonunion contractors by forcing them to comply with various federal and state labor protection laws. The union has been particularly effective at receiving back-pay awards for immigrant workers, who are frequent victims of wage violations—or not being paid at all—by substandard painting and construction firms. For example, Brazilian organizer Fernando Matos tells a story of a Brazilian nonunion drywaller who visited him at his house, and on hearing how the union protects workers, complained of being fired without pay for 17 days of full-time drywall work. Matos repeatedly visited the company owner, negotiated informally, threatened to report him to the state Attorney General's office, and finally recovered the $1,600 owed to the worker. Matos took a photo of the worker holding his paycheck, and placed it in the union's monthly newsletter, *The New England Primer.*[17] Organizing Director Jim Snow states that back-pay liability and fighting unfair labor practice charges can be costly for small and mid-sized contractors, who operate on small profit margins.[18] This helps DC 35 eliminate nonunion competitors, or force them into signing union agreements.

These top-down strategies are important for the union, since bringing in new members without also creating new jobs from union contractors could cause long-term problems. But the Painters Union also seeks to actively recruit nonunion painters. In the past decade, the union has identified recent immigrants as key members of this group.[19] In particular, Brazilians are opting to work in residential painting in the Boston area, which is almost entirely nonunion. Jim Snow describes their influx in painting as "a tidal wave," and states that the DC 35 wants to encourage them to move into the unionized sector.[20]

In an effort to recruit immigrant painters, DC 35 has committed personnel and financial resources to a long-term organizing program. In the past ten years, the union has hired an organizing department with 10 full-time members and a full-time director. Within this group two organizers are Latinos (Cuban and Puerto Rican), one Irish, one Cambodian, one African American, one female (North American), and one Brazilian, all working primarily with their respective communities. The organizing director, Jim Snow, is a white U.S. citizen. Organizer Tony Hernandez describes the staff as "the United Nations."[21] Snow believes that hiring immigrant organizers is the most effective way to reach out to immigrants by overcoming cultural and language barriers.

A second bottom-up organizing method used by the Painters Union is active recruitment of nonunion skilled craftspeople, a practice known as "stripping." This tactic aims to leave nonunion employers with a shortage of skilled workers. It also brings in new union members with a keen understanding of how the nonunion sector works. Organizer Fernando Matos worked for six years as a foreman for a nonunion company, and he brings practical knowledge based on this experience. As a Brazilian immigrant himself, Matos is crucial for reaching out to Brazilians in the union and outside it. He feels there is frequent misunderstanding about union activity in the United States among Brazilians. "They don't know who to trust. Believe it or not, sometimes when I try to hold a meeting about the union, they think we are part of the immigration service."[22] While many Brazilian painters hail from regions with little union activity in Brazil and may consider Brazilian unions to be corrupt, Matos notes, "They quickly realize that things are different here [in the U.S.]. The law is very severe." He recognizes that many of the Brazilian painters lack immigration documents, which makes gaining trust more challenging.

In an effort to educate Brazilians about workers' rights and the benefits of U.S. labor unions, Fernando Matos and other DC 35 staff have held four "community meetings" starting in 2002. The Painters Union co-sponsored these events with the Brazilian Immigrant Center (BIC), and they took place in Catholic churches in Rockland and Framingham, Massachusetts, a town with a large number of Brazilian residents and Brazilian-owned small businesses. Matos recalled, "At the first meeting, we had 150 people. Different ages, different colors, and coming from different fields—some from pizza, some from cleaning. They wanted the money that the union offers." At these meetings, Matos and Fausto da Rocha, the BIC director, give practical tips on keeping records on hours worked, wages earned, and names and addresses of employers. This helps in making claims to the state Attorney General's Office for back pay. Matos notes that the Attorney General's Office does not use legal status against workers when making wage claims, and he does not discourage those lacking documents from joining the union.

The Painters Union has also used the local media to raise awareness about unions in the Brazilian community. For example, Matos has appeared on a Portuguese-language radio program and announced that Boston-area union painting companies are seeking painters. "I gave the numbers [wages], and that was sufficient. I got calls right there, before I left the radio station." In 2003, DC 35 started offering English classes as a way to prepare immigrant workers for the painting and construction workforce. Matos stresses the importance of English skills for painters, noting that communication with the foreman is needed to function on the job site, as well for knowing one's rights and negotiating a raise. "Otherwise, you're like a horse that someone jumps on and makes you run." Matos recognizes that many Brazilians avoid spending time studying English, as they plan to return to Brazil in a few years.[23]

When asked about ties to Brazilian churches, Matos explained that he is a pastor himself. Two years ago, he started a congregation in the basement of his home in Revere, and it recently relocated to a larger building in Chelsea, which was once a factory. Matos became a pastor in 1994 in Massachusetts and worked with Pastor Oriel de Jesus at the *Assembleia de Deus* in Somerville, a large Brazilian church near Boston. Matos' congregation is independent and has about 25 members, all of whom are Brazilian.

After attending a service and talking with several members, I found that many of the men work as painters but none aside from Matos are in the Painters Union. Several said they lack the English skills needed to join the union, but hope to join in the future. There did not seem to be any specific program to help them become members. One woman who works with her husband cleaning houses explained that the church serves as a place for congregants to share information about job openings, rooms and apartments, and to pass out food and clothing to newcomers. These jobs are mostly in housecleaning and residential house painting, which do not require immigration documents.

Matos views his work as a pastor and as union organizer as separate, and says he does not use the church to recruit union members. But his position in the church is clearly beneficial in gaining respect and prestige in the Brazilian community, which strongly values church participation (Martes 2000). This could go a long way in encouraging the trust needed for workers to act collectively and join a union, especially when they are also faced with the challenge of seeking a foothold in a new country.

Teamsters Local 25

The International Brotherhood of Teamsters (IBT) Local 25 in Charlestown, Massachusetts, is also recognizing the importance of bringing immigrants into its ranks. This local is one of the oldest in the IBT and its jurisdiction covers an area roughly corresponding to Greater Boston.[24] In addition to trucking and freight, the local covers occupations such as warehousing, parcel delivery, bus drivers, car haulers, car rental employees, forklift operators, shipping and receiving clerks, oil burner technicians, and certain manufacturing jobs such as making corrugated boxes.

According to Steve Sullivan, Local 25 Education and Training Director, the local's membership has fluctuated between 9,000 and 9,500 in the past several years.[25] The local has an organizing department, although with the recent departure of Amy Battisti-Ashe, community organizer and English as a Second Language (ESL) instructor, there are no full-time organizers on staff devoted to building new membership. He explains that currently organizing is mostly "reactive," meaning that the union responds to calls from workers who actively seek representation. He advocates employing rank-and-file members to organize by talking to workers on job sites, but the union does not use this tactic systematically. Among the local's staff members who do some organizing, none is bilingual.

Despite this, Sullivan observes that demographic shifts occurring in many jobs represented by the union mean that recruiting recent immigrants is crucial for membership growth. Local 25 today includes workers with diverse national origins, including Irish, Italians, Haitians, Somalis, Albanians, Salvadorans, Mexicans, Cambodians, and Brazilians. Sullivan adds that workers of particular national origins often cluster in specific job categories, for instance Local 25's bus drivers division is almost entirely Haitian, and Somali members mostly work for car rental agencies at Logan Airport. Brazilian members also work for airport car rental companies such as Hertz and National, as well as for UPS and in field maintenance for Massport. However, Local 25 does not keep data on the country of origin or immigrant status of its membership. The application to join the union does not require this information.

According to Amy Battisti-Ashe, Local 25 began actively seeking to organize immigrant workers in September 2001. At this point, Local 25 president George Cashman made a decision to reach out to immigrants, and the local initiated an ESL program in the union hall. The local made classes available to members, their families, and people from surrounding communities. Battisti-Ashe explains that the local used the classes as an organizing tool. In addition to helping union members grasp English, Battisti-Ashe taught about the U.S. labor movement and the importance of unions. For instance, during the Justice for Janitors strike in Boston in 2002, one firm's management tried to hire immigrant workers as replacements. Students in Local 25's ESL classes had learned "if you need work, look for a job where workers are not on strike."[26]

Coinciding with developing an ESL program, Local 25 began to publish bilingual (English/Spanish) articles in its newsletter, *The Spokesman*, and added a Spanish page to its website. The union also began supporting pro-immigrant national policies. For instance, in October 2002, Local 25 sent seven members to Washington, D.C. as part of AFL-CIO's national "Reward Work" campaign to pressure Congress to support undocumented immigrants' ability to earn legal status. In October 2003, Local 25 sponsored a bus for the Immigrant Workers' Freedom Ride, and sent 25 members to a rally in New York City.

Steve Sullivan emphasizes that bringing in community members for ESL, citizenship, and Commercial Drivers License classes is a key tactic for expanding membership. He has pushed the local to offer these classes to the broader community rather than only union members as a way to open the union hall to the outside and educate potential members about the benefits of unions. Speaking of the need to reach out to immigrants, he explains, "If we let them learn how to drive a truck on our dime, they won't forget us. This is like planting a forest one tree at a time."

In February 2003, Local 25 collaborated with the Brazilian Immigrant Center (BIC) to offer a series of bilingual workshops at the immigrant center. The goal of these workshops is to educate Brazilians on the unions' activities and the benefits of becoming a member, such as obtaining health coverage and improving working conditions, plus access to a credit union, an investment plan, the union's driving school, and educational programs such as citizenship classes. Sullivan also explains the basics of collective bargaining at these events. One recent workshop held at BIC was billed as "*Você quer ser caminhoneiro*?" (Would you like to be a truck driver?) and focused on the local trucking industry. It featured tips on acquiring a Commercial Drivers License and on specific jobs and companies with union contacts. These workshops are open to the community, and information about them in Portuguese and Spanish has been posted on Local 25's website.[27]

Despite this progress in reaching out to Brazilians and other immigrants, Local 25 has not deepened its relationship with these communities. For instance, the union has not had direct contact with any other Brazilian organization aside from the Brazilian Immigrant Center. Sullivan explains, "We haven't gone specifically after Brazilians as Brazilians. We haven't gone to that community and said 'we need 30 of you for UPS.' But we have told them that UPS is a hiring company right now." Battisti-Ashe notes that a change in Local 25's leadership in April 2003 led to a "circling of the wagons." She describes a pattern in which the union makes overtures to an immigrant community, takes a stand on a piece of pro-immigrant legislation, but then backs off after complaints from some segments of its membership. For example, BIC is actively organizing support for the Driver's License Bill (House Bill 2292), which would enable immigrants to hold a license with consular identification in place of a Social Security card. Battisti-Ashe notes that the union does not officially support this bill, although tacitly the leadership agrees with its provisions. "Our official position is not to take a position," she observes.

Battisti-Ashe points out the Teamsters' model of organizing can be confusing for many Brazilian workers. The union organizes workers using the craft model, so that one must be in a particular occupation to join the local. One must work at least 30 days for a company with a Teamsters contract to become a union member, a practice known as "closed shop." In Brazil, a worker can join any union, regardless of employer. In the workshops given at the BIC, Local 25 staff members explain that it is more difficult to join a union in the United States than it is in Brazil. Furthermore, Sullivan and Battisti-Ashe find that many Brazilians lack familiarity with unions, either in Brazil or the United States, which may cause distrust.

In order to face this challenge, Sullivan wants to employ rank-and-file members as organizers to talk with nonunion workers. Immigrant union members can effectively use their language skills to reach workers of the same nationality. Sullivan has explored holding meetings at the union hall every Monday night for two hours, to which a different immigrant group would be invited each week. In addition, he aims to leverage funding from the Mayor's Office for New Bostonians and the state Department of Education to open a computer lab at the union hall for adult education courses open to union members, their families and community members. Although these ideas have gained support from Local 25 leadership, they are not yet being implemented.

United Food and Commercial Workers Local 1445

The United Food and Commercial Workers (UFCW) Local 1445, affiliated with the AFL-CIO, has recently increased its outreach to immigrant workers. This local, based in Dedham, Massachusetts, represents 15,000 workers in food processing, healthcare, recycling, uniform manufacturing, food retail and wholesale trade. Local 1445's jurisdiction covers much of northeastern New England. Along with four other UFCW locals, Local 1445 recently negotiated a new contract with Stop & Shop supermarkets, one of its largest employers. In addition, in the past year, Local 1445 staff attempted to organize healthcare workers at Tenet Corporation's Worcester Medical Center.

As with the Painters and Teamsters, UFCW Local 1445 is not content with merely enforcing contracts for existing members but seeks to build bargaining power by organizing new workers. The union added 800 new members in 2003, and hoped to surpass this number in 2004.[28] In order to support this goal, the local invested 30% of its budget into new worker organizing, consistent with AFL-CIO New Voice budget outlay.

In 1996, Local 1445 initiated immigrant outreach by hiring Fernando Lemus, a Salvadoran, to better communicate with the growing Hispanic workforce in supermarkets, a stronghold for the union. Recently promoted to business agent at the local, a job involving negotiating with contractors, Lemus is a role model for other organizers. UFCW currently has an organizing department with four full-time organizers and a full-time director. The director and two organizers are white U.S. citizens, and Tom Fabricio Da Silva, a Brazilian, and Miguel Vasquez, a Salvadoran, have been hired since 2002. DaSilva worked for four years at Stop & Shop and, as the only staff member who speaks Portuguese, he has provided valuable connections with the Brazilian community.

Local 1445 is beginning to recognize the importance of recruiting Brazilians in industries such as baked goods and food retail. Like the other unions in this study, the local does not keep data on numbers of Brazilian members. DaSilva has requested this information, arguing that although Brazilians are often categorized as Latinos, they should be considered distinct. Union meetings are held in English, and the local uses union authorization cards in English and Spanish, but not in Portuguese. DaSilva emphasizes the importance of having organizers of the same ethnic group as workers. "This makes a huge difference—I could not organize Latinos and Miguel [a Salvadoran] could not recruit Brazilians. Brazilians might understand Spanish, but they may not relate to it well."

At the time of this research, Local 1445 was involved in a campaign at a commercial bakery in Woburn, Massachusetts. This campaign began in the spring of 2004, when several Brazilian workers decided to do something about poor working conditions. The bakery supplies large area restaurants and employs 98 workers, all but two of whom are Brazilian. According to DaSilva, the bakery has employed mostly Brazilians for the past 10 years. They may not recruit Brazilians directly, but the managers have been known to say they "like the way Brazilians work." Most likely, managers rely on "word of mouth" to fill the workforce, which includes many with family relations, such as a mother and son, and pairs of siblings.[29]

A group of workers study English part time at the Brazilian Workers Center, an agency in East Boston. Founded in 2001, this nonprofit offers ESL, citizenship classes and workers' rights workshops. Director Paulo Sardinha has invited Matos of the Painters Union and DaSilva to give educational workshops on unions, starting in 2002. Because of this relationship, Sardinha immediately contacted DaSilva at UCFW Local 1445 when the workers revealed their complaints. DaSilva promptly distributed union authorization cards to a worker, who signed up 60 out of 83 workers (an additional 15 employees are in supervisory roles). Given this positive response, DaSilva began to make home visits and filed for an election for UFCW representation with the NLRB, which was set for July 1, 2004.

According to DaSilva, workers' main concerns are wages, safety, job security, and respect at the workplace. "Wages are all over the place—they vary a lot for each worker, and if you are an attractive woman, you'll be offered more." DaSilva added that safety is lax, and workers have been fired without due notice. Most workers receive paid vacation and sick days, but they lack health coverage. With the election date set, Doug Belanger, Local 1445 organizing director, put DaSilva in charge of the campaign full-time. DaSilva states this is the first time a large group of Brazilian workers have joined together to organize in Massachusetts. UFCW represents workers at Carvel Restaurant in the town of Marlborough who are all Brazilian, but they organized it before any Brazilians worked there. He says, "This will be an open door if we win. Most Brazilians will not organize because they are scared, but this will set an example." He added that winning the election is not sufficient and the union wants to negotiate a good contract for the workers.

While Local 1445 has focused on traditional organizing methods such as holding meetings with workers, hand-billing outside the plant, mailings, and holding NLRB elections, DaSilva believes visiting workers in their homes has been an effective tactic in this campaign. This approach builds trust among workers and demonstrates that the union has their interest at stake. It also helps pinpoint the main issues affecting workers, which he uses to shape the campaign. For instance, he finds that health insurance may not be as important as wages to people who are saving money to return to Brazil; but for those intending longer-term residence, healthcare may be a top priority. DaSilva uncovers other problems during home visits, such as overcrowding and other community issues. If workers have U.S. citizenship, he encourages them to vote in local elections. Speaking Portuguese is "extremely important" while organizing, and DaSilva argues that "when it comes down to it, the workers are voting for you—you represent the union, and you help them put a face on the campaign." Miguel Vasquez, who has assisted with this campaign, feels that to organize well "you must be in the field as much as possible talking with people. If you leave the field, you will lose."[30] He has faced difficulties interacting with Brazilian workers, and hopes to study Portuguese for this purpose.

As the campaign progressed, the company fired two workers. One was dismissed for "insubordination" after explaining his use of ice to clean a mixing machine, a task that falls outside his responsibility. According to this worker, he had asked several questions during a mandatory meeting held by the company to discuss the union, and the meeting was promptly adjourned. A second worker was fired after supposedly turning in an expired green card. The company also began hiring several Spanish-speaking temporary workers, which DaSilva felt was meant to alert Brazilians that they would be replaced if they attempted to unionize.

DaSilva recognizes that some workers do not sympathize with the union. "Some don't want to talk to me. They think the company will help sign their immigration papers, so they stay loyal . . . some have worked [at this bakery] for five to seven years." He adds that those opposed to the UFCW often lack exposure to the labor movement in Brazil. In contrast, most workers favorable to the UFCW at the bakery have experience with Brazilian trade unions, such as teachers unions, ironworkers, or in one case, a bus drivers union. To some extent, this breaks down by region, with those from smaller towns in the south central state of Minas Gerais[31] often having less familiarity with organized labor and being less receptive to the Local 1445 drive, while several from Vitória (a city in Espírito Santo) and Rio de Janeiro are more familiar with unions and more interested in joining UFCW. Support for the union also seems to vary with workers' goals for the future. "Some just want to save money and return home, and this creates problems for the Brazilian community because these people avoid issues here in Boston." However, DaSilva notes an example of a woman who moved to a better-paying full-time cleaning job, but she wanted to vote for the union before leaving, in order to support her co-workers.

In addition to organizing workers directly, the union has developed links with immigrant organizations as a way to attract new members, and as a source of support during campaigns. DaSilva sits on the Board of Directors of the Brazilian Immigrant Center (BIC), and frequently visits its office while organizing. While I accompanied DaSilva, he often used the BIC office as a strategic site for meetings, faxing material and other activities. At one point, he printed a letter to the bakery workers on BIC letterhead with the BIC director's approval. DaSilva also visited the Brazilian Workers Center, the organization that connected him to this campaign.

DaSilva believes these links are important for the campaign and the union's work in general. "BIC is a leader in the community, and when they see this letter, they will see that this is part of the community, not just the union by itself." Vasquez believes that "this work requires you to get involved with many different groups." He has spoken at the *Comité de Inmigrantes*, a pan-Latino organization in Chelsea, during a campaign to organize 300 workers at an industrial laundry firm there. In addition, Vasquez has received letters of support from Catholic priests for this campaign, which he feels contributed to its success. In this case, DaSilva explains that this could be a risky tactic, since not all of the Brazilian bakery workers attend the same church. The workforce is divided between Catholics and Protestants, he estimates, adding that "five of the workers are gay, and I don't know if they would like receiving a letter from an [evangelical] pastor."

These relationships between UFCW Local 1445 and immigrant groups seem to be mutually beneficial. Local 1445 helped with fundraising for *Comité de Inmigrantes, La Comunidad*, a group in Everett, *Centro Presente*, a Latino immigrant legal services and advocacy group in Cambridge, Jobs with Justice, an organization affiliated with AFL-CIO, and BIC. In the past several years, the local contributed $1,000 to $1,500 to BIC annually. DaSilva feels that union staff has allowed him to develop leadership within the Brazilian community and to focus on campaigns that directly affect it, such as the Woburn bakery. The 21-year-old organizer feels that he and 29-year-old Vasquez can "bring new blood" into the union. Meanwhile, his position with the union enables him to pursue a personal goal of strengthening the Brazilian immigrant community.

The election occurred on July 1, 2004, and resulted in a tie. The company later challenged the results with the Labor Board, since one of the fired workers had submitted a vote. According to DaSilva, the company is "playing dirty" and accusing him and Vasquez of threatening workers with violence or with calling the INS if they did not vote for the union. This indicates the hostility that unions often face in trying to organize new members in today's workforce. DaSilva and BIC director da Rocha agree that this campaign will affect the way Brazilians in Boston view unions. According to DaSilva, "if we lose, it will show how weak the Brazilian community is. It will show the impact of not having rights, of not having legal status. Part of the reason for this situation is that we are not united, and we are still not respected here." He planned to write about the election results for *A Semana* and the *Brazilian Voice*, weekly newspapers for the New England Brazilian community.

Conclusion

What do these experiences of Brazilian immigrant workers with U.S. trade unions suggest about labor organizations' ability to bring this new group of workers into their ranks? Do they offer any insight into union revitalization and adaptation to the changing conditions of the globalizing economy? This study shows that there is a growing, though limited, trend of Brazilians joining labor unions in the Boston area. The specific cases demonstrate the potential for organizing, albeit on a small scale, among Brazilian immigrants who are entering the Boston area workforce, even under the inhospitable conditions that current unions face. In order to assess unions' success at reaching out to this new segment of the workforce in several distinct industries, we must examine factors other than increases in numbers of Brazilian members, since the unions do not keep reliable data on this. Instead, we can look comparatively at the unions' approaches, their benefits to members and to larger society, and their ability to overcome barriers associated with organizing Brazilians and other immigrant workers.

The Painters Union District Council 35 has shown adaptability in its approach by combining top-down organizing (focused on employers)—common in the building trades—with bottom-up strategies (focused on workers). For instance, they are actively engaging in "stripping" or stealing skilled workers from nonunion firms to work for union contractors. They have done this with immigrant workers, and have even hired several immigrants as full-time organizers. Moreover, DC 35 uses a flexible approach to confront nonunion contractors dispersed across greater Boston and New England. As with other building trades unions, they use a single contract for the entire region, with varying wage rates. The union also emphasizes the role of the regionally based District Council, with 14 local affiliates under its direction. This helps it respond more effectively to market forces affecting the industries they cover. Jim Snow, Organizing Director, notes that in 2003, the union's aggregate work hours have increased, despite a decrease in painting as a whole in New England, both union and nonunion. He feels this accomplishment is "primarily the result of organizing."

This flexible approach is effective in reaching out to painters and construction workers whose employer and location can vary at a given time. In this context, collaboration with community and immigrant organizations serves a dual role of offering support for campaigns, as well as a providing a physical place for these mobile workers to gather. This is particularly helpful for reaching out to Brazilians, who are dispersed in residential enclaves across eastern Massachusetts (see Mitchell 2003). The union shows sensitivity to this in holding community meetings with the BIC in towns such as Framingham with its high proportion of Brazilians.

Along with working with immigrant groups, the Painters Union DC 35 collaborates with other building trades' locals, and meets monthly with the Boston Building Trades Council to share strategy and analysis of the regional construction industry. DC 35 also works closely with state regulatory agencies such as the Attorney General's Office and the Labor Board to file wage and hour violations and unfair labor practice charges. These have in some cases hurt the bottom line of substandard companies, which frequently pay less than agreed-on wages or none at all, and overlook health and safety concerns.

An additional measure of the union's success can be seen in the positive returns to members and to society at large (Lewis and Mirand 1998). DC 35 provides health benefits, health insurance, pension benefits, and annuity accounts to its members. Members also receive elaborate job training, access to a list of 340 signatory companies and timely information on which employers are hiring. Furthermore, the union offers education about workers' rights and ESL classes to recent immigrants, helping them to increase their earnings potential.

As in the case of the Painters Union, UFCW Local 1445 is combining traditional approaches, such as filing for NLRB elections, with innovative methods such as one-on-one home visits. These visits are aimed at building rapport with workers, bridging language and cultural barriers, and educating workers on how unions can offer a democratic voice in the workplace. To do this systematically, the local has committed scarce resources to hiring a full-time organizing staff. Its organizing department includes immigrants who have worked in the industry and can therefore utilize their practical knowledge of working conditions, as in the Painters Union.

Local 1445's organizing department is smaller than the Painters', despite having larger membership (15,000 compared to 4,000). During the baked goods campaign, however, organizer DaSilva mobilized sympathetic workers to talk to other workers. Two workers who were fired during the campaign joined the union payroll to bolster organizing efforts in the days leading up to the election. Deploying workers as organizers in this way helps increase organizing capacity despite a limited full-time staff. It also develops leadership skills and involves members more fully in the work of building the union.

In contrast, staff members of Teamsters Local 25 recognize the benefits of bottom-up organizing approaches that the Painters and UFCW are using, but they have not prioritized or found a way to invest the necessary resources for this effort. The local has not replaced Battisti-Ashe, the ESL instructor and organizer, and the only staff member who spoke Portuguese. Although the local's training director supports grassroots organizing by rank-and-file and full-time organizers, this is not yet occurring on the ground. The Teamsters Local 25 does keep literature in Portuguese on the benefits to joining a union, a list of union contractors, and a Portuguese translation of the Weingarten Rights at the union hall.

These three union locals are similar in the way that they form strategic connections with Brazilian community organizations. All three have ties with the Brazilian Immigrant Center, and the Painters and UFCW also have a connection to the Brazilian Workers Center, the two groups in Boston that deal with workplace issues among Brazilians. The UFCW campaign emerged from the grassroots and reached the union by way of the BWC, where several workers study English. Through the educational workshops that all three locals conduct in collaboration with these two groups, Brazilian workers gain awareness of the U.S. labor movement and acquire skills they can parlay into higher-wage jobs, and better security and benefits. This is the case in unionized painting and drywalling, bakeries and food retail, and freight hauling and other transport jobs.

Notwithstanding these achievements, the unions in this study face significant barriers to recruiting Brazilian immigrants as new members. In the case of the Painters, organizer Fernando Matos concedes that he must confront mistrust from Brazilians about joining unions, despite his close ties to the community. There also appears to be a lack of knowledge about unions among Brazilian painters. While conducting this research, I talked to 12 Brazilian painters at BIC, and to others standing outside a Dunkin' Donuts waiting to be picked up for day labor, and only two of them had heard of the Painters Union. Despite the entry of Brazilians into the more unionized commercial sector of the painting industry, the vast majority work in nonunion, and often informal, residential painting.

Along with the increase of Brazilian painters, there is a sharp growth in Brazilian-owned painting firms. According to Matos and Snow, most of these firms are small, employing under five people, and vehemently anti-union. Referring to an employer for a job at University of Massachusetts Dartmouth, where Brazilian workers were found sleeping at the site, Snow says, "usually you find the most vicious exploiters of a group are members of that same group." Matos points out that of the 340 companies with union contracts only one is Brazilian-owned, despite the existence of hundreds of small Brazilian painting firms.

Although the UFCW does not confront either the informal small firms found in the painting industry or Brazilian employers, the union shares the Painters' challenge of fear and lack of knowledge about U.S. unions among Brazilian workers. For instance, while accompanying DaSilva on house calls, I talked to the bakery worker who had been fired for "insubordination." If he joined, this would be his first time as a union member, whether in Brazil or in this country. He asked me if it was possible for the union to cut paid vacation and sick days, something he had heard in a mandatory meeting held by the employer. In this context, DaSilva and BIC director da Rocha agree that the bakery campaign will strongly affect the way Brazilian immigrants in Boston view unions.

One issue that runs across all three cases is the challenge of organizing an immigrant community that is heavily undocumented. To be sure, lack of a green card or permanent residence status makes it difficult for Brazilian and other immigrants to have a secure sense of rights in their adopted country. DaSilva sees immigrant status as "one of the big walls. We try not to see it as a bad thing; we see them as workers. But the company does use it against us." The Painters Union does not inquire about immigration status, but organizers note that lack of legal papers makes workers more fearful and hesitant to associate with unions.

Sullivan of the Teamsters agrees that Brazilians, much like other first-generation immigrants and particularly those without legal status, do not realize the extent of their rights in the United States. He notes that employers can easily threaten immigrants with notifying Homeland Security if they challenge workplace practices. "Immigrants never, or rarely ever, file an accident report if they get hurt on the job. They don't question the boss" because they are "happy to be anywhere but where they came from." In discussing his aspirations for the Teamsters Union in the future, Sullivan states, "My argument is that the Sullivans, like my name, a hundred years ago, we were the truck drivers and the laborers of the city, and we've established ourselves enough to be able to move forward, so to speak. We're no different from the Vasquezes and the Diazes and the folks that are coming into this country to go to work. We need to embrace them. We need to invite them into our union hall, show them what we do, who we are. Why we believe we are the best union in the country."

Although this finding on undocumented workers as more difficult to organize differs from Delgado's (1993) study of a successful unionization drive among a largely undocumented Latino workforce in 1980s California, Fink's (2003) investigation of Guatemalan workers at a poultry processing plant shows that in some cases workers without legal status may be more fearful of joining unions. Further research could tease out the influence of undocumented status on propensity to unionize among Brazilians in the Boston area, and the specific challenges this category presents for unions. Additional research could also explore the potential synergy between labor unions and Brazilian churches. This could include examining the relationship between the church where Painters Union organizer

Fernando Matos is pastor, and the Painters Union. Such a study could potentially shed new light on the challenges of community formation among Brazilians in the United States, a topic explored elsewhere in this volume. Finally, additional studies could probe the ways that increasing union membership among Brazilian immigrants is changing the Brazilian community in Massachusetts, perhaps increasing social solidarity and other forms of collective action.[32]

Table 1. Summary of Local Unions and Their Approaches toward Brazilian Workers

	Painters Union District Council 35	Teamsters Local 25	UFCW Local 1445
Main occupations represented	Commercial and industrial paining, drywalling, glazing	Trucking and freight, warehousing, car rental agencies	Food processing, food retail and wholesale
Total membership	4,000	9,000	15,000
Estimated Brazilian membership	250–300	40	200
Staff members who speak Portuguese	1	0	1
Website information in Spanish or Portuguese	No, but states that union supports undocumented workers and amnesty for immigrants	Web pages in Spanish and Portuguese	Web pages in Spanish, uses union authorization cards in Spanish
Primary organizing approach	Securing back-pay from nonunion contractors, hiring immigrant organizers	Internal organizing, offering ESL classes	NLRB elections, home visits
Links to Brazilian community organizations	Organized four community meetings held with BIC starting 2002, Brazilian organizer is also pastor at a Brazilian church	Organized workshops with BIC on workers' rights and on obtaining a commercial drivers license starting in 2003	Workers' rights workshops at Brazilian Workers Center starting in 2002, Brazilian organizer is on BIC Board of Directors

Table 2. Frequency of Occupations of Foreign-born Brazilians in Massachusetts

Occupation description	No. observations, n = 396	Percentage
Not in labor market	96	24.14
Restaurant manager	6	1.52
Registered nurse	5	1.26
Restaurant—cook	29	7.32
Restaurant—food prep	5	1.26
Restaurant—dining room attendant, bartender	7	1.77
Cleaning—janitor, building cleaner	9	2.27
Cleaning—maids and housekeeping	36	9.09
Sales—cashiers	15	3.79
Sales—retail salesperson	6	1.52
Office—bookkeeping, accounting, auditing	5	1.26
Office—secretary, admin. assistant	5	1.26
Construction—painters, construction and maintenance	14	3.54
Production—bakers	7	1.77
Transportation—laborers and freight, stock, and material movers, hand	5	1.26
Other		36.97
Total		**100.00**

* listed categories have more than 5 observations, n=396.
(Source: U.S. Census 2000: PUMS 1% sample). Prepared by author.

Notes

1. For more information on the AFL-CIO policies supporting immigrants' rights within a fairly enforced system of legal immigration, see AFL-CIO (2000).
2. Source: 2000 U.S. Census, Summary File 4. I used the code for "Foreign born" under the category "Ancestry: Brazilian" as a proxy for Brazilian immigrants in the Boston NECMA (New England County Metropolitan Area, which includes Boston, Worcester, Lawrence, Lowell, and Brockton). The 2000 U.S. Census records a total population of 5,671,502 in the Boston NECMA, and 740,940 of these are foreign born.
3. In 1990 and 2000, Brazilians who did fill out U.S. Census short forms do not fit into the category "Hispanic/Latino." Those who write Brazilian under the category "Other Hispanic or Latino" are listed as "Non-Hispanic" and their nationality is not tabulated (see Margolis 2003, 54).
4. Teresa Sales' book (1999) on Brazilian immigrants in Framingham, Massachusetts, has been translated into English.
5. This echoes Margolis' observation that the "disjunction between social roots and current employment [for Brazilians in New York City] provides a crash course in downward mobility" (1994, 129).

6. Source: 2000 U.S. Census Public Use Micro Sample (PUMS). Using the 1% PUMS, I prepared a cross-tabulation to match foreign-born Brazilians in Massachusetts with data on occupations and industries. See Table 2 for a summary of the results.
7. The category "Not in the labor force" has 96 cases in the sample, suggesting that a high proportion of Brazilian immigrants are under age 18 and thus would not be counted, or that large numbers work in the informal sector and would also not be counted.
8. This is the case in the public sector and manufacturing, such as automobile and metal industries, in industrialized regions, such as the state of São Paulo.
9. See Clawson and Clawson (1999) for a review essay on factors attributed to organized labor's decline.
10. See Fraser (1991) and Gabaccia (2000) for examples of organizing along ethnic lines in the early 20th century in the Jewish and Italian immigrant communities, respectively. Receptivity to unionization efforts in these cases was often linked to prior experiences with strikes and labor organization.
11. Waldinger et al.'s (1998) analysis of the Los Angeles Justice for Janitors campaign also emphasizes Latinos' and especially Salvadorans' "high level of class consciousness" and willingness to take risks involved in organizing as shaped by experiences in their home countries.
12. Fine notes that the AFL-CIO organizes an average of 400,000 new workers a year, but there were approximately 27.5 million poverty-wage workers in the United States in 2000.
13. In 2003, overall membership of AFL-CIO unions fell by 40,000, but SEIU added 75,000 members and LIUNA added 32,000. See Porter (2004).
14. See The Painters and Allied Trades District Council 35 website, available at: <http://www.iupatdc35.org/Pages?aboutus/html>.
15. The authors note that in the early 1980s, union representation in building and construction industries in the United States fell from a high of more than 80 percent in the late 1940s to 20 percent.
16. This follows practices common in other building trades unions; for a discussion of a similar approach by the Carpenters in Boston, see Safford and Locke (2003, 24–27). Lewis and Mirand (1998) note that nonunion employers can choose to leave the area rather than sign a union contract, but this does not necessarily hurt job growth, especially if it opens up more bid opportunities for union contractors, who can then compete on a more even playing field.
17. Fernando Matos, interview by author, March 26, 2004.
18. Jim Snow, interview by author, March 19, 2004.
19. Mark Lohan, District 35 organizer and student at the University of Massachusetts Boston writes that the Painters Union emerged out of tightly controlled

labor guilds and once restricted its membership to skilled native-born workers. See Lohan (2002).

20. The 2000 U.S. Census lists construction industry painting as one of the most frequent occupations for foreign-born Brazilians in Massachusetts. See Table 2.
21. Tony Hernandez, interview by author, December 11, 2003.
22. Matos, interview by author, March 19, 2004.
23. In his own experience, Matos anticipated staying in the United States for two years, but soon found that it would take longer to save the amount of money he had wanted. He is now married to a Trinidadian, has two daughters, and has no intention of returning permanently to Brazil.
24. Local 25's jurisdiction extends from Lowell in the north to just above Brockton to the south, and Framingham to Wakefield and the city of Boston to the east and west.
25. Steve Sullivan, interview by author, March 10, 2004.
26. Amy Battisti-Ashe, interview by author, December 10, 2003.
27. See Teamsters Local 25 web site, available at: <http://www.teamsterslocal25.com/espanol.html>.
28. Fabricio DaSilva, interview by author, June 30, 2004.
29. The occupation of baker appears more frequently than any other manufacturing job in the 2000 U.S. Census micro sample for Brazilians in Massachusetts. See Table 2.
30. Miguel Vasquez, interview by author, June 22, 2004.
31. A large proportion of Brazilians in Massachusetts are from this state, particularly the region surrounding the city of Governador Valadares, Minas Gerais, as noted earlier. See Martes (2000).
32. Many thanks to Judith Tendler, Sharon Stanton Russell, Richard Locke, Keith Hampton, Leticia Braga, Clémence Jouët-Pastré, and three anonymous reviewers for comments on earlier versions of this chapter.

References

AFL-CIO. 2000. *Building Understanding, Creating Change: A Report on Immigrant Workers' Rights.* Washington D.C.

Brecher, Jeremy and Tim Costello. 1999. "A New Labor Movement in the Shell of the Old?" In *The Transformation of U.S. Unions: Voices Visions and Strategies from the Grassroots.* Ed. R. M. Tillman and M. S. Cummings. Boulder: Lynn Reinner.

Bronfenbrenner, K., S. Friedman, R. W. Hurd, R. A. Oswald, and R. L.Seeber, eds. 1998. *Organizing to Win: New Research on Union Strategies.* Ithaca: Cornell University Press.

Clawson, Dan and Mary Ann Clawson. 1999. "What Has Happened to the U.S. Labor Movement? Union Decline and Renewal." *American Review of Sociology* 25:95–119.

Delgado, Hector. 1993. *New Immigrants, Old Unions: Organizing Undocumented Workers in Los Angeles.* Philadelphia: Temple University Press.

Davis, Mike. 2000. *Magical Realism: Latinos Reinvent the U.S. City.* New York: Verso.

Fine, Janice. 2003. "Community Unions in Baltimore and Long Island: Beyond the Politics of Particularism." Ph.D. diss., Massachusetts Institute of Technology, Cambridge, MA.

Fink, Leon. 2003. *The Maya of Morganton: Work and Community in the Nuevo New South.* Chapel Hill: University of North Carolina Press.

Fraser, S. 1991. *Labor Will Rule: Sidney Hillman and the Rise of American Labor.* New York: The Free Press.

Gabaccia, D. 2000. *Italy's Many Diasporas.* Seattle: University of Washington Press.

Levitt, Peggy. 2001. *Transnational Villagers.* Berkeley: University of California Press.

Lewis, Janet and Bill Mirand. 1998. "Creating and Organizing Culture in Today's Building and Construction Trades: A Case Study of IBEW Local 46." In *Organizing to Win: New Research on Union Strategies.* Ed. Bronfenbrenner, K., S. Friedman, R. W. Hurd, R. A. Oswald, and R. L. Seeber. Ithaca: Cornell University Press.

Lohan, Mark. 2002. "History of the Painters Union." Unpublished Capstone Paper, University of Massachusetts, Boston.

Margolis, Maxine. 1994. *Little Brazil: An Ethnography of Brazilian Immigrants in New York City.* Princeton: Princeton University Press.

———. 1998. *An Invisible Minority: Brazilian Immigrants in New York City.* Boston: Allyn and Bacon.

Martes, Ana Cristina Braga. 2000. *Brasileiros Nos Estados Unidos.* São Paulo: Paz e Terra.

Martes, Ana Cristina Braga and Soraya Fleischer. Eds. 2003. *Fronteiras Cruzadas: Etnicidade, Gênero e Redes Sociais.* Ed. Ana Cristina Braga Martes and Soraya Fleischer. São Paulo: Paz e Terra.

———. 2003. "Na Virada do Milenio: A Emigracao Brasileira para os Estados Unidos." In *Fronteiras Cruzadas: Etnicidade, Gênero e Redes Sociais.* Ed. Ana Cristina Braga Martes and Soraya Fleischer. São Paulo: Paz e Terra.

Milkman, Ruth, ed. 2000. *Organizing Immigrants: The Challenge of Unions in Contemporary California.* Ithaca: Cornell University Press.

Mitchell, Christopher. 2003. "Perspectiva Comparada sobre Transnacionalismo entre Imigrantes Brasileiros nos Estados Unidos." In *Fronteiras Cruzadas:*

Etnicidade, Gênero e Redes Sociais. Ed. Ana Cristina Braga Martes and Soraya Fleischer. São Paulo: Paz e Terra.

Porter, Eduardo. 2004. "What Unions Can Gain from Immigration." *New York Times*, March 28, 2004, Business Section, p. 1.

Safford, Sean and Richard M. Locke. 2003. "Unions on the Rebound: Embeddedness and the Transformation of Building Trades Unions." Conditionally accepted for publication by the Industrial and Labor Relations Review.

Sales, Teresa. 1999. *Brasileiros Longe de Casa.* São Paulo: Cortez Editora.

Sum, Andrew, W. Neil Fogg, et al. 1999. *The Changing Workforce: Immigrants and the New Economy in Massachusetts.* Joint Project of Citizens Bank and Mass-Inc. Boston: Northeastern University Center for Labor Market Studies.

Waldinger, R., C. Erickson, R. Milkman, D. J. B. Mitchell, A. Valenzuela, K. Wong, and M. Zeitlin. 1998. "Helots No More: A Case Study of the Justice for Janitors Campaign in Los Angeles." In *Organizing to Win: New Research on Union Strategies.* Ed. Bronfenbrenner, K., S. Friedman, R. W. Hurd, R. A. Oswald, and R. L. Seeber. Ithaca: Cornell University Press.

Wells, Miriam. 2000. "Immigration and Unionization in the San Francisco Hotel Industry." In *Organizing Immigrants: The Challenge of Unions in Contemporary California.* Ed. Milkman, R. Ithaca: Cornell University Press.

10
The Religious Field among Brazilians in the United States

Paul Freston

Obviously one cannot talk about religious affiliations in the Brazilian diaspora without taking into account the status of the religious field in Brazil itself.[1] In those terms, Brazil can be portrayed in many ways. It can be described as the largest Catholic country in the world, but also as the world capital of Spiritism. And at the same time, a fact that is probably less well known, it now has the second largest community of practicing Protestants in the world (after the United States). That is in absolute numbers, not in percentage of the population. In addition, Brazil has the largest community of Pentecostals[2] in the world (herein I shall treat Pentecostals as a sub-set of Protestants, and indeed as the largest segment of the Brazilian Protestant community). One in every nine Brazilians is now a Pentecostal; one in every seven in the state of Rio de Janeiro.

What are the main trends in the religious field in Brazil? From the official censuses the first trend is the decline of Catholicism. This is obviously a relative decline because it started from a position of monopoly as the official and traditional religion. But in the 2000 Census Catholicism was down to 73.7%, having lost ten percentage points since the 1991 Census. This decline seems to be continuing in the early twenty-first century. In the state of Rio de Janeiro, Catholicism (that is, the percentage of the population prepared to admit to an at least nominal Catholic affiliation) was already down to 57% in 2000, so by the next census there may well be a minority in that state that even calls itself Catholic, let alone actually practices the religion.

The second trend is the rise of Protestantism and especially of its Pentecostal forms. In the last census, Protestants were 15.5%; if one assumes that the rate of increase of the 1990s has persisted until today (2006), that would mean something like 17 or 18%. Over two-thirds of these Protestants are Pentecostals. And the third trend is the rise of the category known as "no religion," which covers a multitude of unorthodox individualistic spiritualities as well as agnostics and atheists (who would seem to be a smallish minority of people with no religion). Those with no religion came to 7.3% in the 2000 Census and are also expanding rapidly.

Other religious groups, inasmuch as they appear in the census (an important proviso), do not amount to very much: Spiritism 1.4%, Umbanda 0.25%, Candomblé 0.8%.[3] Obviously, that does not reflect anything like the reality of their influence in the country; it merely reflects the way people reply to the question that the census asks, which does not allow for multiple affiliations and does not ask about practice. By no means is the cultural influence of the Afro-Brazilian religions reflected in the census figures. But in terms of the two largest categories, Catholics and Pentecostals, it is important to note that Catholics are now disproportionately elderly, rural, male, and light-skinned, whereas Pentecostals are disproportionately urban, younger, female, and darker-skinned.

Research on Religion in the Diaspora

Religion in the Brazilian diaspora[4] has been the object of very few studies and is now one of the most glaring gaps in the study of Brazilian emigrants, both for its intrinsic interest and because of the social role of religion among migrant populations. Unlike African churches in Europe and Hispanic and Korean churches in the United States, which have been studied a great deal, there has been little study of Brazilian religions outside Brazil. So this is another form of invisibility for Brazilian immigrants: even at the academic level they fall through the cracks. For example, the PARAL network in New York is "a network of scholars committed to a comparative study of religion among the peoples of Latin American heritage living in the United States," but it completely ignores Brazilians. Brazilians, it seems, are not people of Latin American heritage! Various authors have approached Brazilian diasporic religion tangentially, whether as part of broader studies of religious transnationalism or of broader studies of Brazilian immigrants. Peggy Levitt (2002a) has studied the religious transnationalism of various communities in the Boston area, including Brazilians from the town of Governador Valadares in the state of Minas Gerais, a major supplier of Brazilian emigrants. In addition, there is an ongoing study at the University of Florida coordinated by Manuel Vásquez, looking at Brazilians and other groups in Florida. As for specialist works on Brazilians in the United States, religion has merited some comments in Margolis (1994) and a chapter in Martes' book (2000) about Massachusetts. But in general it has been surprisingly unstudied.

What needs to be looked at? Evidently, the composition of the diaspora population can affect the way that the religious field will be transplanted. The social composition in terms of class, age structure, gender, color, in terms even of the country of destination—all these factors may affect the way that the religious dimension of the host country is transplanted or not to the diaspora. So one task is to compare the Brazilian diasporic religious field with what happens in this area in Brazil. Secondly, it can be compared from one country of destination to another (between the United States, Europe, Japan and Paraguay, for example), with a discussion of what might cause the differences. In addition, there is the question of how religion affects migratory flows. Do certain religions encourage migration by offering new perspectives, by providing networks for recruitment, by reducing the economic and psychological costs of emigration, by influencing the choice of destination? And does migration itself affect religiosity? Classically, it was often thought that the migratory state—the condition of migrancy—tended to diminish religiosity, especially when moving to a more secular context than the one the person came from. The migrant loses contacts and constraints and the net result is a process of secularization. Or, on the other hand, does migrancy accentuate religiosity as a form of cultural defense? Or does it simply transform it from one form to another? Or does it remain the same?

In addition, there is the question of the effects of diasporic religion. Does the diasporic religion remain contained within the ethnic group? Or does it overflow, as it were, and influence the religious aspect of the host society? Is there any possibility that the religious field in the United States could be influenced by the immigrants' religion (obviously not only by Brazilians, because they are not numerous enough, but in conjunction with other, much more numerous immigrants)? It is still far too common to talk of American Christianity when talking basically about white American Christianity. Not only are African Americans left out but also all the ever more numerous immigrant Christians and their descendants. While it has often been commented that the flood of immigrants to the United States since 1965 has undoubtedly led to the pluralization of the religious field due to the presence of other religions, the vast majority of immigrants are Christians of one type or another rather than Muslims, Hindus or Buddhists. So rather than the pluralization of religion, the flood of immigration has led to the pluralization of the Christian variants.

Brazilian Religiosity in the United States

In the diaspora, some Brazilians presumably practice their religiosity in non-Brazilian contexts. In the United States, for example, some might go to Anglophone churches. But it would seem that the great majority practice in a specifically Brazilian context. That seems to be the case even when an easy possibility for not doing so exists. For example, in Framingham (Massachusetts), the American town with the highest proportion of Brazilians in its population, there was an older Portuguese population. The Catholic Church already celebrated a Portuguese mass, and the first Brazilian Catholics who arrived went to it. But once a substantial Brazilian community had been established, the churchgoers started a Brazilian mass at a separate time from the Portuguese one. So even where there are linguistic similarities, a specifically Brazilian context still ends up being created. The same is true in Portugal itself, where the great majority of Brazilian evangelicals set up their own churches rather than go to existing Portuguese ones.

In the diasporic situation, it seems as though organized religion both expands and contracts. It expands in the sense of churches fulfilling many other functions in addition to the usual ones: familial, sociocultural, linguistic (preservation of the language), economic, political (representation and organization), medical, and other functions. The churches expand to fulfill these other functions vis-à-vis the relative lack of other state and civil society institutions among the immigrants. That of course may be a temporary void which over time may be reoccupied by other institutions. However, it is an extremely important function, particularly in the early years, and the void is never in fact totally reoccupied. This expansion of functions applies both to Catholic and Protestant (or evangelical) churches, although in different ways due to their diverse social and organizational characteristics and theological traditions. (In Portuguese, "protestante" and "evangélico" are generally used as synonyms.[5])

At the same time organized religion in general contracts and seems to be weaker than in the homeland. This is first of all due to geographical dispersion. The Brazilian community in the United States is fairly dispersed geographically, rather than concentrated in ethnic enclaves. Secondly, the contraction of organized religion reflects the newness of the situation. In addition, it reflects the busyness of people's lives; the average immigrant works very long hours, and if both spouses are in the United States, they usually both work. Finally, it is due to the temporary mentality which says "we are not really immigrants, we're not really making our home here, we're just here temporarily to work and go back home," a return which usually ends up being repeatedly delayed. The result of this contraction is that it is unlikely (at least in the first generation) that levels of organized religious practice are as high as in Brazil.

However, this contraction of organized religious life does not take place uniformly across the religious spectrum. Instead, we often see a greater Christianization. Of course, the religious field in Brazil is highly Christian, but it seems to be even more so in the diasporic situation. Other currents are greatly reduced, or even virtually absent in organized form in relation to Christian (Catholic and Protestant) practice. The second change is a greater Protestantization of the Christian field. In other words, amongst the Christian churches, the Protestant ones seem to attract a higher percentage of churchgoers than they do in Brazil. And thirdly, there is a greater pentecostalization of the Protestant field. Pentecostals are already two-thirds of Protestants within Brazil, but once again, in the diaspora that percentage seems to grow even more. Even churches which are not obviously Pentecostal in name take on Pentecostal features among the immigrants. (In fact, the same is true of the Catholic world, where the Catholic Charismatic Renewal is very influential in the diaspora.) To the extent, therefore, that organized religion exists in the Brazilian diaspora, it is far more heavily Pentecostal than in the homeland.

Protestantism and Migration

When it comes to religious percentages, comparison with Brazil is not easy. There is an obvious problem in comparing the Brazilian census, which is based on self-identification, with figures for participation in religious organizations in the diaspora, which are based on practice. We cannot produce percentages for the diaspora comparable to those in the census. To illustrate the problem, we can ask: is the percentage of Protestants higher or lower in the diaspora than in Brazil? From what we know of immigrants generally and Brazilian immigrants in particular, one can cite good *a priori* reasons for both answers. And the main problem, of course, is that there are no firm statistics regarding how many Brazilians we are talking about.

Some authors, including Martes and Margolis, estimate that Protestants are more numerous, relatively speaking, among Brazilians in the United States than in Brazil, which of course begs the question whether Protestants emigrate more, or whether emigrants convert more. Or, indeed, whether both of these processes occur. Other observers, however, including many

Protestant pastors, claim that there is a much lower proportion of Protestants here than in Brazil. In the case of the pastors, that may be a self-serving answer which helps to justify their own work. In addition, it may be based on the unperceived contradiction between the heavy demands for participation which pastors of Brazilian churches traditionally make and the busyness of the immigrants' lives, which does not allow them to be as active in religious communities as they would be at home. Pastors may therefore find it harder to mobilize their flocks than they are used to, and perceive this as a diminution in the percentage of Protestants.

What reasons would there be for believing there to be a smaller percentage of Protestants among Brazilians in the United States than in the homeland? One reason would be that a very high proportion of the immigrants are from the state of Minas Gerais, which has a relatively low percentage of Protestants compared to the national average. Another reason might be that many immigrants are young males, a category which is relatively under-represented in Protestant churches. And a third reason might be the geographical dispersion of Brazilians in the United States, the long working hours and other factors related to the immigrants' condition of life, which might make some people abandon their active religious participation (even if they do not cease considering themselves to be Protestants).

On the other hand, one can think of many reasons for supposing a higher percentage of Protestants here than in Brazil. First, because the Protestant churches are famously good at helping to overcome the difficulties of immigrant life (see e.g. Levitt 2002b regarding Latinos). This applies both to the psychological challenge of creating and maintaining the positive attitudes and ethic of hard work and initiative, which are essential to success and even to survival, as well as to the practical questions of establishing networks which can assist the immigrant in finding places to live and work. As one of the few contexts in which broad networks of (at least relative) trust can be established, these churches make the immigrants' lives easier in a series of practical ways.

Second, it is possible that Protestants do migrate more. We can talk of an analogy between religious migration and physical migration, the idea of an elective affinity between religious and physical mobility. Protestant evangelical discourse values social mobility and a break with tradition. And if you have broken with tradition by changing your religion, why not break with tradition by emigrating as well? A third argument for supposing the strength of these churches in the diaspora is the relative lack of other Brazilian institutions for socialization and information-sharing within the immigrant community, a void which the churches fill. In addition, of course, the churches can offer locations for reinforcing Brazilianness. Even though the Protestant religion is not the traditional Brazilian religion, it has effectively been "naturalized," and the automatic identification of Brazilianness and Catholicism no longer holds. So these churches can be locations for reinforcing Brazilian identity and the Portuguese language (especially for parents concerned that their children grow up knowing Portuguese[6]), as well as offering safe networks relatively free of competitiveness. There are a lot of complaints in the Brazilian community (as in many immigrant communities) that Brazilians exploit other Brazilians. The expectation of solidarity is not met in the broader community, but is reconstituted, at least relatively, in the churches.

Catholicism versus Pentecostalism in the Diasporic Situation

Another factor in the presumption of Protestant strength in the diaspora has to do with the other side of the coin, so-called Catholic slowness (about which more below). This Catholic slowness in occupying spaces leaves them open to be occupied by other churches. This contrasts with how scholars of global Pentecostalism have referred to it as a religion made to travel, as in many ways an ideal religion for transnational migrants. Pentecostalism is a translatable religion and not at all territorial, being based neither on a national church structure of dioceses and parishes, which is very difficult to uproot and transplant, nor on shrines and places of pilgrimage, which are also difficult to uproot. As a nonterritorial religion, it is very flexible. In addition, many aspects of its doctrine, symbology (of the pilgrim, for example), organization, ethics, mechanisms of social control that the churches try to inculcate, as well as mechanisms of self-control which the church members try to incarnate—all these favor the objectives of the immigrants in situations where they really cannot afford to lose their way too much because they are living precariously. Another thing which favors Pentecostalism is its abundant and localized supply. Very often people will go to any functioning religious community that is just down the road, especially if they are financially strapped or bent on saving all they can. So rather than going to perhaps the only place where they can hear mass in Portuguese, which may be 40 miles away and only once a month, they will go to the Pentecostal church just around the corner. And why is Pentecostal supply so localized? Largely because it is a lay religion, not dependent on religious specialists who may be in scarce supply locally.

How Many Protestants?

Based on my research, it seems reasonable to estimate (fairly conservatively) that there are currently (2006) around 800 Brazilian Protestant churches in the United States.[7] If one estimates an average membership of sixty people, which is also a conservative estimate as there are some very large churches as well as many tiny ones, that would mean 48,000 members of Brazilian Protestant churches in the United States. If we use the lower end of the estimates for the total Brazilian population in the United States, 700,000, that amounts to about 7%. Even if we add the small number of Brazilians who practice their religion in non-Brazilian churches, the end result (say, 8%) is still lower than the figure of Brazilians who proclaim themselves to be Protestant in Brazil (15.5% in the 2000 Census; probably around 17% today). However, we must remember that the latter figure is based on self-identification, whereas our estimate for Brazilians in the United States is based on effective participation. From what we know of the (comparatively very high) propensity of Protestants in Brazil to practice their religion (around three-quarters claim weekly practice), and if we allow that practice is probably lower in the diaspora because of busyness and dispersion, then we end up with a percentage of Protestants that is either slightly lower or very similar to that which obtains in Brazil. In other words, if we assume that weekly practice in the diaspora is lower than in Brazil (say, 50%), then the 8% who effectively participate may represent a Protestant community in the diaspora of around 16%.

However, what this Protestantism represents in terms of the organized religious field in the diaspora is much higher. Compared to the other confessions, the Protestant (and especially Pentecostal) churches grow in importance amongst Brazilian emigrants, whether in the United States or in Japan, Paraguay or Western Europe. This brings us back to what I referred to earlier as Catholic slowness. Let me exemplify this phenomenon. When I went to do research in London (the city where I grew up and know fairly well), I fully expected to find five or six Brazilian Protestant evangelical churches in London. Instead, I discovered 30. And what about a Catholic presence? I discovered the existence of one Brazilian Catholic priest who celebrates mass in Portuguese in four different locations and is virtually impossible to contact. I e-mailed him once before I went to London, and he replied, "Oh, yes! Here is my telephone number. Call me when you arrive." On subsequent trips I tried calling him several times on each occasion, only succeeding in reaching a recorded message in English and Portuguese (without even the possibility of leaving a message). Now, if I am a Brazilian immigrant in London going through a crisis of some sort, that is not a great deal of help. I am more likely to resort to one of the 30 evangelical churches, whose pastors (many churches have more than one) are easily reached. Another example is Santa Rita, a town in eastern Paraguay of 11,000 people, 90% of whom are Brazilians. There are 16 Brazilian Protestant churches, ranging across the spectrum from the Lutheran Church to the neo-Pentecostal Universal Church of the Kingdom of God. And there are just two Catholic priests, one Brazilian and one Italian, who also serve four surrounding towns. Similar examples can be given from Japan. Of course, the Catholic communities that do exist tend to be bigger than the average evangelical church. In addition, over time the Catholic presence grows and that is why I refer to slowness rather than absence. The Catholic Church ends up establishing a presence, but it takes some time. Thus, the Brazilian Apostolate of the Boston archdiocese is now up to about fourteen communities, and the clergy is increasingly Brazilian (at the beginning, they were often returned American missionaries). But wc can say that in general the difficulty that the Catholic Church has found in following the diaspora is an extension of its difficulty in following population movements within Brazil.

The current maps of the different religions in Brazil show clearly that Catholicism and Pentecostalism are diametrally opposed. Catholicism has difficulty on the urban peripheries and on the agricultural frontiers, which are precisely places of population movement. Presumably, its weakness in those areas has to do with its territorial structure and clericalism. And of course, its institutional resources are getting ever scarcer, in terms of Catholics per priest. Another factor is the lack of a tradition in Brazilian Catholicism of contributing financially, which stems from its traditional status in Brazil of a very well-endowed semi-official religion. The idea of giving money to a voluntary institution which depends on your contributions is new to Catholic immigrants, whereas it is already the norm in the case of Protestant immigrants.

Other Religions in the Diaspora

The presence of other Brazilian religions in the diaspora is timid. In Japan, for example, one secular Brazilian journal is full of advertisements for evangelical churches, replete with times of services, addresses and telephone numbers of the church and the pastors, and even their web pages. Often there are numerous locations for each church. In the middle of all these adverts, there is one for a Spiritist group, which, instead of offering locations and telephone numbers, offers the reader a mailing address to obtain . . . a computer disk. Similarly, in one of the secular Brazilian journals published in London, there are pages and pages of advertisements for evangelical churches, and tucked away in the middle there is one advertisement for an Afro-Brazilian *terreiro* (temple), with an address and telephone number. My call was answered by an Argentinian woman speaking Portunhol (a mixture of Portuguese and Spanish), who said the *terreiro* was run by a *pai-de-santo* (priest) who was an Italian who had done an internship in Brazil. And this *terreiro* was actually located in Brixton, not a center of the Brazilian presence in London but a heavily Afro-Caribbean area. So this is a fascinating example of religious globalization: a Brazilian religious temple in England run by an Italian with an Argentinian assistant and (one presumes) with basically an African and Caribbean clientele! But as a demonstration of the strength of this religion amongst the Brazilian diaspora community, it obviously does not represent a great deal. With regard to Kardecist Spiritism, there are several dozen centers in the United States, although it seems that many of them were started by, and are largely frequented by, Portuguese or (Spanish-speaking) Latinos. So although there is a Spiritist presence in the Brazilian community, it is much smaller than its strength in Brazil would lead one to expect.

A Theology of the Undocumented

In view of the relative predominance of evangelical churches in the diaspora, it is worth asking how these churches work (theologically and pastorally) with the fact that the vast majority of their members (and sometimes even the pastors) are undocumented. While Brazilian Catholicism is well known for its theology of liberation, and Brazilian neo-Pentecostal churches have become famous for their theology of prosperity, neither of those theologies is really fundamental for the churches operating in the context of the Brazilian community in the United States. The basic underlying theology which they all need is what I would call a theology of the undocumented. While this theology is necessary for the Catholic churches as well, it is especially important for the evangelical churches because of the pronounced moralism which generally typifies them. In other words, how do churches that are usually very moralistic and legalistic, very concerned with being on the right side of the law, function when they know that the great majority of their congregation is in the country illegally and has broken several laws and told several lies in order to get here? What pastoral treatment do they give to this question? What sort of theology do they develop, explicitly or implicitly?

One almost never hears an explicit and systematic treatment of this question in public evangelical fora, but from interviews and other sources it is possible to piece together a rudimentary theology of the undocumented. This is a mixture of theological, historical and pragmatic arguments, many of which are, of course, not unique to Brazilian immigrants. The theological arguments stress that God created a world without borders. Borders are man-made and should not be absolutized and can therefore be ignored. In addition, Jesus was an illegal immigrant in Egypt, and the migration motif has been part of the biblical history of salvation since Abraham. And the Jews are instructed in the Old Testament to treat the "resident alien" with generosity and respect. The historical argument states that the United States is a country built on waves of immigration, of which they are merely the most recent but no different qualitatively from the previous waves. Why should the descendants of previous immigrants be able to prevent current ones from entering? In other words, the only American government with a moral right to prohibit immigration would be a government of Native Americans. Or, in the words of one pastor interviewed: "Which is better, to come from São Paulo on a tourist visa and overstay your visa, or to come from Britain in 1690 on a boat when nobody had to have a visa, kill a few Indians and steal their land?" And finally, the pragmatic arguments go along the lines of: "we are illegal not because we want to be but because we're obliged to be. We're not actually doing anything illegal. We are good citizens working hard, and doing our best to get legalized. We are doing jobs that Americans don't want and, in any case, as the Americans exploit the whole world, why shouldn't we be allowed to do these underpaid jobs? And, after all, this is all a game. The government makes laws which it does not really wish to enforce because the economic effects would be drastic. So the government is really an accomplice in an elaborate game of make-believe. If it really wanted to expel all the illegal immigrants, it knows where they are." Indeed, it is said that in the week after the terrorist attacks of 2001 many undocumented Brazilians lost their jobs because the employers were worried that the authorities would really start enforcing the laws. But the following week they were all hired again because everyone realized that nothing was going to happen.

Most pastors seem to work pastorally from the existing situation: "I have to work with my people where they are, rather than from an ideal situation." Generally they encourage people to move in the direction of legalization where possible, but it is very rare to hear any questioning of the moral right of their undocumented flock to be in the country. Evidently, apart from anything else, the pastors realize which side their own bread is buttered on. However, some Brazilian churches that have links with existing American denominations have encountered incomprehension. One pastor told me that the American co-pastor in his church (which was divided between a Brazilian and an American congregation) was horrified when he found out that 70% of the Brazilians were illegal. But this same Brazilian pastor concluded that the Berlin Wall, the old wall of shame, had fallen, but the new wall of shame was the one along the border with Mexico.

How all this functions at the individual level can be gauged from the account of one Pentecostal immigrant who told me that he was arrested once for a traffic violation and his undocumented condition was discovered. He was ordered to appear for a deportation hearing but never did so. He then commented very revealingly that all that had happened because he was "outside the will of God" at the time. At first, it might have appeared that he was making an ethical judgment on his condition of illegality as a reflection of being distant from the will of God, but in fact his meaning was quite different. What he was saying was that he was only caught by the authorities because he was outside the will of God; otherwise, he would never have been caught. It was the disgrace and tension of being caught that was the result of his distance from God; there was no negative ethical judgment at all on being undocumented or disobeying the American authorities.

The Future of Religion in the Diaspora

In conclusion, what can we say about the prospects for the evolution of religion in the Brazilian diaspora? In the first place, the future of religion in the diaspora will depend on the future of religion in Brazil. In the short term, the latter will continue to be characterized by the decline of Catholicism, but obviously that decline has limits. There is a solid nucleus that is not going to be eroded, and in any case the Catholic Church is slowly changing in order to meet the challenge of pluralism and prevent further erosion. Secondly, Pentecostalism and Protestant churches in general will continue to grow, but it should be noted that for every two people who leave Catholicism only one becomes Protestant. So the trend is not towards the constitution of a Protestant majority in Brazil, but rather towards a pluralist religious field consisting, perhaps, of a still sizeable Catholicism (even if retaining under 50% of nominal adherence), a large but very pulverized Protestant field, and finally a considerable sector of non-Christian religions and nonbelievers.

In the second place, the future of religion in the diaspora will depend on whether new immigration continues apace or whether it slows down and a stable community develops which over time will be dominated by the second generation. How will that second generation behave religiously? Will it follow the Latinos, amongst whom the second generation has a higher percentage of evangelicals than the generation that immigrates, and the third generation even more so? Or will they follow a trajectory of secularization? What will "second generation" mean in a globalized world with far easier opportunities for various forms of transnationalism and less pressure to assimilate on the classical model? And finally, how much will Brazilian diasporic religion influence the religious field of the host countries? In the case of the United States, will American Christianity be affected at all (at least locally in areas such as Massachusetts) by the presence of Brazilian Christians—both Protestant and Catholic—in its midst?

Notes

1. "Religious field" refers to the idea of a social space in which agents and institutions struggle for ascendancy. The data on the Brazilian religious field are drawn here from diverse sources. This chapter also draws upon my own fieldwork among Brazilian immigrants in the United States and other countries, mostly carrried out between 2002 and 2005.
2. Pentecostals are an enthusiastic form of Protestant Christianity, emphasizing the contemporary manifestations of gifts of the Holy Spirit such as speaking in tongues, divine healing, prophecy, and exorcism of evil spirits.
3. Spiritism, also known as Kardecism, was introduced from France in the mid-nineteenth century. Largely middle-class, it combines spirit-mediumship and reincarnationist beliefs with a particular understanding of the Christian gospels. Candomblé is an Afro-Brazilian religion, although by no means restricted now to people of African descent. Umbanda was developed in the early twentieth century as a self-consciously Brazilian integration of Afro-Brazilian, indigenous and Spiritist elements.
4. I use this term in quotation marks, as it is not consensual among scholars of Brazilian emigration. It is, nevertheless, a useful shorthand for referring to all Brazilians outside Brazil.
5. In fact, most Brazilian Protestants are evangelicals in the Anglophone sense, defining evangelicals as a sub-set of Protestants distinguished by (according to British historian David Bebbington's [1989] working definition popular among recent scholars) four emphases: conversionism (need for change of life), activism (evangelistic and missionary efforts), biblicism (a special importance to the Bible, though not necessarily the fundamentalist idea of "inerrancy") and crucicentrism (centrality of Christ's sacrifice on the cross).

6. For a broader discussion of language patterns between generations of Brazilian immigrants, see Chapter 13, "Two Languages at Play" by Kátia Mota.
7. This estimate is a composite of information obtained (and a critical evaluation of the plausibility of this information) from a variety of sources: a) interviews with Brazilians in the U.S., whether participants in the Protestant field or knowledgeable outside observers; b) lists of Brazilian churches (often with addresses, telephone numbers and websites) in the United States as a whole or in particular localities, or pertaining to particular denominations (e.g. www.metodistalivre.org.br, www.aibban.org, www.linhaberta.com, www.confradeb.com); c) advertisements in the Brazilian secular media in the United States; and d) news items in Brazilian evangelical publications.

References

Bebbington, David. 1989. *Evangelicalism in Modern Britain.* London: Unwin Hyman.

Levitt, Peggy. 2002a. "Redefining the Boundaries of Belonging: Thoughts on Transnational Religious and Political Life," paper presented at the Institute for the Advanced Study of Religion, Yale University.

———. 2002b. "Two Nations Under God? Latino Religious Life in the United States." In *Latinos: Remaking America,* pp. 150–164. Ed. Marcelo Suárez-Orozco and Mariela Páez. Berkeley: University of California Press.

Margolis, Maxine. 1994. *Little Brazil.* Princeton: Princeton University Press.

Martes, Ana Cristina Braga. 2000. *Brasileiros nos Estados Unidos.* São Paulo: Paz e Terra.

Part Three

A NEW GENERATION OF PEOPLE AND RESEARCH

11

Between "Cultural Excess" and Racial "Invisibility": Brazilians and the Commercialization of Culture in Newark

Ana Y. Ramos-Zayas

Adriana Pereira had arrived with her parents and sister from Belo Horizonte in the mid-1990s. In the hallways of East Side High School in the Ironbound neighborhood of Newark, New Jersey, Adriana and I had the first of many conversations. Adriana explained how "Brazilian culture" was very popular in the United States. She commented:

> "You have American people saying we're really hot. Not only really hot as in attractive, but more like that we're caring people. When you meet someone, we hug, we kiss. And that's really true. Because the American people, the Black people, they're really . . . I never saw an American going to their friends and hugging them, kissing them, you know. They don't do that like we do. And they see that as something that is Brazilian, Brazilian culture. I think they like that. They have an image of Brazil, and it's all the good things of Brazil. They don't see any of the poverty or crime, just the beach and Carnival, Rio!"

Adriana's comment was one of many instances in which the Brazilian residents of the Ironbound with whom I spoke deployed an image of "cultural excess," which I define as the representational and ideological strategies through which certain bodies are viewed as overflowed with meanings and never naturalized.[1] In the context of the Ironbound, a neighborhood considered Newark's "Little Portugal," cultural excess served to claim a space for Brazilians in the U.S. multicultural landscape. The Brazilians whom I interviewed understood that the image that whites and Blacks had of them was one of hyper-culture, of a Brazilian culture that was highly commodifiable and appeared more like postcards of landscapes than an expression of human reality. In the context of the Ironbound, strategies of marketing culture and re-signification were central to the transformation of landscapes and identities (see Lefebvre 1991).

In this chapter I examine how Brazilians in the Ironbound deployed cultural excess as a strategy to get *closer* to a locally constituted form of "Americanness," rather than to separate themselves from dominant views of what "being American" is. I suggest that the Ironbound, which until recently had been a stronghold of Portuguese migrants and Portuguese-Americans, served as an immediate model of how culture could be successfully commodified, even in a city otherwise considered "decrepit," "dangerous," and "ugly," like Newark. I argue that many Brazilians in the Ironbound have constructed Brazil in multicultural terms, as a "country of immigrants" and a "racial democracy," so that Brazilian multiculturalism was not incompatible with images of the United States as a multicultural society. Nevertheless, cultural excess also served as symbolic capital among a Brazilian population that considered the United States as a country in which full citizenship was only available to (racially unmarked) suburbanite whites and Newark Blacks, who constituted a political elite and force in the predominantly Black city.

Whereas the cultural-excess strategy may seem initially effective in constructing Brazilians as "racially invisible"—particularly in the contexts where Brazilians resurrected ideas of racial democracy, miscegenation, and an avoidance of a "Hispanic" identity—the strategy was limited by how other Latinos and Portuguese residents of the Ironbound racially and culturally marked Brazilians.[2] While the Portuguese viewed Brazilian cultural excess as evidence of primitivism (akin to how whites view Blacks, or colonial powers viewed their subjects), other migrants from Latin America and the Caribbean viewed Brazilians as "Hispanic." Puerto Ricans, in particular, did not see the Portuguese language as a barrier to *Latinidad*, given that many Puerto Ricans, being second- or third-generation U.S.-born themselves, don't speak Spanish and distinguished between Latino identity and language. Brazilians in Newark appeared to inhabit an imperfect space in which they constructed themselves as culturally excessive (rejecting an American blandness, but producing a non-threatening hyper-cultural self-image), while other local residents, particularly the Portuguese and other Latin American migrants, constructed "Brazilianness" in explicitly racial terms (Ramos-Zayas 2001).

In a letter she had written to a friend back in Belo Horizonte, Mariela Pereira described Newark in light of a trip she had made to Florida to visit an American boyfriend whom she had met on the Internet. Mariela wrote:

> "Newark is a very strange city. It's only fifteen minutes by train from Manhattan and yet it seems like another country. For one, EVERYBODY speaks Portuguese (from Brazil and from Portugal) and sometimes they don't understand each other . . . it's hilarious. I know people who have lived in Newark for over ten years and they don't speak English or have ever been to Manhattan. The houses are old and some of them are falling into pieces . . . I bet that Rocinha [a favela in Rio] has better places than those I've seen in Newark, and cheaper too. Other houses that are not as old were constructed by the first Portuguese that arrived here and have a style with tile of images of Catholic saints under the windows . . . Newark is dirty, old, and full of people from Governador Valadares and rude and ignorant Portuguese people, but at least they have pão de queijo in each corner."

Mariela explained that her friends back in Belo Horizonte assumed she lived in New York.

> "Nobody knows about New Jersey; they know about New York, the bigger city. Newark is more like a ghetto of mineiros. Do you think people in Brazil would understand if I tell them that I left Brazil to come to America to live in a place where everybody speaks Portuguese? No, of course not!"

The life experiences of Brazilians in Newark suggest that it is important to recognize that the class background of Brazilian migrants to the United States varies by region of settlement as well as by town of origin and legal status. As a Brazilian priest mentioned:

> "The wealthier, more professional Brazilians settle in Manhattan. The other ones, who are not as wealthy or who come with family, settle in Queens. Manhattan means that you have 'made it' here. Those who are really poor are the ones who come to New Jersey. In New York you find Brazilians from everywhere in Brazil, many are from the bigger cities, São Paulo, Rio. In Newark you find the poorest ones, mostly from Minas, who get here without any money and with children to support, or at least with some of their children along."

In these working-class families, economic need contributed to the centrality of paid employment in the daily lives of Brazilian (and other working-class Latino) youth, who oftentimes felt that their academic responsibilities in high school and their future higher-education aspirations were compromised, to various degrees, by the financial demands of their households, and that their interest in pursuing higher education was thwarted by the fact that they did not qualify for federal assistance because of their legal status (see also Sales and Loureiro's discussion of the "school versus work" dilemma, in this volume).

Cultural Excess: Avoiding "Americanness" and the Commercialization of Culture

Given the particularities of Brazilian migration to Newark, the cultural excess attributed to Brazilians was noteworthy because elected officers and the media in the city rarely viewed Brazilians as a group characterized by poverty, even when some Brazilian residents were in fact struggling to make ends meet. In an interview that appeared in *Brazilian Voice* (April 2002), Newark's mayor, Sharpe James, remarked:

> "The Brazilians are coming on quite strong in the United States –see how many are opening their own businesses? They possess so much energy, and they are so proud of their cultural heritage . . . I saw Brazilians parading down Ferry Street with their colorful costumes and folk dancing . . . I believe that what we should now do is extend that field of inclusion into the political arena with naturalization and electoral participation. . . . [The plans for development in the Ironbound neighborhood] will mean the general renaissance of the East Ward and the filling-in of urban space . . . Brazilians are known for playing soccer, so recreational spaces are quite important."

The areas that Brazilians inhabit were not considered stigmatized "inner-city" spaces, like the rest of Newark, but spaces "rich" in culture and commercial potential–spaces that deserve to have soccer fields and which are characterized by street parading in colorful costumes.

The real estate value of properties in the Ironbound did not depend on the desirability of the too small, too close-together houses, but on the area's commercial sector and cultural life, validated by the fact that more and more "real Americans" and the mainstream media emphasized the area's ethnic restaurants and culture as a marketing strategy. In fact, the cultural capital of foreign business was reasserted throughout the period of my fieldwork in the Ironbound. For instance, Vicente, a Galician resident of the Ironbound, showed me a letter he had sent to the editorial board of a local newspaper in which he expressed his sentiments regarding the recently opened chain stores in the area:

> "I love Ferry Street! I love, specially the way it used to be. ONLY foreign business!!! Lately I've seen American business taking over some spots on Ferry Street. Two big exemples: Dunkin' Donuts is at the building where a great Portuguese restaurant used to be . . . Castelo's Restaurant closed its doors for another American chain to take another 'slice' of Ferry from us. So here is my request to the [Ironbound community organization]: Get together with owners of business in Ferry St. to make this to be a new law in the city. DO NOT LET ANOTHER BUSINESS TAKE PLACE AT FERRY STREET IF THEY AREN'T A PORTUGUESE, BRAZILIAN, ITALIAN OR EVEN A HISPANIC PLACE. THE FEELING OF "NOT BEING IN AMERICA" MUST GO ON FOREVER!!!!!!!!!!!!!!!!!!!!!! [Caps in the original]"

A vehement opposition to the opening of more "American restaurants" was not only a legitimate concern over the destitution of small, family-owned businesses in the area, but also the fear that the Europeanized, working-class area will eventually turn into a "white trash" area or an "inner-city" neighborhood. The impossibility of commodifying an "American" identity, even despite its association with chain restaurants, was evident in the general proclamation that "even Hispanic" businesses should be favored over "American" ones. Somewhat ironically, the cultural strategy deployed by the Portuguese (and to a lesser extent, the other Europeans) in the Ironbound centered on catering (literally and figuratively) to the dominant U.S. society. There was a great emphasis on "showing Americans" and tending to Americans (showing them "our rich culture," as a Brazilian newspaper put it). While Americans are perceived as generally "cultureless," the Portuguese, Brazilians and other Latin American residents viewed each other as part of distinct, even monolithic, cultural groups, whose cultures could be marketed in various commercial forms. Yet whose culture was to be promoted was a point of contention, especially between Brazilians and Portuguese, currently the two groups that have most successfully opened ethnic restaurants and shops in the area.

In an effort to present a national Brazilian "culture" that was commodifiable and appealing not only to Ironbound residents, but more generally to dominant U.S. society, Brazilians drew from regional and racial group cultures in Brazil—from *comida mineira* to *Capoeira* to Carnival parties to beach wear—to offer a unified national culture devoid of regional or racial specificity. Similar strategies have been noted in studies of Brazilians in Massachusetts (Sales 1999) and California (Beserra 2003; Ribeiro 1997). This resonates, for instance, with Gustavo Lins Ribeiro's study of Brazilian transnational identities in San Francisco. As Ribeiro (1997) notes, these images of Brazilian culture are not only the stereotypes that dominant U.S. society has of Brazilians, but also the way Brazilians themselves construct their identities in a mainstream interethnic (and heavily racialized) system. The construction of a "comunidade brasileira de São Francisco," as imagined by its members, requires the production of spaces and strategic scenarios for the dissemination of images and the development of a "cultural intertextuality" that inserts Brazilians into a U.S.-based politics of difference. Many Brazilians in Newark favored a hegemonic Rio identity, not only because Rio offered a more popularly recognizable form of Brazilianness in the United States, but also because Rio (and São Paulo)—in contradistinction to other Latin American cities—were privileged for being urban and cosmopolitan, especially among Brazilian migrants from rural areas of Minas Gerais viewed as "backward" by many Brazilians, especially by Brazilian youth.

Every single comment I heard, from Portuguese and Brazilians alike regarding the differences and conflict between the two groups was ultimately a gendered comment. For instance, Cristina, an eighteen-year-old woman from Belo Horizonte who was very involved in a local evangelical church, described the image that the Portuguese had of Brazilians in Newark: "They think that we're all putas [sluts]. That we only want to steal their husbands. And they think this because they see a lot of Brazilian women working in bars and go-go places. But just because people work in those places doesn't mean that they are prostitutes. That's what they [the Portuguese] don't understand." Likewise, Fatima Sales, a mathematics teacher who had migrated from Portugal as an infant, commented on the heavily gendered components of conceptions of Portuguese "traditionalism" and Brazilian "modernity":

> "The guys you'll see them, they'll wear the shorts and they'll wear the flip-flops. They think it's cool to wear their flip-flops to school, I think it's a danger [AY: Why is it a danger?]. Well, what if they trip down the stairs or something falls on their feet? Then we have an accident . . . The girls, you know, wear very short, tight clothing, and the Portuguese in this community look at them and . . . The perspective the

> Portuguese have of the Brazilian is that they are very loose, they are very fast, simply because they look a certain way. That's not necessarily true, because I know a lot of Brazilian families and they are very strict with their children. But [the Portuguese] have that perception."

Even when questions about the relationship between Brazilians and Portuguese were not presented in terms of explicit questions about gender or sexuality, the responses were invariably suggestive of the ways in which "being Brazilian" and "being Portuguese" in Newark were always gendered and sexualized identities.

While cultural excess is a strategy partly facilitated by constructions of modernity and traditionalism in the Ironbound, these constructions unfolded amidst conflicts and contradictions, and were oftentimes challenged in all their problematic expressions. More than rejecting or conforming to a stereotyped image of Brazilians common in the United States, many Brazilians felt that what was at stake were claims over space, the deployment of urban identities, and constructions of difference and sameness. Not only were they a part of an image game that complied with popular reductionist visions of Brazilian culture, but also a similar tension developed between a strategic, market-mediated image of Brazilian culture and a belief that these images were in fact inherent, quasi-biological or ecologically-based traits. Sometimes the warm weather was to blame for Brazilian temperament or clothing style, for instance. Likewise, every single comment I heard, from Portuguese and Brazilians alike, regarding the differences and conflicts between the two groups was fundamentally a gendered comment.

This insistence on Brazilian cultural excess is not entirely new. Anthropologist Roberto Da Matta coined the term "a jeitinho brasileiro" (roughly translated as "a Brazilian way") to describe "a style, a way of being, a mode of existence that, despite being founded in universal qualities, is exclusively Brazilian" (in Tosta 2004, 580). Nevertheless, cultural excess involved the deployment or insistence on this "jeitinho" not as a way of being, but as a *strategic way of presenting oneself and performing one's identity* to meet specific, locally determined goals, including the cultural production of space and configurations of urban identities. Brazilian cultural excess was highly predicated on the actual or perceived exposure of young women's bodies in spaces indirectly marked as un-Brazilian, including Ferry Street, the main commercial thoroughfare of the Ironbound, as well as institutional sites like East Side High School, the only high school in the neighborhood. My research in Newark suggests the need to expand our understanding of cultural work (and how the cultural worker is produced and to what end) to include the everyday experiences of Brazilians who may or may not limit their displays of Brazilianness to organized folkloric celebrations such as parades and carnivals. More significantly, the highly gendered conception of Brazilian culture must also be considered in light of multiple configurations of localized conflicts over access and resources.

The perspectives of Brazilians—especially Brazilian women—as potentially problematic were accentuated not only in relation to their participation in the festivities (and daily life) of the presumably more honorable and unproblematic Portuguese residents, but also in light of an increasing perception of Brazilians as "illegal immigrants" in the increasingly nativist post-9/11 United States. In fact, illegality marked the boundaries of the otherwise positive view of foreignness and cultural commodification in the Ironbound. At the time of my ethnographic study, few people in the Ironbound, or in the state of New Jersey for that matter, seemed to associate "illegal" migration with the Portuguese, despite the increasing references to "illegal aliens" in everyday legal and community discourses in the past decade or so (De Genova and Ramos-Zayas 2003). The ways in which the stigma of "illegality" is imposed in rather arbitrary ways onto populations from different countries depending on the historical period is beyond the scope of this discussion (see De Genova 2002). What is relevant here is that while even after 9/11 illegality did not seem to shape the everyday life of the Portuguese (the largest undocumented group in New Jersey), Brazilians and other Latin American groups in Newark expressed great concern over deportation.

Racial Invisibility: Brazilian Youth, Latinidad, and a New *Mestiçagem* (?)

Brazilians were caught between a strategy of cultural excess in the commercialization of culture in the Ironbound logic (and in connection to the area's Portuguese residents), on the one hand, and a quest for racial invisibility when faced with the U.S. racializing discourse which rendered them as "closer to Hispanic," on the other. These two mutually constitutive positions—between cultural excess and racial invisibility—were more clearly articulated in the context of the local public high school. For Brazilian youth, cultural excess was a way of being part of a Brazilian Ironbound community, while the high school was a place for performing Americanness and racial invisibility to various degrees of success.

The quest towards racial invisibility or selective racial visibility involved a combination of discursive and ideological strategies, which included, first, drawing on Brazil's national myth of racial democracy, while blaming American Blacks for their explicit discourses on "race" and civil rights; secondly, focusing on the otherness of "Hispanics" by emphasizing Brazil's role as a global economy, in contradistinction to the "lesser" Caribbean islands or Latin American states from which other Newark migrants hailed; and, finally, cultivating ambiguous images of U.S.-born Latinos, particularly Puerto Ricans, as evidence of alternative forms of citizenship (Ramos-Zayas 2003, 2004). Brazilians in the Ironbound in turn claimed space by emphasizing their culture –or even cultural excess—vis-à-vis the less desirable lack of culture of white Americans, while deploying various degrees of racial invisibility when in contact with Black Americans and other Latinos, particularly Puerto Ricans. Brazilian modernity simultaneously praised Black bodies and insisted on Brazilian's racial invisibility in a context that values cultural excess (see Schein 1999). In the context of these racial performances, Puerto Ricans played an important role given their position as U.S. citizens, oftentimes English-dominant, and a numerical majority among Latinos in Newark. For Puerto Ricans, speaking Spanish, for instance, was not an exclusive requirement for Latinidad. Interestingly, the patterns that Santos Mota, in this volume, notices regarding the generational variations in how Brazilians in Framingham viewed (and deployed) code switching, bilingualism, and the pragmatic usage of Portuguese among youth resonate with the case of Brazilian youth in Newark, as well as with perspectives on language usage among Puerto Ricans (Urciuoli 1996; Zentella 1997).

Despite some spaces where a tenuous form of Latinidad developed, Brazilians tended to view themselves as different from those whom they considered "Hispanic." Nevertheless, Newark's Ironbound, with its insistence in the culturalization of commercial space, presented a more complicated case than studies of Brazilians in the Northeastern U.S. describe regarding Brazilians' positioning vis-à-vis a white-Black binary. On the one hand, Brazilians emphasized that they were not "Hispanic," a term in fact associated with racism and social stigma, and they only used Latino to suggest a common geographical area or foreign status (Beserra 2003; Margolis 1994; Marrow 2003; Meihy 2004). Nevertheless, many Brazilians also avoided being considered white in the context of the Ironbound, where cultural excess opened commercial and social opportunities and being "just white" was considered undesirable.

As Mario Petrino, an Italian-American school administrator at the local high school, commented: "The kids who are from South American countries don't see the Portuguese here as Americans . . . They might see some of the *Black* kids as American kids, in their places of work." The predominantly Portuguese population at East Side High School was still positioned somewhat outside a reified American mainstream. This demonstrated how "white" and "American" have become slippery categories in contexts where recent migrants and U.S.-born minorities coincide.

In addition to signaling Portuguese as different from white, many Brazilians rejected identification with Blackness, except in instances when Blackness was equated with urbanness, a desired attribute deployed in contradistinction to the rural "folksiness" of other Latin American immigrants. Hence, while whites and Blacks were considered more American than the Portuguese and Latin American populations, "just white" or "just Black" identities were generally not viewed as desirable even if they could perhaps have provided an alternative for Brazilians to avoid being racialized as "Hispanic." A main proposition here is that, while Brazilians appeared to position themselves as distinct from (and superior to) "Hispanics," they nevertheless developed an alternative identity through an U.S.-bred version of *mestiçagem.* While Brazilians did not see themselves as Black, white or "Hispanic," they did acknowledge that the "real" Americans would most likely consider them "Hispanic" or, depending on phenotype, Black, but not white. Sharing urban space and occupations with "Hispanics," many U.S.-born and migrant Brazilians in Newark explained how the stigma associated with this term was usually also applied to them. The "Hispanic" label in Newark was not only limited to Spanish-speaking immigrants. In fact, "Hispanic" was a term most frequently used to refer to Puerto Ricans, most of whom were English-speakers and U.S. citizens, rather than a term limited to other Latin American populations perceived to be more indigenous or from rural areas.

This distinction between different levels of "Hispanicness" became more evident in a conversation with Bruna, Alena, and Paula, three Brazilian students at the Ironbound High School. When I asked them whether Brazilians got along with those they considered "Hispanic," the following conversation ensued:

Bruna: The guys think we are hot. Because they are like always screaming things in the street . . . they are like that. [Things like] Bonita mamacita. You cannot imagine, they are like they never saw a woman before in their lives.

AY: What is their background? Do you distinguish between different nationalities?

Bruna: No, I don't, they look like the same, my boyfriend used to say that they have mala forma, como se fala? They are all of the same size,

the same style . . . It's like when there is a whole bunch of Chinese people you don't see like any difference . . .
Alena: But that's about the Mexicans. Not everybody is like that. None of my friends look like that. My Puerto Rican friends don't look like that.
Bruna: Some of them I look I can't say if they are Puerto Ricans or Ecuadorians, Uruguayos, Paraguayos, Bolivianos, they are all the same. The mira, mira . . . [Laughter] just the miras, miras,
Paula: Not everybody just the Mexicans: mira, mira, mami, mirale el culo.
AY: But there aren't that many Mexicans here at the school.
Alena: No, not in the school . . . But like you see it on Murray Street. Go there at six thirty, seven o'clock in the morning they are all going to construction.

A main tentative proposition here is that the new version of *mestiçagem* involved the racialization (and disavowal) of other Latino nationalities in very particular ways, so that some migrants are deemed superior to others. Moreover, Brazilians are engaging the Portuguese *as Portuguese* in their own process of producing a Brazilianness in the United States, rather than acknowledging only the racial groups most commonly representative of U.S. racial formation—that is, Blacks, whites, Asians, and "Hispanics."

Cosmopolitanism and *Mestiçagems* in the Formation of Brazilian Identities

Although many Brazilians in Newark rejected the "Hispanic" category, they also questioned the desirability of being positioned as either Black or white. Rather than subscribing to these racial categories, many Brazilians developed a discourse on race that relied on two somewhat complementary perspectives in a quest for racial invisibility. On the one hand, Brazilian discourse on race in Newark, perhaps predictably, insisted on the moral superiority of Brazil as a country, and Brazilians as a people, in the conception of a racially equitable society. Various versions of Brazil's "racial democracy" discourse were deployed in most of my conversations with Brazilian migrants and, to a lesser extent, U.S.-born Brazilians, in which ideas of *mestiçagem*, color blindness, and a racial triad were elaborated in contradistinction with the U.S. more racist system. On the other hand, however, most Brazilians in Newark challenged the very desirability of Americanization, as the route by which an immigrant has to shed a vaguely configured traditionalism and embrace U.S. modernity. Instead, many U.S.-born and migrant Brazilians in Newark insisted that their own cosmopolitanism and modernity, unlike that of migrants from other Latin American countries, was related to the role of Brazil in the global world system. Among many Brazilians in Newark, narratives abounded about how Brazil was, like the United States, a country of immigrants and how, unlike other parts of Latin America, it never had a colonial mentality or considered their Portuguese colonizers superior.

I asked Ursula and Renata, two Brazilian students who were members of ESHS volleyball team, whether they saw a difference between Blacks and whites in the United States. Ursula commented: "Oh yes. There's a lot of racism. I was talking about that with some friends. Because everything started in the 1600s. The slaves coming from Africa and all that. And after that you see that the Black people are the poor people. The really white people are very racist, because they don't want to be around Black people. They see that the Black people are troublemakers, rob them." Then Renata added: "But Black people are racist too. All they talk about is discrimination, racism, complaining and complaining all the time. This is very different about the U.S. . . . In Brazil we have all the colors. And the other countries around Brazil too. All the colors. So that was very different when I came here. Because we never see white people here. Sometimes we see a white person, and it's always Hispanish or from a Latin country, you know. So the only Americans we see here are Black." To Brazilians, Puerto Rican and Black discussions on "race" and "discrimination" were viewed as racializing and contradictory to an image of Brazilian culture as folkloric and commodifiable that appeared more acceptable in the United States. Brazilian culture only became symbolic capital by retaining an unthreatening, folkloric, commodifiable quality, and avoiding a more explicitly political stance regarding racial inequality, which the discourse around Latinos and civil rights has deployed. As Ribeiro notes, "Brazilians, as recent arrivals to the global migratory scene, must gain a greater understanding of what it means to be a minority in a socio-political and economic situation strongly marked by race and ethnicity. This is a process relatively difficult for people socialized on deeply-rooted racial ideologies that pretend to dilute difference, specially if one considers that these emigrants are generally white, middle-class Brazilians" (1997a, 19). At stake, thus, is the structural relation between the changing contours of Brazilian identity in Newark and the formation of an imagined community capable of providing a sense of citizenship in an interethnic context.[3]

Conclusion

In this chapter I have examined the boundaries of whiteness, of exclusion and inclusion into systems of power and privilege, as manifested in the everyday lives of Brazilians (and, to a lesser extent, other South American groups) residing in the Ironbound, an area considered the Portuguese neighborhood of Newark. Demographic changes—including the increasing influx of South American migrants, particularly from Brazil—have altered the multiple configurations of "becoming American," not only among the newcomers, but also among the old-time Portuguese and Spanish residents of the area. In their interaction with one another, Brazilians and Portuguese created a liminal state of "not quite whiteness" and reshaped this space in ways aimed at avoiding Blackness precisely by rejecting conventional notions of American whiteness. Brazilian newcomers positioned themselves in this space by alternatively deploying their cultural excess—as individuals and as a group globally considered (hyper-cultural, sexualized, etc)—in contradistinction to competing logics of racial invisibility or selective visibility. Instead of subscribing to the white-Black racial polarity which they associated with the United States, Brazilians developed ways to expand a system of whiteness that include configuring white identity in racialized, not naturalized terms, and developing alternative formulations of belonging, especially by the use of commercial culture and deployments of Europeanness to mark the social space of the Ironbound.

Cultural excess, critical in the production of a much-romanticized ethnic enclave, in fact served to cater to upper-class whites. (An example of this was when Governor Christine Whitman was photographed Christmas shopping in the Ironbound. The newspaper clipping was displayed at Riviera's Bakery, a popular culinary landmark on Ferry Street.) While the Portuguese in Newark attempted to maintain an Old World image to sustain the commercial viability and character of the Ironbound, the Brazilian newcomers also deployed a cultural excess that asserted their modernity and the global capital attributed to Brazilian culture. Brazilian cultural excess was strategically performed, partly to attain racial invisibility in a context in which the Portuguese were likely to racialize Brazilians as closer to Black or closer to "Hispanic."

Nevertheless, commercially viable images of culture and cultural excess were truncated by accusations of "illegality" that generally viewed Brazilians as "closer to Hispanic," even when the Portuguese also experience a high level of "illegality." As suggested by national newspaper and the mainstream media, Brazilians are central actors in the processes of "white flight" or even targets of U.S. nativist sentiments. Brazilians' insistence on performing their own cultural excess as a strategy to gain symbolic and material capital appeared curtailed by a racialization process that positioned Brazilians as closer to "Hispanics" rather than to other European-ancestry groups. The cultural excess Brazilians deployed was thus a less effective strategy toward cultural distinctiveness (vis-à-vis other Latin American migrants) when issues of "illegality," perceived to be a "Hispanic" trait, were raised. The strategy of cultural excess does not necessarily challenge the modernist claim that being "modern" is being "race-less"; moreover, there's also an investment in the Ironbound in not being modern, since modernity is associated with being Black. The uses of "culture" in the neoliberal state must be examined in all their various aspects.

Notes

1. This work is part of a book-length ethnographic project on how Brazilian and Puerto Rican youth in Newark, New Jersey, Belo Horizonte (Brazil), and Santurce (Puerto Rico) socially produce space, understand citizenship, and construct ideas of race. Methodologically, the project examines the lives of students, staff, parents, and community leaders affiliated with two high schools in Newark, one in the largely Brazilian area of the Ironbound, and the other one in North Broadway, a predominantly Puerto Rican area. For a discussion on the so-called 1.5 generation of Brazilian youth, especially in the context of U.S. public schools, refer to Sales and Loureiro in this volume.

2. It is important to explain that "Hispanic" and "Latino," terms often used to describe the U.S.-born populations of Latin American and "Hispanic" Caribbean descent, have distinctly different origins. The term "Hispanic" was coined by the U.S. Census Bureau in the 1970s to group the predominantly Puerto Rican and Chicano/Mexican American populations, and thus was a label imposed from above to racially mark a population characterized as "Spanish-dominant" and immigrant. Conversely, Latino was a term used by community leaders and activists to politically organize populations of Latin American and "Hispanic" Caribbean descent around a presumed common identity and cultural markers (specifically, a common Spanish language). Brazilians are not considered "Hispanic" by the U.S. Census, nor do they share the Spanish language with other Latin American groups. Nevertheless, because Latino also implies a common geographic region, including South America, Brazilians often describe themselves and are described by others as Latino. Moreover, contemporary studies have pointed to the inadequacy of using the Spanish language as a basis for assuming a Latino identity, given that many U.S.-born or U.S.-raised Latinos are English-dominant or English

monolinguals, and even those who do speak Spanish separate themselves from other groups by focusing on differences in accents, word usage, and colloquial speech (De Genova and Ramos-Zayas, 2003). Hence, the continuously expansive definition of who is Latino or "Hispanic" creates various opportunities for Brazilians to self-identify or be identified by these labels. As some authors have pointed out, both labels are inadequate to capture the diversity of experiences of the people they signify. For further discussion on these subjects, see Calderón 1992; De Genova and Ramos-Zayas, 2003; and Oboler 1995.

3. Howard Winant (1992) has also remarked that "U.S. multiculturalism makes it more similar to Brazil's perception of itself." Puerto Ricans are guides on how to achieve this, as Puerto Ricans could be considered the ultimate "multicultural (colonial) subjects." A question that begs attention in the context of Latinidad in Newark is: to what degree are Puerto Ricans an "epitome" of U.S. *mestizaje*? Puerto Ricans embody the whiteness of U.S. citizenship and English language skills and place of birth, in the case of second and third-generation. Puerto Ricans also embody the Blackness associated with being urban, getting along with Blacks, living in areas considered tough, and being racialized as similar to Blacks. Most Brazilians considered both Blacks and whites as American, while they considered Puerto Ricans as Americans in some ways but not in others. How is this an organic, localized *mestiçagem*? Does this suggest that Puerto Ricans' ideas of *mestizaje* and Brazilian idea of *mestiçagem* are different? Would someone like Peter Wade agree that all "types" of racial democracy ideologies are just not the same? Could there be conflicts among different racial democracy ideologies? These are some questions that will be addressed elsewhere (Ramos-Zayas, forthcoming).

References

Beserra, Bernadette. 2003. *Brazilian Immigrants in the United States: Cultural Imperialism and Social Class.* New York: LFB Scholarly Publishing.

Calderón, José. 1992. "'Hispanic' and 'Latino': The Viability of Categories for Panethnic Unity." *Latin American Perspectives* 75(fall), 19(4): 137–44.

De Genova, Nicholas. 2002. *Working the Boundaries: Race, Space and Illegality in Mexican Chicago.* Durham: Duke University Press.

De Genova, Nicholas, and Ana Y. Ramos-Zayas, 2003. *Latino Crossings: Mexicans, Puerto Ricans, and the Politics of Race and Citizenship*. New York: Routledge.

James, Sharpe. April 10, 2002. Interview that appeared in *Brazilian Voice*, under Voices that Must Be Heard, Edition 17, and was translated into English by Matthew Corey.

Lefebvre, Henri. 1991. *The Production of Space*. Oxford: Basil Blackwell.

Margolis, Maxine. 1994. *Little Brazil: An Ethnography of Brazilian Immigrants in New York City.* Princeton: Princeton University Press.

Marrow, Helen. 2003. "To Be or Not to Be (Hispanic or Latino): Brazilian Racial and Ethnic Identity in the United States." *Ethnicity* 3(4): 427–464.

Meihy, José Carlos Sebe Bom. 2004. *Brasil Fora de Si: Expêriencias de brasileiros em Nova York.* São Paulo: Parábola.

Oboler, Suzanne. 1995. *Ethnic Labels, Latino Lives: Identity and the Politics of (Re)Presentation in the United States.* Minneapolis: University of Minnesota Press.

Ramos-Zayas, Ana. 2001. "Racializing the 'Invisible' Race: Latino Constructions of 'White Culture' and Whiteness in Chicago." *Urban Anthropology* 30(4): 341–380.

———. 2003. *National Performances: The Politics of Class, Race, and Space in Puerto Rican Chicago.* Chicago: The University of Chicago Press.

———. 2004. "Delinquent Citizenship, National Performance: Racialization, Surveillance, and the Politics of 'Worthiness' in Puerto Rican Chicago." *Journal of Latino Studies* 2:26–44.

———. forthcoming. *Cartography of Racial Democracy and Urban Emotional Landscapes: Puerto Rican and Brazilian Youth under Neoliberalism.*

Ribeiro, Gustavo L. 1997a. "Street Samba: Carnaval and Transnational Identities in San Francisco." A paper presented at the BRASA IV Congress, Washington, D.C., November 12–15.

———. 1997b. "Vulnerabilidade e Ambiguidade. Cidadania na Situção de Emigrante em São Francisco, California." Unpublished paper written for the Institute for Global Studies in Culture, Power and History, Johns Hopkins University, Baltimore, Maryland.

Sales, Teresa. 1999. *Brasileiros longe de casa.* São Paulo: Cortez Editora.

Schein, Louisa. 1999. "Performing Modernity." *Cultural Anthropology* 14(3): 361–395.

Tosta, Antonio Luciano de Andrade. 2004. "Latino, eu? The Paradoxical Interplay of Identity in Brazuca Literature." *Hispania* 87(3): 576–585.

Urciuoli, Bonnie. 1996. *The Semiotics of Exclusion: Puerto Rican Experiences of Race, Class and Language in the U.S.* Boulder, CO: Westview.

Winant, Howard. 1992. "Rethinking Race in Brazil." *Journal of Latin American Studies* 24(1): 173–192.

Zentella, Ana Celia. 1997. *Growing Up Bilingual: Puerto Rican Children in New York.* Malden, MA: Blackwell.

12

Between Dream and Reality: Adolescent and Second-Generation Brazilian Immigrants in Massachusetts[1]

Teresa Sales and Márcia Loureiro

In the 1980s Brazilian society started experiencing the phenomenon, unknown until then, of the emigration of large numbers of its citizens to other countries, triggered off by the economic crisis the country was then going through. As is common knowledge, this phenomenon led to the establishment of numerous communities of Brazilian expatriates in various countries, especially the United States, and particularly the states of New York, Massachusetts, Florida, and Connecticut.

Twenty years after that migratory outflow began, it can be seen clearly that the move of Brazilians abroad, once begun, took on a momentum of its own. Researchers on migration issues (Margolis 1994; Sales 1999; Martes 1999; Assis 1999; Fusco 2001) indicate similarities between this phenomenon and that experienced by other national groups, whereby the social support networks that gradually form in both the countries of origin and the countries of destination operate as factors for support and attraction for subsequent migrant waves. Allied to this process, of course, are economic aspects (especially, better employment opportunities and much higher wages) as well as other factors that affect individuals′ or families' decisions to emigrate. Sales (1999) points out a further similarity between Brazilian expatriates and those from other immigrant communities: the gradual transition from a group that initially consisted largely of young men venturing alone to another country, to a community where the presence of families becomes more and more common as a result of family reunification. What follows are redefinitions of the temporal expectations of the migration in favor of staying for longer periods in the destination country.

As a consequence of this change in demographic profile, the Brazilian community in the United States today has a segment that deserves special attention since it shows specific characteristics and needs. The teenagers born in Brazil who emigrated as young children (as the result, it should be noted, of decisions they were not consulted on) were later educated in the United States, acquiring academic training and cultural identity very similar to those of immigrants from other countries and to those of young Americans. Portes (1996b) refers to them as "immigrant children," who are different from "children of immigrants," the latter being defined as children born in the United States to immigrant parents or born abroad but taken to the United States at a very early age. According to Portes, immigrant children constitute the second generation, or the "one-and-a-half" generation, as he prefers to call them.

In the 1990s further studies were made of the processes of adaptation of immigrants to American society, this time with special attention to young people and adolescents belonging to the "new" second generation. This group is considered new in the sense that it is part of the recent migration of Latinos and Asians that intensified in the United States as of the 1960s. These immigrants were also considered a new generation due to their ethnic/racial characteristics. Their visibility (for example, the presence of non-Anglo children in schools) distinguishes them both from natives and from the descendants of earlier migrants. As a major milestone in the return to such studies, several field research initiatives were conducted by a number of well-known researchers regarding international migrations in the United States. This work resulted in the publication of a special issue of *International Migration Review* (vol. 28, Winter 1994). Two years later these same articles were re-published in a book organized by Portes (1996a). Carola and Marcelo Suárez-Orozco (1995 and 2002) also made an important contribution to the study of this new second generation.

By way of an introduction it might be good to emphasize certain questions brought up in these and other similar and complementary works that would seem to be useful for studying the Brazilian case that we intend to treat in this chapter.

The importance of studying the second generation of immigrants is stressed by several different authors. According to Portes (1996c), the consequences of immigration in terms of assimilation fall on the shoulders of this second generation, which can either become integrated into the mainstream American middle class, as did their European predecessors, or else become part of a multi-ethnic underclass. This is one of the trends observed in the new second generation. It is this generation, and not the first, that determines whether or not the mother tongue will be retained, whether the population dependent on welfare will grow, whether it will undergo cultural transformations, and whether the level of inter-ethnic marriages will decline or increase, for example. There was a process of loss of ethnicity, language, and culture of origin in the migrations of Europeans to the United States, as well as ascension upward through the labor market, a process that was concluded with the third generation (Sowell 1981; Alba 1985). This is the process so often referred to in many works as the melting pot.

Regarding language, for example, the process of assimilation began with the first generation learning only enough English to survive. The second generation then spoke the language of origin at home, in community groups, and English at school and in public life in general. (Thus far, the Brazilian immigrants in the United States have done just this.) The third generation then permanently adopted English at home, at work, and everywhere else, leaving behind once and for all the original language of the earlier generations (Portes and Schauffler 1996). Because the second generation had closer contact with their ethnic group, and especially because of its bilingual upbringing, there was a fear on the part of American society in general, as well as the authorities, that English was being rejected in favor of other languages. But the study mentioned above showed that this fear was unfounded; the great majority of the children and teenagers in bilingual programs became fluent in English, and their knowledge of two languages became a cultural advantage.

Two topics often emerge regarding the second generation. On the one hand, there is the adaptation of its members to the receiving society, related to concerns as to the real perspectives for their being assimilated, and, on the other, correlated with first, their performance in school. The reality that leads to the return to these topics is the incontestable empirical fact that between 1980 and 1990 immigration was responsible for 39% of the total growth of the population of the United States (Rumbaut, 1994). Taking into consideration immigration itself and the high relative rates of fertility among immigrants, it is estimated that the total number of children born to Latin-American and Asian parents in 1990 was 16.4 million (Portes 1996c).

According to the analyses carried out by some authors, the perspective of assimilation of the so-called new second generation today is different from that of second generations in the past, in two different aspects. First, in that the descendants of the last great immigration began their life in the United States in low positions but rose and even surpassed the WASPs

(Lieberson 1980), partly because of their ethnic-racial status. Secondly, and this also explains the upward mobility of those first immigrants, the country was going through a different economic phase. According to Kelly and Schauffler (1996), positive results from assimilation can be seen in the first stages of United States capitalism, when the immigrants provided the labor force needed for an expanding economy. The internationalization of the economy, however, changed the context in which this type of assimilation in the Ford era took place, when workers saw their simple acceptance into the labor market as a first step toward success. Today, with widespread outsourcing, many obstacles have arisen on the road to socioeconomic insertion into a receiving society. Kelly and Schauffler question whether the more recent Asian and Latin-American immigrants will be able to repeat the success story of their predecessors.

In the same vein, the Suárez-Orozcos (2002) note that in earlier periods, wages for jobs in the industrial sector allowed workers, including immigrants, to enjoy a middle-class life style with little formal education. This perspective becomes less likely with each decade, and, in this regard, the statistics are clear. According to the United States Census Bureau, the average annual wage of male workers between the ages of 25 and 34 who had not finished high school in the year 2000 was approximately US $19,000, US $26,000 for those who had finished high school, and US $42,000 for those who had received four years or more of college education.

The interest behind the "open doors to migration" policy in developed countries (Portes 1996c) has always been to guarantee advantages and benefits to employers, who could then hire cheap and abundant labor without having to assume any responsibility for the workers or their families. That is, since the origin of the migration process, the division of labor had been that the employers hire the workers, the state takes care of the families, and the rest is left for the future. Thanks to an economy in expansion and a number of other associated factors, the migrants at the beginning of the twentieth century were successful, but such a prosperous future is doubtful for the new migrants, due to the restructuring of industries and to the continuing existence of racial prejudice today. In other words, the great majority of this poor non-Anglo second generation depends on resources from the families and communities they move into.

The perspectives indicated by Hirschman (1996) regarding the integration of the new second generation into the U.S. economy are even gloomier. Hirschman questions the classical hypothesis of "adaptation = Americanization," according to which the longer an immigrant stays in the United States the farther he or she will progress socioeconomically and the less he or she will resemble the ethnic group of origin. This position is based on analyses of the performance of the new second generation of post-1965 immigrants who arrived from Asia and Latin America. During the 1980s and 1990s, migrants came face to face with an economic situation where most job opportunities were in the service sector, involving low-paid jobs and limited opportunities for moving up the social ladder.

These pessimistic perspectives about the possibilities of upward mobility for this new second generation become more explicit through the concept of segmented assimilation developed by Gans (1992) and by Portes and Zhou (1993). The new second generation, according to these authors, experiences downward mobility according to the extent to which they are absorbed into the African American or Latino populations living in neighborhoods of concentrated poverty. Such segmented assimilation, in turn, leads to limited opportunities in the job market (implicated in the transformations of the U.S. economy as well) and below-average performance in school.

Some more recent research has tried to counter this interpretation of the second generation, such as the work of Perlmann and Waldinger (1997), Farley and Alba (2002), and Kasinitz, Mollenkopf and Waters (2002). Evoking comparisons to the parameters of assimilation of the second generation of European migrants at the start of the 20th century, Perlmann and Waldinger show how even the "best-prepared" immigrants from that previous migration—such as Jewish newcomers—had some difficulty in acculturating rapidly; they conclude that the new post-1965 second generation immigrants do not encounter greater hardship than their predecessors. Research by Farley and Alba demonstrates how, within the various second-generation immigrant groups of today, many surpass the first generation of their parents in terms of educational and occupational outcomes as well as economic status. Based on field research in New York, Kasinitz, Mollenkopf and Waters are more emphatic in countering the perspective of segmented assimilation as a model of downward mobility. To them, the so-called native minorities can offer access to institutional supports that are able to promote successful experiences for the new second generation. Contrary to the perspective of segmented assimilation, intergroup contact provides a positive dimension that creates a new kind of multiculturalism and social inclusion.

In a study on Vietnamese immigrants, Zhou and Bankston III (1996) discuss the adaptation of the new second generation from the point of view of social capital, and are also more optimistic as to this adaptation. Their opinion is that the social capital in the family and the community enabled the second generation to be successful in school and in their professional lives. The thesis they present is that the second-generation Vietnamese immigrants in the New Orleans region, through constant involvement of all the families, develop a strong ethnic identity, behavior patterns and expectations determined by the community. For these authors, social capital is more important than human capital, and the individual characteristics of the parents are an important factor in the adaptation and integration of the young immigrants.

An additional issue with regard to the second generation is their school performance, which has been the focus of a number of studies. Perlmann and Waldinger (1997) hold that research on immigration is slowly changing from focusing on recent arrivals to studying immigrant children. This change in focus is apparently the result of the visible presence of immigrant children in schools and also, for many of them, their participation in the labor market, as we shall see farther below in regard to teenage Brazilian immigrants.

One research project on immigrant students was held in two regions with considerable migratory presence, namely, San Diego, California, and Miami Dade and Broward (Fort Lauderdale) counties, in Florida. This research was based on a broad sample of 5,127 respondents from Asia, Latin America and the Caribbean. To be included in the sample a student had to be foreign or, if born in the United States, to have at least one parent of foreign nationality. One important study resulting from this research was done by Rumbaut (1996), who analyzed the subjects′ ethnic identity, self-esteem and segmented assimilation. Another significant study, by Kelly and Schauffler (1996), dealt with the assimilation of these immigrants. The latter study correlates school performance with the different ethnic groups.

Another important study was conducted by Carola and Marcelo Suárez-Orozco (1995) on students in an area of origin (Guanajuato, Mexico) and in the United States. This study included recent migrants from Mexico, Mexican Americans, refugees from Central America, Cuban Americans and Puerto Ricans, and compares these ethnic groups with respect to the following items: unemployment rate, rate of births out of wedlock, and proportion of poor families. With this research the authors attempted to show how the theories of assimilation and acculturation of immigrants are insufficient due to their "closed" propositions concerning a phenomenon they consider open and dynamic, in that it flows from one generation to the next and affects the experiences of the first and the second generations in different ways. Another conclusion of the study comes very close to what has been seen in the case of the Brazilians: that the children of the first-generation immigrants absorb the anxieties, ambitions, dreams and conflicts of their parents. Since the parents do not have a mastery of English, they feel unable to help their children in activities such as school assignments, and this becomes a reason for great anxiety and a feeling of incapacity and shame. For this same reason, the parents often restrict their children's activities and seek to minimize the influence the receiving society has on them.

None of the studies that are briefly described here took the second generation of Brazilian immigrants into consideration, since this migration is quite recent and because Brazilian teenagers are a very small minority, virtually invisible in American society. Little by little, however, their presence has become more clearly demarcated, largely because of communities formed through ethnic companies in the cities where the immigrants have tended to concentrate, such as Framingham and Somerville in the Greater Boston Area, and the Allston neighborhood in Boston itself. In addition, some of the bibliography on the topic has become available in English (Margolis 1994; Goza 1994; Sales 2003; Beserra 2003).

This chapter is intended to fill this gap based on the limited data available at present. In the next section we quantitatively present certain characteristics of the new second generation of Brazilian immigrants. In the third section, based on field research on adolescents, especially in schools, we analyze their insertion into American society through school and work, a topic that is further examined in the fourth section of the article. Finally, in the conclusion, we reconsider some of the assumptions explored in the introduction to observe the case of Brazilian immigrant adolescents in Massachusetts.

Massachusetts-born Brazilians

The second generation we refer to consists specifically of children born to Brazilian immigrants in the United States. But since this immigration flow is recent, having occurred over the last 20 years (considering that it began in the mid-1980s), it is not yet possible to obtain a significant sample of this second generation that could be interviewed in the field.

But there is great interest in this group, since it consists of the people who will give contours to one of the most recent migratory processes in the United States. We therefore went in search of data from vital statistics in the United States and from the Brazilian Consulate General in Boston in order to show, at least quantitatively, how the second generation of Brazilian immigrants in Massachusetts has been constituted.

In Table 1 we present the number of children registered at the Brazilian Consulate in Boston and the number of children of Brazilian mothers, according to data from the Massachusetts Department of Public Health (DPH). As one can see, there are fewer children registered at the Consulate than those who have Primary Care Perinatal Data Forms on file at the DPH (Bureau of Family and Community Health, Office of Statistics and Evaluation), an institution that kindly provided crossed data for this research.

Table 1. Children Registered at the Consulate General of Brazil in Boston (1998–2002) and Children of Brazilian Mothers Counted by the Massachusetts Department of Public Health (1998–2001)

Year	Numbers from the consulate	Numbers from the DPH	Growth rate DPH
1998	463	683	
1999	644	799	17%
2000	708	1,033	29%
2001	697	1,282	24%
2002	696	–	
Total	3,208	3,797	

Sources: Massachusetts Department of Public Health and Consulate General of Brazil in Boston

Considering that the jurisdiction of the consulate includes not only the state of Massachusetts but also the states of Maine, New Hampshire, Rhode Island, and Vermont, the difference in data might be even greater because the statistics from the DPH refer only to Massachusetts. And a number of other factors might cause the data obtained from the consulate to be less complete than those provided by the DPH.

First, children of Brazilians may be registered at consulates in other cities, even if they were born in the area under the jurisdiction of the consulate in Boston. (The opposite can also occur, that is, children born outside the jurisdiction of the consulate in Boston can be registered there. According to the regulations, all Brazilian consulates in the United States are authorized to register the births of Brazilian children born in any state in the United States.) In addition, there may be Brazilian parents who prefer not to register their children at the Brazilian Consulate, and there is no way to measure this eventuality. According to first-hand accounts by personnel at the consulate, many parents put off registering their children until it is absolutely necessary, such as when the need for a passport arises.

The numbers registered on the Primary Care Perinatal Data Forms also fail to reflect all the Brazilian children born in Massachusetts, only those whose mothers are Brazilians. Children whose fathers are Brazilian or of Brazilian descent, but whose mothers are of other nationalities, are not registered as Brazilians. As posited by Rumbaut (2004), there can be significant differences in cohort size depending on whether this mother-centric or a father-centric rule is used to identify second-generation youth.

Even with all these drawbacks, these are the data we have, and they can at least give an idea of the growth of the second generation of Brazilians in Massachusetts. Considering that the data from the consulate would seem to be incomplete, we have used statistics from the DPH to calculate the annual growth rate of this second generation.[2] As can be seen in Table 1, this rate was 17% between 1998 and 1999, 29% between 1999 and 2000, and 24% between 2000 and 2001. We would need a longer temporal sequence to verify whether this fall in the growth rate from 2000 to 2001 was a merely occasional factor during these two years or if the trend will continue in the future, meaning a reduction in the growth of the second generation as compared with the two preceding annual periods. Based on the field observation of the authors of this present article, all indications are that this growth has continued in more recent annual periods.

The most interesting data is provided by the Primary Care Perinatal Data Forms, and is specifically related to our interest regarding the second generation of Brazilian immigrants in Massachusetts. These data can be seen in Table 2 and will now be analyzed.

The first aspect to be underscored in the data on this table is the extreme dispersion of the births of Brazilians throughout the state. This geographical diversity is even more visible in the original table provided by the DPH, which served as the basis for the construction of the more concise Table 2. This table shows that, although sometimes few in number, children born to Brazilian mothers in Massachusetts were registered in almost all the cities and towns in the state.

However, there is a higher concentration in some regions than in others, especially in the Greater Boston Area, where a little over one third of the children born during this period were registered. Framingham stands out among these towns and cities in the metropolitan area, with 13.78% of the children, followed by Boston and Somerville, each with a little over 8%.

The table of Brazilian towns and cities provided by the DPH demanded detailed work of comparison with the data from the Brazilian Demographic Census of 2000 in order to correctly identify the Brazilian municipality of origin of each mother, also taking into account many errors in the DPH records. The Brazilian municipality of Governador Valadares, for example, is spelled 12 different ways, probably depending on the parents

Table 2. Children of Brazilian Mothers by Town or City of Birth in Massachusetts between 1999 and 2001

Town/City	Number	%
Framingham	429	13.78
Boston	267	8.57
Somerville	260	8.34
Everett	185	5.94
Lowell	165	5.29
Worcester	154	4.94
Marlborough	149	4.78
Malden	95	3.05
Revere	85	2.72
Barnstable	64	2.05
Milford	58	1.86
Lynn	55	1.77
Brockton	53	1.70
Fall River	51	1.63
Chelsea	50	1.60
Medford	48	1.54
Peabody	45	1.44
Hudson	44	1.41
Cambridge	43	1.38
Ashland	43	1.38
Yarmouth	38	1.22
Weymouth	37	1.19
New Bedford	32	1.02
Cities with from 10 to 30	349	11.20
Cities with fewer than ten births	315	10.11
Total	**3,114**	**100.00**

Sources: Massachusetts Department of Public Health and General Consulate of Brazil in Boston

who registered the children and the American functionaries who made the registrations. For the purposes of this study, we listed only those Brazilian municipalities where more than 30 children were born in Massachusetts of Brazilian mothers. They are Governador Valadares (state of MG), 183; São Paulo (SP), 162; Rio de Janeiro (RJ), 137; Belo Horizonte (MG), 117; Curitiba (PR), 64; Criciúma (SC), 51; Conselheiro Pena (MG), 49; Goiânia (GO), 44; Vitória (ES), 44; Ipatinga (MG), 37; and Anápolis (GO), 36. Six of these 11 municipalities are capitals of important states in Brazil and four are cities in the State of Minas Gerais, led, as might by expected, by Governador Valadares.

The information regarding the Brazilian municipalities of origin of the mothers allows us, of course, to determine both their states and regions of

Table 3. State of Origin of Brazilian Mothers Who Gave Birth to Children in Massachusetts between 1999 and 2001

Town/City	Number	%
Minas Gerais	7299	39.988
São Paulo	2277	12.455
Paraná	1699	9.277
Rio de Janeiro	1644	8.999
Santa Catarina	1277	6.966
Espírito Santo	1088	5.922
Goiás	1077	5.877
Bahia	500	2.744
Federal District	244	1.322
Rio Grande do Sul	233	1.266
Pernambuco	222	1.211
Pará	155	0.822
Mato Grosso do Sul	122	0.666
Mato Grosso	77	0.388
Ceará	77	0.388
Paraíba	55	0.277
Maranhão	55	0.277
Piauí	44	0.222
Rio Grande do Norte	44	0.222
Rondônia	44	0.222
Tocantins	44	0.222
Sergipe	33	0.166
Alagoas	33	0.166
Amazonas	11	0.055
TOTAL	**18,244**	**100.00**

Sources: Massachusetts Department of Public Health and General Consulate of Brazil in Boston.

origin. Let us first look at the states of origin of the Brazilian mothers (Table 3).

Most Brazilian mothers in Massachusetts come from the state of Minas Gerais, with 40% of the cases. Far behind, with only 12% of the cases, is the state of São Paulo and, close behind, Paraná and Rio de Janeiro (9% each). The states of Santa Catarina (7%), Espírito Santo (6%) and Goiás (6%) also proved important. Although there is a high concentration of mothers from Minas Gerais, explained by the weight of this state as the region of origin at the beginning of the migratory flow from Brazil to the United States, 24 of the 27 states in Brazil are represented. This data backs up the qualitative observations made during the fieldwork that showed an increase in the number of areas of origin in Brazil.

Table 4. Regions of Origin of Brazilian Mothers Who Had Children in Massachusetts between 1999 and 2001

Region	Number	%
Southeast	1,228	67.4
South	319	17.5
Central-West	150	8.2
Northeast	103	5.6
North	24	1.3
Total	1,824	100.0

Sources: Massachusetts Department of Public Health and General Consulate of Brazil in Boston

Table 4 summarizes the data in Table 3 by region of origin of the Brazilian mothers. The great concentration of the Southeastern Region of Brazil should be noted, as over three-fourths of the Brazilian mothers in Massachusetts come from this section of the country. Jointly with the Southern Region, which responds for 17.5%, the two represent 85% of the Brazilian women who gave birth in Massachusetts. This showing is possibly very close to what was seen in the fieldwork observations regarding the migratory flow from the areas of origin in Brazil to the United States. Behind the Southern Region comes the Central-West, with less than half the number shown by the South, followed by the Northeast and, finally, by the North. It is interesting to note that in a partial sample of the Brazilian migratory flow, all the regions in Brazil were represented as places of origin of mothers who had children in Massachusetts during the period covered by Tables 3 and 4, namely, from 1999 to 2001.

Teenage Immigrants

Strictly speaking, the adolescent population discussed here is comprised of persons who migrated with their parents to the United States when they were children or teenagers; as mentioned in the Introduction of this volume, they would more accurately be characterized as members of the "1.5" generation. Most of them therefore had their first socialization while still in Brazil. The data for this analysis were obtained from two sources: 1) a study we conducted between September and December 2000 through qualitative interviews with young people at schools, churches and associations; and 2) a quantitative survey conducted in 2002, based on a questionnaire sent to public schools in Massachusetts conducting bilingual English-Portuguese programs. The phase of the qualitative interviews, which were held with teenage Brazilian immigrants themselves and with persons responsible for educational programs, was carried out by Teresa Sales while associated with the David Rockefeller Center for Latin-American Studies, at Harvard University. The second stage, the application of the questionnaires, was conducted with the collaboration of Márcia Loureiro, who sent and received the questionnaires.

A sample of 45 respondents participated in the stage of the qualitative interviews. In 2002, 73 questionnaires were answered. All interviewees were high-school students in towns and cities of the Greater Boston Area. In 2000, the students were from high schools in Somerville, Medford, Cambridge, Watertown, Framingham and Everett; in 2002, from high schools in Framingham and Marlborough.

As can be seen in Table 5, which covers all the data discussed above, the proportions of male and female students in our sample were almost identical. Their ages vary from 13 to 20, with the greatest number being between 15 and 16 years old (44%).

Table 5. Gender and Age of Adolescent Respondents in Greater Boston, 2000 and 2002

Age	Male	Female	Total	%
13 and 14	10	14	24	20.3
15 and 16	29	23	52	44.1
17 and 18	19	18	37	31.4
19 and 20	2	3	5	4.2
Total	60 (50.8%)	58 (49.2%)	118	100.0

Sources: Interviews in 2000 and Questionnaires in 2002

The fact that the questionnaires were filled out by and the majority of the interviews were held with students in bilingual programs at high schools caused a certain bias in the data, since the sample consisted only of teenagers who had been living in the United States for a relatively short time. This is because it is usually the more recent arrivals who are registered in the bilingual programs. Obviously, the longer a student has been at a school in the United States, the more likely he or she is to leave the bilingual program and move into the school's mainstream program. This is undoubtedly why our sample has such a high proportion of adolescents who had been in Massachusetts for one year or less (41%) or two years or less (70%), as can be seen in the accrued attendance in Table 6.

As can be seen in Table 7, these adolescents, like the Brazilian mothers of children born in Massachusetts (Table 4), came from all regions in Brazil, with the highest proportion being from the State of Minas Gerais

Table 6. Period of Arrival of the Adolescents in the Greater Boston Area, 2000 and 2002

Time since arrival	Number	%	Accrued %
Less than 1 year	26	22.0	22.0
1 year	23	19.5	41.5
2 years	34	28.8	70.3
3 to 4 years	16	13.6	83.9
5 to 6 years	10	8.5	92.4
Over 7 years	8	6.8	99.2
Born in the U.S.A.	1	0.8	100.0
Total	118	100.0	

Sources: Interviews in 2000 and Questionnaires in 2002

Table 7. Region of Origin of Adolescents in the Greater Boston Area, 2000 and 2002

Region of origin	Number	%
South	12	10.2
Southeast (except Minas Gerais)	21	17.8
Minas Gerais	47	39.8
Central-West	23	19.5
North and Northeast	14	11.9
United States	1	0.8
Total	118	100.0

Sources: Interviews in 2000 and Questionnaires in 2002

(40%), which is in the Southeastern Region of Brazil. Different from Brazilian mothers of children born in Massachusetts, however, the second most common region of origin of these adolescents, comprising 20% of the sample, is not the South but the Central-West. Here too the highest concentration is from the State of Minas Gerais, which was classified separately to give visibility to its importance as a region of origin of the teenagers in these studies.

In answer to the question about where they would rather live, the majority (52%) of the 72 students who filled out the questionnaires said they prefer the United States, whereas 39% said they would rather live in Brazil. Nine percent stated they would like to live in both countries. It is interesting to juxtapose these answers with those given to another question on the questionnaire, of an even more subjective nature, formulated as: "When you think about Brazil, what comes to mind?" The 71 responses were classified as follows: family (38%), being homesick [*saudades*] (31%), a number of aspects that we classified jointly as positive factors (27%), and a number of factors we classified as negative (4%). But in relation to the United States, the answers were quite different: better future (33%), a place to work (29%), positive factors (22%), and negative factors (16%).

There is an apparent contradiction between the preference for living in the United States and the image of the United States for the Brazilian teenagers who answered the questionnaire. Whereas the image of Brazil puts the family in first place, followed by being homesick, and 27% of positive factors, with only 4% of negative factors, the image of the United States is more related to the future and to a job, but shows a higher rate of negative factors than Brazil (16%) and a lower rate of positive factors (22%). When confronting these two questions, this second generation is similar to the first generation of their parents, most of whom have a more positive image of Brazil but are more inclined to stay in the United States due to objective factors that relate their professional life to its U.S. context.

Finally, two facts stood out in the interviews with the adolescents in 2000: the importance of work in their everyday lives, and their aspiration to go on to college after finishing high school. In view of the dilemma of returning to Brazil or staying in the United States, which is the same problem their parents have, these young people must also face the problem of work versus study. The questionnaire applied at the schools in 2002 took into account the analyses of the data provided by the interviews held in 2000 (Sales 2001), which indicated these facts and dilemmas.

In the next section of the article we will approach the first of these aspects in the lives of the immigrant Brazilian teenagers living in the United States, namely, study versus work.

Study and Work

Daniela is 16 years old and studies at Somerville High School. Every day she gets out of school at 2:30 P.M. and then takes three buses to get to work at the Student Center at MIT by 4:00. There she is a cashier at a small grocery store frequented primarily by local students. The store has two other employees, who are also Brazilian immigrants in her age bracket and who also work as cashiers. Both she and her colleagues are occasionally asked to do other tasks, such as prepare sandwiches, salads and sauces that are very popular among the hurried students who are their customers. Daniela works from 4:30 to 9:30 or 10:00 at night, and has no fixed time for leaving. She gets home at 10 or 11 P.M., in time for dinner, after everyone else in the house has eaten, then puts her school materials in order for the next day and, if she has some absolutely urgent assignment, spends some extra time studying. The next day she may doze off a few times during the less interesting classes, waiting for Saturday to come around, the only day she has the morning and part of the afternoon free. On Saturdays she can have lunch with her family at home and even go to some typically animated Brazilian get-together after work. She is also on the job all day Sunday (her day off is on Thursdays) and at night she tries to keep her homework assignments up to date, which is almost always impossible.

Daniela's routine is quite common among the 45 young people interviewed in 2000. A little over half (55.6%) of them work regularly and 22% have jobs on weekends or have worked and are now looking for a new job. Therefore, almost 80% have working experience, in other words, they have had a job as a component of their everyday life. Only ten respondents, or 22%, have had no experience at all in a job, and all of these ten were in the youngest age bracket, between the ages of 13 and 14 (Sales 2001, 363).

Among the 73 students at Framingham and Marlborough High Schools who answered the questionnaire in 2002, 40 (54%) were working, 31 (43%) were not, and 2 (3%) did not answer. This shows a smaller proportion of workers as compared with the 45 respondents to the questionnaire of 2000, which asked a slightly different question "Do you now work or have you ever had a job?" Since the questionnaire was less precise than the interview, where the interviewer could check answers and spend more time with the respondents, those who answered the questionnaire may not have paid full attention to the second part of the question, about whether they had ever worked. Even so, over half answered the question affirmatively.

We are thus dealing with a sample of student-workers. Although American high-school students commonly have jobs, they usually work only on the weekends and during vacation times, within the labor laws for minors. Youngsters between 14 and 16 are only allowed to work on Saturdays and Sundays, whereas those between 16 and 18 may also work during the week, but only until 10 P.M. However, the laws are not always complied with in the case of undocumented immigrant workers. Many of these minors, even those under age 16, work long hours after school, between six and eight hours daily, a situation that obviously limits their progress in school. Many teachers and advisers mentioned the constant problem of Brazilian students who sleep during classes.

The work of these teenagers is mainly in the services sector (especially at luncheonettes and restaurants) and in commerce (especially at supermarkets). Of those who were working in 2002, 74% were in the services sector and 26% in commerce. The questionnaire applied in 2002 also contained three questions about the work of the immigrant Brazilian adolescents. The first was: "How much did you earn last week?" Of those who answered this question (only 31), 58% said they earn up to 150 dollars, 19% stated they earn between 150 and 200 dollars, and 23% said over 200 dollars. The second question was: "Who did you get your current or last job from?" Of the 34 students who responded, the majority (41%) said they found their job on their own. In sequence, friends (22%) and mothers (12%) were the most common sources. Other family members—fathers, siblings, uncles/aunts and cousins—are mentioned infrequently. The third question was: "What proportion of your salary goes to your family?" Of the 38 who answered, 42% said nothing went to the family. Eighteen percent said they hand over one-fourth of their earnings to the family, 24% give half, 13% hand over their entire salary, and 3% said they don't always contribute. This question was included only on the questionnaire, and was not part of the script for the interviews, held two years earlier. In the interviews, however, it was possible to go deeper into the meaning of work in the lives of these adolescents.

For them, work is, above all else, an absolute divide between life in Brazil and life in the United States; this difference can be attributed to both issues of cultural context and of age at migration (Rumbaut 2004). Of the 45 respondents in 2000, only three (7%) had had working experience in Brazil before emigrating. The proportion of those who answered the questionnaire in 2002 was higher. Thirteen respondents (18%) of the 73 answered in the affirmative.

For these teenagers, Brazil is the world of the extended family consisting of grandparents, uncles, aunts and cousins who stayed behind, the world where they were children, where they only played or only studied without having to work, and life was guaranteed by the adults. As one of the respondents stated, "There we had fun." In the United States they belong to the adult world through their labor.

But work in the United States also means a doorway to the world of consumption, which had never been so available before. Many of the respondents made it clear that they did not work out of necessity but to have a little extra cash and for the possibility of buying their things without having to ask their parents for money.

The meaning of work for these adolescents varied between those who stressed the importance of "having their own money for consumption" (approximately half the sample) and another half who also see work as a way to help support their families.

Fabiano, age 17, studies at Somerville High School and supports himself designing T-shirts. He got his present job through his aunt, who was the friend of a department head. Fabiano came to the United States two years ago and has had his present job for a year. He says he works because he has to pay the rent for the house where he lives with his mother, who has been in the States for only two months. He likes his job because he feels he is learning a profession, and wound up his interview by saying, very seriously: "I work to be able to support myself."

The main references in the life of these teenagers are the Brazilian community and their families, where this work schedule affects their entire life, including weekends. For the Brazilian immigrants, including the teenage workers, days off are usually during the week and hardly ever on weekends. Only going to church competes with working on the weekends.

Bruno, age 14, studies at the Middle School in Watertown and works in a supermarket. He carries boxes, cleans the store and sometimes works as cashier when things are especially busy. He works from 6 P.M. to 9 P.M. and on the weekends his schedule depends on arrangements with the boss, who is an immigrant of Hispanic origin who lives in his building and knows his family very well. Bruno stays at school from the time classes let out until 2:30 in the afternoon, when it is time to go to work, but the extra hours spent at school are not very profitable in terms of study. He plays sports, especially soccer, and is on the school soccer team.

Both in the case of Daniela and, especially, of Bruno, it is clear that the work the immigrant teenagers do is very flexible. With the exception of school hours, all the rest of their time is organized by the employer, not only in terms of tasks, but also in determining the times they can leave. Daniela is a cashier, but she also makes sandwiches and salads. By definition, Bruno is "a jack of all trades." He was hired to do the heavier work of cleaning and carrying boxes, but sometimes he is called on to take care of the check-out stand. In addition, on the weekend his time depends on arrangements with his boss. Many of the respondents referred explicitly to this type of schedule where there is no set time to leave.

Juliana, age 17, studies at Somerville High School and works every day at a dentist's office, where she is the secretary. She works from 3:30 till 8:30 or 9:00 P.M., depending on how busy the office is. If things are extra-busy, she may have to stay until 9:30 or 10:00, until the office is closed and she has sterilized everything. "And can you handle all your homework?" "No, not all of it. I do part of it, the part for the strictest teachers, those who get after us more."

This double responsibility of work and school is related to the objectives and values these young people have. Influenced by the immigrant environment they live in, their objective in school has a very practical meaning for them: they especially intend to *learn English* and, as soon as possible, *earn money* by getting a good job. The perspective of earning money is fascinating for most of them, a completely new side of life in comparison with their life in Brazil.

Work is a central aspect in the life of these immigrant adolescents. Most of those who are not working yet are only 13 and 14 years of age, and their perspective is that, sooner or later, they also will be involved in the labor market, even while they are still in school. Work is also the main link of their insertion into both the Brazilian immigrant community and the family.

In this world permeated by the common denominator of labor, many parents have neither the time nor the interest to follow up on the school life of their children, and this aspect is directly related to the same factor that leads the younger generation to work after school. This is the world of work, the world of earning money and consuming, and it is the mainspring of the everyday life of these immigrants. School, in the context of this world of work, is only the place where their children will be better equipped for a life of labor—especially, it is where they will learn English. Sandra, age 18, a student at Somerville High School and a cashier at McDonald's, serves as an example of this climate in immigrant families:

> "I don't know if I should stop studying after I finish high school or if I should try to get into college. Because at home there's a lot of pressure for me to work. I've always wanted to study, but there's always somebody trying to get me to leave school. This is what makes me so undecided."

This view of school as a place where children can learn English and thus be better equipped for an immediate life of work also permeates the choice by parents in terms of the type of school their children attend (public schools in all cases). And, among the public schools, they prefer those that *do not have a bilingual program,* for the child to come into contact with the English language as fast as possible. In the United States the neighborhood of residence determines the choice of school, so many of the immigrants ended up studying in bilingual schools, understandably located in neighborhoods with large numbers of immigrants. But today this question is no longer as relevant since the bilingual programs have been phased out in Massachusetts.[3]

It is interesting to note the opinion about this point expressed by several of the adolescents interviewed in schools with bilingual programs in 2000:

> "My stepmother thinks the bilingual program is wrong. But I think (but I don't say anything to her) that we have to have our own language. If we study only English we'll forget Portuguese. Some kids I know are forgetting their Portuguese, they don't use any more punctuation. They forgot it. That's why I'm in favor of this program that lets you keep up on your own language and learn another one too. For me, I don't want to forget Portuguese, ever."

Another respondent gave a similar opinion:

> "Here nobody has a passport [she is actually referring to the student visa]. Here nobody has any documents. So you come here but you end up going back to Brazil, isn't that what happens? And how are you going to go back speaking just English? You get a job and the guy asks you to write something and you're going to make a mess of it. It'll be hard. So it's good for you to keep both languages, don't you think?"

On more than one occasion, both in the interviews with guidance personnel and psychologists, and from observing Citizens´ Council Meetings sponsored by the Brazilian Consulate, the question came up about the lack of interest by parents in the performance of their children at school. And there is a feeling of neglect on the part of the children because the parents spend all their time working or at church.

In the immigrant universe that has this common denominator of work, school ceases to be a place for the children and adolescents to prepare for life in the future. It becomes part of the more immediate project of equipping them for work and consumption, a world that is divided between school and the long hours that the adolescent immigrants spend working each day.

Conclusion

It is important to note that this study only examines the second generation of Brazilian immigrants within the section on children born in Massachusetts, utilizing data from the Massachusetts Department of Public Health and the General Consulate of Brazil in Boston; within this section, the analysis in purely quantitative. Brazilian immigration to the United States is one of the relatively most recent cases (mid-eighties). For this reason, it has not yet been possible to conduct qualitative research with the second generation: the children who have one or both Brazilian parents but who were born in the United States and are therefore legally American.

One must be cautious, therefore, when using the bibliography on the second generation referenced in the introduction to analyze the Brazilian case, as that bibliography refers to the true second generation while our interviewees are actually first-generation adolescents. They are the biological second generation of their immigrant parents, but not in the sense defined by migration studies. Nevertheless, as most are adolescents who came as children with their parents to the United States and who are embedded in the North American school system, it is pertinent to consider in this conclusion the various aspects of these adolescents' adaptation to North American society, especially as they relate to assimilation. Another aspect of great importance covered in the aforementioned studies relates to their performance in school. However, we did not specifically cover the theme of schooling with these Brazilian immigrant adolescents, which deserves a comparative study with other migratory groups.

While they are not technically part of the second generation, the Brazilian adolescents interviewed acted as such in terms of their use of English. Studies (such as Mota, this volume, and Rumbaut 2004) have shown that there is a certain consistency in the use of the host country's idiom by immigrants: the first generation learns only what is necessary for survival, the second generation uses the native language at home and in community group settings while using English at school and in all other environments of American socialization, and only the third generation definitively adopts English. All interviews were conducted in Portuguese, especially because they were conducted in social spaces where native language use was common: meetings at churches and Portuguese classes in bilingual programs. However, even in these environments, we commonly noted the use of various expressions in English, in the middle of a sentence in Portuguese. In other more spontaneous settings, in which we were only observers (such as at social gatherings after mass and religious celebrations), it was common for adults to speak in Portuguese while the children and adolescents spoke in English amongst themselves. It is as if there were two codes for these children and adolescents: the code for communicating with parents, relatives and friends of their parents in Portuguese, and the code for communicating amongst themselves (siblings and friends) in English.

Dominating a skill that their parents do not have, that of the English language, creates distance between generations. These adolescents are proud of knowing English, it is a sort of triumph in their lives. The situation commonly occurs whereby these youths are called upon to help their parents in settings where English is needed, such as at a medical appointment or a meeting at school. This ability is reinforced through affirmation within their family and in the community. However, this ability does little or nothing to aid in their integration in American society. Portes (1996c) affirms that the consequences of assimilation are established in the second generation, which can integrate into the mainstream of the North American middle class, or can intensify a multi-ethnic underclass, the latter being one of the tendencies which the author observed in the new second generation. The Brazilian immigrant adolescents we observed confirm this tendency. Although their mastery of English confers status within the family and the community, it does not contribute to integration into American society. In school, their integration only occurs amongst other Brazilian nationals and other Portuguese language groups, especially Cape Verdeans, who equally participate in the bilingual programs. They do not even reach the level of socializing with Hispanic groups, against which they hold the same stereotypes as their parents.[4]

We saw that almost 80% of the adolescents interviewed and 54% of those who responded to the questionnaire at the schools worked. The type of work is very similar to that of their parents, meaning predominantly in low skill jobs. The only difference is that they divide their time between work and school and therefore work fewer hours than their parents. But taking into account the hours spent working and the hours spent at school and studying, these are adolescents who work as hard as their parents. Their relationship with North American society is marginal: as workers in an employee relationship, and as students who only socialize with their ethnic group and with others who speak their same (Portuguese) language.

Finally we would say, as Carola and Marcelo Suárez-Orozco (1995) would, that the adolescents we studied, children of first generation immigrants, are the recipients of the anxieties, ambitions, dreams and conflicts of their parents. Because the latter do not dominate the language and especially because they are wholly focused on their intense work activities, they are unable to accompany the educational life of their children. And because these children do not have American citizenship, they may even dream of continuing their studies at a university, but the American legal system places almost insurmountable barriers in the way of the fulfillment of these dreams. Between dream and reality, these Brazilian adolescents end up with the same reality as their parents, a hard life of work that, for them, has started earlier.

Notes

1. A prior version of this chapter appears in J. L. Falconi and J. A. Mazzotti (eds.), *The Other Latinos: Central and South Americans in the United States.* Cambridge, MA: Harvard University Press, 2008.

   Teresa Sales is Professor at the State University of Campinas (Universidade Estadual de Campinas) in São Paulo, Brazil; Márcia Loureiro was Diplomat and Brazilian Adjunct Consul in Boston from 1999 to 2003.

   The authors would like to thank Maria Alice Smolka for her suggestions regarding the Department of Public Health data, and Fábo Hirano and Roberta Perez for their help in inputting the data for the questionnaires.
2. These data are more reliable, although they do not take into account children whose fathers are Brazilian but mothers are not.
3. However, some school systems (such as Framingham) have been able to maintain their programs through campaigns at the local level.
4. To assert themselves as hard workers, first-generation Brazilian immigrants adopt the stereotype that American society holds regarding Hispanics, considering them a lazy group that takes advantage of the American welfare system, while only they, the Brazilians, are a hardworking people, recognized as such by American society (Sales 1999).

References

Alba, R.D. 1985. *Italian American: Into the Twilight of Ethnicity*. Englewood Cliffs, N.J.: Prentice-Hall.

Assis, G.O. 1999. "Estar aqui . . . , estar lá . . . : uma cartografia da emigração valadarense para os EUA." In *Cenas do Brasil migrante.* Ed. Sales, T. and Reis, R., São Paulo: Boitempo Editorial.

Beserra, B. 2003. *Brazilian immigrants in the United States: Cultural Imperialism and Social Class.* New York: LFB Scholarly Publishing LLC.

Farley, R. and Alba, R. 2002. "The New Second Generation in the United States." *International Migration Review* 36(3).

Fusco, W. 2001. "Redes sociais na migração internacional: o caso de Governador Valadares." *Cadernos NEPO*, Campinas, NEPO-Unicamp.

Gans, H. 1992. "Second Generation Decline: Scenarios for the Economic and Ethnic Futures of the post-1965 American Immigration." *Ethnic and Racial Studies* 15(2).

Goza, F. 1994. "Brazilian Immigrants to North America." *International Migration Review* 28(1).

Hirschman, C. 1996. "Studying Immigrant Adaptation from the 1990 Population Census: From Generational Comparisons to the Process of 'Becoming American.'" In *The New Second Generation.* Org. Portes, A. New York: Russell Sage Foundation.

Kasinitz, P., Mollenkopf, J., Waters, M. 2002. "Becoming American/Becoming New Yorkers: Immigrant Incorporation in a Majority Minority City." *International Migration Review* 36(4).

Kelly, M.P.F. and Schauffler, R. 1996. "Divided Fates: Immigrant Children and the New Assimilation." In *The New Second Generation.* Org. Portes, A. New York: Russell Sage Foundation.

Lieberson, S. 1980. *A Piece of the Pie: Blacks and White Immigrants since 1880.* Berkeley: University of California Press.

Margolis, M. 1994. *Little Brazil.* Princeton: Princeton University Press.

Martes, A.C.B. 1999. *Brasileiros nos Estados Unidos—um estudo sobre imigrantes em Massachusetts.* São Paulo: Paz e Terra.

Perlmann, J. and Waldinger, R. 1997. "Second Generation Decline? Children of Immigrants, Past and Present—a Reconsideration." *International Migration Review* 31(4).

Portes, A. (org.) 1996a. *The New Second Generation.* New York: Russell Sage Foundation.

———. 1996b. "Preface." In *The New Second Generation.* New York: Russell Sage Foundation.

———. 1996c. "Introduction: Immigration and Its Aftermath." In *The New Second Generation.* New York: Russell Sage Foundation.

Portes, A. and Schauffler, R. 1996. "Language and the Generation: Bilingualism Yesterday and Today." In *The New Second Generation.* Org. Portes, A. New York: Russell Sage Foundation.

Portes, A. and Zhou, M. 1993. "The New Second Generation: Segmented Assimilation and Its Variants." *The Annals of the American Academy of Political and Social Science,* vol. 530.

Rumbaut, R.G. 2004. "Ages, Life Stages, and Generational Cohorts: Decomposing the Immigrant First and Second Generations in the United States." *International Migration Review* 38(3).

———. 1996. "The Crucible Within: Ethnic Identity, Self-esteem, and Segmented Assimilation among Children of Immigrants." In *The New Second Generation.* Org. Portes, A. New York: Russell Sage Foundation.

———. 1994. "Origins and Destinies: Immigration to the United States since World War II." *Sociological Forum* 9(4).

Sales, T. 1999. *Brasileiros longe de casa.* São Paulo: Cortez.

———. 2001. "Segunda Geração de Emigrantes Brasileiros nos EUA." In *Migrações Internacionais—Contribuições para Políticas.* Org. CNPD. Brasília: CNPD.

———. 2003. *Brazilians Away from Home.* New York: Center for Migration Studies.

Sowell, T. 1981. *Ethnic America: A History.* New York: Basic Books.

Suárez-Orozco, C. and Suárez-Orozco, M. M. 1995. *Transformations: Migration, Family Life, and Achievement Motivation among Latino Adolescents.* Stanford: Stanford University Press.

______. 2002. *Children of Immigration.* Cambridge: Harvard University Press.

Zhou, M. and Bankston III, C. 1996. "Social Capital and the Adaptation of the Second Generation: The Case of Vietnamese Youth in New Orleans." In *The New Second Generation.* Org. Portes, A. New York: Russell Sage Foundation.

13

Two Languages at Play: Language Boundaries in the Speech of Second-Generation Brazilian Immigrants

Kátia Maria Santos Mota

In this chapter I discuss some aspects of language behavior in a bilingual situation of recent immigrants moving between two cultural frameworks in the United States: their Brazilian Portuguese-speaking families and the larger English-speaking world. My key questions in developing this study were: how do the two languages function in relation to the acculturation patterns of the group? What factors contribute to the development of either stable or transitional bilingualism? How can speech events reveal the role of each language in social situations? Having this in mind, I present some conclusive data from ethnographic research done as part of a doctoral project at Brown University (Mota 1999).

Working with twelve Brazilian immigrant families living in Somerville, Massachusetts, I was able to cover different aspects of their acculturation process in reference to language behavior: the parents' L2 (second language) acquisition, the maintenance or gradual loss of children's L1 (first language) competence; families' discourse patterns in L1/L2 related to ethnic identity formation; and the contribution of social domains for bilingual competence development. My intention here, however, is to describe the basic patterns of G2 (second generation) bilingual behavior, highlighting the pragmatic role that each language plays for communication in different social domains, as well as the symbolic power that each language possesses in dealing with territories of identity affiliation.

This case study presents the perspective of the immigrant family. I register parents' and children's voices with the intention of describing their language behavior relative to their perceptions of living between their past life in their country of origin and the new challenges they face in their host country. I use a qualitative approach, with data gathered through questionnaires, guided and open-ended interviews, and participant observation in community events.

The target group of this paper consists of the children of the families involved in the research—twenty-four children/adolescents—who represent the first G2 in this group. The group's profiles (ten boys and fourteen girls) are represented in the following chart:

Chart 1. Twenty-four G2 group children

Group's Profiles	Age	Residence in the U.S. (years)	Schooling in Brazil (years)	Schooling in the U.S. (years)
Boys	2–19	2–10	0–6	0–10
Girls	7–17	3–7	0–7	2–7
Group Means	10.9	5.8	1.9	4.4

Focusing on a G2 Brazilian immigrants study done in Danbury, Connecticut, Menezes (2003) proposes three groups based on the age of arrival in the United States.

Table 1. G2 Brazilian Immigrant Youth (Menezes)

Group 1	Those who were born in Brazil, lived part of their childhood and attended school there where they became literate in L1; they came to the U.S. at an older age and started the experience of living in the host country by following Brazilian-oriented cultural values.
Group 2	Those who were born in Brazil but came to the U.S. at a very young age; they were actually socialized in the host country, and their memories of Brazil are mostly based on their parents' perspectives, which is part of the collective imaginary of Brazilianness.
Group 3	Those who were born in the U.S., are considered American citizens by their families and Brazilian communities, and are most likely to feel detached from Brazilian ethnic traditions.

Portes (1996) refers to the first group as "immigrant children" while the other two are members of the second generation, but in Portes and Rumbaut (2001) the second group is more specifically called the 1.5 generation, and the third one corresponds to a strict definition of second generation. The age limit to distinguish between the first two groups is not clearly defined, but Marrow (2003) refers to the 1.5 generation as the foreign-born children who enter the United States after the ages of 5 or 6 (but before 12). In a more rigorous perspective, assuming that the age of arrival in the host country plays a relevant role in determining the level of assimilation, Rumbaut (2004) points out that there are three groups among those children that were born in the foreign country: a) those who arrive in early childhood (0–5), labeled the 1.75 generation; b) those who arrive in middle childhood (ages 6–12), labeled the 1.5 generation; c) those who arrive in their adolescent years (ages 13–17), labeled the 1.25 generation. Given the small size of my sample, I follow the distribution by Menezes (table 1) to present my subjects as: group 1 (N = 12 [50%]); group 2 (N = 9 [37.5%]) and group 3 (N = 3 [12.5%]). Considering that the study includes all three groups, not having in the scope of the research any comparative data among the groups, I treat all my subjects as "second generation" (G2), meaning children of Brazilian immigrant parents (G1). This fact does not exclude, in a further study, the possibility of reviewing my data analysis by comparing the three groups' language behavior.

Bilingualism and Immigrant Families

Studies on bilingualism and immigrant groups, focusing on bilingual competence and its manifestation in social domains, can contribute greatly to describing the process of adaptation among G2 members, since language knowledge and use is one of the outcomes of this process (Portes and Rumbaut 2001, 22). Assuming that language functions as a highly visible marker of ethnic identity, preservation of L1 among immigrant groups often represents, in private and public spheres, resistance to cultural assimilation that has not always been seen as the best road for socialization in the host country. It is acknowledged, however, that the association of language to ethnicity does not always happen in a linear way; in most of the situations it is subjected to continuing and multifaceted changes related to the sociohistorical movement of the group. Therefore, in a particular time of history, language can assume its primordial ties to the group's collective identity, while in another time it can play an exclusively symbolic role (Eastman 1984).

In the historic evolution of the United States, in spite of the continuous discourses about the desire/need of preserving ethnic traditions among immigrant groups, it is clearly perceived that the Anglo-American cultural way of living has been socially imposed as the most acceptable model that emerges throughout the acculturation process. Assimilation to the new cultural patterns seems to be inevitably seen as the most efficient way of promoting social mobility. The fast pace in which assimilation becomes a reality, however, can threaten intragroup solidarity and cultural tradition preservation, resulting in a high level of probability of L1 loss.

Classical researchers such as Fishman (1966) and Veltman (1983) have shown that L1 loss is likely to occur in G2 immigrant families of various ethnic groups, although they point out that this is never caused by the group's voluntary intention of assimilation. On the contrary, great efforts made by the ethnic communities and the families themselves to maintain L1 have been documented. In a recent study of new waves of immigrants, Rumbaut (2004) analyzes English language proficiency among a large population of first-generation immigrants from non-English speaking countries, and the results show that 37% of those who arrived in the United States in early childhood and 15% of those who arrived in middle childhood have declared they speak English only; in this sense, the process of L1 extinction follows a very rapid pace.

The adoption of bilingualism turns out to be an outcome of the intersection of two identities. Language does not represent exclusively a symbolic value of ethnic primordial ties; it expands to be manifested in public space as a pragmatic component of self-interested ethnic identity formation. By making a language choice, the individual not only feels or reinforces group affiliation; s/he takes action in order to get the advantages of being identified as a member of a specific group (Eastman 1984). From this perspective, the use of language in speech events represents acts of identity, as it reveals not only attitudes concerning the members of a specific language group, but also the way the individual pictures his/her personal identity while confronting alterity. By facing a new cultural paradigm one can more clearly perceive differences and similarities in ways of interpreting values and attitudes, as well as become more conscious of effective behavior in intercultural settings, as Agar (1994, 20) points out:

> "Culture is no longer just what some group has, it's what happens to you when you encounter differences, become aware of something in yourself, and work to figure out why the differences appeared. Culture is an awareness, a consciousness, one that reveals the hidden self and opens paths to other ways of being."

Given strong outside family pressure for language assimilation, the maintenance of Portuguese competence for G2 Brazilian immigrants can be seen as a difficult challenge not likely to be achieved. The sense of identification and the desire to be acknowledged as members of the Brazilian community seem to be the most important reasons for the young Brazilians I followed to either adopt or reject Portuguese in daily life. The decision to become bilingual comes as part of a life project that integrates the confluence of two nationalities, two different cultural worlds, and two possibilities of acting in multiple social identities.

Research on Brazilian immigrants in the United States reveals a state of "in-betweenness," since the desire to work here in order to assure their future life in Brazil gives them an ambiguous position of being both sojourners and immigrants. Although the latest studies have shown that the number of Brazilians with permanent residence in the United States is growing, most of the interviewees admitted that while this country is their workplace, their ultimate goal is to return to Brazil (Margolis 1994, Reis and Sales 1999). In spite of some inconsistency revealed in their actual behavior, the parents in my study show three coherent positions associating their needs to become bilingual with their intentions regarding living in the United States or returning to Brazil:

Table 2. Parents' Goals Regarding Families' Destination.

Orientation	No. of families
The ones that have made the decision to stay in the U.S. but acknowledge the importance of keeping Brazilian cultural tradition alive.	7
The ones that keep high expectations to return to Brazil as soon as they get enough money to justify the migration experience, but acknowledge the importance of L2 learning and incorporate American cultural components in order to facilitate their inclusion in the labor market when returning to Brazil.	4
The ones who feel high insecurity of not knowing the best thing to do and oscillate between the two possibilities.	1

In all three positions, despite different motivations, the immigrant parents saw bilingual competence for their children as a social advantage, a form of cultural capital, a family investment that can benefit their children's future personal and professional lives. Thus L1 maintenance becomes a goal in each of the categories presented. In the first group, L1 assumes the role of ethnic tradition preservation and reinforcement of family ties; in the second group, in spite of the great value given to L2 as an instrumental tool for financial success, L1 competence assures the reintegration to the school system when returning to Brazil; and in the third group, the development of bilingual competence, seen as a necessary condition in order to allow the family to be able to make their own decision for keeping the two languages alive, broadens the possibilities of either staying in the United States or returning to Brazil. Although they presented different supporting arguments in favor of bilingualism, their motivations were clearly stated, keeping a certain degree of unity in terms of the desire to reconcile the two languages and cultures as part of the family socialization process.

To achieve bilingual competence it is necessary to carry out both L2 acquisition and L1 maintenance. What do parents think about G2 bilingual competence? What expectations do they have about G2 language development? During the initial contact I had with the families, a questionnaire about "family socialization process in the U.S." was filled out by the parents. To register their perceptions and expectations regarding their children's language development, parents were asked to respond to the following six statements:

Table 3. Parents' Perceptions and Expectations of Children's Language Development

Statements	No. of families
We think that it's important to keep the children's Portuguese competence.	9
We believe that children are becoming perfectly bilingual.	8
We want our children to learn English as soon as possible.	4
We are not forcing our children to learn English.	2
We believe that our children will naturally choose one language.	1
We believe that our children will definitely lose Portuguese.	0

It is evident that parents believe that their children's process of language socialization will probably follow an "additive bilingualism" model in which the acquisition of L2 does not threaten the maintenance of L1 (Lambert 1972). In responding to the questionnaire, none of the families showed any concern about the possibility of children losing Portuguese. During the ongoing process of conducting the research, though, I could see how fragile their opinions were with respect to their children's L1 maintenance. Toward the end of the research, with parents feeling more comfortable with my presence, I could ask them about their actual beliefs about the perspective of G2 achievement of stable bilingualism. They affirmed that in a very short time of living in the United States, English had already become their children's primary language, and showed doubts about the preservation of Portuguese. None of the families assumed that Portuguese would continue to be their children's dominant language. Seven families affirmed that G2 immigrants can already be considered English-dominant speakers, and five families believed that only for a certain period of time would their children be able to show balanced proficiency in both languages. They seemed uncertain about future trends for bilingualism achievement. Their perceptions, unfortunately, match with research data found for other immigrant groups in the United States (Portes and Rumbaut 2001).

Most of the families believe that parents are responsible for keeping their children's Portuguese alive, as the school system, even in bilingual education programs, reinforces language assimilation towards English monolingualism. At the time of my research (1995–1996) I could already register the starting point of parents' sense of frustration with bilingual education programs, citing their lack of educational quality and social commitment. The dysfunctional aspects, stressed by parents, are presented in Mota (2002); the result of this process is pointed out in a more recent study done by Sales and Loureiro (in this volume), which assumes that parents prefer English. Currently, the new Massachusetts state legislation after "Question 2" requires schools to have ELLs (English language learners) instructed through Sheltered English Immersion, giving no primary language education. Without social support, parents feel insecure and show great difficulties in dealing with their children's language behavior. By affirming that their goal is to be successful within the North American society as well as to maintain loyalty to their ethnic heritage, parents reveal a state of living in constant tension, which influences their orientation towards G2 language behavior. It was my intention, then, to register during participant observation the occurrence of any of the following situations:

1. Parents fostering language shift, with the consequent loss of L1, as the best alternative for G2 to be successful in the new country;
2. Parents preserving a high degree of attachment to their previous Brazilian life and stressing the importance of their children's L1 maintenance as a form of resistance to the assimilation process; and
3. Parents valuing their experiences in both native and host countries and expressing the desire for their children to become bilingual/bicultural and to learn to function adequately in both "in-group" and "out-group" worlds.

Although most of the parents declared themselves in favor of bilingualism, families could not be fitted exclusively into any of the above mentioned categories. An oscillation from one category to another, depending on specific communicative events, was the most registered pattern, demonstrating their decisiveness and persistence together with expressions of uncertainty and ambiguity.

Social Settings and Language Domains

Fishman (1972) calls attention to the fact that L1 can only have a chance to survive in a situation of "diglossia," with a correlation between specific social domains and the exclusive usage of each language in a model of "linguistic complementary functions." This language behavior is what he calls "stable bilingualism." In my research, participant observation was done in five social domains (family, work, school, leisure, church), aiming at the identification of domains which could enhance L1 maintenance for G2 Brazilian immigrants. The following analytical categories were used: exclusively Portuguese / predominantly Portuguese / both languages in similar balance / predominantly English / exclusively English. However, none of the domains could be clearly characterized as having both languages in balanced proportion.

Table 4. Social Domains and Language Behavior

Social domains	Language Behavior
Work and school	represent the greatest likelihood of L2 assimilation and consequent L1 loss, reinforcing "subtractive bilingualism" (L2 acquisition causes L1 loss).
Leisure time (reinforcing friendship ties)	shows evidence of the presence of a strong language boundary between parents' and children's way of socializing with friends; while the parents keep the conversation "exclusively Portuguese," children gradually change over time into "predominantly English" or "exclusively English."
Family and church	were the most conservative social domains in terms of L1 loyalty, being "predominantly Portuguese" and "exclusively Portuguese," respectively.

To speak English at school is a matter of personal survival, to be socially integrated. To show an English accent close to that of native speakers confers status and respect; it is an intelligent way of getting rid of silly jokes coming from American classmates or even old-timer Brazilians. In public spheres English becomes the unmarked language—the most acceptable way of speaking—the cultural capital that, according to Bourdieu (1994), represents a valuable social investment. Those who are speakers of a language with high social status receive their language skills as part of their cultural capital, while children coming from a minority language environment with lower social status have to overcome a stigmatized language/culture inheritance. In this perspective language choice functions as a tool in the struggle for power in interpersonal relations.

Bourdieu emphasizes the role of the school as an agent of reproduction of the existing distribution of cultural capital, which values the high prestige language varieties. Even though most of the G2 subjects in the study had attended bilingual education programs, parents critically pointed out that such programs did not really help them develop L1 competence because of their low level of quality in terms of educational requirements. These are labeled "transitional" bilingual programs, meaning that the teaching in L1 functions only as a bridge for mainstreaming students. Therefore, the label "bilingual" does not avoid promoting a quick assimilation since it does not adopt any kind of pedagogy leading to bilingual/bicultural identity formation.

Brazilian parents believe that they can exert a great deal of influence to help G2 maintain its Portuguese competence. Some of the practices included: directly acting as language teachers at home, keeping strong connections to relatives in Brazil, and preserving a significant Brazilian cultural presence at home, especially with the habit of family getting together to enjoy Brazilian TV programs. I registered many situations in which the parents transformed their homes into schools and became effective teachers in order to fulfill their desire to keep their children competent in L1. Unfortunately, as Saunders (1988) notes, their teaching methodology and other strategies of overcorrecting their children can actually function to impede the presence of L1 in familial discourse practices. Some strategies are more successful than others (Mota 2004), and while parents knew their successes were limited, they continued their struggle.

> "It depends on the parents keeping the language alive. If parents have this as a goal they can maintain Portuguese at home. But the more we want to do it in our own way the more we see it's not the way they want. We do our best. We'll see if this takes root." (Ms. Souza)

Often, however, their efforts fail. School and family settings can become dissonant language territories by imposing either language on children's communicative practices.

> **I:** Which language do you prefer to speak?
> **F:** I don't know. At school we speak more English, but we feel like speaking Portuguese, but we can't because we're already in the last year of bilingual class. At home, we feel like speaking English, but we have to speak Portuguese. It's very difficult.
>
> (Interviewer and Fernanda, 8)

The participation in church life does not seem to be anything imposed by parents; it is indeed interesting to listen to children speaking about their sentimental ties concerning church activities. For the children, as for their parents, the church represents the place where they can make real friends and enjoy most of their social life; at the same time, they believe that it is important to preserve the church space as typically Brazilian, and therefore there is no resistance to speaking "exclusively Portuguese" there. Eight families, including both parents and children, are involved in leadership positions in church events. Even the youngest children, who insist on speaking English at home, declare that "at church English does not fit well." Practices in church often reinforce Portuguese maintenance. Carol, age 15, teaches Bible school to children on Sundays. She told me that all her students who speak only Portuguese in class are rewarded by receiving candy at the end of the class. She believes that they like it and accept this rule because they seem to understand how important it is to preserve their language ties with Brazil. Another interesting experience was presented by the Souza family, whose children go to Bible school three times a week, where Portuguese is the only spoken language. The mother believes that this is the best way for them to preserve not only the oral language but also the written one, considering that every week they are required to keep a journal with notes taken from the classes. Not surprisingly, church socializing strengthens friendships. Carol, for instance, stated that "the friends I make at school cannot be called real friends, so I feel much happier to go out with my friends from church. We do have more fun together."

To speak Portuguese does not always mean that children/adolescents feel especially Brazilian; sometimes they present themselves to others as Brazilian for particular reasons in specific circumstances. A similar explanation can apply to the choice of English. Working with G2 Brazilian immigrants and using the categories proposed by Gumperz (1992) utilizing the ethnography of communication approach, I could identify the following reasons for choosing between English or Portuguese:

Table 5. Social Reasons for Language Choice

Social Reason	Language Choice
The social domain where the action takes place	the most appropriate language is English except when conversation happens at home or at church
The person to whom the conversation is addressed	"linguistic solidarity" to the language of the other speaker if s/he is older and more respected
The topic of conversation	Congruence of language/cultural components tends to be preserved (i.e., things referring to Brazil are more adequately expressed in Portuguese).

The observance of such systematic linguistic rules does not follow a linear manifestation; incongruent situations normally occur as signs of subjective discourse intentionality of which the speaker may be unaware. Besides the three factors listed (the social domain, the topic of conversation and the kind of interlocutors), the speech acts of bilinguals can carry various intentional meanings when using either language, when code-switching in the same speech event, or when code-mixing by borrowing language components that can interfere in the other language's phonological, morpho-syntactic or semantic systems. According to this understanding of sociolinguistic behavior, this study has identified the following categories of language behavior in the daily routine of the boys and girls included in the research.

Communicative Patterns in G2 Speech

Monolingual speech (Portuguese / English)

This communicative pattern normally occurs when interacting with a monolingual speaker in a setting that is "exclusively Portuguese." It was observed, however, that with G2 Brazilian immigrants the maintenance of symmetrical communication (both speakers keeping the same language in the conversation) occurs when the other speaker is American and cannot speak Portuguese, but not when talking to monolingual Portuguese speakers. In this situation there is a loss of symmetrical communication; the G2 bilingual keeps switching into English even knowing the other person cannot speak English, showing that the dominant language holds a more considerable social status and at the same time conveying the idea that someone "not speaking English" can barely be socially integrated. When conversation starts in Portuguese, as soon as the child or adolescent perceives that his partner can understand English, s/he changes automatically to a speech that can be either "predominantly English" or "exclusively English." As Regina, age 9, told me, "The language that flows more easily is English."

The tendency to keep the conversation more in English than in Portuguese can be explained by three possible reasons: the low level of tolerance for non-English speakers; the need to be self-represented as an English speaker by establishing ethnic boundaries through language; or the ability of knowing how to exclude the other person as participant in the conversation. All these aspects can come out together, especially in younger children who are losing L1 competence mostly because they are influenced by their older siblings, and in those children/adolescents who, no matter the age, search for a more quickly acquired assimilation and to establish distance from their Brazilian heritage.

Bilingual speech as intergenerational boundary

In many communicative events there appears to be a growing gap among parents and children's interpersonal relations, especially because English becomes the children's major language long before parents achieve competence in L2. The inversion of social roles between parents and children comes as a natural consequence; children assume an authoritarian voice by wedding their identity to the Anglo-American community, while parents fear losing the family tradition. Subtractive bilingualism, as a result of school's reinforcement of L2 acquisition in detriment of L1 maintenance, seems to be the main path followed by immigrant children, even at a high cost of breaking family interaction (Wong-Fillmore 1991).

Although parents declare that they try to encourage their children to develop their attachment to both cultures and languages, in many situations it was possible to observe that their attitudes do not always contribute to facilitate it. Indeed, they present a discourse full of statements in which the use of L1 represents a symbolic tool for parental manifestation of power within the home environment. Reinforcing the point that the acculturation process in a foreign country leaves them in a very fragile emotional state, especially when they admit that their children are experiencing a considerably fast assimilation movement towards the Anglo-American culture, parents continuously express a feeling of "losing their children," which is marked by the different parameters of language choice among family members. This is the case of Ms. Pereira, who has been living in the United States for five years and does not show interest in learning English because she believes that it would make her children forget Portuguese; in her opinion it is more important to keep the family unity by forcing them to speak Portuguese than to give herself the chance to learn English. By doing so, she gives up the opportunity for integration into the Anglo-American world by learning to communicate better within the local community. Therefore, the adoption of Portuguese as the home language acts as a means of preserving parental authority as well as a guarantee to make possible the family's return to Brazil.

In reality, L1, a minority language in the host country, is more likely to be retained if three relevant factors are present: positive individual attitudes towards the language; a large amount of favorable social interaction with L1 speakers; and perception of personal benefits linked to the use of L1 (Gardner 1985). In the particular case of this group of families, however, it was observed that the quality of social interactions between parents and children has been strongly harmed because of parents trying to impose the use of Portuguese at home. In many situations children do not speak Portuguese spontaneously, but they are constantly forced to use L1 to show respect to their parents.

Not being aware that authoritarian positions in language choice can contribute to L1 loss (Saunders 1988), parents react negatively when children address them in English or manifest American behaviors. Moreover, parents can send confusing messages by swinging from one extreme to another in their attitudes about the United States or, conversely, Brazil. Worried about their children's future, they can be extremely critical of their children's ignorance about Brazilian culture or alienate their children by comparing their progress in school with their nephews and nieces in Brazil.

In reference to language choice in intergenerational discourse within the family setting, three language phenomena in G2 discourse patterns were observed in the families of this study:

Table 6. Family Discourses and Language Choice

Family Discourses	Language Choice
Communication among siblings	tends to be "exclusively English"
Children's communication with parents	older children and girls tend to address their parents more often in Portuguese than younger children and boys
Triangular communication	older children function as interpreters for their younger siblings in order to access their parents

> "With my Brazilian friends that speak English I always speak in English. I only speak Portuguese when they don't speak English. But if I'm at home, then I think I speak more Portuguese even with my friends, because we're at home and at home it's more Portuguese. But, I don't know, I speak more English with my brother. Even with my mother I speak English sometimes, but she doesn't understand me. Then I have to speak Portuguese." (Karina, 16)

Karina talks about her language behavior at home, assuming that in her circle of friends English comes to be the dominant language, but showing efforts to keep Portuguese as the home language. However, her inconsistency and insecurity about speaking Portuguese are also evident. Her phrasing "I have to speak Portuguese" shows the feeling of duty she has towards L1 loyalty.

Code-switching in bilingual speech

In conversations among bilinguals, many speech sequences of code-switching spontaneously occur in daily conversation. A constant flow of the two languages seems to be the most natural way of conveying meanings for a life in two places, revealing not only better competence in either language for certain semantic fields, but also the "in-betweenness" of identities in transitional/stable moments of life. The two languages may assume complementary social roles or establish conflict zones of aiming to reach a wider space in personal/social identities. Code-switching should not be seen as the speaker's inability to preserve the autonomy of the two language systems, but as part of an interaction process making communication easier and more informally conducted, as bilinguals can make use of either language to convey meanings at a faster pace. Although it is possible to predict occurrences of code-switching according to factors such as the topic of the conversation, the institutional space, the social context, the speakers' identities, etc. (situational speech), code-switching can also be a manifestation of metaphorical purposes, to call attention to specific language-related meanings in order to assure a more emphatic kind of discourse. Many studies of bilingual communities have shown the occurrence of code-switching as both a communicative tool and a means of preserving collective identity. Gumperz (1992), for instance, views code-switching speech more as an outcome of the speaker's ability to manage the two languages for self-interested communicative purposes than as a form of language behavior determined by situational settings.

> "Talking with Brazilians is funny because you don't know when we change from Portuguese to English. Sometimes in a ten-word sentence, five are in Portuguese and five in English. We can understand each other, but it sounds weird. Especially when we are angry, then everything gets mixed up, it can't be separated. When one doesn't find the word in Portuguese, then you say it in English and when it doesn't come out in English, then you say it in Portuguese. That's why I have more Brazilian friends. It becomes easier to speak two languages than just speaking one." (Erica, 13)

Erica shows that bilingual competence can be seen as an advantage in communication; she expresses the idea that it's easier to communicate when you have two languages available. One can understand this as an intermediary phase of L2 acquisition, but it is also evident that by dealing with two languages, the cultural universe of the speaker can be expanded through different language-related meanings. In her opinion, the bilingual speech enables her to better express emotions which can facilitate friendship ties. Although acknowledging the advantage of being bilingual, she is aware that code-switching may be characterized as a "strange, weird way of speaking," maybe because of the stigmatizing concept of "language purity" or the prejudice of mixing language belonging to a low prestige ethnic group. G2 Brazilian immigrants show a certain ambiguity by admitting that code-switching is their normal way of speaking, but at the same time show feelings of inferiority. If their speech is weird, how do they see themselves as being binational? The same perception is evident in Clara's statement:

> "Generally with my friends I speak two languages. When I write a letter to them I mix everything. Sometimes I use a word that I know better in Portuguese and sometimes one that I know better in English. Then I get used to mixing the two languages. People think that it's weird." (Clara, 13)

Code-mixing in bilingual speech (overlapping)

Parallel to code-switching, a common language behavior when languages are in contact is code-mixing or the borrowing of linguistic components, such as phonological, morphological, syntactic or semantic items, which are incorporated into the system of the other language. From the examples I registered I found that English components are more frequently inserted into Portuguese than the reverse, that is, L2 interference on L1 shows that the dominant language "invades" the space of L1. The opposite direction, Portuguese interfering in English speech, happens when the child/adolescent is newly arrived and acquires interlanguage patterns of communication, but as long as they become socialized in the host country, they reach fluency in English and decide to use the language not only to communicate more easily but also as a means of facilitating their social inclusion in the United States. At this point G2 members tend to preserve their L2 discourse without L1 interference, while their L1 performance receives a growing interference of L2.

Expressions such as "vou fazer uma aplicação para o College" (I'm applying for College) clearly shows that the false cognate words "application" and "College" are the ones that most easily can be incorporated into the L1 speech, because they can be easily accepted in the L1 lexicon structure while carrying the L2 meanings. There are also many examples of linguistic extension or creation of neologisms. When speaking Portuguese, new words, borrowed from English stems, are adopted, such as the very interesting example of "bisar" which comes from the English expression "be busy" that is transformed into a verb with morphological endings in Portuguese. By using the word on a daily basis it tends to expand lexically and assume other meanings that are not predictable in the original word in English, as it is shown in Carol's speech, which finishes using "bisado" (very busy) as a synonym of "doidona" (very crazy).

> "It's very funny. We say that 'That girl is bisando me too much,' that she's really on me since she's taking up my time. A friend of mine from Brazil was on the phone and said to her 'Erica doesn't stop 'de bisar' me.' She asked: 'She doesn't stop what?' I answered: 'de bisar . . . Ah! Sorry, it means that she is bisando me, she's always on me,' I don't think she understood anything. I said, 'She got bisadona. She got crazy.'" (Carol, 15)

Many other examples can be registered in the Brazilian community dialect: words taken into Portuguese as "disha," "parkear," "vaquear," instead of the Portuguese words "lavanderia," "estacionar," and "aspirar," because of the interference of the English words "dishwasher," "to park," and "vaccuum cleaner." I could also register some even stranger examples of code-mixing when Carol told me that her friends invent new Portuguese expressions such as "Eu cambequei pra casa" taken from the English expression "I came back home."

This phenomenon of code-mixing has been frequently observed in the Brazilian community's way of speaking among adults. I believe that G2 speech with code-mixing probably follows the parents' interlanguage patterns, especially when addressing adults. I did not notice many of these occurrences in conversation among G2 members. It is important to point out the need for linguistic studies which can better describe the Brazuca dialect (Brazilian English) in terms of the generative rules that both generations tend to follow.

Language and Power in Bilingual Speech

We can "do things with words" (Austin 1965); that is, by using a certain kind of discourse, intentionally or not, we can cause a shift in a conversation not only at the cognitive or emotional level but also on the performative level—the power to take or transform actions by using discourse strategies. Language choice can work out very well at the pragmatic level of communication; by choosing either L1 or L2 the individual is able to give different connotative and social meanings to the selected messages.

Foucault (1996) has shown that language is never neutral; the struggle for power is a struggle for the control of discourses. Language practices, including language choice, can be interpreted as acts of repression, domination, or disempowerment. Utilizing a similar perspective, Fairclough (1989) presents his theoretical contribution—Critical Language Analysis—in which the power conveyed in verbal messages can be discovered by following a set of analysis categories. Any text, spoken or written, can reveal intentions of controlling the interaction either by overt linguistic features or by the "between the lines" messages. His theory presents a structured means of developing awareness of hidden levels of language.

Supported by the above theoretical assumptions that associate language with power, I decided to register the meta-linguistic awareness of my G2 population by conducting interviews in which they were asked to critically reflect on their language behavior, specifically language choice, during their speech acts. This was done in order to find out if they are conscious of the manipulative power of using bilingual competence for self-interested purposes. The outcomes suggest that their linguistic analysis was quite consistent with my data interpretation; their statements clearly present evidence of their meta-linguistic competence, in that by choosing either language they can convey extra-verbal intentions. The data collected were categorized in five discourse intentions, which can be illustrated by samples of G2 speech acts.

Language as a tool for controlling parents' behavior

Interviews with parents revealed much frustration and complaints that "there is no order in the house," the reason being that their children's dominant language is turning out to be English. Many embarrassing situations exposed G2 power of dominating turn-taking in the conversation, correcting the mother's way of speaking English, making fun of the parents' linguistic ignorance, etc. Children very soon understand that by being competent in L2 they can hold the role of decision-maker in family affairs.

> **Ms. Ferreira:** Sweetie, you had a meeting at school last week and you didn't tell me.
> **Daughter:** And could you speak English with my teachers?
> **Ms. Ferreira:** They always have interpreters at the meetings.
> **Daughter:** I didn't know about the meeting.

Portes and Rumbaut (2001, 119) show that in a study done with G2 of different ethnic groups in the U.S., "while a foreign language is spoken in almost all immigrant homes, 72 percent of the children had opted for

English as their preferred means of expression in junior high school, with the figure increasing to 88 percent by the time of high school graduation." Parents' rudimentary knowledge of English, combined with children's refusal to speak the home language, provides an indicator of dissonant acculturation. According to Portes and Rumbaut (2001, 127): "In the extreme, fluent communication across generations ceases, opening the way for affective separation and weakening of parental authority."

Language as instrumental motivation for professional career

To achieve success in both processes of L1 maintenance and L2 acquisition, motivation and attitudes are important factors to be considered. Motivation, according to Gardner (1985), can be divided into two types: integrative and instrumental. The first relates to the desire to belong to a social group or to be able to establish interpersonal relations within the language group, and the latter deals with the idea of making personal and professional investment through language proficiency. Asking my G2 sample of Brazilian immigrants about the importance of being competent in Portuguese, their answers clearly reveal their bicultural experience of being Brazilian in their sentimental ties, and American in a more work-oriented way. At first they cling to the integrative motivation, to be loyal to the Brazilian community, but they also express their instrumental motivation for knowing Portuguese to "get a better job." With the evolution of the world economy and the U.S. position in it, L1 competence is perceived by G2 immigrants as a benefit in the labor market.

> **I:** What's the importance of learning Portuguese?
> **C:** Everyone has their own reason. If you have Brazilian friends, that will help you. I think it's very good to know other languages to communicate, to get a better job. Parents should help the kid to learn another language. Especially here. The longer you stay here, the more immigrants will come, the more you will need to learn other languages.
>
> (Interviewer and Candice, 17)

The interviewee's voice reflects, in Bourdieu's (1994) terminology, her awareness about the "profit" that the native language can provide in the growing linguistic "market" of a "globalized world." In the interview, Candice, and all other adolescents, admitted that English proficiency assumes the highest position for the labor market, no matter where they live, whether in Brazil or in the United States. Their language beliefs, however, do not guarantee their success in professional life. Sales and Loureiro's study (in this volume), by using a large number of subjects in a more advanced phase of Brazilian migration movement, shows in a quantitative survey that for the second generation "work is above all else, an absolute continental divide between life in Brazil and life in the United States." In their conclusion, however, the authors affirm the paradox that for Brazilian G2 English mastery does not mean integration into American society and, consequently, does not assure equal conditions to the mainstream youth for achieving better jobs. This finding is corroborated by the sociolinguistic assumption that states that language itself does not determine reality, but it mirrors the dynamics aspects of collective social life.

Language as symbol of national identity

Language choice can represent a symbolic distinction between "we" and "they" groups. According to Romaine (1994, 36), "speakers display what may be called 'acts of identity,' choosing the groups with whom they wish to identify." In contemporary societies national identities have been losing their primordial role of being attached to a specific national group, since other forms of identities have emerged creating other kinds of affiliation such as gender, race, profession, religion, etc. Hall (2000) has pointed out that the globalization process of networking people from all different parts of the world has resulted in what he calls the "denationalization process," giving rise to the emergence of transnational identities which are characterized as hybrid, and more flexible and adjustable to collective and individual social interests and needs. He also calls attention to the fact that when groups or individuals feel marginalized, they tend to reinforce their in-group unity by marking their presence through ethnic revitalization. In that case, the ethnic language becomes a relevant and visible symbol of belonging. Following a similar interpretative perspective, Tsuda, cited in Phillipson and Skutnabb-Kangas (1996), states that two language paradigms exist in the contemporary world: linguistic imperialism through English monolingualism in institutional settings, and linguistic ecology through the revitalization process of minority languages. This has been defined by Paulston (1992:24) as "In hard times, man will cling to his language and ethnic group; in times of plenty, man pays little attention to resource like ethnic languages." Through the migration process, many immigrants become aware of preserving their national identity and keeping L1 alive. Language then plays the role of group unifier as well as being a symbolic tool for strengthening the group socialization process in the host country.

> "I'm interested in learning Portuguese. I think it's very important for a person's education. If I am Brazilian and I'm not good at Portuguese, that's ridiculous. Like many Americans who don't know English well. Now I can see how important it is for me. Before I didn't care. It's a matter of identity." (Clara, 13)

My G2 informants follow the position affirmed by Clara, since they are conscious of the importance of Portuguese competence to feel Brazilian. However, the discourse strategy she used by comparing Brazilians to Americans in terms of the need for language strategy shows her intention to put the two groups on equal terms, although in many parts of the interview she recognized that L1 maintenance is much easier when the language has high social prestige. This is not the case for immigrant minority languages. In her statement three speech intentions can be clearly identified: to associate L1 competence with the individual's level of education; to state that L1 competence is important for every language group; and to express the fact that immigrants become aware of the need for affirming identity through L1 competence. It is not possible, however, to know if such positions are consciously recognized or if they come as the hidden message of feelings and needs to protect or convince herself of the benefits for her self-improvement brought on by the migration process.

Language as strategy of establishing exclusion

By making use of language games of power, the minority language becomes a powerful tool for excluding others in public spaces, assuring the delimitation of ethnic territories in which there is an intentional inversion of dominance—the Anglo-American group becomes "the foreigner / the outsider." L1 functions as the "marked language"—the unpredictable language in this specific speech event—carrying all the discourse intentions of the speaker. A very interesting episode elucidates this discourse category: getting on a bus in Somerville by late afternoon, a group of five Brazilian adolescents were seated in the back. At the beginning they were talking in English about a TV program, but suddenly one of them changed the conversation to criticize some teachers' attitudes at school and, by changing the topic, they automatically switched to Portuguese. By doing so, they were able to express what they wanted, showing their emotional state out loud. In situations like the one described, the minority language acts as "a secret code" making the other passengers of the bus (except me) feel ignored or intentionally excluded. In this particular speech event, language can be seen not only as a means of excluding others, but also as a strategy of affirming ethnic identity, of assuming the right to make visible the presence of the ethnic group in the foreign land.

Language as an emotional space

Expressions of emotions, considered by MacKey (1968) as one of the basic internal functions of language, can be manifested through language choice in which the individual selects the language with the most meaningful lexicon for expressing feelings of anger, aggression, fear, depression and other psychological states. Grosjean (1982) presents relevant examples which show the relationship between language choice and mental activities, emotional expressions, and reactions to stressful situations. He adds, for instance, that "swearing in one language is easier than in the other, either because it is the bilinguals' first language or because the bilingual feels freer to do so in that language" (Grosjean 1982, 278).

> **I:** In what situations do you like and don't like to speak Portuguese?
> **E:** When I'm in class and there are Americans around, and I'm angry or nervous, then I feel like swearing in Portuguese. But if I'm at home and get nervous, then I feel like swearing in English. Like in the math class, I swear a lot in Portuguese. Also when someone bothers me, if he's American, I want to swear in Portuguese, and if the person is Brazilian, then I feel like swearing in English.
>
> (Interviewer and Erica, 13)

> **J:** At school I speak in Portuguese sometimes when I'm angry.
> **I:** To whom do you speak Portuguese when you're angry?
> **J:** To nobody. I speak to myself.
>
> (Julia, 10, and interviewer)

The inner speech comes, consciously or not, in one specific language, the one which carries the emotional burden of the experienced situation; the speaker can act without censorship and can also impede others from reacting. The monologue type of discourse is then able to preserve private identities, to avoid the sharing of meanings, and to reject social interaction.

Language as expression of a sacred niche

As a consequence of the church functioning as the most traditional social domain for L1 maintenance, G2 Brazilian immigrants develop their religious affiliation exclusively in Portuguese. The religious space becomes particularly important for family integration, in such a way that the language acquired by parents during childhood does not have to compete with L2.

This is shown in Fabio's telling me that Portuguese is the language of his prayer moments and that during his dreams his mother comes always speaking Portuguese. The same happens with Marcos, age 7, the only child who constantly refused to speak in Portuguese during my interviews, who admitted that he only knows how to pray in Portuguese.

> **I:** Do you like to pray in Portuguese or in English?
> **M:** Portuguese.
> **I:** And do you really pray in Portuguese?
> **M:** Every night.
>
> (Interviewer and Marcus, 7)

When using language in private spheres, L1 is usually chosen as the most adequate way of registering messages in the most intimate domains of human behavior, confirming Spiro's (1955) assumption that the first learning experiences at home are the last ones lost throughout the assimilation process.

Conclusion

In the various communicative events involving G2 Brazilian immigrants, L2 dominance, which gradually becomes a symbol of success in the host country, is apparent. L1 maintenance becomes fragile as the assimilation process takes place; family values and personal beliefs are left behind as a result of internal and external pressures towards the strengthening of a new identity.

Bilingualism can become transitional or stable depending on the level of G2 attachment to family tradition: a rigid pattern of ethnic affiliation, "imposing" either language, enhances L1 loss, while a more flexible ethnic affiliation allows the confluence of the two languages as symbolic of acceptance of hybrid ethnic identities. My findings support those of Portes and Rumbaut (2001, 133) who conclude in their study of G2 ethnic groups that G2 bilinguals represent the most effective type of language adaptation to enhance family connection, in contrast to monolinguals, either in L1 or L2, and limited bilinguals.

Thus, even considering that the natural trend of language development among the G2 sample of this study is towards L2 monolingualism, the empowerment of the Brazilian community can open new possibilities to involve the youths in sociocultural activities, giving them the opportunity to become fluent bilinguals. During the interviews there were many relevant moments of L1 revitalization showing an interesting oscillation between identities.

> "I feel even more Brazilian because here there are a lot of different Brazilians. In Brazil everybody knows the same things that you know. Here you learn more new things, ways of speaking Portuguese, the differences in accent. In Brazil if someone said to me 'o' trem' I wouldn't know what it meant and here I know that 'trem' is the way that 'mineiros' speak. You learn to know who is who, the differences, people's habits. I feel more Brazilian. You value yourself more. Here I value being Brazilian." (Carol, 15)

To the perception of this young immigrant the linguistic diversity of Portuguese speakers could only become visible with the experience of living in a foreign country and having to socialize with Brazilians coming from all different regions. In this respect, the migratory movement can enlarge the understanding of the country of origin, by making cultural encounters with other ways of being Brazilian. Even knowing that Carol's experience does not represent the great majority of Brazilian adolescents, it is worth mentioning that the need to strengthen Brazilian ties in the foreign country, probably as a survival strategy in the initial phase of migration, can enhance L1 revitalization and reinforce the acceptance of multiple Brazilian-American identities.

References

Agar, M. 1994. *Language Shock: Understanding the Culture of Conversation.* New York: William Morrow.

Austin, J. L. 1965. *How to Do Things with Words.* New York: Oxford University Press.

Bourdieu, P. 1994. *Language & Symbolic Power.* Cambridge, MA: Harvard University Press.

Eastman, C. M. 1984. "Language, Ethnic Identity and Change." In *Linguistic Minorities, Policies and Pluralism,* pp. 259–76. Ed. J. Edwards. New York: Academic Press.

Fairclough, N. 1989. *Language and Power.* London: Longman.

Fishman, J. (Ed.). 1966. *Language Loyalty in the United States.* The Hague: Mouton Humanities.

Fishman, J. 1972. *The Sociology of Language.* Rowley, MA: Newbury House Publishers.

Foucault, M. 1996. *A ordem do discurso*. São Paulo: Loyola.

Gardner, R. C. 1985. *Social Psychology and Second Language Learning—The Role of Attitudes and Motivation*. Baltimore: E. Arnold.

Grosjean, F. 1982. *Life with Two Languages: An Introduction to Bilingualism*. Cambridge, MA: Harvard University Press.

Gumperz, J. 1992. *Discourse Strategies*, Cambridge, UK: Cambridge University Press.

Hall, Stuart. 2000. "Quem precisa da identidade?" In *Identidade e Diferença*, pp. 103–33. Ed. T. T. da Silva. Petrópolis, RJ: Vozes.

Lambert, W. E. 1972. *Language, Psychology, and Culture*. California: Stanford University Press.

MacKey, W. 1968. "The Description of Bilingualism." In *Readings in the Sociology of Language*. Ed. J. Fishman. The Hague: Mouton.

Margolis, M. 1994. *Little Brazil—An Ethnography of Brazilian Immigrants in New York City*. Princeton, NJ: Princeton University Press.

Marrow, H. 2003. "To Be or Not to Be (Hispanic or Latino): Brazilian Racial and Ethnic Identity in the United States." A qualifying paper submitted in partial fulfillment of requirements for a Master of Arts in the Department of Sociology. Harvard University.

Menezes, G. H. 2003. "A segunda geração de brasileiros em Connecticut." In *Fronteiras Cruzadas: etnicidade, gênero e redes sociais*, pp. 157–73. Ed. A. C. Braga Martes and S. Fleischer. São Paulo: Paz e Terra.

Mota K. S. 1999. *Imigrantes Brasileiros nos Estados Unidos: trajetórias de identidades em uma situação de bilingüismo*, doctoral thesis, Brown University.

———. 2002. "Políticas de Educação Bilíngüe na escola e na família: cenários de competitividade lingüística." Presented at Associação Nacional de Pós-Graduação e Pesquisa em Educação (ANPED), Caxambu, MG.

———. 2004. "Aulas de Português fora da escola: famílias imigrantes brasileiras, esforços de preservação da língua materna." In *Cadernos CEDES* 24(63): 149–63 (maio/ago.).

Paulston, C. B. 1992. *Sociolinguistics Perspectives on Bilingual Education*. Clevedon, U.K.: Multilingual Matters.

Phillipson, R. and T. Skutnabb-Kangas. 1996. "English Only Worldwide or Language Ecology?" *TESOL Quarterly* 30(3): 429–52 (fall).

Portes, A. (org.) 1996. *The New Second Generation*. New York: Russell Sage Foundation.

Portes, A. and R. Rumbaut. 2001. *Legacies: The Story of Immigrant Second Generation*. Berkeley: University of California Press.

Reis, R. and T. Sales (org.). 1999. *Cenas do Brasil Migrante*. São Paulo: Boitempo.

Romaine, S. 1994. *Bilingualism*. Cambridge, MA: Blackwell.

Rumbaut, R. G. 2004. "Ages, Life Stages, and Generational Cohorts: Decomposing the Immigrant First and Second generations in the United States." *International Migration Review* 38(3): 1160–1205 (fall).

Saunders, G. 1988. *Bilingual Children: From Birth to Teens.* Philadelphia: Multilingual Matters.

Spiro, M. 1955. "The Acculturation of American Ethnic Groups." *American Anthropologist* 57:1240–52.

Veltman, C. 1983. *Language Shift in the United States.* The Hague: Mouton.

Wong-Fillmore, L. 1991. "When Learning a Second Language Means Losing the First." *Early Childhood Research Quarterly* 6:323–46.

14

Brazilian Immigration to the United States: Research and Issues for the New Millennium

Maxine L. Margolis

It has been nearly two decades since Brazilians started emigrating to the United States in large numbers. Since research began on this new migration stream in the early 1990s, this is an appropriate time to review the emergent themes surrounding Brazilian immigration to this country: these include demographic issues, questions about identity and concerns surrounding employment, social class, community and community organization, religion, studies of return and the second generation. In this chapter I will also briefly review problems following 9/11 with particular reference to what I see as a brake on transnational behavior. Along with providing an overview of recent studies on these topics, I will also suggest areas for future research.

Demographic Issues

By 2001 nearly two million Brazilians were living abroad, a 27 percent increase from 1997. Of these, between 800,000 and 1.1 million Brazilians resided in the United States (Salgado 2001). But one would never know the size of the Brazilian population by looking at the figures from the 2000 U.S. Census, which managed to count a mere 212,000 Brazilians in the entire country, and this despite the fact that, for the first time, data from the census was meant not only to identify those born in Brazil, but also to include those born of Brazilian parents in the United States. Similarly, the more recent 2004 American Community Survey only located some 282,000 Brazilians in the United States.

Given the dubious national figures, it comes as no surprise that state and local data on Brazilian numbers are also suspect. To provide a specific example: in 2001 fellow anthropologist Nancy Foner had just finished editing the second edition of her book, *New Immigrants in New York City*—first published in 1987—when I learned that the new edition, like the old, would not have a chapter on Brazilians. I sent her an e-mail asking why Brazilians were again excluded. She replied that she was only including recent immigrant groups of significant size and that, according to official statistics, Brazilians in New York City were far too few in number.

Her decision was based on data from the 1999 Current Population Survey which estimated that there were only 7,000 Brazilians in New York City's Primary Metropolitan Statistical Area and 20,000 Brazilians in the larger Consolidated Metropolitan Statistical Area which includes New York, New Jersey, Pennsylvania, Delaware and Connecticut. Again by way of comparison, the Brazilian Consulate in New York City estimated that in 2003 about 300,000 Brazilians were living within the New York consular district which covers these same five states. Hence the Current Population Survey's count of 20,000 Brazilians contrasts with the Consulate's estimate of 300,000 Brazilians in precisely the same geographical area, a majority of whom, consular officials believe, live in New York City. Even in Queens, the area of greatest concentration of Brazilians in New York City, Brazil is not listed among the top 20 source countries of the foreign-born (Lobo and Salvo 2004).[1]

Similarly, despite the high percentage of undocumented individuals in the Brazilian community, the U.S. Department of Homeland Security's estimates of the resident unauthorized alien population do not place Brazil in the top 20 countries of origin, thus implying a resident population of fewer than 30,000 undocumented Brazilians in the entire country. Perhaps there is something to be said for invisibility!

But while most critics of official figures of Brazilians living in the United States cite such undercounts, at least one believes that overestimates may also be a problem. An editorial in a south Florida Brazilian newspaper claims that many of the numbers bandied about in the Brazilian press are exaggerations. For example, 200,000 Brazilians are said to live in Florida, with perhaps a quarter of them in Pompano Beach and Deerfield Beach—adjacent communities with large concentrations of Brazilians. Since the combined population of these two towns is 130,000, this would mean that with some 50,000 Brazilians living there, over one-third of the population is Brazilian, likely a significant exaggeration (Nunes 2001).

But there is no doubt that the undercount is a far greater concern. One reason for it according to Tereza Costa (in press), the New York Consulate's liaison to the Brazilian community, is the fear with which many Brazilians greeted the 2000 Census forms.[2] The number of Brazilians contacting the

Consulate doubled as they tried to verify a widespread rumor that a mass deportation would immediately follow publication of the 2000 Census data. And since Costa believes that perhaps 70 percent of Brazilians in the New York Consular district are "sem papel" (without papers), that is, undocumented, it is little wonder that many refused to fill out census forms.

Aside from numbers, another intriguing demographic phenomenon is the expansion of the Brazilian population in the United States from metropolitan areas in the Northeast, Florida and the West Coast to smaller communities, including ones that are not usually associated with immigrant settlement. For example, there is a burgeoning Brazilian population in Atlanta and its suburbs–perhaps numbering as many as 30,000—as well as Brazilian communities in such unlikely places as Goose Creek and Mount Pleasant, South Carolina[3] (Celestino 2005).

Not only are Brazilians settling in a greater variety of locales in the United States; in recent years many have become involved in secondary migrations both within and across state lines. The moves are made because of job availability, the cost of rent and/or considerations of climate. Some Brazilians have moved from New York City to New Jersey, Connecticut, and Pennsylvania, while in New Jersey others have left Newark to take jobs in smaller communities in the state like Riverside and Burlington. In Massachusetts Brazilians now live throughout the state, not just in the Boston metropolitan area. Then, too, many Brazilians in Broward County, Florida—Pompano Beach and Deerfield Beach—are secondary migrants from the Northeast who moved to the Sunshine State, which many say they prefer because of the weather (Jansen and Siqueira 2005; Suarez 2003; Siqueira and de Lourenço 2004).

In some cases there is a downside to such migrations. Leaving New York City, for example, and "moving to the other side of the river"—a reference to New Jersey—is viewed as a "setback" if one is to be considered an immigrant who has "made it." It is common for Brazilians in New York City to refer pejoratively to Brazilians who live in Newark and other less fashionable locales. In the words of one Brazilian, "it was horrible to have to leave Manhattan and go live with the Brazilian crowd (*brasileirada*) in Queens" (quoted in Costa 2004, 13). A similar association between social status and place of residence is reported among Brazilians in south Florida, where those living in Broward County are looked down on as poorer and less educated by those who reside in Miami (Resende 2002, 2005). So "the other" now appears to be those other Brazilians who live in what are considered to be less desirable parts of several American metropolitan areas.

Not only is there greater diversity as to where Brazilians are settling in the United States, there is also a wider range of origins in Brazil, as pointed out by Siqueira and Jansen in this volume. Whereas during the early years immigrants from Minas Gerais dominated the migration stream, today immigrants from Mato Grosso, Rondonia and Roraima—regions that were never traditionally considered sources of immigrants to the United States—are fanning out in small communities in New Jersey, Florida and elsewhere. Goias, Paraná, and Santa Catarina have also become major immigrant-exporting states. As Cristina Martes (2000) noted, Brazilians in her Massachusetts study came from sixteen states and the Federal District. The number of places sending out immigrants has expanded to the extent that emigration has become a national phenomenon in Brazil.

The Question of Identity

No one interested in the massive undercount of the Brazilian population in the United States can fail to make reference to the question of Brazilian identity. Uncertainty about Brazilian identity not only helps explain the undercount, it also clarifies the general invisibility of Brazilian communities in this country. Let me give one glaring example. Rodolfo Acuña, a respected expert on Mexican immigration, wrote in 2003: "Brazilians are considered Latinos; however, Brazilians speak Portuguese and they do not have a strong national presence in the United States."

Many researchers have analyzed how Brazilians conceive of themselves vis-à-vis other populations in the United States, most especially Hispanics (Beserra 2005; Davis 1997; Fleischer 2002; Marcus 2004; Margolis 1998; Marrow 2002; Martes 2002; Ribeiro 1999; Sales 1998). Several have suggested that Brazilian identity is problematic in part because, as anthropologist Darcy Ribeiro (2000) observed many years ago, "the Brazilian people see themselves as unique, as singular."

This observation helps explain why it is so difficult for Brazilians to accept their inclusion in other groups. Because of this reluctance, one researcher has argued that Brazilians in the United States have created a distinct identity, what he calls a "*Brazuca* identity" (Tosta 2004). *Brazuca* is a colloquialism for Brazilian immigrants in this country that first appeared in print in the late 1980s (Bicalho 1989). Brazilians adopt stereotypes that already exist in American society and use them to distance themselves from Hispanics. As a consequence, *Brazucas* have played two contradictory roles: the role of the exploited minority and the role of transmitter of the dominant class ideology.

Then, too, Brazilians only become fully conscious of their identity after they leave Brazil. In Brazil, Brazilian national identity is taken for granted; it is an abstraction that is rarely a signifier since those one meets on a daily basis are all likely to be Brazilian. Typically, in Brazil an individual's reference point is not nationality but city or state of residence or social class. But while national identity in Brazil is a given and seldom noticed, Brazilians abroad are classified as foreigners from a distant and exotic land (Margolis 2008). "Brazilians learn Brazil only after they come to the United States," write de Lourenço and McDonnell (2004). Most migrants bring with them regional cultural images that are only superseded by national ones—the Brazilian flag, *capoeira*, 7th of September Independence Day celebrations, Brazilian music and cuisine—once they arrive in the United States (Vieira this volume).

Some interesting questions surrounding Brazilian identity are raised by several contributors to this volume. We have Davis's suggestion, for example, that Americans held distinct images of Brazil decades before Brazilian immigration to the United States began, images with which immigrants now have to contend. Playing on these understandings, Beserra notes that in constructing a national identity in a foreign setting like Los Angeles, Brazilians have a choice between "exoticization" and "latinization." She believes most prefer the former because, owing to widespread discrimination against Latinos in the United States, being identified as a Brazilian "exotic" is deemed advantageous. In a similar vein, Ramos-Zayas argues that Brazilians use a "cultural excess" strategy to avoid being classified with Hispanics whom they see as being associated with poverty and marginality.

How does racial identity play out in this mix? A study by Fazito and Martes (2004) found that in the United States Afro-Brazilians who were used to being called by terms like "mulata" and "morena escura" were nonplused by the American category "non-white." But this uneasiness is not limited to people of color because, as the authors point out, most Brazilians are classified here as Hispanic, Latino or Other—all "non-white" categories from an American perspective. Similarly, McDonnell and de Lourenço (this volume) note that many of the Brazilians they interviewed in Boston thought of themselves as "white" when they lived in Brazil, but took on a new racial identity—that of "Brazilian"—once in the United States.

Confusion over identity also has practical consequences. Although researchers agree that Brazilians widely reject a Hispanic label and affirm their distinct national identity, no one to my knowledge has investigated the consequences of this rejection for political life. As the Hispanic population in the United States grows and its political activities and organizations multiply, will Brazilians continue to separate themselves from these efforts? In Massachusetts, rather than building ties to local Hispanic groups, Brazilians seem to be strengthening their connections to the Portuguese community through organizations like MAPS, the Massachusetts Alliance of Portuguese-Speakers (Martes 2004). But what about Brazilians in those parts of the United States that lack other Portuguese-speaking populations? Are they more likely to make common ground with Hispanics to achieve common goals? This is another question that calls for research.

A generational issue also comes into play here. First-generation immigrants tend to maintain strong ties to Brazil and reject ethnic and racial labels that might detract from their national roots. First and foremost, they regard themselves and want to be regarded as Brazilians, certainly not as Hispanics and rarely as Latinos. National identity is highly salient for this generation and is the primary reference for socializing and for collective activities.

But what alliances might be forged in the next generation and beyond (Suárez-Orozco 2004)? To answer this question we should look more closely at issues surrounding ethnicity, nationality, and identity in the second generation, which some researchers have in fact begun to do. Helen Marrow (2004), for example, has found that second-generation Brazilians are much more willing to identify themselves as Latinos than are their parents.

At this point, however, so many scholars have dealt with ethnic and national identity among Brazilians that, as a research issue, I would like to see identity laid to rest for a while, at least for first-generation Brazilians. But identity must remain a focus in the political realm, as a cause that should engage community activists. While I agreed with Marcus's (2005) suggestion that we should lobby for the 2010 Census to include a category, "Yes, I am Brazilian," I have since found out that we will not have to wait that long. Beginning in 2005, the American Community Survey replaced the long form of the U.S. Census and included questions about country of birth and ancestry.

The Employment Picture

The employment picture of Brazilian immigrants does not seem to have changed a great deal since the first years of the exodus from Brazil. Brazilians are still overwhelmingly employed in services: women as housecleaners and child minders, men in restaurant work, construction, painting, landscaping and more recently, carpentry (Margolis 1998). Moreover, the nature of these jobs has not changed. For example, a recent study of the New York restaurant industry found that most restaurant workers—at least 36 percent of whom are undocumented—earn less than $20,000 a year and that very few of these jobs provide benefits or opportunities for upward mobility (Greenhouse 2005).

Then, too, evidence suggests that some of the same issues that inspired Brazilians to go abroad a decade or more ago are still in play today. Research on Brazilians in south Florida, for example, found that an important issue for many immigrants is that they are overqualified for the jobs they hold. That is, Brazilians trained as lawyers, doctors, architects and in other professions express great frustration because their expectations of professional success were thwarted by Brazil's job market, frustration which spurred them to emigrate in the first place (Alves and Ribeiro 2002).

But let us turn to the brighter side of the employment picture. I know that at least some Brazilians—perhaps a considerable number—who have been in the United States for longer periods of time and who have green cards, have moved up the occupational ladder. While I am aware of such "success" stories in New York City and elsewhere—Brazilians who own businesses or hold white collar and professional positions—no one, to my knowledge, has systematically investigated occupational mobility among long-term residents, yet another potential area for future research.

While the jobs that most Brazilians hold have not changed, a recent study has revealed certain employment practices of which I was previously unaware. José Carlos Meihy (2004) describes two job arrangements in New York City that have not been reported elsewhere. One is the practice of "rented jobs." To cite his example: a Mexican immigrant employed as a groundskeeper by Columbia University at $12.00 an hour, "rents" the job out to an undocumented Brazilian to whom he pays $4.00 an hour, keeping $8.00 for himself and remaining free to engage in other remunerative activities. Needless to say, employers are kept in the dark about such arrangements.

It is unclear how widespread the other practice was since it appears to have ceased after the attacks on 9/11. Here the Brazilian owner of a cleaning company brought several working-class women at a time from northeast Brazil to New York City to work as housecleaners. The company owner had "contacts" at the American Consulate, meaning that all the women were able to secure visas to come to the United States as tourists. When they arrived they were housed in an apartment in Queens paid for by the cleaning company, which also paid for their round-trip airfare and trained them to become housecleaners. According to Meihy, since some of the women were illiterate, cleaning products were color coded according to their use. The women were brought to and from work by other employees of the company and their movements were otherwise restricted. They averaged one cleaning job a day for which they received at least $60.00, of which 70 percent was kept by the company. After a few months of work and before their visas had expired, the women returned to Brazil with $1,000 to $1,500 in their pockets, a great deal of money to poor Brazilians. With 9/11, however, the practice came to a halt as it became much more difficult to secure tourist visas.

Social Class and Immigration

So that was a case of Brazilians from very modest backgrounds coming to the United States to work. It is, in fact, an example of a more widespread phenomenon. Some recent Brazilian immigrants have not suffered from the sort of downward job mobility experienced by their compatriots who arrived earlier. The reason is that the work they do in the United States is not very different from what they did in Brazil. Unlike earlier immigrants who tended to belong to the urban middle class, some more recent émigrés have working-class roots in small towns and rural areas. As Costa (in press) found in her analysis of recent consular data, over a quarter of the Brazilian women employed as maids in the United States had been maids in Brazil, while about 10 percent of the men working as waiters had held similar positions back home. Of course, the attraction of American jobs, however undesirable from the point of view of working conditions, is that they pay wages that are many times what similar jobs pay in Brazil.

Others have also noted that many recent immigrants come from more humble backgrounds than their trail-blazing predecessors. For example, Luciana Andreazzi (2004), a school psychologist in Framingham, Massachusetts, points to the "different Brazils" she has encountered in her work—the urban, educated, middle class Brazil and the rural, poorly schooled, excluded Brazil. Similarly, Heloisa Galvão (Souza 2002; Souza 2004), founder of the Brazilian Women's Group in Boston, also notes that poorer, less educated Brazilians from interior towns are now arriving there. These poorer immigrants who earlier had no access to either the information or the resources of middle class immigrants, now have both thanks to friends and relatives from the same towns in Brazil who are already established in the United States.

But one might well ask: how do Brazilians of such modest means come to this country, especially given the current difficulty in obtaining tourist visas and the high cost of entry via Mexico? One answer is that groups of some twenty to thirty Brazilians already in the United States get together monthly and contribute money to fund future immigrants. In a set sequence one member of the group receives the entire fund, which is then used by a relative or friend to pay for passage to Mexico (including the services of a *coyote)* or for plane fare and the costs of obtaining a tourist visa. When the new immigrant arrives and finds work, he—and it is usually a he—begins repaying the amount he received to come here. The system not only helps new immigrants pay off their debts and start saving for the return home, it also eliminates potential threats from *coyotes* to turn them over to immigration authorities if the debt is not paid in a timely manner. Finally, members of the group help newcomers to find work so that they too can begin contributing to the fund to finance other Brazilians who want to emigrate.

Community and Community Organization

This arrangement might be called a group investment fund, and it is one of the very few associations—formal or informal—reported among Brazilians in the United States. With a handful of notable exceptions, researchers in New York, Massachusetts, Florida and California have found no secular organizations set up to assist Brazilian immigrants.

Just as nearly all academics who have done studies on Brazilian immigrants have noted their problematic identity, so too virtually all have commented on the fractured nature of Brazilian communities. Several fissures that inhibit community solidarity appear to be present among Brazilian populations in the United States. Evidence suggests, for example, that Brazilians who arrived earlier in the migration stream—say ten or more years ago—tend to disparage more recent arrivals for being less educated and coming from more modest backgrounds. Brazilians in places where immigration began earlier sometimes have a negative image of their newly arrived compatriots, whom they see as opportunists without a sense of community. According to Teresa Costa of the Brazilian Consulate in New York, a similar divide exists between the relatively few Brazilians who have become American citizens and those who have not. These "Brazilian Americans" sometimes attribute the same negative characteristics to the Brazilian immigrant population as a whole that Brazilians tend to attribute to Hispanics. That is, those "other Brazilians" are "not to be trusted" and are "only out for themselves." In order to get a better understanding of community dynamics, a fruitful area for future research might look at relations between old timers, including those who have become U.S. citizens, and more recent immigrants.

The issue of community among Brazilian immigrants and community-based institutions or rather the lack thereof has been dubbed "Brasphobia." In 2003 an informal conference with that title was organized by the Brazilian Rainbow Group in New York City. I gave a presentation about what I call the "discourse of Brazilians bad mouthing each other" (Margolis 2003). Part of the discourse is the refusal of some Brazilians living in the United States to identify themselves as Brazilian. I found this in the Brazilian community in New York City, and it also has been reported by researchers in Boston and Florida (Margolis 1994a; Martes 2000; Resende 2002, 2005). As one immigrant in south Florida told anthropologist Rosana Resende, who was inquiring about his nationality, "I *was* Brazilian."

Brazilian immigrants themselves complain of the lack of a community ethos and compare themselves unfavorably to other immigrant groups in this regard. However, partly contradicting the litany of complaints is actual behavior, that is, the reality that Brazilians could hardly survive the immigrant experience without the aid and comfort of other Brazilians. One of the most salient features of Brazilian immigrant populations in the United States is the apparent contradiction between ideology and behavior. While examples of non-communitarian actions certainly exist, it is also true that Brazilian immigrants overwhelmingly rely on each other to navigate the multiple hurdles of immigrant life.

One researcher (Brown 2005) has come up with an intriguing thesis concerning community and ethnic cohesion among Brazilian immigrants. He suggests that they have experienced less fragmentation than what he calls "ethnic ambivalence," a simultaneous celebration of "Brazilianness" by individuals and small groups with a feeling of alienation towards this same Brazilianness when referring to the Brazilian immigrant population at large. Brazilians have high regard for themselves and their compatriots in terms of a strong work ethic and general decency, but have negative views of Brazilians as employers and community leaders. In short, the same individuals express positive views of Brazilians individually and negative views of Brazilians collectively. This, Brown argues, explains why they overwhelmingly prefer American to Brazilian employers and are usually reluctant to participate in events organized by the larger community.

Given such ethnic ambivalence, it is essential to cite what I referred to as the "notable exceptions" to the lack of community organizations among Brazilians in the United States. Aside from the widely acclaimed Brazilian Immigrant Center in Allston, Massachusetts, that has been fighting for workers' rights for over a decade, other community-based organizations include the Aliança Brasileira dos Estados Unidos in Connecticut that provides members an I.D. card that looks similar to a driver's license and a $20,000 life insurance policy. The Brazilian Rainbow Group in New York, although initially formed to aid gay and lesbian immigrants, has reached out and offered advice and aid to the immigrant population at large, making it the only such organization in that city. Then, too, despite the general lack of community groups, Kirshner (this volume) notes that three Boston labor unions have made efforts to organize Brazilians there and suggests a "potential synergy" between labor unions and the Brazilian churches in that city.

Religious Issues

This brings us to a discussion of religion in Brazilian immigrant communities. While, as we have seen, there is a dearth of secular organizations among Brazilians in the United States, this is definitely not the case of religious-based groups. Again, most of those who have done research on Brazilian communities here are struck by the burgeoning number of churches in them, particularly evangelical churches.

In the brief discussion here I am relying in part on recent field work in south Florida led by a team of University of Florida researchers and their Brazilian counterparts (Vazquez and Williams 2003). The researchers located thirty-nine churches with Brazilian congregations in Broward County alone, only one of which was Catholic; the rest were Protestant, the majority Pentecostal (Alves and Ribeiro 2002).

How to explain the plethora of religious institutions? Part of the appeal of these ethnic-based churches is that they are not limited to a specifically religious dimension but also play important social and support roles. The ethnic churches augment social life through many kinds of recreational activities—parties, community meetings, national celebrations, sports events and the like. These activities help construct ethnic identity in public spaces so that, in essence, they recreate Brazilianness in a foreign setting.

The churches, moreover, are sources of information about jobs, housing, and other aid intended to help Brazilian immigrants. The social role churches play as sources of information and solidarity may explain why in the United States—in contrast to Brazil—roughly as many men as women attend church services. And the support can be very specific. Immigrants from the same church or the same town in Brazil may receive material assistance from the church's members from the same region (Alves and Ribeiro 2002). Given this, future research might investigate whether or not co-religionists also play a role in arranging emigration to the United States.

Martes (2000) in her research in Boston came to a similar conclusion about the roles churches play. The churches are not only the center of social life; they also provide a good deal of practical aid to immigrants. She explains the success of the evangelical churches, in particular, by citing the fact that, unlike the Catholic Church, the evangelical churches are entirely dependent on their own members for financial support, which makes them less hierarchical and less centralized than their Catholic counterparts. Since evangelicals fund church facilities themselves, a strong feeling exists that this is "our space," one built especially for Brazilian believers. Moreover, as Freston notes in this volume, the religion emanating from these churches is "non-territorial" and therefore well suited to transnational migrants because it is not linked to a specific location and does not rely on national church structures like dioceses. Also it is easily reproducible and far less dependent on religious specialists than Catholicism. Finally, Martes suggests that the actual discourse of the evangelical churches is comforting to immigrants; by encouraging hard work and lauding prosperity and social mobility, such religious discourse is decidedly attuned to their own aspirations.

In a later study Martes (2004) notes the importance of religious communities in providing what she calls a "captive market" and a "customer base." This is especially true of evangelical business owners who have a better chance of drawing customers from their own churches than Catholics do. This may be one reason why the percentage of evangelicals among Brazilian business owners in the greater Boston area is much higher than their share of the Brazilian population.

With regard to future research on these issues, I agree with Kirshner's call (this volume) for an analysis of the ways in which Brazilian churches perform civic and political functions, including the limits of their engagement in those areas.

Studies of Return

Because of the recentness of Brazilian emigration, there are as yet few studies of return. In fact, I know of only two in depth studies on returned immigrants. One is my 1997 research in Rio de Janeiro on Brazilians who had lived in various parts of the United States and then returned home (Margolis 2001). My main focus was the impact the immigrant experience had had on returned migrants. Many of the topics they discussed in the interviews with me had a collective leitmotif, an idealistic conception of what life is like in the contemporary United States. This representation of American society, in turn, colored their perceptions of Brazil, amplifying and intensifying complaints about life back home.

Several related themes emerged in what I call the "discourse of return." One is impunity and corruption. Simply put, returned immigrants complained about the lack of law enforcement in Brazil and the impunity with which laws are broken along with political and judicial corruption. These conversations often segued into discussions about crime and the uncertainty and fear it inspired in returned immigrants. As one seven-year resident of New York now living in Rio de Janeiro told me: "I don't know which was my bigger mistake, having gone to America in the first place or having returned home."

The other study is Sylvia DeBiaggi's analysis of how the values and attitudes acquired in the United States impacted the lives of Brazilians upon their return home. With a primary interest in gender roles, DeBiaggi interviewed returnees in Belo Horizonte and Governador Valadares, Minas Gerais and Criciúma, Santa Catarina. She found that a majority of women felt that their relationships with their husbands had been better in the United States—there they were more independent and enjoyed more equality in the division of household tasks—but that because of cultural and family pressures, they had had to resume more traditional roles upon their return to Brazil. Many resented their loss of autonomy and spoke wistfully of their years in the United States. DeBiaggi concludes "that going home is a very stressful experience for family members who do not realize that the return to the country of origin is actually a new migration with all the new dislocations that that implies" (2004, 162).

The New Generation

When I did my initial field research in the late 1980s and early 1990s, the issue of second-generation Brazilians in the United States did not arise because a majority of the Brazilian immigrants I interviewed were young, unmarried, and very few had children (Margolis 1994b). Moreover, in the 1990 Census over 93 percent of Brazilians were foreign-born, reflecting the recency of this migration stream (Marrow 2002). Now with the passage of time scholars are making their first forays into research on the new generation of Brazilians, most of whom can be more precisely described as the "1.5 generation," that is, Brazilians who came to the United States as young children and are now adolescents (Portes 1990; Suárez-Orozco and Suárez-Orozco 2001).

I find what little research has been done on this generation somewhat contradictory. One study suggests that many second-generation students have different expectations from their parents (Johnson 2004). The parents—who say they plan to return to Brazil someday—are willing to work in low-level jobs because they see them as temporary. But many Brazilian adolescents envision their residence in the United States as long-term or permanent and assert they would be dissatisfied working in the same sort of low-wage service jobs held by their parents.

Yet despite their aspirations and often excellent school records, the undocumented status of many in this younger generation presents a serious handicap. One of the biggest challenges facing Brazilian adolescents is that despite having lived in this country for many years, if they want to attend a community college or state university they must pay out-of-state tuition because of their irregular status, tuition which can cost two or three times more than that paid by legal residents (Souza 2004). Then, too, since they are international students, they are not eligible for federal financial aid or scholarships. One example of the consequences of this handicap: an undocumented Brazilian who was valedictorian of his 2005 high school class in Massachusetts was unable to enroll in a public university because his parents could not afford out-of-state tuition and he was ineligible for other financial aid. Although a brilliant student with a bright future in computer science, he and his family were forced to return to Brazil so he could enroll in a tuition-free federal university there (Woolhouse 2005; see also de Oliveira 2005).

As a result of these barriers and the great personal frustration that often results, an indeterminate number of young Brazilians have become high school dropouts. In fact, Brazilian adolescents in Massachusetts have among the highest dropout rates of any immigrant community in the state (Andreazzi 2004). Writes researcher Mary Helen Johnson of the long-term consequences: "For first and second generation immigrants, restricted access to higher education will directly affect their potential future earnings . . . and their incorporation into the host society (2004, 101)."

But contrasting with the finding that Brazilian adolescents tend to reject the employment trajectory of their parents is Teresa Sales' (2001) and Sales and Loureiro's research (this volume), also in Massachusetts. They suggest that many in this new generation reproduce the path of the parental generation in terms of employment and values. Some young Brazilians not only go to school full-time, but most—80 percent in fact—also have extensive work experience. Moreover, they work in jobs similar to those of their parents; in supermarkets, restaurants, construction and as housecleaners and baby sitters. And it is work that most distinguishes their lives in this country and Brazil. While in Brazil they were children playing and going to school, in the United States, because of their labor, they are part of the adult world.

Work, in turn, opens up the world of consumerism to these adolescents. About half used their earnings to help support their families; the rest worked not from necessity but to have their own money to do as they wished. Like the Brazilian immigrants I interviewed in New York City in the early 1990s, these young people cited the ability to earn so much more money in so much less time as the key motivation for living in the United States (Margolis 1994b).

Within this environment school is secondary, Sales believes, and parents who work long hours have little time to oversee their children's schooling. Education is viewed instrumentally, as a way of learning English in order to earn money, rather than as an end in itself. Relatively few see it as preparation for moving up the occupational ladder. As a result, the future of these young people in terms of their insertion in the U.S. labor market looks very much like that of their parents. While with experience they may eventually get somewhat better paying jobs, many are likely to remain confined to the unskilled service sector of the urban economy (Sales 2001).

This general lack of mobility for Brazilians in the American job market has been confirmed by Scudeler (1999). Then, too, other evidence suggests that Sales is correct in her prediction that without higher education Brazilians are likely to be mired in the low-wage sector of the U.S. economy. As a result of shifts in the American labor market which have led to a steep decline in high paying, unionized factory jobs—jobs typically held by those with only a high school education—today a man with a college degree earns, on average, 81 percent more than a man with only a high school diploma (Egan 2005).

What have we learned about younger children, including those born in the United States who have little or no familiarity with Brazil? For some Brazilian immigrants, a U.S.-born child redefines their expectations of impermanency in this country and enmeshes them more firmly in American society. Many baptize their U.S.-born children with American names—Michael, Anthony, Jennifer, John and Linda were popular among Brazilian immigrants in Danbury, Connecticut. Moreover, such children often serve as liaisons to American society, as interpreters for their parents in medical consultations[4] or when buying a car or renting an apartment. The child's voice may be recorded on the answering machine and children answer the phone for parents not comfortable speaking English (Menezes 2003).

But parents also express frustration about trying to ensure that their children remain fluent in Portuguese when they are immersed in American media and surrounded by English- (or Spanish-) speaking friends. As Mota notes in this volume, many parents try to preserve a significant Brazilian cultural and linguistic presence at home by having the family watch Brazilian television programs together. One Brazilian immigrant in New York City told me that all of her Brazilian friends with children subscribe to TV Globo, the Brazilian television network, hoping that their daughters and sons will become "hooked on" Brazilian *telenovelas* (widely popular evening soap operas) and maintain or improve their Portuguese. Children's lack of literacy in Portuguese is also a worry to many parents, especially those with specific plans to return to Brazil.

After 9/11

Finally, we turn to 9/11 and how the traumatic events that day shaped the experience of Brazilian immigrants in this country. Three critical issues affecting Brazilians and other immigrants have emerged post-9/11: documentation, entry into the United States, and shifts in transnationalism.

One serious problem for immigrants since the attacks in New York and Washington is the issuance of driver's licenses. Prior to that fateful day many states did not require a Social Security card before a driver's license was issued. But since then most states have made it more difficult to obtain or even renew licenses without proper documentation. Since a driver's license is not only required to operate a vehicle and take out car insurance, but may be needed to open a bank account, get a credit card, enter a federal building, rent an apartment, and travel, the lack of a license presents ongoing problems in daily life. Said one Brazilian about the current situation: "It is better to be deported than to live here without a driver's license. Without it we become invisible. Having [a license] . . . is the closest you can get to being American. Only the green card is better" (quote from Costa, in press).

Several schemes have surfaced in the Brazilian community to meet the demand for these documents. While a driver's license normally costs about $50, some Brazilian immigrants have paid as much as $800 to get a license using false documents. Then, too, organized "tours" have been arranged to states where it is easier to get a license; such excursions can cost as much as $3,000. Between 2000 and 2002 one Brazilian operating in the Northeast and southern United States sold over 1,700 counterfeit social security cards for $2,000 to $2,500 each, earning over $4 million for his efforts. His arrest enabled U.S. authorities to trace hundreds of illegally obtained driver's licenses held by Brazilians, licenses which were then canceled (*O Estado de São Paulo* 1999; Mineo 2003).

Since 9/11 the awarding of driver's licenses to undocumented immigrants has emerged as a political issue in the United States. While immigrant advocacy groups have been lobbying to allow undocumented immigrants to obtain driver's licenses, arguing that this makes sense because it insures that immigrants will have passed a driver's test and know the rules of the road, anti-immigrant groups have been just as vehement in opposing the awarding of such documents to "illegal aliens." Most alarming to immigrant advocates is the Real ID Act which was passed by the U.S. Congress in May 2005. Once fully implemented, the legislation mandates that applicants for drivers' licenses in *all* states must prove they are in the United States legally.

Moreover, a few local officials have taken it upon themselves to challenge the residence in their communities of Brazilians and other immigrants who lack driver's licenses or documents proving they are living legally in the United States. For example, although immigration control is a federal responsibility, in Danbury, Connecticut, the mayor sought to deputize the state police to enforce immigration laws. Similarly, the police chief in a small town in New Hampshire has invented his own border control policy; he has given orders to arrest undocumented immigrants charging that they are "trespassing" in his community (O'Leary 2005; Powell 2005).

But the repercussions of 9/11 have been much broader than its impact on driver's licenses and the actions of a few scattered officials. Entering the United States also has become much more problematic for foreigners. The growing number of Brazilians arriving here via Mexico is an issue that has not been dealt with at length by academic researchers, although Siqueira (this volume) cites data suggesting that over 75 percent of Brazilians coming to the United States after 2000 either entered via Mexico or flew into this country with false passports. The entry phenomenon has received widespread attention in Brazil and in some U.S. border communities. Anyone who has been following reports in the Brazilian media knows that there has been a large increase in the number of Brazilians entering clandestinely via Mexico (Maisonnave 2005a; Sotero 2005). And in 2005 George W. Bush defended the hardening of U.S. immigration policy by specifically citing statistics on the decline in the number of undocumented *Brazilians* picked up on the U.S.-Mexican border (Dantas 2005).

To cite some figures: in 2003 more than 5,000 Brazilians were detained at the border—up from 1,300 in 2000—and the numbers have skyrocketed since then. In 2004, 8,600 Brazilians were detained, and for the eight months ending in May 2005, over 22,000 Brazilians were picked up on the U.S.-Mexican border. In April 2005 alone, 4,800 Brazilians were detained—an incredible 160 a day—more than ten times the number detained during the same period the previous year (Gilot 2003; Kammer 2005; Maisonnave 2005b).[5]

How to explain this spectacular increase? Evidence suggests that Brazilians—and others as well—are now taking advantage of a loophole in U.S. immigration law. According to international law, when OTMs ("other than Mexicans," in the parlance of U.S. immigration law) are stopped at the border, they cannot be sent back to Mexico. Since the United States is very short of detention space, very few of those apprehended are imprisoned. This is an eyewitness account of what transpires:

> In the silvery-blue light of dusk, 20 Brazilians glided across the Rio Grande in rubber rafts propelled by Mexican smugglers who leaned forward and breast-stroked through the gentle current.
>
> Once on the U.S. side, the Brazilians scrambled ashore and started looking for the Border Patrol; finding it led to a quick and well-rehearsed surrender. "We used to chase them; now they're chasing us," one Border Patrol said as he frisked the Brazilians and collected their passports.
>
> What happened next explains the odd reversal.
>
> The group was detained overnight and given a court summons that allowed them to stay in the United States pending an immigration hearing. Then a Border Patrol agent drove them to the McAllen [Texas] bus station, where they continued their journey into America.
>
> The formal term for the court summons is a "notice to appear." Border Patrol agents have another name for it. They call it a "notice to disappear" (Kammer 2005).

Upward of 98 percent of undocumented immigrants detained in this way do not show up for their court appearances. Since Brazilians have learned the procedure, that is, that they automatically will be let go once they receive the court summons and then are free to travel to their final destination in the United States, they are intentionally trying to get caught by the Border Patrol. It is estimated that, on average, for every would-be immigrant stopped at the border, another three make it through safely. As such, the increase in the number of Brazilians detained may simply be an artifact of a change in behavior.[6]

Paradoxically, it is those with fewer resources who are unable to secure tourist visas that are more likely to make the trip to the United States via Mexico, a trip that can cost up to $9,000. Then, too, because poorer Brazilians have more difficulty getting tourist visas, it is said that "the law of three suits" (*a lei de três ternos*) operates among American consular officers in Brazil. If a would-be tourist has the same suit on in his passport and visa pictures and during his visit to the U.S. Consulate—rather than three different suits—this means he is poor and really intends to immigrate, not just visit—and so is denied a visa.

Finally, to conclude this discussion, I want to cite a wider problem: the 9/11 attack's effect on transnationalism. One of the most salient features of transnational migration is the movement of international migrants back and forth between home and host countries. While the frequency of such international travel varies with geographical distance and financial resources, one of the basic ingredients of transnational behavior is that international migrants do not leave their home countries never to return (Glick Schiller, Basch, and Szanton Blanc 1992).

Since 9/11 it has become much more difficult for Brazilian immigrants—unless they have green cards—to be transnationals, that is, to travel easily back and forth between the United States and Brazil. While what I previously called "yo-yo migration," the remigration of Brazilians to the United States who had purportedly returned home for good, was still possible prior to 9/11, with growing strictures on the issuance of tourist visas and greater control at airports and borders, such travel has become ever more problematic (Margolis 1994b, in press).[7] Seasonal workers illustrate the predicament that some Brazilians find themselves in, that is, those with jobs in construction and landscaping who typically are employed only part of the year. Where they once returned to Brazil during the slow winter months when work was scarce, today they cannot risk such travel and are forced to remain in the United States even if unemployed.

Teresa Costa, the liaison to the Brazilian community in the New York Consulate, says she receives daily calls from frantic Brazilians at JFK airport who have been barred from entering or re-entering the United States. In nearly all cases, they are denied entry even if they have valid visas and passports because by overstaying the time limit of their visas on a previous occasion, they were living here illegally and are therefore prohibited from returning. Air manifests are now screened in advance, and passengers may be sent back to Brazil upon entry if there is evidence that they were undocumented in the past (Boyle 2004).

These constraints seem to have changed the nature of Brazilian migration. The majority of Brazilian immigrants to the United States—past and present—have always claimed they would eventually go back to Brazil after they saved a requisite amount of money, even though many delayed the return home for years or even decades. But today many recent immigrants, realizing that once they return to Brazil they must stay, have been meeting their monetary goals in three or four years and then actually going home for good.

This is notably different, however, from the situation of Brazilians who have lived in the United States for five or ten years and who remain undocumented. Simply put, they are caught in a vise. Since it has become so difficult to come and go from this country, they are loath to risk returning to Brazil only to find they cannot get a job or otherwise support themselves there. Even immigrants who have lost jobs here are reluctant to return to Brazil without the savings they had planned, knowing they are also likely to be jobless back home. This feeling of entrapment has caused profound depression in some Brazilians, a feeling that they have "lost their place," that they cannot return to Brazil because if they return they cannot survive, and if they stay in the United States, they cannot live.

Notes

1. Two researchers suggest that a more reliable headcount of immigrants would look at local statistics like housing permits and school enrollments (Justich and Ng 2005).
2. For a discussion of the reasons for the undercount in the 1990 U.S. Census—which likely holds true for the 2000 Census as well—see Margolis (1995).
3. The 2000 U.S. Census counted only 865 Brazilians in the *entire* state of South Carolina, yet in Goose Creek alone there are at least two stores entirely devoted to Brazilian products.
4. Discussing medical issues in American clinical settings can be particularly discomfiting for Brazilian immigrants who are not fluent in English and who have a different sense of time. See Jouët-Pastré, Ribeiro, Guimarães and Lira in this volume.
5. While one might assume that immigration enforcement in the workplace increased after 9/11, as it did at the U.S.-Mexican border, that is not the case. In fact, in 2003 Immigration and Customs Enforcement arrested only 450 undocumented immigrants in the workplace, down from 14,000 in 1998 (Porter 2005).
6. Since its first episode aired in March, 2005, "América," whose central character is smuggled across the Mexican border and finds work as an exotic dancer

in Miami, has become Brazil's most popular evening soap opera (*telenovela*). Some have suggested that it may have played a role in the increase in the number of Brazilians detained along the U.S-Mexican border.

7. Still, transnational behavior has not vanished entirely. For example, sending remittances to the home country is often seen as a mark of transnationalism and in one 2004 survey over three-quarters of Brazilian immigrants in Massachusetts were sending remittances to Brazil (see Martes, this volume).

References

Acuña, Rodolfo F. 2003. *U.S. Latino Issues*. Westport, CT: Greenwood Press.

Alves, José Claudio Souza and Lúcia Ribeiro. 2002. "Migracão, Religião e Transnacionalismo: O Caso dos Brasileiros no Sul da Flórida." *Religião e Sociedade* 22(2): 5–90.

Andreazzi, Luciana. 2004. "Brazilian Immigrants: The Ecological Matrix of Social Exchange, Resources & Vulnerabilities." Paper presented at the Conference on Brazilians in the U.S.: Another Invisible Latino Diaspora. Aliança Brasileira nos Estados Unidos, Central Connecticut State University, New Britain, April 16.

Beserra, Bernadete. 2005. "From Brazilians to Latinos? Racialization and Latinidad in the Making of Brazilian Carnival in Los Angeles." *Latino Studies* 3(1): 53–75.

Bicalho, José Vitor. 1989. *Yes, Eu Sou Brazuca*. Governador Valadares, Minas Gerais: FUNSEC.

Boyle, Michael. 2004. "Immigration Law, Legal Resources Available." Paper presented at the Conference on Brazilians in the U.S.: Another Invisible Latino Diaspora. Aliança Brasileira nos Estados Unidos, Central Connecticut State University, New Britain, April 16.

Brown, Peter. 2005. "The Ambivalent Immigrants: Brazilians and the Conflict of Ethnic Identity." Senior Honors Thesis in Sociology and Brazilian and Portuguese Studies, Harvard University, Cambridge, MA.

Celestino, Helena. 2005. "EUA Impedem Brasil de Instalar Consulado." *O Globo*, February 24.

Costa, Maria Teresa Paulino. 2004. "Algumas Considerações Sobre Imigrantes Brasileiros na Jurisdição do Consulado Brasileiro de Nova York." Mimeo. New York: Consulado Brasileiro.

———. in press. "Some Considerations on Brazilian Immigrants under the Jurisdiction of the Brazilian Consulate in New York." In *Brasileiros no Exterior: Caminhos da Cidadania*. Ed. Bela Feldman-Bianco and Carlos Vianna. Campinas, São Paulo: Editora da Unicamp.

Dantas, Iuri. 2005. "Bush Elogia "Remoção Rápida" de Brasileiros." *Folha de São Paulo*, November 30.

Davis, Darién. 1997. "The Brazilian-Americans: Demography and Identity of an Emerging Latino Minority." *The Latin Review of Books* (spring/fall): 8–15.

DeBiaggi, Sylvia Dantas. 2004. "Homens e Mulheres Mudando em Novos Espaços: Famílias Brasileiras Retornam dos EUA para Brasil." In *Psicologia, E/Imigração e Cultura,* pp. 135–164. Ed. Sylvia Dantas DeBiaggi and Geraldo José de Paiva. São Paulo: Casa de Psicólogo Livaria e Editora.

De Lourenço, Cileine and Judith McDonnell. 2004. "The Politics of Identity: Brazilian Women Workers in Massachusetts." Paper presented at the meetings of the Latin American Studies Association, Las Vegas.

De Oliveira, Patricia. 2005. "An Immigrant's Dream." *Boston Globe,* June 11.

Egan, Thomas. 2005. "No Degree, and No Way Back to the Middle." *New York Times,* May 24.

Fazito, Dimitri and Ana Cristina Martes Braga. 2004. "O (In)devido Lugar—Narrativas de Imigrantes Negros Brasileiros Sobre Raça e Cidadania." Paper presented at the annual meetings of the Associação Nacional de Pós-graduação em Ciências Sociais (ANPOCS), Caxambu, Minas Gerais.

Fleischer, Soraya. 2002. *Passando a América a Limpo: O trabalho de housecleaners brasileiras em Boston, Massachusetts.* São Paulo: Annablume Editora.

Foner, Nancy, ed. 1987. *New Immigrants in New York City.* New York: Columbia University Press.

———. 2001. *New Immigrants in New York City.* Rev. ed. New York: Columbia University Press.

Gilot, Louise. 2003. "More Brazilians Crossing Border." *El Paso Times,* May 11.

Glick Schiller, Nina, Linda Basch, and Cristina Szanton Blanc. 1992. "Transnationalism: A New Analytic Framework for Understanding Migration." In *Towards a Transnational Perspective on Migration: Race, Class, Ethnicity and Nationalism Reconsidered.* Ed. Nina Glick Schiller, Linda Basch, and Cristina Szanton Blanc. Vol. 645, pp. 1–27, *Annals of the New York Academy of Sciences,* New York.

Greenhouse, Steven. 2005. "In $8 Billion Restaurant Industry, a Study Finds Mostly 'Bad Jobs.'" *New York Times,* January 5, p. B7.

Jansen, Tiago and Carlos Eduardo Siqueira. 2005. "Brazilians Are Everywhere in New England." Paper presented at the National Conference on Brazilian Immigration to the United States. David Rockefeller Center for Latin American Studies, Harvard University, March 18–19.

Johnson, Mary Helen. 2004. "Undocumented Students in the Boston Brazilian Community." In "Giving Voice to a Nascent Community: Exploring Brazilian Immigration to the U.S. through Research and Practice." Ed. Clémence Jouët-Pastré, Megwen Loveless and Leticia Braga. Working Paper no. 04/05-2. David Rockefeller Center for Latin American Studies Cambridge: Harvard University.

Justich, Robert and Betty Ng. 2005. "The Underground Labor Force is Rising to the Surface." New York: Bear Stearns Asset Management.

Kammer, Jerry. 2005. "Loophole to America." *San Diego Union-Tribune*, June 4.

Lobo, Arun Peter and Joseph J. Salvo. 2004. "The Newest New Yorkers 2000." Population Division, New York City Department of City Planning.

Maisonnave, Fabiano. 2005a. "Estranhos no Paraíso." *Folha de São Paulo*, January 6.

———. 2005b. "Captura de Brasileiros nos EUA Decuplica." *Folha de São Paulo*, May 5.

Marcus, Alan P. 2004. "Brasileiros em Massachusetts, E.U.A.: A Identidade Étnica de uma Minoria Invisivel." Paper presented at the meetings of the Brazilian Studies Association (BRASA), Rio de Janeiro, June 9–12.

———. 2005. "Brazilians in Framingham: Notions of Place and Ethnicity." Paper presented at the National Conference on Brazilian Immigration to the United States. David Rockefeller Center for Latin American Studies, Harvard University, Cambridge, March 18–19.

Margolis, Maxine L. 1994a. "A House Divided: The Absence of Community Organization Among Brazilian Immigrants in New York City." Paper presented at the 92nd annual meeting of the American Anthropological Association, Atlanta.

———. 1994b. *Little Brazil: Brazilian Immigrants in New York City*. Princeton: Princeton University Press.

———. 1995. "Brazilians and the 1990 United States Census: Immigrants, Ethnicity and the Undercount." *Human Organization* 54(1): 52–59

———. 1998. *An Invisible Minority: Brazilian Immigrants in New York City*. Boston, MA: Allyn and Bacon.

———. 2001. "With New Eyes: Returned International Immigrants in Rio de Janeiro." In *Raízes e Rumos: Perspectivas Interdisciplinares em Estudos Americanos*, pp. 239–244. Ed. Sonia Torres. Rio de Janeiro: Editora 7 Letras.

———. 2003. "Brasphobia." Forum on Brasphobia. The Brazilian Rainbow Group, Hunter College-CUNY, New York, December.

———. 2007. "Becoming Brazucas: Brazilian Identity in the United States." In *The Other Latinos: Central and South Americans in the United States*. pp. 210–227. Ed. J. Falconi and J. Mazzotti. Cambridge, MA: Harvard University Press.

———. in press. "Brazilians in the United States: The Aftermath of September 11." In *Brasileiros no Exterior: Caminhos da Cidadania*. Ed. Bela Feldman-Bianco and Carlos Vianna. Campinas, São Paulo: Editora da Unicamp.

Marrow, Helen B. 2002. "To Be or Not to Be (Hispanic or Latino): Brazilian Racial and Ethnic Identity in the United States." Paper Presented to the Brazilian Studies Mini-Seminar: "Brazilians Outside Brazil: Brasileiros fora do Brasil." University of Miami, Coral Gables, April 8.

———. 2004. "Coming to Grips with Race: Second-Generation Brazilians in the United States." Paper presented at the meetings of the Brazilian Studies Association (BRASA), Rio de Janeiro, June 9–12.

Martes, Ana Cristina Braga. 2000. *Brasileiros nos Estados Unidos: um estudo sobre imigrantes em Massachusetts*. São Paulo: Editora Paz e Terra.

———. 2002. "Brazilians in Boston: Race and Ethnicity." Paper presented at the Symposium, What About the Other Latinos? Central and South Americans in the United States. David Rockefeller Center for Latin American Studies, Harvard University, Cambridge, April 5.

———. 2004. "Transnational Institutions and Ethnic Entrepreneurship." Paper presented at the meetings of the Business Association of Latin American Studies, Babson College, Boston.

Meihy, José Carlos Sebe Bom. 2004. *Brasil Fora de Si*. São Paulo: Editora Parábola.

Menezes, Gustavo Hamilton. 2003. "Filhos de Imigração: A Segunda Geração de Brasileiros em Connecticut." In *Fronteiras Cruzadas: Etnicidade, Gênero e Redes Sociais*, pp. 157–173. Ed. Ana Cristina Martes Braga and Soraya Fleischer. São Paulo: Editora Paz e Terra.

Mineo, Liz. 2003. "Illegal Immigrants in a Panic Over Scam." *Metro West Daily News*, March 9.

Nunes, Jorge Moreira. 2001. "Quantos Somos, A Final de Contas?" *AcheiUsa*, 1(11) (July).

O Estado de São Paulo. 1999. "Imigrantes brasileiros nos EUA têm carteira de motorista cassada." October 27.

O'Leary, Mary E. 2005. "Danbury March Shows Support for Immigrants." *New Haven Register*, June 13.

Porter, Eduardo. 2005. "Social Security: Migrants Offer Numbers for a Fee." *New York Times*, June 7, pp. A1, C3.

Portes, Alejandro, ed. 1990. *The New Second Generation*. New York: Russell Sage.

Powell, Michael. 2005. "New Tack Against Illegal Immigrants: Trespassing Charges." *Washington Post*, June 10.

Resende, Rosana. 2002. "Tropical Brazucas: A Preliminary Study of Brazilians in South Florida." Paper presented at the Mini-Seminar, Brazilians Outside Brazil: Brasileiros Fora do Brasil. University of Miami, Coral Gables, April 8.

———. 2005. "Fragile Threads." *Hemisphere* 15 (Summer): 4–6.

Ribeiro, Darcy. 2000. *The Brazilian People*. Gainesville, FL: University Presses of Florida.

Ribeiro, Gustavo Lins. 1999. "O Que Faz O Brasil, *Brazil*: Jogos Identitários em San Francisco." In *Cenas do Brasil Migrante*, pp. 45–85. Ed. Rosana Rocha Reis and Teresa Sales. São Paulo: Boitempo.

Sales, Teresa. 1998. "Constructing an Ethnic Identity: Brazilian Immigrants in Boston, Mass." *Migration World* 26(5): 15–21.

———. 2001. "Segunda Geração de Emigrantes Brasileiros nos EUA." In *Migrações Internacionais: Contribuições Para Políticas*, pp. 361–374. Brasilia: Comissão Nacional de População e Desenvovimento.

Salgado, Eduardo. 2001. "Eles Fogem da Bagunça." *Veja*, July 18, pp. 94–100.

Scudeler, Cristina. 1999. "Imigrantes Valadarenses no Mercado de Trabalho dos EUA." In *Cenas do Brasil Migrante*, pp. 193–232. Ed. Rosana Rocha Reis and Teresa Sales. São Paulo: Boitempo.

Siqueira, C. Eduardo and Cileine de Lourenço. 2004. "Brazilian Immigration to Massachusetts: Newcomers to a Foreign Land." Paper presented at the meetings of the Latin American Studies Association, Las Vegas.

Sotero, Paulo. 2005. "EUA querem frear invasão via México." *O Estado de São Paulo*, February 20.

Souza (Galvão), Heloisa. 2002. "Brazilians in Boston: Before and After 9/11." Paper presented at the Symposium, What About the Other Latinos? Central and South Americans in the United States. David Rockefeller Center for Latin American Studies, Harvard University, Cambridge, April 5.

———. 2004. "Brazilians in New England: A Changing Profile and the Consequences of 9/11." In "Giving Voice to a Nascent Community: Exploring Brazilian Immigration to the U.S. through Research and Practice," pp. 93–97. Ed. Clémence Jouët-Pastré, Megwen Loveless and Leticia Braga. Working Paper no. 04/05-2. David Rockefeller Center for Latin American Studies, Cambridge: Harvard University.

Suarez, Ana Veciana. 2003. "Brazilian Community Growing Strong in Broward." *Miami Herald*, April 9.

Suárez-Orozco, Carola. 2004. "Brazilian Immigration: Introduction." In "Giving Voice to a Nascent Community: Exploring Brazilian Immigration to the U.S. through Research and Practice," pp. 17–18. Ed. Clémence Jouët-Pastré, Megwen Loveless and Leticia Braga. Working Paper no. 04/05-2. David Rockefeller Center for Latin American Studies, Cambridge: Harvard University.

Suárez-Orozco, Carola and Marcelo Suárez-Orozco. 2001. *Children of Immigration*. Cambridge, MA: Harvard University Press.

Tosta, Antonio. 2004. "Latino, *eu*? The Paradoxical Interplay of Identity in *Brazuca* Literature." *Hispania* 87(3): 576–585.

Vazquez, Manuel and Phillip Williams. 2003. Project Summary, "Latino Immigrants in Florida: Lived Religion, Space, and Power." Ford Foundation Grant, Center for Latin American Studies, University of Florida, Gainesville, Florida.

Woolhouse, Megan. 2005. "A Valedictorian Without a Visa." *Boston Globe*, June 3, pp. A1, B5.

INDEX

A

B

L

M

T